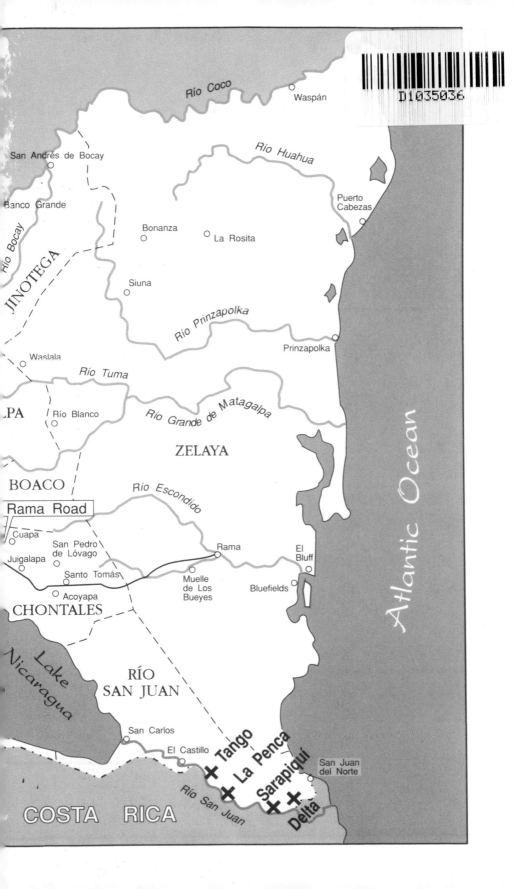

EVERYBODY HAD HIS OWN GRINGO

EVERYBODY HAD HIS OWN GRINGO

The CIA & the Contras

GLENN GARVIN

Foreword by P.J. O'Rourke

BRASSEY'S (US), INC.
A Division of Maxwell Macmillan, Inc.

WASHINGTON · NEW YORK · LONDON · OXFORD
BEIJING · FRANKFURT · SÃO PAULO · SYDNEY · TOKYO · TORONTO

Brassey's (US), Inc.

Editorial Offices
Brassey's (US), Inc.
8000 Westpark Drive
First Floor
McLean, Virginia 22102

Order Department
Brassey's Book Orders
c/o Macmillan Publishing Co.
100 Front Street, Box 500
Riverside, New Jersey 08075

Brassey's (US), Inc., books are available at special discounts for bulk purchases for sales promotions, premiums, fund-raising, or educational use through the Special Sales Director, Macmillan Publishing Company, 866 Third Avenue, New York, New York 10022.

LIBRARY OF CONGRESS CATALOGING-IN-PUBLICATION DATA

Garvin, Glenn.
    Everybody had his own gringo: the CIA & the Contras/Glenn
Garvin; foreword by P.J. O'Rourke.
        p.   cm.
    Includes index.
    ISBN 0-08-040562-2
    1. Nicaragua—Politics and government—1979–
2. Counterrevolutionaries—Nicaragua—History.   3. United States.
Central Intelligence Agency.   4. Counterrevolutions—Nicaragua—
History.   I. Title.
F1528.G37   1992
320.97285—dc20

                                                                91-31555
                                                                CIP

10   9   8   7   6   5   4   3   2   1

PRINTED IN THE UNITED STATES OF AMERICA

In 1986, during a trip to Managua, I was standing on a crumbling street corner with another journalist, trying to hail one of the rusting taxis that periodically limped by. Across the street, a barefoot but neatly dressed little girl eyed us for a few minutes, then crossed to us. "Are you gringos?" she inquired shyly. When we confirmed it, she had a hopeful question: "Do you know my mother? She lives in San Francisco—that's in the United States, I think."

Even though we didn't know her mother, the girl stayed to chat for a few minutes. Her name was Mercedes, she was eight years old, and she lived with her grandparents, who were very old. Her mother had gone to San Francisco a year earlier, to find a job. Sometimes she sent postcards with pictures of the ocean on them. And when would her mother come home? "When things are better," Mercedes answered gravely, and then she was on her way.

This book is for Mercedes, in hopes that things are better.

Contents

Foreword

Glenn Garvin exhibits an impressive understanding of the culture of Central America. I know this because he once saved my life in Panama or, anyway, kept me from being sentenced to years and years in jail there. Actually what he did was talk the police out of giving me a traffic ticket, but it was impressive. This was before Operation Brave Dog, or whatever, had rid the world of Manuel Noriega. In those days the reasonably courageous members of the anti-Noriega National Civic Crusade were in the streets battling the fairly vicious pro-Noriega "Dignity Battalions," and I was covering the moderately dramatic resulting disturbances for *Rolling Stone*. Driving from a tear-gassing to a water cannonade, I turned left on a red light. A Panamanian motorcycle policeman gave chase. Now, I thought, for what is 200 years of Yankee imperialism in Central America if I can't get away with a minor infraction of the motor vehicle laws in the middle of a riot in a place that would be nothing but an "isthmus" clue in an acrostic puzzle except for a canal we American taxpayers bought them? So I took off. Surely I could lose one cop. And certainly the rest of the Panama City police force was too busy whacking demonstrators in the tibias with night sticks to bother about a misdemeanorous gringo fleeing the scene of a left turn. But the police in Panama know that bad driving is an even worse problem than revolution in Central America. In ten minutes there were enough cops behind us to make a Burt Reynolds movie.

While this was going on, Glenn Garvin had the extremely bad luck to be riding in my car. I remember him giving me various pieces of good advice such as "For Chrissake stop, you asshole!" When the Panamanian policemen ran me to earth, Glenn got out of the car and, with his hands in the air, exhibited that impressive understanding of the culture of Central America. Glenn talked to the policemen in Spanish. And talked. And talked and talked. Over the course of an hour those policemen went from murderous pigs to angry fuzz to exasperated flatfeet and finally turned into bemused but good-natured officers of the law who let me off with a warning. Glenn has never explained to me how he managed this. He says all he was doing was describing to the Panamanians, in vivid detail, what an arrogant cake-eating pecker-wit ofay prostitute-mothered *norteamericano* earthworm I am.

In *Everybody Had His Own Gringo,* Garvin puts his understanding to better use. This is the first honest, clear-eyed, and objective account of the guerrilla war against the Sandinistas. Though it is not, thank God, a dispassionate book. Garvin isn't one of those modern wet and foggy writers who confuses objectivity with not knowing right from wrong. To be objective is to tell the truth. And one of the truths told here is that communism is an evil philosophy. People who subscribe to communist beliefs—even the silly type of communist beliefs that animated the Sandinista supporters—hate individuals and free- dom. People who subscribe to communist beliefs need to be disarmed, removed from power, and exiled to some isolated place where they can do no harm, someplace like the 1992 Democratic presidential campaign.

Thus *Everybody Had His Own Gringo* is well supplied with villains. It's also admirably short of heroes. Garvin shows us contra political leaders whose vanity and quarrelsomeness turned contra governance into something like an International Convention of First Wives. He provides unforgiving portraits of those contra battlefield commanders who got their military tactics from the Iraqi air force or their human rights briefings from 2 Live Crew. Garvin describes how the U.S. State Department carried the same pragmatic savvy to Central America that Woodrow Wilson brought to Versailles. And he sketches a Reagan administration that, though it knew what needed to be done in Nicaragua, alternated between comatose inattention to the subject and letting an unhousebroken National Security Council chew the slippers of statecraft and mess on the rug of constitutional law. Then there's the CIA, which seemed to be using the anti-Sandinista resistance to conduct an experiment on U.S. intelli- gence officers concerning the long-term effect of excessive testosterone on idealists with IQs of less than 80. Even Barry Goldwater—not a person usually caught with toes of terra cotta—is seen dumbly blustering in the Senate about the 1984 CIA mining of Nicaraguan harbors. It was this pointless outburst that opened the floodgates of liberal sewage that brought us the Boland Amendment.

Garvin puts all the fools and their follies into perspective. He indulges in no heavy breathing over Iranian arms deals or the small change those deals produced for the contras. He fails to be shocked that hungry partisans short on ammo might sell a few drugs. He gives the American and European "Sandalistas" the shortness of shrift they deserve. (This is the only book ever written about the contras that doesn't mention Benjamin Linder.) Garvin also resists the temptation to call down the wrath of God on the moral flab of cynical mugwumpery of Congress, which changed its mind about support for the contras at least five times, this doing more damage to the cause than the whole Sandinista army and all its Soviet guns. Nor does Garvin urge that the pro-Ortega human offal in the American intelligentsia be hanged from lamp- posts. He doesn't even point out that Bianca Jagger has cellulite.

As a result of Garvin's laudable restraint, we have a book that focuses on the contras themselves, on regular people who took up arms to gain freedoms. These men and women kept fighting—in spite of being hunted by the largest army in the history of Central America, in spite of being shunned by the smug democracies of the West, in spite of often useless and always self-serving "help" from the United States. And these men and women may have to keep on fighting because, as Garvin points out, the war with the Sandinistas isn't over in Nicaragua.

Glenn Garvin's story of the contras is a reminder that the only thing that stands between the slime pit of totalitarianism and the liberties of individuals is individuals themselves. The contras were and are imperfect, human, ordinary —just like us. But would we have the courage to leave our homes and families and go into the hills and fight for years for the Rights of Man? What if freedom-hating collectivists took over *our* government and began meddling in every part of our lives, taxing us into poverty, abolishing our property rights, infusing our educational system with godless nonsense? . . . In fact, we probably ought to be headed for the hills right now.

P.J. O'ROURKE
SHARON, NEW HAMPSHIRE

Preface

All day long we squatted under the grapefruit tree, listening to the dull thunder of the artillery on the other side of the mountain, and wondered what the Sandinistas were shooting at. They might be firing at random—sometimes they did that, launching their expensive Soviet rockets out into the trackless jungle to pulverize monkeys and coconuts—but the shelling had been going on for hours now. It seemed more likely they were blasting away at the contra patrol that was supposed to meet our little group of journalists here but was now thirty-six hours late. Finally, in the late afternoon, the artillery stopped. And a few minutes later, six figures in dusty olive green appeared at the top of the ridge and headed down the crusty dirt road toward us. Even a mile away we could see the sun glinting off the cruel curves of their rifle clips. There was just enough time for us to panic.

"Look, I know it's kind of late to be thinking about this," I said, squinting at the approaching soldiers. "But how are we going to tell if those guys are Sandinistas or contras?"

"I don't know," replied Ambrose Evans-Pritchard, the thin, scholarly reporter from the *London Spectator*. "Everybody wears the same uniforms and carries the same guns."

It had never occurred to us, when the contras told us to meet them on this remote mountaintop in Nicaragua, that they would schedule a rendezvous in an area where the Sandinista army was active. After all, the idea was to show reporters how freely they could move around the northern part of the country.

"If they're Sandinistas," asked Sue Mullin, the free-lance photographer who was the other member of our little group, "what will they do?"

"I'm not sure," I said. "But they might wonder what three gringos are doing hanging around in the middle of a combat zone thirty miles from the nearest town."

By now we were whispering. The soldiers were only a few dozen yards away.

We peered at them for a sign—maybe the tiny red star pins that Sandinista officers wore on their caps or the grinning-skull insignia patches that *Soldier of Fortune* magazine reporters handed out in the contra camps. But the thick layer of dust made it impossible to pick out any details. We tried to look nonchalant; yes, Lieutenant, we're just out here interviewing this grapefruit tree.

The first soldier stopped, tilted his camouflaged cowboy hat up, and gestured at me. "Hey, amigo," he said. "Can you tell me" —*here it comes,* I thought, *he's going to ask me Daniel Ortega's middle name, and when I don't know it we'll all be arrested as CIA agents*—"has there been any shooting up the road today?"

"No, no, all quiet," I answered. The soldier smiled, nodded, and walked on, followed by his five companions. As they walked away, I realized that we *still* didn't know who they were. They might even be our contra patrol, assuming from our studied indifference that we weren't the right gringos and they would have to look further.

As the soldiers trudged on, Ambrose walked over to a nearby peasant shack, where a toothless old woman had been watching our encounter. "*Señora,*" he asked, "do you know if those soldiers were Sandinistas or contras?"

"Sandinistas, of course," she said and went back inside her hut. We could hear her in there with her husband, laughing, and I could just picture the conversation. *Imagine that, Juan, those gringos think they're going to explain the war in Nicaragua to the world, and they can't even tell one army from another. No wonder the North American congress can't make up its mind.*

For the past 135 years, Nicaragua has been a kind of geopolitical mind-altering substance. American politicians and journalists go there, sample the local politics, and immediately start babbling in tongues. It began with William Walker, the nineteenth-century adventurer who declared himself president of Nicaragua, and it continues right up through this morning's newspaper. My favorite recent example was the late American actor Gary Merrill, who until shortly before his death could often be found haunting the coffee shop of Managua's Hotel Inter-Continental, wearing a dress, and proclaiming to one and all that the Sandinista party newspaper *Barricada* "contains more truth than you find in the *New York Times* in a year." Although, he conceded, the crossword puzzle wasn't as good.

No portion of Nicaraguan history has been discussed more, and understood less, than the confrontation that began shortly after the Sandinista National Liberation Front seized power in 1979. When the Sandinistas began reconstructing Nicaraguan society—creating the New Man, as they liked to refer to it—they encountered a stubborn resistance that grew, eventually, into a full-fledged civil war.

I covered that war for six years as a newspaper correspondent. And it never failed to amaze me how Americans of all ideological stripes used it to project their own political fears and fantasies. The most hallucinatory part of the American debate concerned the people who were fighting the Sandinistas—the contras, as they came to be known. Americans who had never been within a thousand miles of a contra felt free to label the group either as a gang of rapists and murderers cooked up in one of the CIA's basement laboratories, or as tropical Thomas Jeffersons who wanted nothing more than to translate the U.S. Constitution into Spanish. The irony was that both pro- and anti-contra Americans seemed to think that, for better or for worse, the contras fought to further the political goals of the United States. Nicaragua hardly entered into the equation from either side.

I spent much of the war with the contras. I went inside Nicaragua with their patrols, visited their border camps, drank coffee in their safe houses in Honduras and Costa Rica, and camped out in the lobby of their Miami political office. I flew in the rickety little planes of their air force and ate mystery meat with them along the Río Coco. The more time I spent with them, the less they resembled either the crude caricatures of the American Left or the civics-book pinups of the American Right.

They were brave men and women who fought, mostly, because they believed that the Sandinista revolution had injured them, their families, or their friends. American money may have paid for their guns, but it did not cause them to leave their farms to fight against a professionally trained and outfitted army. Relatively few of them had a sweeping political ideology in the way that Americans customarily understand that term. But their complaints—about rationing, about interference with their church, about the price the government paid for their coffee beans, about the attempts to turn their children against their way of life—did translate into a grass-roots ideology: the right of an individual to go his own way rather than submit to the direction of a powerful state. For years, the anti-Sandinista movement struggled against the label "contra," believing it negative, but in a curious way it was appropriate: The contras did not necessarily agree on what they were for, but they were absolutely unanimous about what they were against. The *New York Times* once dismissed their feelings as "simple peasant reaction." But when revolutions are fought, the simple peasants do most of the dying.

This is a book about the contras: who they were, why they fought, how their U.S. allies helped and hindered them. It is not a book about the Iran-contra scandal or how policy was made in Washington. Most of the Americans who move through these pages were not top policymakers but the grunts of the Central Intelligence Agency and the State Department, the people who had to translate Washington's grand rhetoric into a workable policy on the ground. Readers interested in a richly detailed behind-the-scenes look at the Sandinistas will also be disappointed; like most American reporters, I had little access to the nine *comandantes.* (The forthcoming book *Inside The Sandinistas,* by top FSLN defector Roger Miranda and the Hoover Institution's William Ratliff, should at last lift the curtain that has always surrounded the party's upper echelons.)

Quite the reverse was true with the contras. I have spoken with hundreds of them over the years, from the top political leaders to fourteen-year-old boys barely taller than their AK-47s. Many of them devoted generous amounts of time to the preparation of this book. They include Roberto Amador, Frank Arana, Enrique Bermúdez, Walter Calderón, Adolfo Calero, José Francisco Cardenal, Alfredo César, Octaviano César, Adolfo Chamorro, Edgar Chamorro, Pedro Joaquín Chamorro, Roberto Espinosa, Edwin Hooker,

Alvaro Jerez, Mary Layton, Bernardino Larios, Edgard Macías, Ernesto Matamoros, Mariano Mendoza, Pedro Mora, Luis Moreno, Tirzo Moreno, Noel Ortiz, Alfonso Robelo, Julio Solórzano, Mario Sacasa, Marta Sacasa, Octavio Sacasa, and Hugo Villagra. Others in and around the contra movement who shared their recollections with me include John Hull, Geraldine Macías, Steve McAlister, Felix Rodriguez, and John K. Singlaub. Many of these individuals graciously talked with me knowing full well that my account would be sharply at odds with their view of events.

I also had the cooperation of numerous U.S. diplomats and intelligence officers. Most of them suffered some damage to their careers through their involvement in a program that ultimately proved a political pariah, and none was anxious to be named here. I hope that for most of them the opportunity to see the story of the contras told, not as that of a tropical Hell's Angels but as the story of a legitimate political-military movement, will compensate for the lack of acknowledgment. A word about my use of names of CIA personnel is in order here. The Intelligence Identities Protection Act makes it a crime to reveal the true identities of officers in the CIA's clandestine services. I have used the real names of CIA officers only when they have already been publicly disclosed elsewhere; otherwise I have used the pseudonyms by which the contras knew them. One other note: When conversations are recounted verbatim, I either witnessed them myself or got a detailed account from someone who did.

Two Nicaraguan historians, Esteban Duque Estrada and Alejandro Bolaños-Geyer, provided numerous documents and plenty of advice to a gringo trying to understand their country. Rita McWilliams and June Erlick reviewed portions of the manuscript. Murray Flander skillfully cut red tape to help me obtain government documents. University of Arizona journalism professor Jacqueline Sharkey did the same in the academic world despite knowing that the political content of my book would appall her—a true friend. Shannon Mohac retrieved literally thousands of newspaper clippings from every nook and cranny of Washington. Don McKeon at Brassey's believed a book about Central America could be interesting, even if no one else in the publishing world did. And a special word is due Jack Shafer of Washington's *City Paper*, who advised me to buy a computer from a company that promptly went bankrupt and then chose a word processing program for me that periodically devoured my entire text.

My colleagues in the Central American press corps did me countless favors and kindnesses over the years. Perhaps my largest debt is to Phil Evans, then the assistant managing editor of the *Washington Times,* who in 1983 sent me to Central America even though I then didn't speak a word of Spanish. I don't know whether he was demonstrating supreme confidence in my reporting ability or just hoping that I wouldn't come back. Either way, he introduced me to the most fascinating story of my career. My traveling companion and Spanish-speaker on that first trip was Peter Jones, now with the Voice of America, who during a month in Honduras managed to teach me two sentences: *Donde está el baño?* (Where is the bathroom?) and *No despare, soy periodista* (Don't shoot, I'm a journalist). Eight years later they are still the most key phrases in my Spanish lexicon. Between 1986 and 1988, when I was running the newspaper's bureau in Costa Rica, the "San José pool"—Reid Miller and

Pauline Jelinek of the Associated Press and Mike Drudge of the Voice of America—shared my trauma during the hundreds of pointless press conferences and incomprehensible interviews that made up the daily work of a Central American correspondent.

Every preface I've ever read contains the phrase "without whom this book could never have been written." This one will be no exception. Sue Mullin took pictures, did interviews, clipped, filed, kept track of Spanish punctuation, located lost notes, and cleaned up after the consequences of Managua's tainted public water supply. Without her, there would have been no book.

Prologue:
July 19, 1979

Toño cursed the beams of sunlight that were breaking through the gray and tracing eerie shapes in the morning fog. Already he could pick out the three little boats trailing behind him. And if Toño could see them, so could the Sandinistas. "How much farther to El Salvador?" he called to the Nicaraguan Coast Guard commander at the wheel of the patrol boat. The commander shrugged; after a night of heavy fog and endless zigzagging, he wasn't sure either.

Toño—his real name was Walter Calderón, but everyone, even his own mother, knew him by his radio call sign—was a lieutenant in the Nicaraguan National Guard. But, he reflected grimly, his commission was about to lapse. Anastasio Somoza, the Guard's commander in chief, had fled Nicaragua two days before, and the army had quickly disintegrated. Now the guerrillas of the Sandinista National Liberation Front were closing in all over the country. Nearly all the big provincial capitals—León, Jinotega, Estelí—had already fallen. By now, Toño supposed, Managua might be in Sandinista hands too. Certainly it did not look good when he left there two days ago. Snipers were even firing into the main Guard headquarters.

It had all fallen apart so fast, like a peasant's mud hut when the river rises. Toño had been fighting on the war's southern front, a narrow strip of plains along the border with Costa Rica, where both the National Guard and the Sandinistas had placed their best commanders. On the southern front there was no guerrilla warfare. Instead, several thousand troops from the two armies were slugging it out there in an agonizing war of fixed positions, soaking the same few hills with their blood in a series of attacks and counterattacks that had been going on for months. The National Guard was short of replacement troops and, even more critically, ammunition—nearly all of Somoza's international allies had turned their backs on him after the Carter administration began making it clear that it wanted him to leave. The Sandinistas, on the other hand, were receiving a steady stream of weapons, ammo, and men from sympathetic

1

regimes in Cuba, Venezuela, and Panama. Despite all that, the National Guard hadn't given up any territory. On Saturday, July 14, when Toño was sent to the military hospital in Managua for treatment of an acute case of dysentery, he still thought the Guard was winning the war.

However, when he left the hospital the next morning to visit the Bunker, the Guard headquarters perched on a hill behind the pyramidal Inter-Continental Hotel, Toño found the fortress-like compound oddly deserted. A few brusque orderlies were scurrying though the compound, but they had no time for Toño. Finally, at one of the gates, a distraught sentry recognized him. "Lieutenant," he blurted, "the cabinet members and their families are going to the airport! They're taking their luggage, even their dogs and cats. All these people are leaving Nicaragua—when are we leaving?" Toño, stunned, had walked away without a word.

Outside, the scene was even more surreal. Managua's dusty streets, usually thronged with street vendors peddling fried meat and sodas and peasants hawking produce from the countryside, were almost empty. The only vehicles were National Guard jeeps racing from ambush to ambush. (The Guard had no secure radio channels, so the Sandinistas listened in on their every move.) The sound of intermittent gunfire crackled in the distance.

On Monday, July 16, Toño finally tracked down half a dozen other young lieutenants from his class at the military academy. Everyone was appalled at how much the situation had deteriorated. "The problem is Somoza," one of the young officers declared. "The whole world hates Somoza, so everyone is willing to throw us to the communists. But it's our fault, too—we have let ourselves get into the situation of being a private army that defends one family." And the Sandinistas had made the most of it; the Guard's international image was terrible. There were nods of agreement. But what could be done about it?

One of the men suggested kidnapping Somoza's son, who commanded an elite Guard unit and could usually be found right there in the Bunker. If they had the younger Somoza—known as El Chigüín, the kid—in custody, the junior officers would disrupt Somoza's control of the Guard and be in a good position to strike some kind of bargain to buy time. Not with the Sandinistas, who were communists and wanted the Guard's blood. But possibly with the middle-class businessmen who also opposed Somoza and had been cooperating uneasily with the Sandinistas for lack of an alternative. Or maybe even with the gringos themselves. The only thing that was certain was that once they had El Chigüín, his father would do as he was told. "Somoza will do anything for El Chigüín," one officer said. There were murmurs of agreement. They set a meeting for the next morning to work out a plan.

But when Toño returned to the small apartment in the Bunker Tuesday morning, July 17, he found he was the only one of the young lieutenants still left in Managua. All the others had been transferred to the various crumbling fronts the night before. There had been orders to transfer Toño, too, but because he had spent the night at the military hospital, no one had been able to find him. Somebody must have found out about the plot—but it no longer mattered. Somoza and El Chigüín had fled the country just before dawn.

Toño jumped into his jeep and drove to the little three-room house where his wife, Lua, lived. "Grab some things," he said. "We're leaving Nicaragua." Almost the instant the words left his mouth, the phone rang. A friend from Toño's class at the military academy was calling from Puerto Somoza, forty-five miles away on the Pacific coast. A Sandinista arms-smuggling boat had just been captured, and he was guarding it. If Toño would pick up his friend's wife in Managua and drive her to Puerto Somoza, they could all escape in the boat.

The drive, which should have lasted two hours, took all day. Toño kept wheeling the jeep onto rough dirt tracks and into bean fields, doubling back and traveling miles out of the way to avoid Sandinista roadblocks on the main highways. They arrived in Puerto Somoza as the sun went down; the boat, already loaded with fifteen other Guardsmen, left as soon as they boarded. But the Nicaraguan Coast Guard spotted them a couple of hours later, boarded the boat, and took the men to a jail in the northern port city of Corinto.

Early the next morning—Wednesday, July 18—Colonel Pallais, the Guard commander in nearby Chinandega, was summoned. He was furious at the men. They were traitors, leaving their country at a desperate moment. The only reason he wasn't going to have them shot was that he needed all the soldiers he could find; there was a report that the Sandinistas were planning to land a large unit near Corinto during the next few hours. "I'm going back to Chinandega to get some troops," the colonel barked. "And you're joining them, whether you want to or not."

The colonel left for Chinandega, twelve miles away. Toño and others waited impatiently in their cells; they weren't anxious to rejoin a dying army, but in jail they couldn't even defend themselves if the Sandinistas should arrive. Four hours later, the local Coast Guard commander nervously unlocked their cells. "The colonel was ambushed on his way back from Chinandega," the commander told Toño. "He's dead. His unit was wiped out. And there's no one left to defend the town." His words trailed off into silence. Toño thought he could hear gunfire in the distance. "Look, I've got a boat," the commander said. "But my job here has been to rescue fishing boats. I don't know anything about combat. Help me escape."

Again the Guardsmen swarmed into a boat. But as they were pulling away from Corinto, they cruised right past a Panamanian ship unloading armed men onto the beach—the Sandinista force that the dead Colonel Pallais had been worried about. The Sandinistas immediately turned their mortars and heavy machine guns on the Coast Guard patrol boat as the captain madly twisted the wheel at torturous angles to escape. Toño crouched on the deck and fired his FAL rifle uselessly at the shore. *I've fought these bastards four years in the jungle,* he thought, *and now I'm going to get killed in a naval engagement.*

Miraculously, the patrol boat, though pockmarked by bullets and shrapnel, got away. The captain pushed it far out to sea, trying to avoid bumping into another Sandinista craft. As they meandered through the darkness without lights, they encountered another Coast Guard patrol boat, then two fishing boats, all loaded with fleeing National Guardsmen—about one hundred men in all, many of them with their families. But what might have been a formidable

3

force on land would be a pathetic collection of sitting ducks if the Sandinistas found them on the water, Toño knew. Now, with the Thursday dawn breaking, they were vulnerable again.

Suddenly there was a burst of excited chatter from the front of the boat. Toño walked to the bow. The captain, for the first time in their brief acquaintance, was smiling. He gestured up ahead, and Toño saw a mist-shrouded coast. "That's La Unión, El Salvador," the captain said. "We've made it." For the first time since he boarded the boat, Toño put his rifle down and slumped against a bulkhead. As the tension drained away, slowly replaced by exhaustion, it occurred to him that no one had wished him a happy birthday. He had turned twenty-four the day before, sitting in the Coast Guard jail.

As they neared the port, Toño saw small boats approaching from every direction, all of them loaded with uniformed National Guardsmen. On shore, a crowd of curious townspeople had gathered to watch the arrival of the bedraggled remnants of what until a few days ago had been the most feared army in Central America. Vendors did a brisk business in tortillas and Coca-Cola; children raced excitedly along the docks. As the captain began tying up the boat, Toño put one foot up onto the wooden pier and prepared to step ashore.

"Hey," a young woman called out to him. "Are you a National Guardsman?"

"Yes, I am," Toño replied.

"How could you kill women and little children?" the woman shouted. *Welcome to exile,* Toño thought to himself as he climbed onto the pier.

"The war is over," Edén Pastora told the dozen men seated around him in the makeshift command post near Peñas Blancas, the tiny customs post on the Pan-American Highway between Costa Rica and Nicaragua. "Somoza has left the country, and the National Guard has abandoned its positions. There is nothing between us and Managua." There was a stunned silence. Some of these men had been fighting the National Guard for twenty years. Could it really be over?

Adolfo Chamorro, better known by his nickname of Popo, was as shocked as anyone. But his mind was already grappling with the logistical problems of victory. As chief of transportation, it would be up to him to move the six hundred Sandinista guerrillas fighting here on the southern front the eighty-five miles to Managua. As though he had intercepted the thought, Pastora's eyes locked on Popo. "Anybody who wants to take their family, we do it," Pastora said. "Mobilize all of our vehicles." That more than tripled the number of people Popo would have to transport, but he didn't blink. When Commander Pastora, the star of the revolution, wanted something, you didn't argue.

Pastora was the best known of all the Sandinista commanders, the one who always went before the television cameras when foreign reporters needed new video footage. But none of the men begrudged him the publicity. Pastora was a military genius. Hadn't he proved it the year before by seizing the National Palace, in the heart of Managua, with just two dozen men? Since then, everyone in Nicaragua knew *Comandante Cero,* Commander Zero. And Pastora, unlike most of the other top Sandinista leaders, was not a communist.

4

That fact was important on the southern front. Most of the subordinate commanders here, while politically left of center, were not communists either. (Popo, who had owned a Managua appliance store before he became a guerrilla, certainly had no use for Marxist economics.) Many didn't even consider themselves Sandinistas. A few of the commanders, in fact, suspected that the Sandinistas had deliberately concentrated all the politically unreliable troops on this one front where they could be carefully watched. The military commanders in the north were nearly all hard-core communists. Even here in the south, there were four senior Cubans in the headquarters building in Liberia, Costa Rica. And a staff of forty advisers from Cuba and communist guerrilla organizations in Argentina and Chile consulted with the southern front commanders on strategy and managed the seventy-five-piece artillery unit. None of the foreigners had attended the meeting of commanders, Popo noted with satisfaction; if the war was really over, maybe they would be going home.

It took Popo six hours to round up his fleet of one hundred trucks, jeeps, and cars, most of them stashed safely over the border in Costa Rica. It didn't make his job any easier that all the troops were going crazy, firing their rifles in the air in a deafening chorus of celebration. Finally, late in the afternoon, the convoy headed up the Pan-American Highway for Managua. But the going was slow. Every 1,500 feet or so the trucks had to stop while troops got out and swept the fields along the road for National Guard stragglers and diehards. Around midnight, as the men searched a meadow south of Rivas—still more than sixty miles south of Managua—Popo began to feel uneasy. At this rate, thousands of troops from the north would arrive in the capital before Pastora. The radicals would be in a position to dictate the future of the revolution.

Popo took Pastora aside. "Look, let's stop before we get to Managua, in Masaya," he suggested. "We stay there, with our men fully armed and our artillery intact, and we negotiate the direction of the new government." Pastora exploded. "Commander Zero does not betray his partners!" he shouted. "Say it again and I'll have you shot!"

Popo was quiet the rest of the way to Managua. But he couldn't banish a nagging little thought: *I hope this thing doesn't get out of control.*

Tirzo Moreno heard the news as he drank his morning coffee. The Honduran radio station said that the National Guard had broken and run, like a bunch of old women. The war was over. "I don't believe it," Moreno snorted to his brother. "Those guys will never give up." But the shortwave station in Costa Rica was saying the same thing. And then they heard it on the Voice of America, too. A smile began to creep over Moreno's face. His side had won.

Not that Moreno had been a fighter. On his small farm near Wiwilí, about a dozen miles south of the Honduran border, the war usually seemed remote— something for the people in the cities. Moreno just went about tending his small cattle business, buying livestock from the peasants around his little mountain town and then getting it to the slaughterhouses down south. There was, however, a Sandinista camp located a few miles north of Wiwilí, so sometimes patrols from one side or the other stopped at Moreno's farm, looking for food or

5

water. He was hospitable to both armies—what could you do when men with guns showed up?—but Moreno was more partial to the Sandinistas.

He particularly liked the Sandinista commander who called himself El Danto, a tough cottonpicker from Chinandega whose real name was Germán Pomares. A lot of the Sandinistas were kids from the city who seemed to have some kind of personal grudge against Somoza, but Pomares had been a campesino, a peasant. Moreno liked that; his parents were campesinos who had practically broken their backs to get him some education and a chance to go a little further in life. Now, not yet twenty-five, Moreno was making as much money on a single cattle deal as his parents used to earn in a year.

The radio said that the Sandinistas were in Managua, and the new revolutionary junta was flying in from Costa Rica. Moreno wondered if El Danto would have a high position in the new government. Actually, El Danto was already dead—he had been killed in an attack on Jinotega two months earlier, but the Sandinistas kept it secret to protect morale. But Moreno didn't know that yet. Today the future seemed unlimited. "I think that in a few days I'll go to Managua," he told his brother. "I want to see what the new government looks like."

1 | *Maldito País*

When he retired as a guerrilla commander in 1933, after six years of cat-and-mouse games with the U.S. Marines in the rugged mountains of northern Nicaragua, Augusto Sandino summoned a young journalist named José Román. He wanted Román to write a book giving his side of the story, Sandino said. Román eagerly agreed, and for weeks they traveled the mountains together, visiting Sandino's camps, where his 1,800 guerrillas were preparing to exchange their guns for plows and hoes. Sandino told the whole story: how he stole his first few hundred weapons, with the help of a half-dozen hookers; the terrible slaughter at the battle of Ocotal, where the Marines called in the first dive-bombing attack in history, and Sandino's men thought the sky was full of demons; the flippant telegrams he sent to the Marine commanders, signed "your obedient servant, who ardently desires to put you in a handsome tomb with beautiful bouquets of flowers."

And Sandino had a question for the young journalist—who, he knew, spoke English. There was an English phrase the Marines used a lot when they were talking about Nicaragua's heat, mud, insects, rain, and guerrillas. *Goddamned country*—what did that mean, exactly? In Spanish, Román replied, it would be *maldito país*. Sandino roared with laughter. That, he said, has to be the title of your book. And it was.[1]

Nicaragua's bad luck began perhaps ten thousand years ago. The country's very first historical artifacts are the "Footprints of Acahualinca," embedded in hardened mud along the shores of Lake Managua: the tracks of a small family, fleeing across the beach from an erupting volcano. Ever since, Nicaraguans have been dodging one plague or pestilence after another. Earthquakes, volcanoes, hurricanes, torrential rains, suffocating heat, stifling drought; natural catastrophe is a regular visitor to Nicaragua.

So, too, is political catastrophe, decidedly noncelestial in origin. Since declaring independence from Spain in 1821, Nicaragua has been at war more often than not, sometimes against its neighbors but more frequently against itself. In recent times, Nicaraguans of all ideological stripes have tried to portray their country as the innocent victim of repeated foreign interventions, mostly by the United States. The fact is that when foreign armies have come to Nicaragua, it has almost always been at the invitation of one group of Nicaraguans who wanted help in making war on another group.

For the country's first 150 years, most of its troubles stemmed from its two dominant political parties, the Liberals and Conservatives. In theory, the Conservatives—old Spanish aristocratic families—stood for agriculture and the political preeminence of the Catholic church. And the Liberals—bourgeois businessmen—stood for commerce and restricting the Church to theology.

Actually, any real political distinction between the two groups was quickly lost. They divided up along geographical lines (Granada, in the south, was the Conservative stronghold, and León, in the north, the Liberal) and family lines (genealogy is of paramount importance in Nicaragua). The only issue was control of the mammoth government patronage machine, which no one bothered to contest in elections; no ruling party ever conceded defeat. Instead, the two parties quickly developed into armies headed by *caudillos*—strongmen —that mercilessly slaughtered one another's supporters. Between 1824 and 1842, the two parties fought seventeen major battles that produced eighteen heads of state.

In 1845 Nicaraguans embroiled foreigners in their political wars for the first time when the Conservatives inflicted a major defeat on the Liberals with substantial aid from the governments of El Salvador and Honduras. The Liberals went in search of their own foreign sponsor. And in 1855, they found him: William Walker, a Tennessee-born soldier of fortune who had recently been frustrated in his attempts to conquer Mexico. He landed on Nicaragua's Pacific coast in June with fifty-eight Americans. Within four months his troops—reinforced with another two hundred or so gringos—had destroyed the Conservative army. He promptly declared himself commander-in-chief of Nicaragua's national army and then had himself elected president. His rule was so brutal, and his territorial lust so obvious, that all five Central American countries—Nicaragua, El Salvador, Honduras, Costa Rica, and Guatemala— quickly united against him. Four years later, the defeated Walker was executed by a Honduran firing squad.

Walker is often portrayed as a prototype for the U.S. interventions in the twentieth century. He was nothing of the kind. The U.S. government opposed his Latin American adventures, thwarted several of his expeditions, and refused to recognize his presidency in Nicaragua. Walker actually *threatened* U.S. economic interests in Nicaragua—he seized the steamship-and-railroad line of Cornelius Vanderbilt, by far the major American investment in the country. Walker was simply a foreign mercenary hired by the Liberal Party, which knew all along of his imperial ambitions. Walker's contract called for him to receive 52,000 acres of land if the Liberals won the war, and his army was "guaranteed forever the privilege of bearing arms."[2]

If Walker's exploits have become a propaganda football in recent years, at the time Nicaraguans knew exactly who was responsible. The Liberal Party was totally discredited, and Conservatives ruled—more or less peacefully—from

1857 to 1893. Then a rebellion by Liberal general José Santos Zelaya started the cycle again. His tumultuous rule lasted sixteen years before dissolving into a new round of wars between Conservative and Liberal generals that dragged on over two decades and brought U.S. troops to Nicaragua five times—three times to protect U.S. citizens when hostilities threatened, twice to shore up compromise coalition governments menaced by rebellious party generals. The ghastliest conflict was the one launched by Conservative general Emiliano Chamorro in 1925, a horror even by Nicaragua's bloody standards. Travelers reported streets littered with bodies, where the only living things were vultures and pigs gnawing on corpses.

In 1927 U.S. president Calvin Coolidge sent his envoy, Henry L. Stimson, to mediate peace talks. Assigned the absurdly difficult task of hammering out an agreement that would end the fighting and lead to stable future governments chosen in free and peaceful elections, Stimson—defying all odds—came up with a compromise that everyone accepted. The Liberals would get control of six of the country's sixteen departments, or provinces, in return for laying down their arms. The United States would supervise the 1928 elections. And a new, apolitical, national army would be formed with American help to replace the Liberal and Conservative armies that turned every presidential transition into a war.

Well, *almost* everyone accepted it. Augusto Sandino, one of the Liberal generals, refused. He promptly withdrew to Nueva Segovia Department, along the Honduran border, and began a guerrilla war that lasted until 1933.

Sandino has been the subject of even more historical distortion than William Walker, much of it generated by the Marxist-Leninist party that took his name thirty years after his death. To start with, Sandino was not a simple peasant, as he is often romantically portrayed; he came from a relatively well-to-do farming family. And he was not a particularly successful guerrilla. In five years of warfare, he inflicted only forty-seven combat deaths on the Marines. The Marines, on the other hand, may have killed as many as three hundred of Sandino's troops in the very first battle of the war.[3] Sandino survived the war, but he didn't accomplish much more than that.

Moreover, Sandino's reputation as a Nicaraguan nationalist has been considerably enhanced. His celebrated anti-*yanqui* sentiments developed after the war began and were more of a personal grudge than anything else. He refused to go along with the 1927 peace agreement not because it was American-backed but because he thought the Liberals were on the verge of military victory and shouldn't negotiate anything away. Even so, he offered to lay down his arms—several times—if the United States would impose an American military government before the 1928 elections, rather than merely supervising them.[4]

Sandino was not overwhelmingly popular. At the beginning of his war, he had a good deal of support among fellow Liberals in the northern provinces, but it waned after a Liberal won the 1928 elections. For their part, Conservatives never thought of Sandino as anything but a vicious outlaw. His troops murdered Conservatives and looted their property whenever possible. One favorite

9

Sandino technique: cutting the victim's throat, then pulling his tongue down through the slit so it dangled on his chest like a necktie. He killed prisoners of war and even murdered a civilian peace negotiator to whom he had given a safe-conduct pass.[5]

Perhaps the most fraudulent thing of all was the appropriation of Sandino's name by the Sandinista National Liberation Front in 1961. The modern Sandinistas were committed communists. Sandino, although his defiance of the United States made him the darling of the international Left, was never a communist. To the extent that he had any ideology, Sandino mixed leftist anarchism with a peculiar mysticism. He believed he was the reincarnation of Julius Caesar (he changed his middle name from Calderón to César in honor of the emperor). He claimed he gave orders to his men on the battlefield through ESP. And he predicted Nicaragua would be the site of Armageddon, where armies of angels and demons would do battle alongside more temporal troops.[6] Really, though, there was no such thing as *Sandinismo*. When Sandino was murdered in 1934, his movement vanished. In the end, he was just another *caudillo*.

As one *caudillo* died, another was being born. Anastasio Somoza was about to launch a dynasty that would last four decades and three Somozas; that would bring Nicaragua unprecedented prosperity, but at the same time turn it into a family farm; that would modernize its economy, but leave its political culture more backward than ever.

The odd thing was that Somoza was a failure at everything he attempted until he decided to try his hand at political tyranny. Car salesman, counterfeiter, and outhouse inspector—every one of his career moves ended in disaster and sometimes perilously close to jail. He had only two qualifications to be president of Nicaragua: He spoke excellent English, because he had attended business school in the United States; and he danced a stylish tango. The former enabled him to work as Henry Stimson's interpreter as Stimson negotiated out the 1927 peace agreement. And the latter endeared him to the wife of Matthew C. Hanna, the U.S. ambassador to Nicaragua. When the Nicaraguan government began setting up its new, apolitical National Guard, Hanna successfully backed Somoza for the commander's job.

The creation of the National Guard is arguably the most disastrous foreign policy initiative in the nearly two centuries that the United States has been dealing with Latin America. Stimson, Hanna, and the other U.S. diplomats wanted to get rid of the political armies that had kept Nicaragua almost continuously at war for ninety years. Instead, they created something much worse: a highly trained and well-equipped army that owed its loyalty not to a single party but to a single *family*.

In January 1933, after supervising two peaceful and reasonably fair presidential elections, the U.S. Marines left Nicaragua, this time for good. Within a month, the new president, Juan B. Sacasa (Somoza's uncle by marriage), negotiated a peace treaty with Sandino. Sandino's troops disarmed, except for about one hundred men who would form a constabulary. In return, they got control of about fourteen thousand square miles of northern Nicaragua, where Sandino planned to build agricultural cooperatives.

If either Sandino or Somoza intended to live up to the peace agreement, it couldn't have been for more than a few fleeting moments. When Sandino's 1,800 men "disarmed," they turned in only 361 weapons.[7] Soon Sandino was lobbying Sacasa to put the Guard under his control. Somoza and the Guard officers, on the other hand, made no secret of their contempt for the peace pact and their loathing for Sandino. Rumors that they were plotting a coup against Sacasa reached both the presidential palace and the U.S. embassy.

Before launching a coup, however, Somoza wanted to make sure that Sandino's army was out of the way. On February 21, 1934, on their way home from a dinner hosted by President Sacasa, Sandino and three of his officers were arrested by National Guardsmen, driven to the Managua airfield, and machine-gunned. It took Somoza two years to get around to toppling his uncle the president and staging phony elections to legitimize his own rule.

There were three Somozas in all: the old man, nicknamed Tacho; his oldest son, Luis; and a younger son, also named Anastasio Somoza and known as Tachito, Little Tacho. (Occasionally, to vary the routine, the Somozas made a loyal family retainer the president, but no one ever doubted who was running the show.) They were all educated in the United States, and often they seemed fonder of the States than they were of their own country. They even talked like the gangsters in the American movies that they loved. When Tacho was shot by an assassin in 1956, his final words to the U.S. ambassador were, "I'm done for."[8]

The Somozas raised theft to an art form. In the earliest days, they simply had the National Guard seize land they wanted. As time passed they grew more sophisticated—loaning themselves government money to buy estates and businesses; buying remote jungle property cheap, then building roads and railroad lines to it with public funds. By the 1970s, the family estimated its own fortune at $100 million.

They were all bullies, and vulgar bullies at that. In 1944, the old man ended a student demonstration by shooting a few of the kids and throwing another two hundred or so in jail. When Managua's society ladies staged a decorous protest march to try to get their sons and husbands out of jail, Tacho sent a mob of whores into the street to slap them around.[9]

The family rule always rested ultimately on the National Guard. But the Somozas did not dominate Nicaragua by brute force alone. They were also cunning manipulators. They consistently co-opted their opponents with money or partnerships in phony coalitions. They bribed opposition factions to form splinter parties and confuse elections. And they relentlessly played the American card. They curried favor with the United States whenever possible and, even more important, gave the appearance of having U.S. support even when it didn't exist.

Popular mythology has it that the Somozas were puppets propped up by the United States to do its bidding in Central America—that is, "He's a son of a bitch, but he's *our* son of a bitch," as Franklin Roosevelt is (apocryphally) supposed to have said of the first Somoza. There certainly were times when Washington found the Somozas useful allies: during World War II, when the fanatical anti-Nazi sentiments of old Tacho were a welcome contrast to pro-German stirrings in Panama; in 1953, when he let the United States use Nicaragua as a base for the agitation that eventually toppled the leftist regime of Jacobo Arbenz in Guatemala; or in 1961, when the gringos needed a launching pad for the Bay of Pigs invasion and Tachito and Luis gladly provided one.

Almost as often, however, the United States was trying to distance itself from the Somozas. State Department archives from the late 1930s and late 1940s are full of cables and position papers that debate how to discreetly signal disapproval of Tacho Somoza without returning the U.S. government to a position where it arbitrated every Nicaraguan political dispute. The United States periodically demonstrated its displeasure by chopping foreign aid to Nicaragua while increasing aid to neighboring countries.

Military aid, meanwhile, was almost unheard of. Often Washington refused even to sell Somoza weapons on a cash basis. And during the early 1950s, the United States persuaded England and Canada to join in an arms embargo against Nicaragua—an embargo broken by several Latin American governments. The Somozas themselves understood what was happening. "What advantage do we get from being friendly?" Tacho complained in 1954 after the Eisenhower administration blunted his attempt to overthrow the government in neighboring Costa Rica. "You treat us like an old wife. We would rather be treated like a young mistress."[10] U.S. policy on arming the Somozas did not change until the early 1960s, when Fidel Castro began attempts at subversion throughout the region.

Rarely, though, did a Somoza speak like that in public. Regardless of how cool relations were with Washington, the Somozas strove at all times to preserve the image of firm American support. If it didn't exist, they fabricated it. The week before he murdered Sandino, Tacho made sure he was photographed at a baseball game with the U.S. ambassador. That seemed to make his claim afterward that the Americans told him to kill Sandino plausible, even though it was totally untrue.

Tacho was assassinated in 1956, and Luis became president; Luis died of a heart attack in 1967, and Tachito became president. And Tachito's son, yet another Anastasio Somoza—El Chigüín—was placed in charge of an elite unit of the National Guard in 1977, clearly in training to become the fourth member of the dynasty. There was no end in sight to the Somozas.

Much of the Nicaraguan population, if not exactly adoring, accepted Somoza rule. While the Somozas could be brutal, they were not significantly worse than the many Nicaraguan presidents who had enforced their rule with party armies. It could even be argued that, as Latin American despots went, the Somozas were relatively enlightened. Among their neighbors, after all, were Maximiliano Hernández, who killed thirty thousand Salvadorans in a single week, and the even more efficient Rafael Trujillo, who slaughtered fifteen thousand people in a day and a half in the Dominican Republic.[11]

Meanwhile, the Nicaraguan economy steadily improved under Somoza family rule. Trade grew and diversified; per capita income rose explosively; infant mortality declined; the percentage of Nicaraguan children in school grew. Leftists in both the United States and Nicaragua often claimed that the Somozas were allowing the United States to rape the country's natural resources, but actually the American share of Nicaraguan exports declined steadily until it was less than 20 percent.[12]

Nonetheless, as Nicaragua was passed from Somoza to Somoza like a family cow, the dynasty built up an impressive stockpile of enemies. By their own count, the Somozas put down twenty-seven revolts during their first twenty-five years of rule, most of them led by businessmen or politicians from the Conservative Party.[13] Every rebellion was quickly snuffed out, often in a matter of hours.

But in 1961 the Somozas encountered trouble from a new quarter: the Left. The country's communist party had always restricted itself to conventional political organizing, insisting that conditions weren't right for armed struggle. The Cuban revolution, however, was turning the communist world on its head. Castro and his chief lieutenant, Che Guevara, were promoting a new, improvisational form of communism; no need to wait for the right conditions, they said, revolutionaries could *create* the right conditions just by making revolution.

That idea had obvious appeal to young Nicaraguan communists who were not enthusiastic about spending decades on pamphleteering and dreary conversations about class consciousness. A few dozen of them quickly joined an expeditionary force organized by Castro to invade Nicaragua through Honduras. The tiny army was immediately detected and crushed, but that didn't dull the enthusiasm of the survivors. In 1961, one of them—a nearsighted, part-time mailman named Carlos Fonseca, who in childhood dreamed of becoming a Catholic saint—got together with a bunch of his friends from school to form a new communist group. There were a lot of arguments over the name, but Fonseca stubbornly wore everyone down until they accepted his choice: the Sandinista National Liberation Front. In Spanish its initials were FSLN.

Later, the Sandinistas would deliberately obscure their origins and their ideology. But there was no doubt that the FSLN was a Marxist-Leninist group from the start. All four founders had dropped out of Nicaragua's communist party because it was too tame. Fonseca and Tomás Borge had been Marxists since 1953; Fonseca had traveled in the Soviet Union and published a book, *A Nicaraguan in Moscow,* in which he confidently predicted that the Soviet Union would soon supplant the United States as the world's greatest agricultural producer because of the Soviets' superior central economic planning.[14] Most of the early recruits had similar—or even more radical—backgrounds. Victor Tirado was a veteran militant of the Mexican Communist Party; Henry Ruiz had attended Patrice Lumumba University in Moscow and spent time in North Vietnam.

Besides communist sympathies, the founders shared something else: they were all well-educated city kids from families that were middle class or better. And when they moved into the countryside—according to Castro, the only proper Latin American environment from which to launch a revolution—their limitations were painfully apparent. They frequently got lost in the unfamiliar terrain; they were ill equipped for its hardships; and the peasants they expected to help them were indifferent or, worse, openly hostile. Nicaragua is the largest Central American country, with fifty thousand square miles of territory, and the campesinos were not short of land. They found Sandinista economic theories suspicious, Sandinista atheism repugnant, and they regularly betrayed FSLN guerrillas to the National Guard. The first two Sandinista military campaigns in the northern mountains, in 1963 and 1967, ended in complete disasters. Their few remaining guerrillas retreated so deeply into the jungle that, for all practical purposes, they ceased to exist.

Meanwhile, the Somoza dynasty was getting into serious trouble without any help from the Sandinistas. Its problems began with a huge 1972 earthquake that killed eighteen thousand people and destroyed most of downtown Managua. Tachito Somoza pocketed much of the foreign aid that flowed into Nicaragua afterward, while he bought up property at bargain-basement prices from stricken owners. While Somoza kept the cash, the National Guard looted relief supplies and then sold them on the black market. For the first time the emerging Nicaraguan middle class began to actively oppose Somoza.

Its antagonism became overwhelming on January 10, 1978. Pedro Joaquín Chamorro, editor of the anti-Somoza newspaper *La Prensa* and the leader of Conservative Party opposition to the dynasty, was driving to work through the empty streets of earthquake-ravaged central Managua when a pickup truck forced his car to the side of the road. Three men jumped out, pumped shotgun blasts through the windshield of Chamorro's Saab, then sped away. His face and chest riddled with buckshot, Chamorro died before he reached the hospital.

The obvious chief suspect to nearly everyone in Nicaragua was Tachito Somoza himself. Even as schoolboys the two men had fistfights; in 1959, Chamorro had launched a brief insurrection against the Somozas. The day after Chamorro's murder, thousands of rioters set fire to Somoza-owned buildings throughout Managua, and soon violent protests spread throughout the country.[15]

As it became apparent that the dynasty might not ride out the storm, the Sandinistas debated their future. The failure of the guerrilla operations in the countryside had split the FSLN into acrimonious factions. One, headed by Tomás Borge—the only surviving Sandinista founder—argued that the FSLN had to stay in the mountains and painstakingly organize for a "prolonged popular war" that might take twenty years. A second, led by Jaime Wheelock—the foremost Sandinista intellectual—contended that it made no sense to organize the peasants because they were a shrinking class. The large majority of Nicaraguans now were wage earners, "proletarians" in Marxist jargon, and the Sandinistas should move into the cities and begin organizing them politically, Wheelock said. It would be a long time before they were prepared to go to war.

The argument between the prolonged popular war faction and the proletarian faction had been going on for years. (Sometimes it was less an argument than a war. At one point Borge issued a proclamation expelling Wheelock and ordering his execution.) But now a third faction emerged. Known as the *terceristas* (followers of the third way), they were led by the dour brothers Daniel and

Humberto Ortega, sons of a Managua importer who was one of Augusto Sandino's original guerrillas. The Ortegas warned that the collapse of the Somoza dynasty could have both grave consequences and great benefits for the Sandinistas. If the Somozas fell under pressure from the middle class, the vast majority of Nicaraguans would see no need for a revolution. Sandinista organizing would be set back years. On the other hand, if the FSLN allied itself with the middle class and played a major role in toppling Somoza, the Sandinistas would be in a good position to influence the direction of the new government.

The *tercerista* willingness to form an alliance with the middle class and the business community has often been cited to prove that the *terceristas* were not really communists but social democrats. Nothing could be further from the truth. The *terceristas* were changing their means, not their ends. Daniel Ortega, in arguing for the *tercerista* strategy, stressed that the alliance would be "tactical and temporary." Humberto Ortega pledged that although the FSLN would have to mute its "slogans of Marxist orthodoxy," it would do so "without losing at any time our revolutionary Marxist-Leninist identity."[16]

The *tercerista* argument finally carried the day after long and difficult negotiations brokered by Fidel Castro, who promised to provide military aid if all three factions united. The Sandinistas immediately abandoned guerrilla warfare in the countryside and moved into the cities, where they had much better success at recruiting. Their efforts were unwittingly assisted by Tachito Somoza, who used his tiny air force to bomb civilian neighborhoods where the Sandinistas were staging operations.

Following the *tercerista* strategy, the Sandinistas toned down their rhetoric and let their non-Marxist allies do most of the public talking. They formed a provisional civilian junta (including Pedro Joaquín Chamorro's widow, Violeta) that apparently had only one Sandinista among its five members. In fact, two others were secret FSLN members, giving the Sandinistas a majority. The junta published a platform of government that promised free elections, full civil liberties, a mixed economy, a national army that would include some former members of the National Guard, a nonaligned foreign policy, and an interim legislative body that would be no more than one-third Sandinista.

The junta served its purpose; even the U.S. State Department, which was frantically trying to maneuver Somoza out of office, supported it. More significantly, perhaps, the Carter administration refused to sell Somoza ammunition to bolster his dwindling stocks and persuaded Israel, Somoza's last international ally, to cut off sales as well. When Somoza resigned on July 17, 1979, most of the National Guard officers' corps buckled and ran. Two days later, the war was over.

On September 21, 1979, two months after the fall of Somoza, Sandinista leaders began a three-day meeting to draw up a blueprint for the new Nicaragua. Their report, though not intended for public circulation, leaked out; it came to be known as "the seventy-two-hour document." In remarkable detail, it set forth the FSLN's plans to cripple Nicaragua's private sector, destroy the "traitorous bourgeoisie," neutralize the Catholic Church, jail and exile Protes-

15

tant clergy, build up and politicize the army, and aid communist guerrilla movements in neighboring countries. Much later the Sandinistas would argue that their most draconian measures were adopted only in response to American support for the contras. But the seventy-two-hour document, which foreshadowed Sandinista plans, was written when there were no contras and the U.S. government was underwriting the new regime to the tune of $120 million.

The most detailed description in the document was that of how the FSLN intended to eviscerate its erstwhile allies in the middle class and the business community. By nationalizing the banks and the export-import business, the Sandinistas noted, they already had "lopped off a strategic portion of the economic power of the bourgeoisie." To finish the job, they would forbid foreign bank loans to the private sector. A rent freeze would "eliminate landlords in such a manner that negotiations can begin for the State to take over all rental housing." And they would not permit "contaminating industry, commerce and private agriculture with North American capital."[17]

The bourgeoisie must come under political attack, too, the Sandinistas noted, but without the rhetoric of class warfare. "We should hit it not by attacking it as a class," the document noted, "but by attacking its most representative elements as soon as they give us the first opportunity."

The reason for all this secrecy was to keep foreign aid flowing from the United States and its allies. This socialist revolution would be built with capitalist money. "Radical moves" would have to wait "because political expediency dictates that more favorable conditions be developed for the revolution, and requires that first the more urgent task of its political, economic, and military consolidation be obtained in order to move on to greater revolutionary transformations."

Nonetheless, there was no shortage of signposts about the revolution's direction. Among the first things the FSLN did was to put the army under control of the party, not the government. The junta issued a decree officially naming it the Sandinista People's Army, and then to drive the point home, another decree said only FSLN entities had the legal right to call themselves "Sandinista." A couple of months later, the civilian defense minister—Bernardino Larios, a former National Guard colonel who had once been arrested for plotting a coup against Somoza—was thrown into prison and replaced by Humberto Ortega.

Freedom of expression was slowly strangled. All the country's television stations were confiscated and put under party control within days of the war's end. The Sandinistas began kicking radio newsmen off the air and regularly shutting down *La Prensa* in early 1980 for stories "detrimental to the revolution." In September 1980 they made it illegal to publish or broadcast stories about "economic stability" or anything "that jeopardizes internal security or national defense."[18]

The "mixed economy" began to disappear, too. The Sandinistas confiscated more than 1 million acres of land in the first two months of the revolution.[19] Much of it belonged to the Somoza family. But then the government began seizing property and businesses because they were "mismanaged" or "under-exploited." Finally, anything of "public utility" was fair game. As a result, the

16

production of beans fell by 25 percent and cotton by 33 percent in the first three years of Sandinista rule. The declines rippled through the rest of the economy as well. But that didn't stop the Sandinistas from doubling military spending from Somoza-era levels.[20] Soviet weapons began arriving within weeks of the Sandinista victory.

The Sandinistas accepted economic aid from the United States and Latin American democracies, but otherwise held them at arm's length. U.S. Peace Corps volunteers were rejected; Venezuelan and Panamanian military advisers were sent home after a polite interval. Soviet and Cuban personnel, however, began flowing into the country. (The Sandinistas had established party-to-party relations with the Soviet Communist party and backed the Soviet invasion of Afghanistan in the United Nations.) The more numerous Cubans were particularly nettlesome to Nicaraguans; they wanted to reorganize the campesinos into collectives, hold political meetings all the time, and set up neighborhood committees that the Nicaraguans considered little more than organized spying. Worst of all, as far as the Nicaraguans were concerned, was their aggressive atheism, an affront in a deeply religious country.

Nowhere were the Cubans received with more hostility than on the Atlantic coast, a predominantly Indian area. When Cubans began replacing Moravian schoolteachers favored by the Miskito Indians, the Miskitos protested. The Sandinistas struck back by sending troops into churches to make arrests, and there were several shoot-outs. In retaliation, in 1980 the Sandinistas relocated three whole Indian villages. About the same time, they postponed Nicaraguan elections until 1985 and redesigned the interim legislative body that would govern the country until then. The Sandinistas, instead of getting one-third of the seats, would have a majority.

Some Nicaraguans turned on the Sandinistas right away. For others, it took time. Shortly after the army was put under party control, Enrique Bolaños, head of Nicaragua's most prominent business organization, went to see his old friend Violeta Chamorro at the junta's offices.

"Violeta, I can't believe you're signing some of these decrees," Bolaños said. "How can you let them have the army? If they have the army, they have everything."

"Ohhhh, Enrique, don't be silly," Chamorro replied in a scolding tone. "They're good boys. You worry too much." As Bolaños left her office, he was worrying even more. These people were going to drag the country back into another civil war.

2 | The Volcano Rumbles

No one remembers, exactly, the day the war began. Almost everyone who was there is dead now. But one day in May 1980, a Sandinista militia commander named Pedro Joaquín González assembled his eighty troops outside their barracks in Quilalí, a small agricultural town in Nueva Segovia Department, about twenty-five miles south of the Honduran border. I've had enough of these sons of bitches, he told the men. I'm leaving. And all eighty of them went with him. In a bit of irony that did not go unnoticed when the high command in Managua found out what had happened a few days later, González and his men moved north into the rugged area around El Chipote, the mountain fortress of old Augusto Sandino himself.

González was a short, serious man of about thirty-five. He had joined the Sandinistas in 1972 and became one of the top lieutenants of Germán Pomares, El Danto. Unlike most of the Sandinista forces, made up of people from the city, the troops of Pomares and González were nearly all humble campesinos. They called themselves *Milpas*, a Spanish acronym for Anti-Somoza Popular Militias that was also a play on words. *Milpa* is Spanish for corn patch, and the name was a boast of their authentic peasant origins.

After the war against Somoza ended, the *Milpas* had become the government's military force in parts of northern Nicaragua. González was made the commander of Quilalí. But the revolution was not turning out the way he expected. He complained to headquarters that the top officers in the new Sandinista army were all from aristocratic families. Cuadra, Castillo, Carrión —these were the same thieving parasites that got rich under Somoza. How was it possible that they were in charge? Where were the campesinos and workers? Headquarters did not reply.

When there *was* word from Managua, it was almost always bad. The small farmers around Quilalí were being forced to join collectives; those who resisted lost their land or went to jail. There were constant political meetings, and the campesinos who didn't attend had difficulties getting the small loans they

18

needed for fertilizer and seed. And the government was even sending new priests to some of the local churches. They seemed to be working from a different Bible than the one the mountain people knew.

After González deserted, he installed his men in a mountain camp, then took a few of his officers to Honduras. Thousands of Nicaraguans had already crossed the border, abandoning their homes rather than submitting to the Sandinistas. Perhaps, González thought, some of them might like to return and fight.

One of the first Nicaraguans he met was Tirzo Moreno, the cattle broker from Wiwilí. Moreno's jubilation at the Sandinista victory had turned sour within weeks. First the new government imposed price controls and other regulations on the cattle industry, making it almost impossible for him to stay in business. Then someone from the Interior Ministry mentioned that Moreno was suspected of selling supplies to the National Guard during the war. The accusatory tone struck Moreno as ridiculous—of course he had sold supplies to the Guard, how could you tell them no without going to prison?—but he wasn't laughing. The Interior Ministry had its own secret police force, and it also ran the "people's tribunals" that were conducting assembly-line show trials of National Guardsmen and those suspected of sympathizing with the Somoza regime. Just about everyone who appeared before the tribunals came out with a thirty-year prison sentence.

A lot of people in Wiwilí were in jail, Moreno knew. And the Miskito Indians who lived along the Coco River to the north had it even worse. Some of them—including Lyster Athders, a member of the Council of Elders that governed the tribe—had been killed. Somehow the plight of the Indians was even more disturbing to Moreno than his own problems. The Miskitos had never asked anything of anyone except to be left alone. What kind of a government would be killing the harmless old preachers on the Council of Elders?

So in September 1979, less than two months after he celebrated the Sandinista victory, Moreno rounded up his few hundred cattle and slipped across the border into Honduras. As the months passed, more and more of his friends and neighbors from Wiwilí joined him in exile, each with a tale more harrowing than the last. Now, eight months later, Pedro Joaquín González was offering him a chance to go back and fight. "With pleasure," Moreno told him.

The timing of their first operation was calculated to drive the Sandinistas wild. During the week of the first anniversary of the revolution, González seized Quilalí, the town where he had been commander. The men rounded up the townspeople to listen to a few propaganda speeches, took some ammunition and equipment from their old barracks, did a little recruiting, and left. Aggravating as it was to the Sandinistas, taking Quilalí didn't amount to much as a military action; since the *Milpas* had deserted, there were few Sandinista soldiers in Quilalí. The next operation had a little more sting to it: The *Milpas* robbed a bank in nearby El Jícaro and afterward engaged in a running gun battle with a Sandinista helicopter.

The business with the helicopter convinced González that he needed some help. His men were armed with hunting rifles and a few beat-up M-16s; as

19

members of a militia force, rather than the regular army, they never had much of an arsenal. But if they were going to fight a real army, González reasoned, they needed real weapons. With Moreno and a few others, he went back to Honduras to make contact with the Argentine embassy. The Argentine military government had just completed its infamous "dirty war" against Marxist guerrillas, killing thousands of people in the process, and no one in the hemisphere hated communists more. Maybe the Argentines would help.

The Argentines were interested. But first, they suggested, González should get together with a few dozen former National Guardsmen who had taken refuge in Honduras and were also looking for a way to fight the Sandinistas. González was reluctant, but he called the Guardsmen. A meeting was scheduled at a hotel in Tegucigalpa, the Honduran capital.

A tense silence enveloped the room as the men—thirty-six Guardsmen, seven *Milpas*—sat down around a circle of conference tables. It didn't last long. "Where did you fight during the war?" one of the Guardsmen asked one of the *Milpas*. "Around Pantasma," the guerrilla replied. The Guard officer jumped to his feet, cords straining in his neck like steel cable. "You shit-eater!" he screamed. "My brother was killed at Pantasma!"

It took several hours before the recriminations and threats finally died down. "We have to work together," Moreno—one of the few people in the room who hadn't fought on either side during the revolution and hence was under no suspicion of having killed or tortured anyone's father, brother, or friend—told the group. "Our cause is the same—ex-Sandinista, ex-National Guard, campesino—we have to fight the Sandinistas together." A tentative agreement was reached, and some men even shook hands. But it was clear to everyone that old grudges would die hard.

A few days later, González told his men he was going to an important meeting in San Bartolo, a village near Quilalí. His old friend Mamerto Herrera, the head of the Interior Ministry in Quilalí, had decided to betray the Sandinistas and supply the *Milpas* with arms. A lot of the men had suspected all along that González and Herrera were in touch with each other. They were close friends; in fact, González was the godfather of one of Herrera's children. And the men had also noticed that when they seized Quilalí in July, the normally ubiquitous Interior Ministry police were nowhere to be found.

González took only one soldier with him to the meeting, a boy of about fourteen, to act as a lookout. "What do I need bodyguards for?" he said when his men protested. "Torrera will provide security." Later the men pieced together what happened that night. González and the boy made their rendezvous with Herrera, who took them to a house in San Bartolo and told them he would return later. Soon after nightfall, the boy glanced out the window and saw Sandinista troops surrounding the house. No one is certain who fired first, but it was a one-sided fight; González and the boy were dead in a matter of minutes. Herrera was seen a few weeks later in Managua, driving a new Mercedes-Benz.

Pedro Joaquín González and the *Milpas* were the first to actually take up arms against the Sandinistas. But anti-Sandinista conspiracies were hatching right and left throughout 1980 and 1981: inside Nicaragua, throughout Central America, in Miami—in fact, just about anywhere two Nicaraguans could meet. The Sandinistas and their supporters would later claim the United States created the armed opposition. The truth is that the idea of armed rebellion occurred spontaneously and simultaneously to several different groups, and all of them went in search of foreign sponsors.

Interestingly, most of the anti-Sandinista groups ruled out (initially, at least) the two most obvious sugar daddies. In 1980, most Nicaraguans assumed that Jimmy Carter's administration was pro-Sandinista. Not only had Carter pulled the rug from under Somoza by refusing to sell him military supplies, but the president also had railroaded a bill granting $120 million in aid to Sandinista Nicaragua through a reluctant Congress. The United States was even the largest single donor to the vaunted FSLN literacy campaign, which taught peasants to read using textbooks including such lines as "The *yanquis* will always be defeated in our country."

The other obvious potential source of money was the Somoza family itself. When Tacho Somoza fled Nicaragua, his first stop was Miami. But his always tenuous relations with the Carter administration quickly frayed even further, and he decided to move along: first to the Bahamas, then Guatemala, and finally Paraguay, where his fellow *caudillo* Alfredo Stroessner allowed him to settle.

But Somoza was far from certain that his time in Nicaragua was over. The only reason he had lost the war, as far as he was concerned, was Jimmy Carter's meddling. And Carter wouldn't be president forever. During Somoza's brief stay in Miami he beckoned Juan Wong, a family friend who had also fled Nicaragua, to his bayfront condominium. Wong would be in charge of making arrangements to reassemble the scattered units of the National Guard. "I can't do it myself, because I'm here under an agreement with the State Department, and they're listening to my phone calls," Somoza said. He gave Wong $500,000 to buy food and medicine for Guardsmen.

Wong and a Guard commander named Pablo Emilio Salazar began touring Central America as Somoza's unofficial ambassadors, trying to convince the governments to accept former Guardsmen into their own armies.

"All the constitutions prohibit foreigners from being in the army," Wong recalled later. "But we were asking them to accept Nicaraguan brigades, so we could keep the men together and maintain discipline. Because I knew, once they got to Miami, forget it. It would be all over. That's only natural." If the units stayed intact, though, they could be mobilized against the Sandinistas later.

This was by no means an easy argument to make in coup-happy Central America, but Salazar was an effective spokesman. Known to the National Guard troops as Commander Bravo, he had been Somoza's best field commander; he kept the Sandinista forces under the command of Edén Pastora bottled up for months, unable to penetrate more than a couple of miles past the Costa Rican border. The military men he spoke to in Central America were visibly impressed with him.

While Wong and Salazar were in Guatemala, they had an argument. Wong wanted to go to El Salvador next; he didn't think Honduras was safe. But Salazar insisted they fly to Tegucigalpa. He wanted to see an old girlfriend from Managua who had promised to meet him there. Her name was Miryam

Baltodano, and she was quite beautiful. She had been a very successful cosmetics saleswoman in prerevolutionary Nicaragua.

What Salazar didn't know was that after he fled Nicaragua at the end of the war, Miryam had taken up with his archenemy, Edén Pastora. One night as Miryam slept, Pastora prowled her house and, tucked away at the back of an overstuffed closet, found a National Guard uniform with Bravo's name on it. The next day, whether through coercion or persuasion, Miryam went to work for the Sandinistas.

So the unsuspecting Bravo flew to Honduras, checked into the Hotel Istmania, and disappeared with a woman. They found him three days later in an empty house a few miles away, his body covered with cigarette burns, his genitals missing, and most of the skin of his face peeled away.

That ended any hope of keeping the National Guard intact on a large scale. But Somoza still tried to hold onto a nucleus of young Guardsmen from the Basic Infantry Training School, known by its Spanish initials EEBI. The elite EEBI had been under the command of Somoza's son, El Chigüín. Somoza invited about fifteen members of the EEBI to go to Paraguay with him; he would pay them $1,200 a month to provide his personal security.

But when they arrived, the Guardsmen found their salaries had been cut to $1,000 and then again to $750. To add insult to injury, money was held out of their checks for rent and electricity in the Somoza compound. They demanded a meeting with Somoza. "If I had known you were such a mean son of a bitch," one of the captains shouted, "I would have been the first one trying to fight against you and kill you, instead of fighting for you!" But it was to no avail. Now that Somoza was paying the bills himself, instead of writing government checks to cover them, he had discovered the virtues of thrift. He wouldn't even use his armored car; the thick steel plating made for lousy gas mileage and heavy tire wear. Disgusted, most of the Guardsmen went back to Miami.

There they began plotting a return to Nicaragua to fight the Sandinistas. They called themselves the Fifteenth of September Legion, after the day Central America won independence from Spain. They talked about getting money and weapons from the military governments in El Salvador, Guatemala, Argentina —just about every possible source except Somoza. No one, the Guardsmen figured, would support a movement that aimed to bring back the Somoza dynasty.

Word of their plans got back to Tacho in Paraguay. Exile, Somoza had discovered, was not nearly as much fun as being a dictator. He was drinking too much and quarreling with his entourage. In mid-September of 1980 he called some of the men at the Fifteenth of September Legion. If they were interested, Somoza said, he would put up the money to back them, no strings attached.

The Legionnaires had told themselves they wouldn't take Somoza money— easy enough to say when none had been offered. Now, however, they would have to do some serious thinking.

They were still talking about it on September 17 when something happened in Paraguay that made it all irrelevant. As Somoza's Mercedes limousine pulled out of his compound, a blue pickup truck darted out of a side street to block its path. A man popped up on a nearby balcony and aimed a Chinese-made rocket launcher at Somoza's car, but it misfired. Another member of the hit squad charged the limousine in desperation, spraying the rear doors with bullets from an M-16. Eighteen shots hit Somoza, who was dead long before the first assassin finally got his rocket launcher working and blew off the limousine's front end.

Years later, the assassins—Argentine communists who trained for the operation in Managua—confided that they were surprised it had been so easy to kill Somoza. They had expected an armored car.[1]

The Fifteenth of September Legion was not the only plot afoot in Miami. New York has skyscrapers, Washington has monuments, Los Angeles has freeways. Miami has conspiracies. Sleazeball gangsters, crazed narcomerchants, pin-striped money-launderers, icy arms merchants: they prowl the little coffee shops of Little Havana's Calle Ocho, the shining steel-and-glass bank towers on Brickell Avenue, the hidden rifle ranges out where the west end of the city falls into the Everglades. It is no coincidence that Miami is the only city in the continental United States with a CIA station.

During the 1960s and 1970s, the chief conspirators were Cuban exiles plotting against Fidel Castro. In the 1980s, however, Miami belonged to the Nicaraguans. In the beginning they were mostly professional soldiers and wealthy Somocistas who had fled the Sandinista revolution.

But there was also a handful of businessmen and professionals who had no connections to Somoza yet mistrusted the Sandinistas. Their numbers grew every month as the leftward march of the revolution became more obvious. They had worked in banks, television and radio stations, construction firms, advertising agencies, law offices, insurance companies; most were in their thirties or early forties, from a generation that had yet to assert itself in Nicaragua. Some had been active in the anti-Somoza Conservative Party, and others had been apolitical.

They began meeting a couple of nights a week to talk about Nicaragua, often at a video production company on Brickell Avenue where Octavio Sacasa worked. Sacasa had managed a family-owned television station before the revolution. As the war neared its end, he was in Los Angeles at an industry convention, buying syndicated programming. While he was away, his wife Marta began spending her evenings fiddling with a shortwave radio, listening to the clandestine Sandinista station. On her thirtieth birthday, Octavio called from California to boast that he just purchased some hot new shows. "Stop buying," Marta said. "I don't think these people believe in private property." The first week the Sandinistas were in power, they seized the Sacasa television station.

Marta Sacasa had never paid much attention to politics in Nicaragua; managing four toddlers kept her busy. But she found exile lonely and Americans peculiarly self-obsessed; when her husband began hosting the weeknight discussion group, she went to a couple of meetings, just for something to do. At first she sat near the door, listening; after a while, she moved into the ring of chairs. Soon she was one of the most animated speakers, fiercely insisting that the only way to reason with the Sandinistas was at gunpoint. "We have created a monster," one of the men confided to her husband one night after she delivered a particularly violent harangue.

The discussion almost always focused on a single theme: Who lost Nicaragua? In later years, the group members would recall those first months as "the time of the guiltiness." In speech after impassioned speech, the finger was pointed in all directions: The National Guard was guilty, for converting itself into a praetorian guard with allegiance to a single family. The Somoza family was guilty, for being so outrageously corrupt. The Liberal Party was guilty, for allowing itself to become a personal vehicle for the Somozas instead of acting like a real political party. The business community was guilty, for turning on Somoza without making sure of the alternative. The arguments would go on for hours.

On May 13, 1980, the discussion group underwent a radical transformation. The exiles were throwing a reception for José Francisco Cardenal, a prominent Managua construction contractor who had just delivered a public slap in the face to the Sandinistas, resigning his post as head of the constituent assembly and flying into exile in Miami.

At the reception, the members of the discussion group zestfully turned once again to their favorite subject. The National Guard had lost Nicaragua, said Fernando Agüero, a dentist and longtime Conservative Party politician. The National Guard was a corrupt, genocidal institution that drove Nicaraguans into the arms of the communists.

"Oh, no, Doctor Agüero," interjected a man from across the room. "It wasn't the National Guard. There is plenty of blame. There were many Nicaraguan people who supported Somoza, many politicians who said they opposed Somoza but in reality practiced *zancudismo* [parasitism]. I think even the Conservative Party once made a pact with Somoza, didn't it, Doctor?" Agüero blanched at that. After leading anti-Somoza riots in 1967 that resulted in hundreds of deaths, the dentist had scandalously abandoned his opposition three years later to join a short-lived power-sharing arrangement with the dynasty.

Hardly anyone at the reception knew the stocky, caramel-colored man arguing with Agüero; he had never attended a meeting of the discussion group. He was a former National Guard colonel who had spent the last four years of the Somoza government in Washington as the Nicaraguan military attaché. His name was Enrique Bermúdez.

After May 13, the discussion group was never the same. The first and most obvious change was that the argument between Agüero and Bermúdez ended "the time of the guiltiness." All Nicaraguans bear some responsibility for what happened, that was the new refrain. This is not the time to fix guilt. This is the time to organize. And there was no longer any question that what the group's members were organizing for was combat; the discussion group's inchoate notions of somehow resisting the Sandinistas had crystallized into a determination to go to war.

The presence of the forty-one-year-old José Francisco Cardenal—"Chicano" to his friends—meant there was something to organize around. Cardenal was well known in Nicaragua (his company had built several of Managua's largest hotels and shopping centers), and as president of the country's largest business organization he also had a degree of recognition outside the country. He had a long, unblemished record of opposition to Somoza. The paunchy, silver-haired Cardenal could be combative—some people thought he could start a fight in a phone booth—but if you were going to try to launch a counterrevolution, you *needed* some combativeness.

But there was still a fundamental division among the exiles over what role the former National Guardsmen should play. It was a debate that would never be fully resolved, that would reverberate throughout anti-Sandinista politics for the next decade. For some Nicaraguans, it was a sincere question, often colored by personal experience, for better or worse, with the National Guard. For others, it was simply ammunition in the struggle for personal power— ammunition that became all the more useful later on when the Nicaraguans discovered what a potent effect it had on Americans.

One school of thought was that any anti-Sandinista movement should be led by civilians. The National Guard long ago had deteriorated into a vast criminal conspiracy and simply couldn't be trusted, according to this argument. It had distorted the face of Nicaraguan politics for forty years. And, in any event, its reputation was so poor that any movement that included the Guard wouldn't be able to attract the support of either Nicaraguans or foreign governments.

The anti-Guard exiles coalesced around a group called the Nicaraguan Democratic Union, or UDN. Some of the UDN leaders, like Chicano Cardenal, were relatively moderate. Their objection to the Guard was pragmatic, having to do with image, and they were willing to accept former Guardsmen in subordinate roles.

Others, however, had a more radical view. One of the most profound critics of the Guard was Edmundo Chamorro. Edmundo and his younger brother Fernando—nicknamed El Negro—were Conservative Party activists who had vehemently hated the Somozas and had periodically mounted small military rebellions against them as far back as 1959. In the late 1960s, the Sandinistas got in touch, hoping the Chamorros would share their gunrunning expertise. A sporadic cooperation began that grew much stronger toward the end of the revolution. El Negro, in fact, pulled off one of the most famous stunts of the war, firing two rockets into Somoza's headquarters from an eighth-floor window of Managua's Hotel Inter-Continental.

The alliance between the Chamorro brothers and the Sandinistas, always tentative, broke up soon after the revolution ended. Edmundo immediately went into exile; El Negro was still working as a car salesman in Nicaragua, but everyone expected him to leave at any moment. And there was no doubt that Edmundo spoke for both of them when it came to the National Guard. The Chamorro brothers had spent too many years fighting those bastards, Edmundo said, and knew very well what a bunch of murderous criminals they were. Sometimes when he talked about it, Edmundo ran his fingers along a thin white scar on his neck, a souvenir from a 1960 shoot-out with the Guard.

Another group of exiles argued that it was crazy to cast aside the military expertise of the National Guard. Why try to improvise when there were people available who knew how to organize an army? It was absurd, these exiles said, to

25

suggest that all seven thousand members of the National Guard had been murderers and thieves. Some were, and some weren't. Making collective judgments about individuals based on the actions of an institution was wrong; that was what the Sandinistas were doing. If the world had been able to separate criminal elements from decent people in the German army after World War II —as it had at the Nuremberg trials—then Nicaraguans ought to be able to do the same.

The exiles in this group included Octavio and Marta Sacasa and the corpulent broadcaster Frank Arana. They had no formal organization, but found themselves working more and more with the National Guardsmen of the Fifteenth of September Legion. While the UDN talked about raising an army, the Legion had actually begun training a few dozen recruits. With money raised from Cuban-Americans, it opened a training camp at the edge of the Everglades. The FBI visited several times, looking for an excuse to shut the place down, but the Nicaraguans made sure all the weapons on hand were legal. The Legion also maintained a much smaller camp in Guatemala.

The Legion had also found a new leader: Enrique Bermúdez, the former National Guard colonel who had quieted the search for the guilty. The Legionnaires had gone looking for a new face at the top because they were finding it difficult to get anyone to take them seriously. Except for pilots and doctors, who were colonels by virtue of their specialties, none of the Legionnaires had risen above the rank of captain in the National Guard. When they tried to arrange a meeting with the top commanders of the Guatemalan army to seek aid, the Guatemalans had refused. Generals, the Guatemalans explained icily, do not meet with captains.

So the Legion wanted a higher-ranking officer. But finding one was more difficult than it seemed. During the final year or two of the revolution, the National Guard had grown increasingly brutal, bombing civilian areas and summarily executing suspected Sandinista sympathizers. Officers linked to those kinds of atrocities were out; so were the notoriously corrupt. Of the few who remained, many preferred trying to make a go of their life in exile to joining a half-cocked guerrilla group with no external support. Gen. Julio Gutiérrez, who had commanded the Nicaraguan unit that went to the Dominican Republic in 1965 as part of the Organization of American States peacekeeping force, turned the Legion down. So did Gen. Fulgencio Mendoza, who had run Nicaragua's telecommunications agency and served as military attaché at several embassies in Europe.

Then someone suggested Bermúdez, who had been the executive officer of the peace-keeping unit in the Dominican Republic. His record was so spotless that the Carter administration, when it was still hoping the National Guard could be kept intact after Somoza's departure, had suggested Bermúdez as a possible commander.[2] Bermúdez, in fact, was one of the few National Guard officers who had achieved some renown in Nicaragua without murdering someone or engaging in spectacular theft. In the 1950s and 1960s, he had been a pretty fair pitcher for the Guard baseball team. After Catholicism, baseball is Nicaragua's religion.

On the day the new Sandinista diplomatic delegation came to take over the

Nicaraguan embassy in Washington, Bermúdez assembled all the official documents in his custody to hand over to the new attaché. He concealed his surprise when the Sandinista official who came to his office was a woman. But his poker face collapsed when the woman spoke; he recognized her staccato Spanish as Cuban. Bermúdez reached into the stack of papers, intending to remove some confidential documents from the Inter-American Defense Board containing an intelligence assessment of the Cuban military. *But what difference does it make?* he thought. *The Inter-American Defense Board has recognized the Sandinista government—it has a communist member now.* He handed the Cuban woman the documents and left. There was one secret, however, that he didn't give away: two cases of embassy liquor were stored in his garage. Keeping the booze, Bermúdez thought, would be his final act of defiance against the Sandinistas.

With his diplomatic experience and his special training in military schools in Brazil, Panama, and the United States, Bermúdez assumed he would have no trouble finding a job with one of the many international agencies headquartered in Washington. But no one would even talk to him. "Everyone loves the Sandinistas," he told his wife, Elsa, one night after another fruitless day of job-hunting. "They're international darlings. And you wouldn't believe the reputation of the National Guard. Everyone thinks that we murdered women and children all day and all night."

Even the Americans turned on him. In December 1979, when Elsa returned to her home in the Dominican Republic for her brother's funeral, the Carter administration refused to give her a visa to reenter the United States. For three months Bermúdez had to stay home watching three small children while he phoned all over the State Department, trying to get help. Bermúdez hadn't agreed before with his colleagues at the embassy that Jimmy Carter had wanted a Sandinista victory in Nicaragua—he thought it was more complicated than that—but it was hard for him to see this visa thing as anything but vindictive. Elsa wasn't even a Nicaraguan.

By the time Elsa got back to Washington, Bermúdez was broke and their home was about to be repossessed. He went to work at the only job he could find: driving a magazine delivery truck around Washington for twelve hours a day. He was forty-seven years old.

The Fifteenth of September Legion got in touch with Bermúdez in spring 1980. After a couple of visits to Miami, he agreed to become the Legion's "political-military coordinator." He sold his home in the Maryland suburbs for about what he still owed the bank. Then he rented a U-Haul truck, loaded his furniture and family into it, and headed for Florida. The truck cost $300. He scraped the money together by selling the two cases of embassy Scotch stored in his garage. As he drove south, Bermúdez chuckled to himself. The Sandinistas were paying for his move.

3 | An Interview with a Tape Recorder

His name was Pedro Ortega, but he liked to be called *Comandante* Juan Carlos. It was no accident that he selected the name of a Spanish king for his nom de guerre; *Comandante* Juan Carlos had been born in Spain and made no secret of his belief that Central America had been in abject decline ever since the conquistadors left. He had moved to Nicaragua in the 1950s and owned a match factory with some members of the Somoza family. In 1980, while the Nicaraguan exile community in Miami was still debating what to do about the Sandinistas, *Comandante* Juan Carlos was already bragging that he had used his considerable fortune to raise an army that would whip the communists. He issued regular communiqués, announcing that his National Liberation Army would be holding a staff meeting at some Managua hotel. Everyone considered him sort of a lovable coot. But when he flew into Miami one day in early 1981 and asked for a meeting with leaders of the exile community, they decided to attend. Maybe, they reasoned, he would give their anti-Sandinista political organization some money.

The meeting took place in a suite at a downtown hotel. *Comandante* Juan Carlos was doing the talking, urging the exiles to join his army and get Nicaragua back on the road to monarchy. In the middle of his speech, one of the *comandante's* young assistants entered the room, clicked his heels and saluted.

"I'm sorry, *Comandante*, but you have a very important call in the other room," the aide said.

"Can't you see I'm busy?" Juan Carlos snapped. "Take a message."

The aide saluted again and marched away, only to return a few moments later. "I'm very sorry, *Comandante*," he apologized. "But Mr. Haig says it really can't wait."

"Ahhh, these gringos," Juan Carlos sighed in exasperation. "Excuse me, gentlemen, I'll get rid of him as quickly as I can."

As Juan Carlos left the room, the exiles stared at each other, wide-eyed. Could this senile monarchist really have forged an alliance with the secretary of state

28

of the brand-new Reagan administration? Maybe there was more to this National Liberation Army than they had thought.

For several weeks Juan Carlos was treated with new respect, befitting a man who could put the U.S. secretary of state on hold. Then the exiles got hold of Juan Carlos's personnel list and discovered that "Haig" was the name of one of his young assistants.

In war, the first casualty is the checkbook. As Nicaraguan exiles in Guatemala and Miami mounted their initial efforts against the Sandinistas in 1980, they discovered that even guerrilla wars cannot be waged at bargain prices. And they also found that most of their own countrymen thought they were nuts. *Los loquitos*, the exiles called them—the little crazy ones, thinking they can declare war on a government that has the Soviet Union behind it.

When *los loquitos* came calling, exile businessmen usually slammed the doors in their faces. When they did agree to listen, it was usually just out of curiosity; rarely did anyone agree to put up any money. Some members of the Somoza family helped out with petty cash—a plane ticket here, $50 there—but real aid was almost nonexistent. Most Nicaraguans thought that trying to fight the Sandinistas was a lost cause.

In desperation, the anti-Sandinista groups looked for foreign sponsors. Representatives of the Fifteenth of September Legion went to Paraguay but came back empty-handed. They contacted Israel in hopes of obtaining a shipload of arms that had been on its way to the Somoza government in mid-1979. The ship had turned back when the United States persuaded Israel to cut off weapons sales to Tachito. But, the Ffifteenth of September men learned, Somoza hadn't actually paid for the arms, only put down a deposit on them.

Chicano Cardenal was also beating the pavement in search of help. He visited Venezuela and Honduras without results. Then he approached the civilian-military junta that governed El Salvador and found its members more receptive. The Salvadoran government was facing an increasingly strong communist insurgency that was being supplied through Nicaragua, and the Salvadorans liked the idea of tit-for-tat. But the Salvadorans decided to channel their aid to Jorge Salazar, a coffee grower who still lived inside Nicaragua. Salazar, an outspoken enemy of the Sandinistas, told the Salvadorans he was going to organize an internal front to fight the FSLN. Two months later, however, Sandinista police gunned Salazar down as he was on his way to meet with his co-conspirators, and the Salvadorans backed away from the whole situation.

The lack of funds didn't stop the Fifteenth of September Legion from setting up a headquarters in Guatemala City. The idea was that Enrique Bermúdez, the public relations face of the organization, would stay in Miami and look for money. Everybody else would go to Guatemala and get about the business of actually setting up a military force. It might also be possible to find some support in Guatemala, where the military and the political right were among the most stridently anticommunist forces in the hemisphere.

29

Two dozen of the Legionnaires moved into a cavernous old house near the Guatemala City zoo. There was no furniture, no heat, not even hot water. The men slept on the floor; they jogged around the zoo every morning in the chilly dawn air, then came home to freezing showers. They begged food by flirting with the ladies who ran vegetable stalls in the open-air market downtown and counted themselves lucky on days when there were two meals.

The situation should have been depressing, but morale was surprisingly high. About the only thing not in short supply at the Legion house was arrogance. Most of the men had been officers in the elite EEBI unit of the National Guard commanded by El Chigüín, the youngest Somoza. They were young, capable, and accustomed to getting their way. And they had the cocky self-assurance of men who had gambled for high stakes and won.

The leader was Justiniano Pérez, who had been a captain and the second in command of the EEBI. Pérez always looked like he had just stepped out of a recruiting poster; even in the middle of the jungle, his uniform seemed freshly pressed. Although he was taciturn—the men called him El Calladito, the silent one—he exuded command authority. His troops thought he was some kind of military god. Even the Somozas had been impressed: Pérez was one of the few officers that they sent a rescue flight for after the fall of Managua.

Pérez had the unquestioned loyalty of the men. That was not necessarily true of some of the other top leaders of the Legion, many of whom were known for their conspiratorial skills rather than their military expertise.

One was Guillermo Mendieta, technically a colonel but really a dentist. Mendieta had been a close friend of the Somoza family, and Tachito had paid for his education. But in 1978, Mendieta tried to engineer a coup against Somoza—not, the men thought, out of any sudden craving for democracy in Nicaragua, but because he sensed Somoza was losing the war and he wanted to be on the winning side. The coup plans were laughable, involving mostly National Guard cooks, chauffeurs, and clarinet players, and Somoza tossed the conspirators in jail for a few weeks then kicked them out of the country. When Mendieta was released, he immediately flew to Libya to plead with Muammar Qaddafi for arms for the Sandinistas. He broke with the Sandinistas after the revolution, when they expropriated all his property. "Mendieta is like a snake—he goes everywhere, and he has a lot of poison," observed one of the other Legionnaires. But Mendieta, like all master conspirators, had a lot of contacts. So he stayed.

Another questionable commodity was Eduardo Román, one of the Legion's few civilian leaders. Román, like Mendieta, had gone through school with Somoza's help. Somoza had even set him up as the manager of Nicaragua's world-class boxer Alexis Argüello. Like Mendieta, Román had turned on Somoza when the picture began to look grim. (His most telling blow against Somoza: getting Argüello to fly a Sandinista flag in his corner during a championship boxing match.) And like Mendieta, Román broke with the Sandinistas not on ideological grounds but because they seized his property.

Román's chief value to the Legion was his association with Argüello. Argüello bankrolled a few Legion projects, most notably a clandestine radio station that the Legion set up in Honduras in February 1981 with $5,000 worth of equipment purchased at a Radio Shack in Miami. The station, which called itself Radio Fifteenth of September, went on the air three times a day on shortwave frequencies. At first the broadcasts were live, until Bermúdez listened to them one day while visiting Honduras. "Sandinista sons of bitches, we're coming to kill you fuckers!" the young announcer shrieked, almost unintelligibly, as Bermúdez blanched. After that, the programs were taped in Miami and carried to Tegucigalpa three times a week by a friendly stewardess on Tan Sahsa, the Honduran airline.

The taped material was only slightly more sophisticated. Marta and Octavio Sacasa made them in a small studio at Octavio's video production company. Marta was usually the announcer. "This is the voice of Free Nicaragua!" Marta would shout. "Nicaraguans, come join our Christian commandos to fight international communism! The time of resistance is at hand!" Crude or not, the slogans worked. After a few weeks, campesinos began showing up on the Honduran border, asking where they could find the Fifteenth of September Legion. And almost without exception, they wanted to meet La Chillona—the screamer. "La Chillona sounds so confident, I know you must have a large army," one of the peasants explained to a Legionnaire officer. In Managua, Marta's mother faithfully tuned in to La Chillona every night without the faintest idea that she was listening to her own daughter's voice.

The Legionnaires began referring to Radio Fifteen as "our first gun." With the recruits it brought in, they opened up a small training site in Esquipulas, Guatemala, a little town near the Honduran border. The Legionnaires sometimes joked that it was appropriate to train in Esquipulas: the town was known mainly as the home of the Church of the Black Christ, where a woodcarving of Jesus had miraculously turned obsidian-black in the sixteenth century. Our troops are surely going to need a miracle or two, the Legionnaires would say. Actually, the town held a less celestial parallel; when a CIA-backed army of Guatemalan exiles overthrew the leftist government of Jacobo Arbenz in 1954, Esquipulas was its headquarters.

As the Legion expanded its activity, the costs went up. The Legion had done a certain amount of networking through the National Liberation Movement, Guatemala's far-right party; two of the party's elder statesmen, Mario Sandoval Alarcón and Lionel Sisniega, contributed money from time to time and sometimes sent deliveries of rice and beans. But the donations barely allowed the Legion to survive. And the men were embarrassed to keep going back to the same people, over and over again, to beg. Something had to be done to ensure the Legion a steady supply of money. Román and Mendieta came up with an idea: "Special Operations," they called it, a more palatable term than "kidnapping" or "armed robbery," which the police might have used.

Román and Mendieta came up with the idea for Special Operations by studying how leftist guerrillas supported themselves when they had no foreign sponsor. The Sandinistas, before receiving large-scale foreign support, had robbed and kidnapped extensively. The Salvadoran guerrillas, before Fidel Castro and the Sandinistas began shipping them arms, were prolific kidnappers; by some accounts they collected $50 million in ransom from

31

abductions during the 1970s. Guatemala's four guerrilla groups, which got Cuban help only sporadically, were still heavily dependent on criminal enterprises to raise money. We have to borrow a page from the communists, Román and Mendieta argued. We are no longer a government army, with the public treasury behind us; we must act like revolutionaries.

At the Legion safe house in Guatemala City, there was little opposition to the idea of Special Operations. To most of the men, armed robbery sounded far more manly and dignified than begging. But when Bermúdez, who was still in Miami, found out, he went wild. "Look, you can do this stuff inside Nicaragua, against supporters of the Sandinistas," he argued. "But if you do it out here, you'll destroy our base of support. No government is going to support us, or even tolerate us, if we're going around kidnapping its people." Mendieta and Román were not impressed. Bermúdez had been in Washington too long, they replied; this was the real world, this was the reality of guerrilla warfare. You had to get your hands dirty.

So the Special Operations squad went to work. About twelve to fifteen of the younger men staged the operations under the supervision of Justiniano Pérez, the picture-perfect captain. They started with bank robberies. To throw off suspicion, only the men who could convincingly imitate Guatemalan accents were allowed to speak during their robberies; and as they left, the Legionnaires scattered leaflets from the Guerrilla Army of the Poor, a Guatemalan leftist group well known for robbing banks. The deception worked perfectly, and soon Special Operations took up kidnapping, too. Then the men expanded to El Salvador, where suspicion would also naturally fall on the local guerrillas. And they even stole cars in the United States and smuggled them to Central America, where they brought premium prices.

In 1981, when the Legion moved its headquarters from Guatemala to Honduras, Special Operations continued. Looking about for a handy target, the men decided to kidnap the young son of Julio Tirado, the owner of Rincón Español, one of Tegucigalpa's pricier restaurants. (Coincidentally, it was a favorite dining spot for many American CIA officers.) Tirado was a Nicaraguan, and the Legionnaires had heard a rumor that he was doing business with the Sandinistas.

Always before, the Special Operations group had kidnapped businessmen, and for the most part they were kept bound and gagged until a ransom was paid. Everything was strictly business. But Tirado's son was only about ten years old, and the men saw no reason to tie him up, especially since he seemed to regard the entire thing as a great adventure. After a couple of days, all the Legionnaires were in love with the boy, and they decided to let him go without collecting a ransom. When he got home, of course, the Honduran police interviewed him and quickly learned that the kidnappers had been Nicaraguans. In less than an hour, Pérez was summoned to Honduran military headquarters. He admitted everything, apparently thinking that because the victim was a Nicaraguan, the Hondurans would brush off the kidnapping. He was wrong. Pérez was quietly expelled from Honduras, along with about half a dozen of the men from Special Operations. Shortly after that, Bermúdez arrived in Honduras; he didn't know all the details of Special Operations, but he had enough information to oust Mendieta and Román.

Pérez had told some of the other officers that he was watching the Special Operations men to make sure they didn't turn into full-time outlaws. He must not have watched closely enough. For years afterward, there was criminal fallout from Special Operations. Pompilio Gadea, who was one of the most enthusiastic Special Operations men, was arrested on drug-smuggling charges in the United States in the mid-1980s. So was Román. And two of the men who kidnapped Julio Tirado's young son, Rolando Monterrey and Jorge Pineda, tried to rob a bank in Hallandale, Florida, on June 16, 1989. When police surrounded the bank, the Nicaraguans opened fire. A policeman was wounded in the shoot-out; Monterrey was killed.

If the activities of the Special Operations unit had ever become widely known, the anti-Sandinista movement might have been crushed just as it was hatching. Luckily for the Fifteenth of September Legion, the story did not leak out. But a few months after the Special Operations campaign was launched, the Legion embarked on another project that did become public and helped create an image of anti-Sandinista forces as mercenaries that would persist throughout the war.

On several occasions, the Legion had contacted the military government of Argentina in hopes of assistance, but the talks had never gone anywhere. But in November 1980, the Legionnaires spoke with a military intelligence officer at the Argentine embassy in Guatemala. His government was deeply dismayed that several leaders of Argentine communist guerrilla groups were living in Managua, the officer said. The Argentines might be willing to underwrite the Legion's fight against the Sandinistas.

First, however, they wanted to see if the Legionnaires were anything but talk. One of the most notorious of the Argentine guerrillas, a man named Mario Firmenich, was commuting between Managua and Costa Rica, where he had set up a shortwave propaganda station, Radio Noticias del Continente. Its signal could reach right into Buenos Aires, and it was driving the Argentine generals into a frenzy. "If you take that radio off the air in Costa Rica," the Argentine officer told the Legionnaires, "we will start helping you."

From a public relations standpoint, involvement with the Argentines was a terrible idea. The Argentine military had an atrocious reputation throughout the hemisphere for its so-called dirty war against guerrillas in the 1970s, during which thousands of suspected leftists disappeared. It would be difficult to sell anyone on the proposition that a movement backed by the Argentines was fighting to bring democracy to Nicaragua. Of course, guerrilla movements must take help where they can find it, and the Legion was not exactly being overwhelmed with offers of aid. But the Legionnaires didn't even seem aware that there might be repercussions from an association with the Argentines, just as they were seemingly unconcerned about the propriety of buddying up to Mario Sandoval Alarcón, the Guatemalan right-winger who was closely linked to death squads in his own country as well as in El Salvador.

33

Even worse than forming an alliance with the Argentines was agreeing to do their dirty work in neutral Costa Rica, a country where the Legion hoped eventually to set up bases. Radio Noticias del Continente was not a Sandinista station; it had nothing to do with Nicaraguan politics; it was operating lawfully with the permission of the Costa Rican government. If the Legionnaires were caught, they would not be able to offer any political justification for their acts; they would have to admit that they were hired guns.

Nonetheless, they agreed to attack the station. The decision was spearheaded by Mendieta and Román, but no one—including Bermúdez in Miami—opposed it. Communists were always acting in international solidarity, the Legion officers reasoned. Now anticommunists would do the same.

The task fell to Hugo Villagra, a short, muscular former National Guard captain in his late thirties. Villagra, who had gone through U.S. Army Ranger and Special Forces training, was one of the best EEBI field commanders; Somoza had entrusted him with constructing the final defensive line north of Managua in the last days of the revolution. And he had a very personal debt to the Argentines: their embassy in Managua gave him asylum after the Sandinista victory in 1979.

Blowing up a radio station, Villagra thought, would barely work up a sweat. He took only six men and several sacks of dynamite to the station, located a few miles north of San José, the Costa Rican capital. But the Argentines had neglected to mention something: Twice previously they had sent groups to attack Radio Noticias del Continente. (In the second assault, a small plane dropped two fifty-five-gallon drums of gasoline mixed with detergent—homemade napalm—through the roof. For some reason the drums didn't explode, but the ruthless nature of the attack provides some perspective on Argentine thinking.) Now the station looked like a military pillbox: thick cement walls dotted with gunports, and barbed wire strung everywhere.

Worse yet, the station staff seemed to know Villagra was coming. As his men approached just before 3 A.M. on December 14, a torrent of gunfire erupted from inside the building. One of the Legionnaires went down immediately, his arm nearly torn off and his intestines dangling gruesomely by his side. Villagra's men traded shots with the radio station staff for twenty minutes before giving up the attack. The gunfire was so intense that they couldn't reach the body of the hit Legionnaire.

They fled to a dirt airstrip outside the town of Liberia, two hours north, where a plane from Guatemala was supposed to pick them up. But the plane never came; and the man they left behind wasn't dead. From him the Costa Rican police learned who the attackers were and their escape plan. Two days later, Villagra and his men were arrested, still waiting for their plane.

In prison, a couple of months later, Villagra got a letter from Mendieta containing a coded message. He shouldn't feel too bad, the letter said, the Argentines were impressed by his courage if not necessarily his tactical skills. They had decided the anti-Sandinistas were serious, and they were going to train fifty of the Nicaraguans in clandestine operations.

* * *

"Look, are you sure this is a good idea?" Roberto Amador asked nervously, looking at the ornate bronze plaque set into the imposing gray stone wall: EMBASSY OF THE UNITED STATES OF AMERICA. "Don't you think we ought to call him first?"

"This guy is my *friend*," Juan Gómez insisted as they walked toward the guard booth. "I never had to call ahead when he was at the embassy in Managua. I just showed up there. He was always happy to see me."

Amador nodded, but in truth Managua seemed long ago and far away. It was hard to believe that it was only eight months ago that he and Gómez had been swaggering colonels, hotshot pilots in the Nicaraguan Air Force. Amador had been one of the last to leave, guiding an overloaded DC-6 along a runway crowded with shrieking refugees and finally coaxing it into the air, delivering eighty National Guardsmen and family members to Honduras.

There was always a shortage of pilots, and it had taken Amador only a few days to find a good job, flying a crop duster over banana plantations in western Guatemala. But then his buddy Gómez had called to say some of the men were forming the Fifteenth of September Legion to go back to Nicaragua and fight. Amador's mouth had gone dry when he heard that. Twice during the last year of the war, the Sandinistas had sent armed men to his house in Managua to kill him. The second time, while Amador was out flying a mission, his wife and children had to sneak out the back door in the middle of the night, like whipped dogs. Now he wanted payback.

But guns and bullets cost money. And Gómez thought they could get it here at the American embassy in Guatemala City. There was a colonel in the military attaché's office who had served in Managua. All they had to do was get inside and explain what they were doing, Gómez had assured Amador, and his buddy would help. Maybe he was right, Amador thought. American politicians were unpredictable, but this would be soldier to soldier.

When they finally talked their way into the embassy, the colonel was waiting in the lobby—tall and blond, a real gringo. He seemed surprised to see Gómez. And when he learned what they wanted, his surprise swiftly turned to amazement and then rage. "Goddamn it, you can't stand in the middle of the U.S. embassy and conspire against a government!" the colonel bellowed. "You've got one minute to get out of here before I call the police!"

Amador and Gómez walked hurriedly back out the door and past the guard booth. When they got to the street, they started to run.

The visit to the U.S. embassy in Guatemala, memorable though it was, was neither the most naive approach to the Americans by anti-Sandinista forces, nor the most catastrophic. Both those distinctions belong to Edmundo Chamorro of the UDN, who in December 1980 decided to contact the incoming Reagan administration about aid. Not knowing exactly how to get in touch with the Reagan people, Chamorro wrote a letter to Richard Allen, whose nomination as the new national security adviser had already been announced. The letter suggested that Reagan fund Chamorro's rebel army and intervene with the government in Honduras or Costa Rica for permission for the anti-Sandinistas to set up bases. Allen sent back a form letter to Chamorro in Costa Rica thanking him "for sharing your thoughts with the President-elect." Worse yet, Allen's letter—sent by regular mail—had no street address or post-office box number on it. Sandinista agents in the Costa Rican post office intercepted it, and it was published on the front page of the FSLN's daily newspaper *Barricada*.[1]

Despite the disastrous Allen letter, anti-Sandinista Nicaraguans could hardly wait for Ronald Reagan's inauguration. They still believed that the Carter administration had helped the FSLN come to power and was enthusiastically supporting the regime. The reality was far more complex. The Carter administration had indeed wanted Somoza to go, but tried to shunt him aside in a way that would not leave the Sandinistas in control. The Carter people proved to be inept Machiavellians, but that did not mean their hearts had been with the FSLN. And as the Sandinistas cozied up to the Soviet Union, Carter began to examine his options in containing them. In spring 1980, he signed a top-secret presidential finding that allowed the CIA to pass several hundred thousand dollars in covert aid to Sandinista political opponents inside Nicaragua.[2]

The finding did not include aid for paramilitary operations, but later in the year, as the Sandinistas sent a torrent of weapons to the guerrillas in El Salvador, the Carter administration seems to have been thinking it over. When the Fifteenth of September Legion opened its first training camp on the edge of the Everglades, there were sometimes visitors: silent gringos wearing mirrored sunglasses who watched everything and said nothing.

It was the arms shipments to El Salvador that most concerned both the Carter administration during its last months in office and the Reagan administration during its first months. At the end of 1980, the Sandinistas had dispatched two hundred tons of weapons by air and sea to the Salvadoran guerrillas, who used the weapons to launch their "final offensive" in January 1981, during Carter's final days.[3] The offensive failed, but to Reagan's people the Salvadoran government appeared to be teetering on the edge. Despite several blunt warnings from U.S. diplomats, the Sandinistas continued shipping arms to El Salvador in fits and starts. Carter had suspended aid to Nicaragua during the Salvadoran final offensive; the Reagan administration soon canceled it altogether.

The anti-Sandinista Nicaraguans, however, had no idea how the subject of El Salvador was dominating National Security Council meetings or how violently the FSLN was being denounced in White House conference rooms. (Secretary of State Alexander Haig even proposed launching a naval blockade of Cuba to cut off the flow of weapons "at the source.") They had no high-level political contacts in the United States; in fact, they had no political contacts at all.

But in the spring of 1981, a North Carolina businessman named Nat Hamrick promised to change all that. Hamrick, who had been in and out of Nicaragua for years and had some business dealings with the Somoza family, knew his way around Capitol Hill's right wing, particularly the office of Senator Jesse Helms. Hamrick arranged for Bermúdez and four other exiles—mostly

Fifteenth of September Legion people—to visit Washington and see if they could stir up any interest in funding anti-Sandinista activities.

The exiles met a few congressional staffers and some reporters during the first two days of the trip, and they felt it was a success. But Hamrick told them these interviews were trivial. "Your most important meeting is going to be with a tape recorder," he said.

The Nicaraguans thought he was kidding, but that afternoon Hamrick brought in a little cassette recorder. Switching it on, he began asking questions about the situation in Nicaragua—what the exiles thought the Sandinistas were up to, what could be done about it. He told them to answer in English. They talked for a while, and then Hamrick left with the cassette. In an hour or so, he came back with a new list of questions. The process went on for six hours. "What's this all about, Nat?" one of the exiles asked as Hamrick left with the cassette for the last time. "This person can't meet with you because it's against the law," Hamrick replied. But he wouldn't say anything more, except that the interview was going well.

None of the exiles ever did learn who was on the other end of the conversation. But a few weeks later, they were summoned to a meeting at Miami International Airport with Vernon Walters, Reagan's new ambassador-at-large and general troubleshooter. "He seemed to know all about us, even though we had never met with him," one of the exiles recalled later. "He was on his way to Argentina, and he told us that although he couldn't be very specific, everything was going to be all right."[4]

That was apparently the first hint of the so-called tripartite agreement between the United States, Argentina, and Honduras. The Hondurans— particularly an ambitious colonel named Gustavo Alvarez, who headed the national police force—had been urging the Americans for months to start supporting the anti-Sandinistas. They were worried about the growth in Nicaragua's army, particularly the Soviet tanks that began arriving in 1980. Alvarez had even wangled a trip to Washington, where he met with CIA Director William Casey to suggest U.S. aid to an anti-Sandinista guerrilla force.

The Argentines were almost as enthusiastic. Their brief contact with the Fifteenth of September Legion had given them a grandiose vision of themselves as an anticommunist leviathan that would patrol the hemisphere against leftist incursions. Enrique Bermúdez had used the training of his fifty men as a pretext to meet with several of the Argentine military leaders. The Americans are a superpower, but they have domestic problems that make it difficult for them to get into the trenches, Bermúdez argued. You can provide the muscle for them. You will be the chief ally of the most powerful nation in the world. To the Argentines, it was like an opium dream—they couldn't get enough.

By July 1981, after a long exercise in shuttle diplomacy by diplomats, intelligence officials, and military men from all three countries, the tripartite agreement was a done deal. The United States would put up the money, the Argentines would supply the advisers, and the Hondurans would offer their territory. But the new partners decided to borrow an idea from Fidel Castro and make aid to the anti-Sandinistas conditional on unity.

Chicano Cardenal was the first one to get the message. He was granted an unexpected audience with Gordon Sumner, a retired U.S. Army general who was Alexander Haig's Latin American specialist. Sumner listened to Cardenal run through his pitch and then said pointedly: "If you expect to get any serious aid, you'll have to get together with the Fifteenth of September Legion."

Sumner didn't elaborate, but Cardenal understood it was more than a hypothetical suggestion. He went back to Miami to tell the rest of the UDN that an alliance was going to be necessary. Most of the UDN politicians agreed; they had begun to sense the difficulty of building an army without the benefit of professional military expertise.

But the Chamorro brothers, Edmundo and El Negro, were reluctant. They would participate in a unified movement, they said, only if former National Guardsmen were restricted to positions as foot soldiers. Cardenal knew the Legion would never agree to that. Besides, he argued with Edmundo Chamorro, it was dangerous using past associations as a litmus test for who could join the movement. "People could just as easily say you were with the Sandinistas," Cardenal pointed out. "Look, Mundo, the important thing is what people think about the future, not what they did in the past. . . . If we exclude everyone who was with the Somozas and everyone who was with the Sandinistas, we're going to have to make an army of Europeans or Africans."

Chamorro still wouldn't accept it. Only he and El Negro could be military commanders, he insisted, because they were the only ones who had fought the Somozas. Cardenal began to wonder how much their obstinacy had to do with ideology and how much with ambition. And putting the military under control of two brothers—a single family—wasn't that just what the Sandinistas had done? Hell, wasn't it just what *Somoza* had done? Cardenal would sign an agreement with the Legion, he decided, and to the devil with the Chamorro brothers.

On August 11, 1981, the pact was sealed in Guatemala. Bermúdez, Justiniano Pérez, and Juan Gómez signed for the Legion; two of Cardenal's deputies signed for the UDN. For the new organization they chose a name suggested by Pérez—the Nicaraguan Democratic Force. A few days later, copies of the agreement began circulating around the Miami exile community. When Edmundo Chamorro got hold of one, he scowled: It was signed *Colonel Enrique Bermúdez*. "Look at this," Chamorro snarled to friends. "That son of a bitch, he wants to continue the National Guard." He quickly dashed off a letter of resignation. Unity had lasted about five days.

4 | War

Noel Ortiz wasn't wild about approaching the ramshackle office that passed for a military headquarters in San Marcos de Colón, the little one-horse Honduran border town, but it seemed better to get it over with. He would tell the Honduran lieutenant inside that he had come here to recruit a guerrilla unit from the bedraggled Nicaraguan peasants who were wandering across the border, fleeing the new Sandinista government in Managua. The Honduran would either give the idea his blessing, Ortiz figured, or throw him in jail. Might as well find out right away.

"We just want to fight the *piricuacos* in Nicaragua," he told the Honduran officer, using a Miskito Indian word for "rabid dog" that people on both sides of the border applied to the Sandinistas. "We don't mean any harm to Honduras."

The Honduran rubbed his chin thoughtfully. "It's okay with me," he said finally. "In fact, I think I have some recruits for you." He motioned Ortiz to follow him through a narrow hallway. On the other side, Ortiz found himself looking into a dark, airless jail cell full of men whose silence radiated hostility.

"How many of you prisoners want to go with this man to fight the *piricuacos*?" the Honduran shouted. The men glared back. Then the Honduran added the fine print: "You can go with him, or we can take you back across the border and deliver you to the Sandinistas." Five minutes later, Noel Ortiz was a commander.

In August 1981, when Enrique Bermúdez got the first fruits of the tripartite alliance—$15,000, delivered to him in Guatemala City by an Argentine intelligence officer—he paid off the back rent on the safe houses and sent the Legion's men to Honduras. There they began trying to recruit the nucleus of an army from the human detritus washing up along the Nicaraguan frontier.

It was a daunting task. There was a handful of bewildered old men who had been minor rural bureaucrats—village mayors, justices of the peace—before

39

the revolution and were now marked as political criminals by the Sandinistas. There were refugees and gypsies, many of whom left Nicaragua with nothing but the clothes they were wearing. And there were the smugglers and rustlers and sneak thieves and men without a past who had always haunted the border.

As Bermúdez soon discovered, the thousands of professionals who had fled Nicaragua—doctors, lawyers, bankers, engineers—were busy building a new life in exile. They weren't interested in getting involved with a banana republic guerrilla army. So instead the FDN recruiters did most of their talking to men who were one step ahead of the police or the Honduran immigration authorities, or, as Noel Ortiz did, to people who had *failed* to stay one step ahead.

Ortiz, a former National Guard pilot, found that Dale Carnegie-style persuasion was not always the best motivation for his new troops. Most of them were rustlers, but one was an authentic killer named Peralta. Peralta had spent ten years in a Nicaraguan jail for murder and escaped in the confused final days of the revolution. He found calisthenics dull and digging latrines beneath his station. He parried direct orders with an airy "fuck you." On about the nine hundredth "fuck you," Ortiz lost his patience.

"Look, you want to fight me?" Ortiz demanded. For the first time, Peralta—a good forty pounds heavier than Ortiz—showed some enthusiasm. "Okay," Ortiz allowed. "We'll fight. If you win, you can leave. If I win, you have to do what I tell you."

Peralta didn't answer; he lunged, knocking Ortiz to the dusty ground and getting his hands around the pilot's throat. Ortiz could hardly hear the screams of the crowd that surrounded them; there was a roaring in his ears. *Okay, God, I better get some help now*, he thought, and smashed his forehead against Peralta's as hard as he could. The larger man sagged, out cold; Ortiz, barely conscious himself, managed to stagger to his feet and pour a bucket of water in Peralta's face. As his eyes opened, the crowd was howling. "He beat you! He beat you!" one old man shouted, waving a finger under Peralta's nose. "Now you got to do what he says." For a while, at least, Ortiz had no more problems.

Not everyone who joined the FDN in the early days was a criminal. There were a few bands of ex-National Guardsmen, and the *Milpas*, the small group of men who fought with Pedro Joaquín González before he was betrayed and killed. With occasional surreptitious help from sympathetic Honduran army officers, some of these groups had staged a few ragged cross-border raids. Bermúdez toured the border for days at a time, courting these pygmy armies. He also talked with dozens of campesinos who had run afoul of the Sandinistas in some way—refused to attend political meetings, maybe, or insulted one of the new "liberation theology" priests sent to their village by the government—and had been lured by the siren song of Radio Fifteenth of September.

Within a couple of months the FDN had assembled a core of three hundred men in four camps along the border. Already, however, Bermúdez was discovering that the wheels of American bureaucracy grind slowly. The promised supplies were nowhere in sight, although it had been months since Bermúdez drew up lists of what he would need. Bermúdez didn't know it, but the aid couldn't begin to flow until Ronald Reagan approved a presidential directive allowing it. On November 23, 1981, he signed National Security Decision Directive 17, which authorized $19 million for paramilitary operations "against Cuban presence and Cuban-Sandinista support infrastructure in Nicaragua and elsewhere in Central America."[1]

While the FDN troops waited, they trained: plinking away at tin cans with rusty .22s and ancient hunting rifles, running back and forth along their crude obstacle courses. More recruits trickled in; by January 1982, Bermúdez had five hundred men and six camps. That was the month the first CIA officer arrived, summoned in the middle of the night from his post at the U.S. embassy in Paraguay. And right behind him was a fleet of C-130 cargo planes, creaking under the weight of twenty-five tons of weapons.

With the weapons, the FDN began training in earnest. And the tripartite alliance—the Hondurans, the Argentines, and the Americans—began to take shape. It was clear to the Nicaraguans that the operation was ramrodded in those early days by the Hondurans or, more specifically, one Honduran: Gustavo Alvarez, who a few short months ago had been a colonel running the national police force and was now a general running the entire armed forces. In Honduras that meant he pretty much ran the entire country. For nearly two years Alvarez had been suggesting that military force was necessary to contain the communists next door in Nicaragua. His personal preference was that the United States send in the Marines, but he was willing to start with halfway measures. And now he was finally getting his way.

Alvarez was delighted to be working closely with the Americans, but many of the people around him thought he valued the Argentine connection even more. Alvarez was a 1961 graduate of the Argentine military academy, and he was a great admirer of the way things were done in Buenos Aires, including the no-nonsense approach to leftists during the "dirty war." As a sort of grisly homage, Alvarez had organized Military Intelligence Battalion 316, the first Honduran death squad. Small potatoes by regional standards (perhaps 120 people vanished or died at the hands of MI-316 over the course of three years in the early 1980s), the death squad nonetheless represented a grim milestone in Honduras, which unlike most of its neighbors had no tradition of political violence.

To work with Alvarez, the Argentines sent about fifteen or twenty officers, commanded by a pair of colonels. The senior officer was Osvaldo Riveiro, a short, squat man whom everyone called Balita, Little Bullet. His executive officer called himself Julio Villegas, although everyone was pretty sure that was a phony name.[2] Riveiro, who had known Alvarez back at the military academy in Buenos Aires, was gregarious and outgoing; the white-haired Villegas was more thoughtful and reserved. They handled all the money. The Nicaraguans—from Bermúdez, needing several hundred dollars for the rent on the Tegucigalpa safe houses, to a foot soldier on leave in the capital, asking for a couple of bucks to see a movie—had to get it from the Argentines.

That was just one of the ways, some subtle and some anything but, that the Argentines let it be known that they were in charge. FDN officers used to tell a story about an Argentine named Juan who, on his vacation, went to see the

Eiffel Tower. Up at the top he was astonished to see his next-door neighbor from Buenos Aires. "What are you doing up here?" Juan asked his friend. "I wanted to see what Paris looked like without me," replied the friend. The arrogance and condescension of Argentines is famous throughout Latin America; Riveiro and Villegas were no exceptions. No Nicaraguan, including the civilians, ever addressed either one of them as anything but "Colonel."

The *éminence grise* in this *ménage à trois*, at least as far as the FDN was concerned, was the Americans. In fact, relatively few of the Nicaraguans even knew at first that the United States was involved. Initially there was just one American—the CIA officer from Paraguay, who called himself Joe. He went to extraordinary lengths to isolate himself not only from the Nicaraguans, but from the U.S. embassy as well. Joe was under what the CIA calls double cover; he entered Honduras under one assumed name, then switched to another once he was inside the country. He never visited the embassy, and in the nine months he spent in Honduras, he could count the number of times he spoke to Nicaraguans on his thumbs.

Joe's single mission was to coordinate the arrival of the twenty-five tons of supplies that the United States flew in: no small task, given that the fledgling anti-Sandinista army had no clerks, no supply officers, no aircraft, no large vehicles—no administrative infrastructure of any kind. There wasn't even anyone to unload the planes as they landed at the Honduran air force base at Palmerola, northwest of Tegucigalpa; most of the FDN troops were out at the border, more than one hundred miles away. The supply effort would have been unmanageable, except for the boundless enthusiasm of Alvarez. He provided hundreds of soldiers to help unload the supply planes. And then he assigned an entire battalion of engineers to build a tent city to store the equipment while Joe figured out how to get it to the border camps.

The American resolve to stick solely to supplying the war effort, however, lasted less than a month. The Argentine military men were all intelligence officers, with little or no actual combat experience. For them to instruct the FDN was the blind leading the blind. The CIA decided to import a dozen or so of its paramilitary experts—"knuckledraggers," in Agency parlance—to train the Argentines before the Argentines trained the Nicaraguans.

The CIA also opened its own direct channel to the Nicaraguans. An Agency officer who called himself Miguel began conferring regularly with Bermúdez. Bermúdez was amused by the high drama accompanying his visits; the CIA man would park blocks away, then come sidling in a back door, looking nervously over his shoulder. It was all a bit too cinematic for Bermúdez. But he liked Miguel, a Puerto Rican who had been in the CIA for a long time and who sometimes spoke bitterly about the changes he had seen during the past ten or fifteen years. "Anticommunism used to be respected, it used to be a good thing," Miguel would say. "Now if you're an anticommunist, people think you're some kind of crazy right-winger." Bermúdez, who was still amazed at the international popularity of the Sandinistas, agreed enthusiastically.

The good personal relationship between the two men did not stop Bermúdez from noticing that Americans, in their own way, could be just as arrogant as the Argentines. Miguel was always saying the FDN would have to do this, the FDN would have to do that. It didn't sound like advice; it sounded like orders. And if Bermúdez protested, Miguel dismissed it: "We learned that in Vietnam."

One afternoon Bermúdez refused to be dismissed. "Your experience in other wars is important," he told Miguel. "But this isn't Vietnam. It's Nicaragua. And you may know Vietnam, but we know Nicaragua." Miguel regarded him coldly. "If you want to go your own way, fine," the CIA officer said in a flat voice. "But what are you going to say if we cut off the aid?"

"I will say it's another Bay of Pigs," Bermúdez retorted. Miguel didn't respond. But his face went pale and then red.

That was neither the first nor the last time Bermúdez argued with Miguel. In fact, it seemed to Bermúdez that he spent most of his time trying to convince his foreign "advisers," both American and Argentine, that Nicaraguans weren't complete idiots.

Bermúdez was painfully aware—because they were always reminding him— that he wasn't a veteran combat commander. While the National Guard fought the Sandinista revolution, he had been behind a desk in Washington; his single brief experience with combat had been in the Dominican Republic more than fifteen years earlier with an Organization of American States peace-keeping force. On the other hand, Bermúdez didn't rise to the rank of colonel by being a total fool. Yet he often had the strange sensation that his voice was electronically scrambled when he spoke to the Argentines or the Americans. They didn't seem to hear him.

There was, for instance, the matter of the supplies. In November, he drew up careful, painstakingly detailed lists of what he needed and gave them to the Argentines who, he knew, would pass them along to the Americans. Some of Bermúdez's requests surprised the Argentines. He asked for Belgian-made FAL rifles instead of the Soviet AK-47s the Sandinistas carried. Wouldn't it be easier, the Argentines asked, to use the AK-47? Then your men could use captured ammunition. But Bermúdez had surveyed his troops, who thought the FAL was a more impressive weapon. It had a longer range and more stopping power, and it made a louder, more frightening noise when it fired. Because his men wouldn't have many machine guns or other heavy weapons, Bermúdez reasoned, the FAL would compensate. The Argentines snickered at the bit about the louder noise, but Bermúdez knew that in a guerrilla war, in which he had to rely on volunteers, psychology counted for a lot. The trainers were thinking like conventional military men; the trainee remembered he was running an insurgent army of peasants.

They argued about the uniforms, too. Bermúdez demanded jungle fatigues for his men, with military canteens and packs. Guerrillas don't wear uniforms, the Argentines maintained. Bermúdez insisted. He had sent patrols into Nicaragua to talk to the peasants; they reported that there was tremendous discontent with the Sandinistas, but the campesinos were skeptical that ragtag guerrillas with no visible means of support could take on the FSLN's Soviet-equipped army. To overcome their disbelief, Bermúdez argued, his men had to look like a sharp, professional force.

The Argentines finally gave in and passed the list of supplies along to the

43

Americans, who had their own ideas. Instead of camouflage fatigues, they sent blue-green workmen's uniforms purchased out of the Sears Roebuck catalogue. Wearing those, the FDN would look spiffy and organized, but would still maintain a civilian image, the Americans explained to a confounded Bermúdez. Even the bluffest gringo, however, offered no rationale for the other purchase from Sears Roebuck. Rather than American jungle boots, as Bermúdez had requested, the shipment contained bright yellow work boots with flat soles. They made a wonderful target for Sandinista artillery; and a guerrilla who tried to walk on a muddy or rocky surface while wearing them quickly went down on his behind.

Bermúdez accepted, reluctantly, the blue-green uniforms. But he demanded new boots. The Americans agreed. It took a mere six months for them to bring in a new shipment.

Word of these hassles rarely penetrated the six base camps along the border, where the mood was upbeat. The men were excited to be exchanging their .22s, antique revolvers, and few old M-16s for real guns and delighted that they no longer had to hide out from the Honduran authorities. There had always been a few Honduran military officers who cooperated with the Nicaraguan exiles, but their support had been marginal and erratic—a couple of guns delivered here, a blind eye turned toward a camp there.

The Hondurans, too, were glad the relationship was being formalized. Some of them had paid a high price for the small help they gave earlier. When there had been slight discrepancies in ammunition inventories at a Honduran outpost in the border town of El Paraíso early in 1981, headquarters sent out investigators. They soon learned that the local commander, a major named Rodríguez, had given a few thousand rounds of ammo to a band of former Guardsmen who were conducting minor raids into Nicaragua. Before the investigators could even report their findings, Rodríguez killed himself.

Now that General Alvarez was in charge, the Honduran military was wholeheartedly committed to the FDN. Bermúdez had cemented the alliance by appointing as his chief of staff a former National Guard major named Emilio Echaverry, who was a classmate of Alvarez at the Argentine military academy. For that matter, Echaverry's presence helped reassure the Argentines, too. He had married the daughter of an Argentine military officer, maintained a home in Buenos Aires, and was in general such an Argentinaphile that his National Guard radio code sign was "Fierro," the name of Argentina's mythic cowboy hero.

By late January of 1982, Bermúdez felt that things were starting to come together. The weapons and supplies were arriving, training was moving ahead at a rapid clip, and he no longer had to dodge bill collectors. The $9,100-a-month budget provided to the FDN by the Argentines, though a bargain price for a guerrilla army, seemed luxurious compared with the old days when the Fifteenth of September Legion had to go begging spoiled vegetables from the Guatemala City market ladies. Bermúdez was even able to get rid of the wheezing, primeval Ford Fairlane he had bought for $300 when he first came to Tegucigalpa; the FDN could afford a new Toyota.

There was only one thing missing from the picture: a war. Near the end of

January, as Bermúdez was trying to figure out the etiquette of announcing a civil war to the world, the Argentines called with a plan.

Colonel Riveiro always claimed that the Argentines came up with the idea themselves. Perhaps so, Bermúdez thought, but the CIA's fingerprints were all over the scheme, too. He knew the Agency was feeling pressure to show some bang for its bucks.

The plan was simple: to blow up bridges on two of northern Nicaragua's major highways. Both bridges were just a few miles south of the Honduran border, so the FDN's still-undertrained forces would not be put to too severe a test. Nor would they have to get in a head-on confrontation with the Sandinista army.

Nonetheless, both bridges were large structures that carried a lot of traffic. The Sandinistas wouldn't be able to cover up their destruction, and because they were seventy-five miles apart it would be impossible to pretend that they had both fallen victim to natural disaster. The CIA and the Argentines could show their bosses some results, and the FDN forces would demonstrate irrefutably to their countrymen that they could deliver a bloody nose to the Sandinistas, Soviet backing or no.

One of the bridges was just south of Ocotal, in Nueva Segovia Department. The other was near Somotillo, on the western side of the country, where only a narrow sliver of Honduran territory separates Nicaragua from El Salvador. The Somotillo bridge lay on the most direct highway route between Nicaragua and El Salvador, and that was another reason Bermúdez was certain the CIA had something to do with this plan. The Sandinistas were shipping weapons to the communist guerrillas in El Salvador along that road, and Bermúdez knew that the Americans were getting more and more worried about El Salvador.

It took almost two months for the Argentines to train the twenty men who were selected to blow up the bridges. They had plans of the bridges from a little-known Pentagon office that had been collecting blueprints and maps for three years, just in case the White House decided to invade Nicaragua.

The Somotillo bridge was assigned to a squad under the command of José Efrén Mondragón, a twenty-one-year-old former National Guard sergeant. The men who went after the Ocotal bridge were commanded by Róger Sandino, a former Guard lieutenant. Under strict orders to avoid Sandinista troops, they took three days of cautious travel to reach their targets. Late the night of March 14, 1982, within a few minutes of one another, the two groups set off their charges of C-4 plastic explosives.

Róger Sandino, at the last minute, decided not to approach the Ocotal bridge himself. And when his men got there, they found that the bridge had undergone some alterations from the blueprints they had studied; they couldn't plant the charges where they had planned. The bridge swayed with the force of the blast, but didn't fall. It would take Sandinista engineers six weeks to reinforce and reopen it.

Mondragón had an even more difficult time. Some of his men deserted the first night. Then, when he reached the Somotillo bridge, the Río Negro was several feet higher than expected because of a heavy rainfall upstream. The

45

men, up to their necks as they waded out to place the C-4, were almost swept away by the swift current. But, Mondragón said later, the higher water may have helped focus the force of the explosion. As he pushed the detonator button, there was a roar like thunder and a swirl of dust. When it cleared, the bridge was gone.

Two days later the men were back in a Tegucigalpa safe house, drinking beer and celebrating the FDN's first victory. Blowing up the bridges had succeeded beyond anyone's imagination. "There is a conspiracy against our people and their revolution, promoted by the current administration of the U.S. government," the Sandinistas said in a decree issued twenty-four hours later. They declared a state of emergency, suspended all opposition political activity and most civil liberties, and ordered news media to submit all stories for advance censorship. In their stories on the destruction of the bridges, the Sandinista newspapers blamed the explosions on *la contrarevolución*, the counterrevolution. In headlines, that was shortened to *contra*. Within weeks, the international press had picked up the term, and the anti-Sandinistas, although they rejected the name for years, could never get rid of it. Nicaragua was at war.

Mondragón was the FDN's first hero. His moment of glory, however, would cost him terribly. Six years later his corpse would turn up, slashed, beaten, and riddled with more than twenty bullets, just a couple of miles from the ruins of the Somotillo bridge. But that story was yet to unfold. For now, an ebullient Mondragón accepted the congratulations of the other men.

The intoxication of success enveloped everyone in the FDN but Bermúdez. He had been excited, of course, when he heard the bombs had gone off and delighted to learn the Sandinistas had declared a state of emergency. But as he was getting ready to go to Radio Fifteen to make a broadcast claiming the attacks in the name of the FDN, Bermúdez got a visit from Miguel, the CIA man. Miguel handed him a communiqué describing the bombings that was signed by the "Authentic Sandino Front."

"What is this?" Bermúdez protested. "There is no such organization. This was an FDN operation."

"Just put out the communiqué the way it is," Miguel answered.

"We'll put out nothing at all before we give somebody else credit," Bermúdez said angrily.

No communiqué was issued. When Bermúdez told some of the other FDN officers the story, they asked what Miguel was driving at. What was the Authentic Sandino Front? "I don't know," Bermúdez shrugged.

But he had suspicions. Edén Pastora, the most revered Sandinista military hero of the revolution, had not been seen in Managua for months. Some people were saying he had deserted the FSLN, that he was in Costa Rica planning to fight against his old *compañeros*. Bermúdez recalled that Pastora, several years before he joined the FSLN, had organized a small guerrilla group called the Sandino Revolutionary Front. That was very similar to the name the CIA wanted to use.

Could the rumors from Costa Rica be true? And could the CIA be in touch with Pastora? Bermúdez wondered, not for the first time and certainly not for the last, just what the Americans were up to.

5 | Commander Zero

He was the most famous military hero of the Sandinista revolution, a commander who slipped into the heart of Managua and seized the presidential palace with only two dozen troops. For three years Edén Pastora was an all-consuming passion of the CIA; the Agency was convinced that he could unseat the same regime he helped put in place. "Nobody got more money, per soldier, than Pastora," recalls one CIA officer, "and nobody was the focus of more of our attention."

It was all part of a seemingly sensible strategy to create a southern front in Nicaragua: to catch the Sandinistas in a vise, with the FDN in the north and Pastora—the famous "Commander Zero"—in the south. Not only would Pastora's experienced guerrilla fighters put intense military pressure on Managua, but his proven political connections to the rest of Latin America would provide an instant base of support from Venezuela, Panama, Costa Rica—all the same countries that had aided the Sandinistas during their revolution.

But somehow the creation of the southern front became a hellish geopolitical black hole that sucked in lives, money, and political careers and never gave anything back. The southern front seemed to conjure up all the worst political traits of Nicaraguans: divisiveness, treachery, parasitism, love of conspiracy. At the paranoid vortex of the storm was Pastora. In the beginning, the CIA officers who recruited him swaggered around the halls of their Langley headquarters like they had just discovered oil. By the end, they were desperately trying to scrape him off, like a loathsome piece of chewing gum that clings to the sole of a shoe.

The conventional wisdom is that the CIA crushed Pastora and cast him aside because the agency couldn't stand working with a genuine Nicaraguan nationalist. Pastora himself is the chief proponent of this line of thought: "I had only one problem with the CIA—I didn't speak English well enough to say, 'Yes sir,'" he once snapped to a reporter.[1]

The truth is more harsh. After nearly three years of American pampering,

47

including seven thousand weapons, millions of pounds of ammo, half a dozen aircraft, and $3.6 million in cash, all Pastora could show for the largess was a militarily impotent organization riddled with Sandinista spies; even his mistress was reporting his pillow talk back to Managua. His army suffered so many catastrophes that some of his strongest supporters began to wonder if he might not be a Sandinista agent himself, sent to cripple contra forces in a key theater of operations. The more charitable simply dismissed him as stupid, disorganized, and insanely egotistical. Either way, in the end they all abandoned him. "Look," says Arturo Cruz, Jr., once one of Pastora's top political advisers, "everyone—not only the Americans—got fed up with Edén after awhile. . . . Tell me one person who *was* close to Edén who *is* close to him today."

Yet his legend persists, in large part because Pastora was both an alluring personality and a relentless self-promoter. He was a ruggedly handsome swashbuckler, a Latin Errol Flynn; maybe the most handsome man ever born in Nicaragua. He certainly would tell you that. And, he'd add, if they ever decided to execute him, they'd have to line him up against the Momotombo volcano, he was such a giant of a man. He used to stage arm-wrestling contests with the champions of each one of his units—with the results fixed, so he could win. He loved to have his picture taken so much that his men sometimes called him *Comandante* Kodak.

Perhaps no other chapter of the war so clearly illustrates the ambiguities, complexities, and exasperations on both sides of the eight-year-long American collaboration with the contras. And many who watched the Pastora story unfold felt that there really was no way it could have a happy ending for either side. "It had to do with two worlds in conflict: the world of rational management, and the magical world of the Nicaraguan *caudillos*, strongmen," says Cruz Jr. "And there was no communicator, no interpreter, who could handle it."

Edén Pastora was born January 22, 1937, in Ciudad Darío, in Matagalpa Department, a land of lush jungle and brutal mountains. His mother came from a well-to-do family and had been educated in the United States, and his father (killed in a boundary dispute when Pastora was seven years old) owned a farm of several thousand acres. They had enough money to send young Edén to a Jesuit boarding school in Granada.

The Colegio Centroamérica had always been a prestigious school, but the class of 1957 would really turn out to be something special; during the 1970s and 1980s, its members would radically reshape Nicaragua's destiny. Besides Pastora, there was also Jorge Salazar, the prominent coffee grower who was murdered by the Sandinistas in 1980. Alfonso Robelo, a self-made millionaire who joined the first revolutionary junta in 1979, was another classmate. And Chicano Cardenal, who made his fortune in the construction business and then gave it all up to fight the Sandinistas, was also a member of the class of '57.

In the 1950s, their political triumphs and failures were still a long way off. But his classmates had already noticed a few things about Pastora. One was that women were always buzzing around him. Another was his mercurial temperament. He seemed to glow with an incandescent rage that sometimes burned right through to the surface. Some of his classmates thought Pastora was angry that he didn't come from one of Nicaragua's imperial families, like the Chamorros or the Cuadras, the social aristocracy that survived even Somoza.

Perhaps, they thought, that was why Pastora was always saying that old Tacho Somoza had personally ordered his father's murder. It was almost like Edén was bragging: Family name or not, my old man was such an *hombre* that Somoza himself had to kill him. (Many years later, Chicano Cardenal asked Edén's older brother Felix about it. "Oh, that's just Edén's bullshit," Felix shrugged. "It was just an argument with a guy in the town.") Edén told the story over and over again. And, he always added, some day he would make the Somozas pay.

So no one was very surprised in 1959 when Pastora dropped out of a Mexican university—he was a lousy student anyway—and joined one of the innumerable armed bands that periodically launched ill-fated insurrections against the Somoza family. Pastora picked a particularly obscure one: the Sandino Revolutionary Front, the first of the modern anti-Somoza guerrilla groups to use Augusto Sandino's name and trademark red-and-black colors. Its single moment of glory was a suicidal attack by thirty-five guerrillas against a National Guard barracks containing three hundred soldiers.

Pastora drifted in and out of various anti-Somoza groups and in 1961 found his way to the FSLN. Two decades later, Pastora would claim that the Sandinistas fooled everyone, including him, about their intentions. "The sad thing is that once in power, the nine leaders of the revolution [the Sandinista directorate] became traitors of Sandinismo," he said shortly after publicly breaking with the Sandinistas in 1982. "In a few short years, they shed the mask of 'pure' revolutionaries, implemented a Marxist-Leninist takeover Stalin-style, creating a totally repressive police state. . . . You asked me how I feel. I feel the same way as all the people of Nicaragua. I feel what all the people of the world feel when they realize that they have been deceived. I feel sadness, anguish, frustration, anger, hatred, and resentment."[2]

Some people may have been deceived by the Sandinistas. For Pastora to claim he was one of them, after seventeen years in and around the FSLN, is ludicrous. Pastora was never a communist, but it didn't bother him a bit to work with those who were, as long as they had guns.

His only objection to the Sandinistas had been that they spent too much time arguing about how many Trotskyites could dance on the head of a pin. Café revolutionaries, Pastora sneered, who would rather split dialectical hairs than make revolution. Action, that was the thing the movement needed. And he was full of grandiose schemes that made the other Sandinistas shake their heads. For example, he had this idea about how a single squad of commandos could seize the whole National Palace, the seat of Nicaragua's government, right in the center of Managua. He suggested it to some of the others in 1970, and those who didn't laugh out loud edged away from him, like he was a lunatic.

It was eight years before the FSLN, in desperation, gave Pastora's plan serious thought. The Sandinistas were worried; their military operations were failing, but strikes and riots—either spontaneous, or directed by other groups oriented toward businessmen and the middle class—were gaining momentum. If the Sandinistas were to remain at the forefront of anti-Somoza activity, they needed an operation that was not only successful, but spectacular—something that would capture the national imagination. In August 1978, the Sandinista leadership gave Pastora the green light to try to seize the National Palace.

Pastora and two dozen guerrillas made their way to Managua. On August 22, they gathered at two safe houses to put on their disguises: National Guard uniforms, complete with the distinctive black berets of the elite EEBI, which supplied Somoza's personal guards. Pastora went over the plan one last time, reminding the guerrillas that they would be using numbers instead of names—the higher the rank, the lower the number. Pastora, as commander, was Zero. A little after 9 A.M. they headed for the palace in trucks painted to look like military vehicles.

The National Palace was anything but palatial, in appearance or in function. Somoza had long since moved his offices to the heavily guarded Bunker complex a couple of miles away. Now the palace—careworn, fading, and boxlike—housed the National Assembly and most of the government offices that ordinary citizens had to deal with on a day-to-day basis: the tax collector, the motor vehicle department, and other petty bureaucracies. At any given moment, there were a thousand or more people, in varying states of confusion, milling around the hallways of the building.

When the trucks pulled up at the palace, Pastora leapt out first. Striding imperiously into the building, he was the perfect portrait of Guard arrogance and officiousness. *"Ya viene El Hombre!"* he shouted—here comes The Man!—the cry that always presaged a visit by Somoza. Behind him, his men confiscated the weapons of the real soldiers assigned to guard the building, a typical security precaution when Somoza went anywhere. No one inside sensed anything amiss—until Pastora burst into the chambers of the National Assembly. "Everyone to the floor!" he yelled, spraying a burst of bullets into the ceiling to show his sincerity.

The gunfire alerted a National Guard squad outside, which promptly counterattacked. But Pastora coolly flipped a grenade into the midst of the assault team, killing four Guardsmen and scattering the rest. In less than three minutes, and without the loss of a single Sandinista, Pastora's loony plan had succeeded. He held the palace.

The negotiations went on for three days, with Pastora frequently threatening to kill his 1,500 hostages, starting with the 50-odd members of the Chamber of Deputies (including several Somoza relatives). The president's military men begged for permission to attack the palace. Somoza, convinced Pastora was a lunatic who would start slaughtering people at the first sign of trouble, chose to bargain instead. Eventually he agreed to release about 50 prisoners, publish several Sandinista communiqués in the Somoza family newspaper, and pay a $500,000 ransom.

Somoza was right about one thing: Pastora was ready to kill the hostages, all of them. "Definitely, oh, definitely yes," he told me five years later. "And Somoza knew it. Our slogan of 'free fatherland or death' was a serious one."

The takeover ended on August 24 when buses came to take Pastora and his commandos to the airport. Thousands of Nicaraguans lined the streets; everybody had heard this Commander Zero talking on the radio throughout the siege, sassing and bullying Somoza in the most outrageous way. As sullen

Guardsmen stood sentry, the crowd chanted "Viva!" Pastora egged them on, waving a rifle in one hand and a clenched fist on the other. He also deliberately dropped the handkerchief covering his face that was supposed to preserve his anonymity. A news photographer caught him as he boarded the getaway plane to safe haven in Panama, the rifle raised over his head in triumph. The picture would become a popular, and highly subversive, poster. The National Palace stunt had not only provided the Sandinistas a much-needed victory; now the revolution had a folk hero.

Lost in all the emotion and bombast was the simple truth about Pastora's assault on the National Palace: It was a terrorist operation, not a military one. He took a large number of innocent people hostage then dared Somoza to attack him. Pastora gambled that Somoza was less ruthless than he was, and won. It didn't prove Pastora was a military genius. It proved he was very brave. It would be some years before anyone sensed the difference.

In the aftermath of the palace takeover, Pastora became for the first time a truly important figure in the Sandinista movement. Not only was he the popular face of the Sandinistas, but the dashing, charismatic Commander Zero proved highly effective at winning international support for the FSLN. Venezuelan president Carlos Andrés Pérez and Panamanian military strongman Omar Torrijos both liked him and stepped up their aid to the Sandinistas; Costa Rican president Rodrigo Carazo, at Pastora's urging, virtually turned over the northern quadrant of his country to facilitate arms shipments. All three men hated Somoza and had been helping the Sandinistas before, but Pastora's presence helped them reassure themselves that a post-Somoza Nicaragua would not be Marxist. Pastora was clearly no communist. After Somoza was deposed, he said, Nicaragua would be a democratic welfare state, like Costa Rica. The sheer force of Pastora's personality convinced the three Latin leaders, and many others, that things would turn out the way he envisioned them.

But however much the Latin presidents wanted to believe it, Pastora was not a member of the Sandinista directorate, where the key decisions were made. In fact, the same characteristics that made Pastora so valuable to the Sandinistas —his Catholicism, his pluralistic politics, and his overwhelming magnetism— had them a little worried. They needed to put Pastora in a leadership post to keep the international support he was bringing them; but it was easy to envision a cult of personality developing around him, one that would pose a threat to Sandinista control of political events. They settled on the high-profile, low-power job of commanding the revolution's southern front, along the Costa Rican border.

It was a cunning solution. The Sandinistas were strongest in urban areas, which lay mostly to the north, and that was where the directorate intended to concentrate its efforts. The south, with few cities and lots of treacherous swamp, would be used merely as a diversion, to pin down some of the National Guard's resources.

The strategy worked. Pastora stayed visible enough to keep the Latin presidents happy, and Somoza moved his best commanders and a major part of his army to the south. The war slogged to a standstill there; each side used artillery to pound the other from static positions. Pastora's troops never penetrated more than a few miles past the border. In the north, meanwhile, the noose drew ever tighter around Managua.

On July 19, as FSLN guerrillas poured into the capital, Pastora's army was still slugging it out with remnants of the Guard. Pastora did manage to join the Sandinista *comandantes* the next day for the victorious ride into the city in a firetruck. When they arrived at the newly renamed Plaza of the Revolution— right in front of the National Palace, the scene of Pastora's great triumph—fifty thousand people stood there, chanting only one name: Zero. Pastora, still grimy and bedraggled from the battlefield, spoke only for a moment. He would, he promised, "remain vigilant at all times so that this revolution is not betrayed or changed." The crowd went wild.

In the months that followed, the Sandinista directorate cleverly distracted Pastora by playing to his mammoth ego. He got an important title—deputy interior minister—and he toured the countryside as a star attraction at political rallies. While Pastora basked in the applause, the directorate consolidated its control. Some of Pastora's friends warned him he was naive, that the hard-liners were taking control, but he ignored it. In late August, the last of Pastora's troops were merged into the new Sandinista People's Army, and his lieutenants quietly removed from command. Even then Pastora did not complain. He was traveling around Latin America, negotiating arms deals, buddying up to Fidel Castro, playing the part of a world leader.

Pastora's disillusionment began during 1980. The rallies were becoming tiresome, and as the Sandinistas turned more and more openly to the Soviet bloc for help, they had less need for Pastora's good relationship with Latin American liberals. Bored, Pastora searched for new conspiracies. He offered to spy on the Sandinistas for the Conservative Party, the largest of the opposition groups. The Conservatives, suspicious of a trap, ignored him.

Pastora claims his growing discontent was ideological, that the Sandinistas were "betraying" the revolution. Almost no one who knew him then agrees. If he was alarmed about the communist direction the Sandinistas were taking, why was his enthusiasm for Castro so boundless? If he was disturbed by the growing influence of the Soviet bloc in Nicaraguan affairs, why did he twice travel to Moscow to help negotiate arms deals? (The second trip was his last; Pastora had too much vodka and reached across the table to toy with the three red stars on Defense Minister Ustinov's uniform. The minister was distinctly unamused.)[3]

Pastora made no public protests, made no attempt to rally his followers in the militia; and except for his abortive plan to spy for the Conservatives, made no effort at all to reach out to the increasingly estranged Nicaraguan opposition groups. Even when he learned that the Sandinistas had detected the antigovernment plotting of Jorge Salazar and were going to kill his old schoolmate, Pastora kept silent.

His silence was prompted by an illusory hope that he might still win a powerful post inside the government—that he might become the tenth *comandante*. Even his admirers could see his ambition. Arturo Cruz, Jr., was working as an economic adviser to the Sandinistas at the time and watched Pastora's relationship with the party hierarchy deteriorate. "Let's face it," Cruz says. "Edén's dissidence began—it had to do with his exclusion from the top directorate, and it was evident by the end of 1980 that he would not get that."

On July 7, 1981, Pastora and a dozen supporters piled into cars and headed south, leaving behind a letter to Humberto Ortega that said Pastora was headed for Guatemala to help the guerrillas there. "I am going to discharge my revolutionary gunpowder against the oppressor in whatever part of the world in which he is found," the letter said, "without it mattering whether they call me Quixote or Sancho." In fact, Pastora and his men were headed to Panama to see his pal Omar Torrijos and plot a course of action.

They decided that some of Pastora's supporters would return to Nicaragua to begin a campaign of spray-painting graffiti: slogans like "Edén is coming." Pastora had the idea that his chum Fidel Castro would force the Sandinistas to take him back in a more important position. Pastora had no idea that, behind his back, Castro referred to him as *El Guajiro*—the peasant.

But the plan was thrown into disarray by the death of Torrijos in a plane crash on July 31. Without his patron's protection, Pastora—at the urging of the Sandinistas—was put aboard a plane for Havana. The Cubans held him under a kind of liberal house arrest for two months. "I went to beaches and nightclubs," Pastora said later. "I had good meals, good wine, and a Mercedes-Benz. They treated me with protocol. I lived in a grand residence, but I was politely discouraged from leaving the country."[4] When his supporters began the spray-painting campaign in Nicaragua, the Cubans forced Pastora to make a videotape disavowing it.

The house arrest might have continued indefinitely—who knows what the Cubans ultimately intended to do with him?—but in October the teenage son of Torrijos, a teenager who had fought under Pastora's command on the southern front, flew to Havana to obtain his release. Once he got out, Pastora really did try to help the Guatemalan guerrillas. He obtained $5 million from Libyan strongman Muammar Qaddafi to finance the war, only to discover that the Sandinistas and Cubans had blackballed him with the Guatemalans.

The whole bizarre sequence of events illustrates how seriously the Sandinistas viewed Pastora. In 1981 there was still no major contra organization, only the Fifteenth of September Legion robbing banks in Guatemala and a few bands of cattle rustlers in isolated mountain hideouts along the Honduran border. But clearly the Sandinistas feared Pastora's capacity to stir popular resentment and resistance.

Even more clearly, the chain of events demonstrates the muddled political judgment, the capacity for self-delusion, and the flair for unpredictability that would later drive the CIA half mad in its dealings with Pastora. At the same time he was complaining about Cuban influence in Nicaragua, Pastora wanted Castro to dictate a change in direction to the Sandinistas. At the same time he was arguing that Nicaragua ought to tend to its own affairs without outside direction, he was obtaining millions of dollars from Qaddafi to launch a revolution in Guatemala. Typically, Pastora saw no contradiction. "I am not a government," he explained. "As a private individual, I can do whatever I want."[5]

Pastora settled in Costa Rica again in late 1981. He was in touch with a growing circle of Nicaraguan exiles, many of them veterans of the revolution who had turned against the Sandinistas. His high school classmate Alfonso Robelo, who had resigned from the Sandinista-controlled junta, became a key adviser. So did Arturo Cruz, Sr., who had replaced Robelo on the junta before resigning himself. And so did a CIA officer named Duane Clarridge.[6]

Pastora and the CIA were not strangers. The Agency first got in touch with Pastora in the waning days of the revolution against Somoza. The Agency was hedging its bets against the failure of U.S. policy; if the Sandinistas won, there would still be someone in the new government that the gringos could talk to. Pastora, who could hardly afford to be caught in direct contact with the CIA at the time, used his aide Carlos Coronel as an intermediary. Coronel came away from the meeting with some money, variously reported as a few thousand to a few million dollars. (Pastora, in a characteristic fit of braggadocio, told his top men that the booty was $20 million, an unlikely sum even in the carefree days before Gramm-Rudman.)

Near the end of 1981, Coronel set up another meeting, this time in Panama. The CIA delegation was headed by Clarridge, who seemed an unlikely choice. He spoke no Spanish and had no Latin American experience; he was known within the Agency mainly for his work fighting the terrorist Red Brigades while he was the station chief in Rome. Now, however, he was the new head of the Latin American division of the CIA's operations directorate.

Oddly enough, Pastora instantly fell in love with Clarridge. Perhaps the officer's incongruity convinced Pastora he was dealing with a real live spy. Clarridge wore a monocle and dressed in pastel-colored Italian silk safari outfits. He drove a bright white jeep with customized license plates that read CONTRA, and no matter how much his superiors screamed about it, Clarridge wouldn't give them up.[7] Conspiracy seemed to ooze from his very pores. Even other spooks found him discomfiting. A CIA assistant division chief once described him to me as "a Mephistophelean presence dressed like an Italian pimp." He was rarely seen without a fat cigar jammed in his mouth—Pastora called him *el hombre del puro*, the man with the cigar.

As much as Pastora loved Clarridge, Clarridge loved Pastora. With Pastora, he had a trophy that would honor any display case at Langley: an authentic revolutionary warrior, a name and face instantly recognizable to everyone in Nicaragua, and a proven success at wooing Latin American liberals who would otherwise be suspicious of any U.S.-backed project. No more need to worry about the National Guard connections of the FDN commanders. In fact, Pastora's old high school chum, Chicano Cardenal, was the FDN's top political leader, which should make unity a cinch.

Clarridge was ready to go to war on the spot. By January 1982, Pastora's organization was collecting $150,000 a month in CIA cash. And during the first two months of the year the Agency shipped him 650 rifles.[8] Clarridge and Pastora continued to meet, in Acapulco and Washington. (One CIA man who did not share Clarridge's personal enthusiasm for Pastora was the chief spook himself, William Casey. Twice Casey was introduced to Pastora in Washington; both times he fell asleep.)

Pastora, too, was ready to fight. But the politicians around him cautioned Pastora against too abrupt a declaration of war. The Nicaraguan population was still exhausted from a two-year-long insurrection; and, perhaps more important, the world community might be reluctant to lend aid and political support to another revolution in Nicaragua so quickly on the heels of the first one. Pastora had to at least offer the pretense of searching for a diplomatic solution.

On April 15, Pastora held a news conference in San José, Costa Rica, to make a public break with the Sandinistas. "Traitors and assassins," he called them, and then catalogued the "political and even moral deviations that endangered the revolutionary process": persecution of the Indians, restrictions on freedom of religion and the press, arbitrary imprisonments and confiscations. He called for all Cubans to leave Nicaragua (and then, perversely, praised "the total unselfishness" of Che Guevara, the Castro lieutenant who was killed while trying to foment a revolution in Bolivia). Finally Pastora said he was "calling for all Nicaraguans to put themselves on a war footing as long as there is a foreign soldier on the native soil." Pastora took particular care to address his words to the Sandinista army and militia; essentially, he was calling for the military to mutiny.[9]

Following the counsel of his advisers, Pastora's carefully crafted statement did not include any overt threat of war. But as soon as reporters began asking questions, Pastora reverted to form. If the Sandinistas didn't shape up, he shouted, "I'll take them out at gunpoint from their mansions and their Mercedes-Benzes!"

Great speech, Clarridge said. Now, meet with the FDN. It was obvious to the CIA that the two fronts had to be united to be effective; and to Clarridge it was obvious who would be running the show. That was why his men in Honduras had ordered Enrique Bermúdez not to use the FDN's name in the communiqué about the bridges at Somotillo and Ocotal that were blown up in March.

So Pastora called Chicano Cardenal. Cardenal was one of the three political directors of the FDN. Along with exiled labor leader Mariano Mendoza—another political director—he agreed to meet Pastora and Robelo at the Hotel Balmoral in San José to talk about unity.

This was the first of many CIA attempts to broker an agreement between the "liberals" on the southern front and the "conservatives" on the northern front. Those labels, which were hurled around so easily by whichever contras felt themselves in a weak position at any given moment and which were then picked up and amplified by a U.S. press corps without the patience to explore the labyrinths of Nicaraguan politics, contained only a nugget of truth. Contra political partnerships, like all other Nicaraguan political alliances, had only a fuzzy relationship to ideology. They depended much more on family trees, personal grudges, and immediate vulnerabilities.

But right away Pastora started accusing Cardenal and Mendoza of forming an alliance with Somocistas. It didn't matter that both men had long, distinguished histories of opposition to Somoza; it didn't matter that Pastora couldn't name a single crime or human rights violation committed by Bermúdez. As far as Pastora was concerned, it was the return of the National Guard, and that was that. (Pastora didn't mention that one of his key aides—in charge of most of his weapons and ammo acquisitions—was Levi Sánchez, a former National Guard general who had been Somoza's last financial officer and was suspected of making off with the contents of several large Guard bank accounts. Sánchez was Pastora's most trusted assistant throughout the contra war, but he always operated from an isolated office in Miami so that Pastora wouldn't have to explain him to anyone.)

Cardenal, never one to shrink from a fight, mercilessly ridiculed both Pastora and Robelo for working with the Sandinistas. *I* always knew they were communists, Cardenal declared. Then he asked Pastora, if we're a bunch of rightists, what is it that *you* believe exactly?

"I am truly a Sandinista," Pastora replied. "I believe in freedom of the press, I believe in private enterprise, I believe in elections."

"You know, Edén, that has a name," Cardenal shot back. "Democracy."

Even Pastora's ally, Robelo, found himself shaking his head in astonishment. Pastora would orate for hours at a time, vaingloriously enumerating his own amazing qualities in the third person: "When Commander Zero comes, people rise, because he's of the people. . . . There used to be a leader in Latin America, Che Guevara. Then he was sacrificed. Then Castro had a chance to be that leader. But he gave himself totally to the Russians. Now there is only one person in Latin America with a chance to be a true leader, Commander Zero."

The talks continued for a week. Cardenal offered (without clearing it with anyone else in the FDN) to make Pastora co-commander of a united contra army, equal in rank to Bermúdez. Meanwhile the political directorate would be expanded to four to include Robelo; that would mean three seats would be held by men who had been anti-Somoza activists and had no connection to the National Guard.

Pastora refused. He wouldn't accept anything less than the total exclusion of former National Guard officers from the movement.

"Come on, Edén," Cardenal exclaimed in exasperation. "If you accept, you'll be running the army in six months. Who do you think people will follow, you or Bermúdez? But I can't just kick Bermúdez out. Right now he's the backbone of the FDN."

The meetings finally broke up with nothing resolved. But Pastora did agree to come to Honduras to meet some of the FDN commanders and political officials, as well as General Alvarez. Difficult though it was for Cardenal to believe, those negotiations were even worse. Pastora opened the meeting by recounting his adventures in National Palace for the group, jumping back and forth across the room with an imaginary machine gun in his hands, making little gunfire noises with his mouth like a boy with a toy rifle. By the time he was finished, General Alvarez was irredeemably lost. Forever after, Alvarez addressed Pastora by his last name, instead of his guerrilla rank of commander—a calculated insult that Pastora understood.[10]

On the second visit, Pastora met with several FDN commanders and political officials. Bermúdez, thinking his presence might be an obstacle, did not attend; he sent a deputy instead. Bermúdez knew how high Pastora's stock was with the CIA and was resigned to the idea of Pastora becoming the military commander in chief. He concentrated his lobbying efforts with the Agency on blocking any attempt to completely exclude former Guardsmen from the movement.

But Pastora continued to self-destruct; his performance at the second meeting all but ended any hope of unity. First the FDN officials watched in fascination as Pastora and his entourage approached their safe house. One of Pastora's men would run ahead twenty or thirty yards, press himself flat against a wall, look carefully around, and then wave his arm for the next man to run ahead. It looked like something out of a World War II movie.

Inside, the FDN officers listened patiently for hours while Pastora explained that they were assassins and torturers who would have to be eliminated if the contras were to win any following inside Nicaragua. Finally, Bermúdez's deputy interjected. "You killed people in Ciudad Darío, you killed people in Granada, you've killed people before," he argued, referring to rumors that Pastora had executed some National Guardsmen in the days after Somoza fled. "What about that?"

"That was unimportant," Pastora said dismissively. "That kind of shooting isn't important, it isn't even worth mentioning." The FDN men exchanged glances. It wasn't exactly a denial. A few minutes later, Pastora explained his vision of the new contra military. It would call itself the True Sandinista Army. "The men will wear red-and-black handkerchiefs," he said, "and we are going to sing the Sandinista Hymn."

At that several of the FDN officials laughed out loud. The CIA wanted to be revolutionary, but no one could quite imagine the Americans attending meetings where everyone would lift their voices in song: *We fight against the Yanqui, enemy of humanity.* The meeting continued for nine hours, but everyone knew it was over.

Back in Costa Rica, Pastora continued to organize. He, Robelo, and a handful of others had formed the Democratic Revolutionary Alliance, or ARDE. They used their CIA money to rent fifteen houses in Costa Rica—including a huge, ornate two-story house in San José's fashionable Escazú neighborhood that would be both a headquarters and Pastora's home—plus a fleet of forty-six vehicles. Every time a bright young Sandinista fled Nicaragua, Pastora called or wrote to recruit him.

Arturo Cruz, Jr., who had resigned his post in Nicaragua's Foreign Ministry because he was tired of parroting the Soviet line on Afghanistan and Poland, got a note from Pastora. "It was a very folkloric letter, a very beautiful type of letter, full of spelling mistakes," Cruz recalled later. Cruz, though disenchanted with the Sandinistas, was reluctant to join any movement that seemed to imply a return to the Somoza days. But the news that Pastora was on the verge of going to war filled him with excitement. He went to San José and was only slightly disconcerted that before entering Pastora's study, he had to be briefed by Edén's cousin, Orión Pastora.

"Are you aware of who you're going to see?" Orión asked.

"Sí," replied Cruz, puzzled. "Edén."

"No," Orión explained solemnly. "You are going to see a man chosen by history."

Once inside, Cruz could hardly pay attention to a word Pastora was saying. "You don't listen to him," Cruz says of the meeting. "You look at him. You are totally fascinated and seduced by the revolutionary mien. . . . It's like a fantasy you are absorbing, okay? And you're not listening to what he is telling you. Basically, you are mesmerized." By the time Cruz left the room, he was sold.

By September it was apparent to Clarridge that contra unity was impossible, at least for the foreseeable future. He went to Costa Rica to meet with Pastora, Robelo, and a couple of others. "It's time you people went to war," Clarridge told the ARDE leaders. "We've been working on this for a year now. We expect some results."

In front of Clarridge, everyone nodded in agreement. Privately, the response was more ambivalent. Some Pastora aides had the quiet suspicion that, without lifting a rifle, Commander Zero had already suffered a major defeat. His highly publicized speech urging insurrection in the Sandinista army triggered few desertions, much less an open mutiny. "I was aware that Pastora would not be the great success people expected him to be for a very simple reason," says one former adviser. "Because the breakdown in the [Sandinista] army and the popular militias that they expected to happen when he announced his dissatisfaction with the Sandinistas, it didn't take place."

Pastora (and, for that matter, many other contra leaders) wasn't paying attention to his own rhetoric. The Nicaraguan army, under Sandinista control, was no longer a Central American stereotype: cranky, highly factionalized, and independent to a wild fault. Now political indoctrination was tight, decision making was extremely centralized, and the chain of command disciplined. The contras didn't realize it yet, but they weren't fighting some banana republic colonel. They were at war with the Soviet bloc.

Another of Pastora's failures was more apparent. The Latin American liberals who were Pastora's most important allies in 1979 were now giving him a very public cold shoulder. Pastora toured South America and Europe looking for support, but everyone turned him down. Portugal's Socialist leader Mario Soares rejected Pastora's overtures; so did Felipe González, Spain's Socialist prime minister. In many countries, civilian leaders refused to see him at all.

Pastora and his coterie were discouraged by the lack of support. And they were alarmed by the success of the FDN, which was continuing to expand its military operations in the north. Pastora's prediction that a group led by ex-Guardsmen could never win support was utterly wrong: thousands of campesinos were flocking to the FDN's Honduran border camps. And while the FDN hadn't really been able to deliver a body blow to the Sandinistas yet, its troops were moving openly and fearlessly throughout a large chunk of northern Nicaragua. If Pastora was going to compete with the FDN for troops and international aid, he had to start fighting.

But when Pastora told his commanders to get ready for combat, he got an unpleasant shock. They wanted to form a general staff, like a regular army, with one man in charge of logistics, another in charge of intelligence, and so forth.

The commanders saw this as simple military logic. Pastora saw it as conspiracy. No way, he told them. Commander Zero is in charge. Commander Zero is a military genius and a popular hero. Who among you presumes to give Commander Zero advice? "You men have been eating too much bacon and living in the city too long," he concluded.

Pastora decided that he needed to bring in someone to set an example. He headed for the Dominican Republic, to find his old chief of logistics, Popo Chamorro.

It hadn't taken long for Popo to see his worst fear—that the revolution was out of control—come true. He held several midlevel posts in the new government in 1979 and 1980, but everywhere he looked, things were going wrong. Confiscations, kangaroo courts, idiotic Bulgarian economic planning, and Cubans running around Managua like it was their private anthill. Meanwhile, one by one, the men who had fought with them on the southern front were going into exile. When Pastora left, too, Popo cheerfully joined the graffiti spray-painting campaign—even though he was certain, as he warned the others, "It's just going to get us arrested." Popo was a prophet. His own imprisonment lasted about two months. When the Sandinistas turned him loose, he moved to Santo Domingo and set up a small business tinting automobile windows.

Now he listened as Pastora presented him with a proposition: Popo would live in a small, Spartan house in San José and collect a salary big enough to feed his family, no more. He would symbolize guerrilla spiritualism. His job would be to set up a camp on the northern side of the Río San Juan, the eastern boundary between Costa Rica and Nicaragua. It took Popo about an hour to accept.

When he arrived in October 1982, the situation was a good deal bleaker than Pastora had described. The other commanders were barely speaking to Pastora, and they begged Popo to support them. Several of the best officers from the southern front of 1979 had already left ARDE. As for setting up a camp—for what purpose? Pastora had only had 150 soldiers, desultorily bivouacked on the Costa Rican side of the Río San Juan. Popo reminded himself that the Sandinistas had started out with less, but still it was hard to feel very optimistic.

But Popo got the camp set up. And soon after the turn of the year, another 2,550 rifles arrived. When the local campesinos heard that guns were available, they began streaming into the ARDE camp.

Popo and some of the other commanders were not eager to hand out the rifles willy-nilly to anyone who asked. After all, weren't they expecting ARDE forces to be bolstered by desertions from the Sandinista army? Wouldn't it be better to hold onto the weapons for those experienced soldiers?

"Nonsense," Pastora decreed. "Commander Zero will arm the campesinos. Commander Zero does not withhold arms from the people." Besides, he added airily, the gringos would always bring more guns.

On April 15, 1983, Pastora declared war.

"My country is once again trespassed upon," his statement said. "It is our obligation in the name of national dignity to expel the interlopers from our soil and restore sovereignty and peace. . . . I declare that if the Cubans, who are today the instruments of intervention and death here in Nicaragua, have not left this sacred soil within two weeks from today, they will end like all others who have dared trespass upon us: dead."[11] The statement was supposedly issued "from the mountains of Nicaragua," although Pastora was really still at home in Costa Rica. Robelo called a press conference in Mexico City to read the declaration, but Mexican authorities expelled him from the country moments before it was to get under way.

Twenty-five years before, the Mexicans had allowed Fidel Castro to raise an army and launch an invasion of Cuba from their shores, and they had long been hospitable to El Salvador's communist guerrillas. Robelo's expulsion was a clear signal: Latin governments would employ a different standard for the contras.

6 | The Monkey-Eaters

You could hear the engine's rumble for miles, and there was plenty of time for Toño to deploy his men along both sides of the narrow dirt road that snaked along the Río Yacalwas. There was plenty of time for him to worry, too. Less than twenty-four hours inside Nicaragua, and if this turned out to be a Sandinista army vehicle approaching, his fledgling unit would get its first trial in combat. Almost all his 240 men were newly recruited campesinos, and although Toño had trained them himself, firing a gun on a rifle range was a lot different than doing it in battle. And the man with Toño's single piece of "artillery"—an M-79 grenade launcher—had never even test-fired a round; the ammo was too scarce. "Remember," Toño reminded him one last time, "that thing doesn't shoot like a rifle. The grenade will travel in an arc, so aim high." The young peasant nodded solemnly. The grenade launcher and an M-60 machine gun across the road were the unit's only heavy weapons.

The vehicle rounded a bend in the road, and the men could finally see it: an olive-green pickup, with half a dozen Sandinista soldiers sitting in the back. Toño willed his trigger finger to be still as the truck lurched along the rutted road; better to wait until it was right on top of his men before springing the ambush, so close that there would be no escape. When it was twenty yards off, Toño took aim with his own FAL rifle, then shouted: "Fire!"

Hundreds of contra rifles roared from both sides of the road. Their muzzle flashes lent a weird glow to the darkened foliage at the jungle's edge and silhouetted the campesino with the M-79 as he stood straight up out of the bushes like John Wayne or some other loony gringo movie soldier, just a few feet from the truck. He fired his grenade launcher almost straight up in the air; as Toño watched the grenade crazily arch thirty feet over the truck, into the jungle beyond, he thought: *home run*. Across the road, the contra with the M-60 had forgotten to unfurl the ammo bandolier from around his neck. As the gun fired, the bandolier jerked the stock up into his throat and held it there as the recoil hurled the contra backward into the jungle, his finger clasped to the trigger, spraying bullets all around.

The Sandinista soldiers were returning fire now. The contra with the grenade launcher, an easy target, was already down, and dozens of the men around Toño bolted for the cover of a single large guanacaste tree. Incensed, Toño grabbed a tree branch and began walloping their butts as they crouched behind the thick trunk. *"Fight, you bastards!"* he bellowed. *"FIGHT!"*

But all along the road, the guns had quieted. The six Sandinista soldiers from the back of the truck were dead; the driver, who had thrown himself on the floor when the shooting started and miraculously escaped injury, had surrendered. *A forty-to-one advantage in troops can overcome a lot,* Toño reflected as he searched the dead men's pockets for documents. He found nothing; they were just six unlucky enlisted men. "Burn the truck," Toño ordered and then sat down by himself under a tree at the side of the road. *Maybe,* he brooded, *the other National Guardsmen are right. Maybe the peasants will never be soldiers. Maybe they* are *just a bunch of monkey-eaters.* Toño wondered if he should turn back.

Until March 1982, almost all the FDN's energies were devoted to political tasks: organizing support in the exile community and securing foreign aid. But after the bridges in Ocotal and Somotillo were blown up, it was time to concentrate on the military part of the struggle. An army had to take the field.

The initial framework for the FDN military force was organized almost totally around former National Guardsmen. Bermúdez was the commander in chief; all the members of the general staff were ex-Guardsmen, and so were the first group of field commanders. Even in those early days, National Guardsmen did not make up the majority of the FDN—of the 500 troops in FDN camps at the beginning of 1982, about 150 were ex-Guard—but they designed the organization and they ran it. They did most of the dying, too; of the original 150, more than two-thirds were dead by 1985.

The National Guard role in organizing the FDN would be a source of constant complaint in the U.S. Congress throughout the war. But if an anti-Sandinista military force was going to get into the field quickly—before the FSLN had a chance to consolidate its hold on Nicaragua—there was little choice. Going to war is not just a matter of picking up guns and heading into the jungle. Supplies must be assembled, allocated, and delivered; communications must be organized; intelligence must be gathered and analyzed. Guerrilla forces can organize from scratch, build slowly, and learn to perform all these tasks through trial and error. But it takes a long, long time. It took the Sandinistas, even with some training from Cuba and the Palestine Liberation Organization, sixteen years to become a militarily credible force. And even then they overcame Somoza only when Panama, Venezuela, and Cuba lent a massive amount of arms and expertise.

In spring 1982, the FDN had five base camps in western Honduras, each of them located just a couple of miles from the Nicaraguan border. (Another base, the Commando School, was a training installation and was not, as a rule, used for staging combat missions. Radio Fifteen, the headquarters of the general staff, and the political offices were all located in Tegucigalpa.) One of the camps was called Pino-1, for the pine trees that dotted its hilly terrain; another was known as Nicarao, after the ancient Indian chief for whom Nicaragua was named. The names of the other camps reflected the National Guard origins of the FDN. Ariel, the easternmost camp, and Sagitario were named for Guard colonels killed by the Sandinistas. Zebra, the westernmost base, took its name from the distinctive striped insignia of the Guard's elite EEBI unit.

Each camp commander staged some military forays into Nicaragua, but these amounted to little more than cross-border raiding parties. Units loaded up with ammunition, hiked inside for two or three days until they found something to shoot at, and then came right back out. The contras had little intelligence from deep inside Nicaragua, and it wasn't until the summer that Bermúdez and the general staff began to realize the breadth of the potential support for the FDN.

It began with a deep reconnaissance patrol by a twenty-three-year-old former National Guardsman named Luis Moreno. Moreno had graduated from the military academy as a second lieutenant just a month before the fall of Somoza and saw action only briefly before he was wounded in the back and hospitalized. A cousin who worked at the Spanish embassy in Managua managed to get asylum for him there. Eventually Moreno slipped out of the embassy and escaped to Costa Rica.

Moreno was a young, intelligent man—he was the head of his class at the military academy—and could easily have gone about building a new life in exile. Instead, he hopscotched the region—Costa Rica, Panama, Guatemala, Honduras—looking for a way to go home and fight the Sandinistas. Like most of the National Guardsmen who joined the FDN, his motives were a tangled weave of ideological, professional, and personal threads. Like nearly all Guardsmen, he was a fierce anticommunist. But it was more complicated than that. Moreno was angry at being forced to leave his country; his whole family was still inside Nicaragua. He was haunted by a Dantesque vision from the last days of the war, when he had seen a Sandinista mob burning a National Guardsman alive in Ciudad Darío. And he felt cheated out of a professional military career that he had trained for during three harsh years in the academy.

When Moreno arrived in Honduras in March 1982, Bermúdez instructed him to pick a nom de guerre. The idea was to protect family members back in Nicaragua by concealing your identity. But it was also a sort of initiation ceremony, the only one the FDN really had. Even Bermúdez, whose participation in the FDN was hardly a secret, had a code name; he was known as 380, his cadet number during his days at the military academy.[1] It made sense to Moreno. He had chosen the name Mike Lima, after the phonetic initials of his name the way it had always appeared on Guard duty rosters: Moreno, Luis.

Three months later, on June 26, the newly christened Mike Lima led fifty-nine men—fourteen former National Guardsmen, six former Sandinista soldiers, and forty-eight campesinos—into Nicaragua. The eclectic nature of the force was deliberate; Bermúdez was trying to meld the FDN's three separate components into a single organization. To avoid the heavy concentration of Sandinista troops across the border from FDN camps, the contras marched far to the east, to a tiny Honduran village along the Río Coco named Banco Grande, before a 2 A.M. crossing into an almost-unpopulated

63

jungle in Nicaragua's Jinotega Department. But it took four hours to cross the river, swollen with summer rains. They were spotted, and the Sandinistas moved troops to the area by helicopter. For more than a week, Lima's men stayed barely one step ahead. On July 4, Lima decided it was time to draw blood. Breaking his unit into teams of three—one experienced soldier with two campesinos—he set a pair of ambushes for the pursuing Sandinistas, who walked right into them. Nine Sandinistas were killed, and the rest fled.

The ambushes threw the Sandinista pursuit into disarray, and Lima's men were able to forge south without any difficulty. Lima soon was in Zelaya Department, where most Sandinista military posts were manned by militia, ill-trained draftees who often fled rather than confront the contras. After Lima was about forty miles inside Nicaragua, he felt secure enough to split his unit into four patrols to gather information.

The first thing he learned was that FDN logistical planning would have to improve if the contras were to stay inside Nicaragua for more than a week or two. His men were short on ammunition, a result of Bermúdez's decision to use the higher-powered Belgian FAL rifles instead of the Soviet-made AK-47s that the Sandinistas carried.

The contras were also low on food and hadn't brought enough money to buy more. They had no medicine for malaria, which was rife in the Zelaya lowlands, and several of the men—including Lima—nearly died. The contras didn't even have bandages for their wounded.

The only reason Lima's unit was able to stay inside was that the local campesinos were tremendously supportive. They kept the contras steadily supplied with food, and when Lima suffered stomach problems from eating undercooked meat, an old peasant woman even produced, like magic, a bottle of Phillips' milk of magnesia. The campesinos bitterly complained that they had to sell their crops to a state purchasing agency, which they were certain cheated them blind; and they were shocked by the public abuse that the Sandinistas were heaping on the Catholic Church hierarchy.

What was more, Lima found that if he turned loose one of his campesino soldiers—a strutting bantam whose nom de guerre was Tigrillo, little tiger—to talk to the peasants, they soon wanted to do more than just complain about the Sandinistas. Even among the short, squat campesinos, Tigrillo was a runt: a shade under five feet tall and less than one hundred pounds. But he seemed to puff up as he started chattering away, like some nutty campesino disc jockey, and after a few minutes the local men would come to Lima asking if he had enough rifles for them. They wanted to join the FDN. Lima was stunned; nobody in the FDN thought widespread recruiting was possible yet, but after a couple of weeks he had to start turning people away. The unit was up to 240 men, and even with what he had captured from the Sandinistas, Lima couldn't equip a quarter of the new recruits.

In early August, Lima radioed Tegucigalpa that he was coming back to Honduras with 180 new recruits, increasing the FDN's size by nearly 40 percent in a single stroke. "Don't bring such a mountain of men," Bermúdez begged in a panicky voice. "The Americans don't want us to grow so much. How can we supply them?"

"Hijo de puta!" the dumbfounded Lima sputtered. "Then what are we doing here? What's the point of all this?"

"Let me call you back tomorrow," Bermúdez urged. "Let me check some things around here."

"I'm coming to Honduras," Lima said. "You can do whatever you want." He switched off the radio.

On August 20, Lima returned with his new recruits. "If I go back for a little while," he told a meeting of the general staff, "I could raise six hundred men." The officers were euphoric. Even Bermúdez seemed giddy, Lima noticed. He wondered what had changed since they talked on the radio.

What had happened was that Lima's news had shocked Bermúdez into doing some hard thinking about his American allies. Bermúdez had come into this business with open eyes; he knew what happened to the Cubans at the Bay of Pigs, when the Americans cut off their air support at the last minute. He had seen the pictures of South Vietnamese desperately grasping for the skids as the last helicopter pulled away from the roof of the U.S. embassy in Saigon.

Right from the start there had been worrisome reminders that the U.S. agenda in Nicaragua did not necessarily match up with the FDN's. In 1981, at the same time the Americans were setting up the tripartite alliance with Honduras and Argentina, U.S. Assistant Secretary of State Thomas Enders was in Managua offering to shut the contras down if the Sandinistas would quit sending arms to the guerrillas in El Salvador.[2] The gringos cared about their security interests, not freedom in Nicaragua.

Bermúdez wasn't too troubled, initially, because of his confidence in the Sandinistas. As long as they kept subverting their neighbors and getting more deeply involved with Fidel Castro and the Soviets, Bermúdez was certain, the Reagan administration would want to supply the contras. Perhaps the United States only intended them as an instrument of cheap containment, but that wouldn't prevent the contras from pursuing their own agenda.

Now, however, there was a disturbing new ingredient in this stew: Edén Pastora. Even though Pastora had acted like a madman and alienated the Hondurans and the Argentines during their meetings in Tegucigalpa, the CIA was clearly still enchanted with him. It seemed entirely possible to Bermúdez that Pastora might try to convince the Americans to cut off the FDN and put all their chips by him. "To the gringos Pastora is *el mimado*," the spoiled, overindulged child, Bermúdez told his general staff. "We are the handicapped ones. We have to grow and grow, in order to be a reality and raise the political cost of being demobilized."

There was no way to match Pastora's political credentials, Bermúdez reasoned, at least in the eyes of the Americans. The only thing the FDN could do was to improve its military strength. The bigger and more powerful it was, the more difficult it would be for the Americans to turn off the spigot. So the word went out: recruit. Bring in as many men as you can. Anybody you can't bring, tell them you'll be back for them soon.

Politically, the growth strategy may have saved the FDN from being strangled in its crib. But from a military point of view, it would eventually lead to some serious problems. While the contras certainly needed more men in uniform—

five hundred troops were obviously never going to be able to defeat a Soviet-equipped army that numbered in the tens of thousands—the FDN also needed to build a political and logistical infrastructure to support a larger army.

Many of the campesinos who would soon be tramping off to Honduras to get a rifle and a blue-green uniform would have served the FDN better by staying in place in Nicaragua. The contras needed civilian collaborators: to serve as an intelligence network, to hide and care for the wounded, to supply food. Later, when it became obvious that the civilian-support side of the war effort had been neglected, the contras would try, not always successfully, to fill the gaps with high-tech solutions borrowed from the Americans.

Those difficulties, though, were years in the future. The recruitment campaign was about to create a more immediate problem: the foul-mouthed, violent, lovable little man who called himself Tigrillo.

His real name was Encarnación Baldivia. In 1977 he and his brother Francisco (who, though older, was thoroughly dominated by Encarnación) abandoned their few acres of coffee bushes near La Concordia, high in the mountains of southern Jinotega Department, and joined the Sandinistas. They fought long and hard against Somoza, and it was more fun than breaking your back in the coffee fields. When the war was over, the brothers stayed in the Sandinista army.

Encarnación began to have his doubts about the revolution in mid-1980, when his unit went to Nueva Segovia to chase around the renegade *Milpas* under the command of Pedro Joaquín González. Encarnación's men never quite caught up with the *Milpas*, but the more he heard about them, the less sense his own role made. Everything this guy González said was true. The new government *was* pushing around the campesinos and messing with their lives. Why should Encarnación be trying to jail a guy who was defending the campesinos? The whole damn revolution was supposed to be about a *better life* for the campesinos.

After a few weeks of fruitless pursuit, Encarnación's unit went back to its base on Lake Apanás for rest and the never-ending political lectures. One morning a Cuban officer from Managua was talking about religion and where it fit into the revolution. He went on and on about poverty and the tough life of the campesino, a subject on which Encarnación hardly needed instruction. But the Cuban barely mentioned God at all. What kind of religious lecture was this? At the end of the talk, when the officer asked if there were any questions, Encarnación got up on his stubby feet. "What about God?" he queried. "God doesn't exist," the Cuban answered, looking surprised. "The only reality in Nicaragua is the Sandinista revolution." Encarnación sat back down, nodding wisely. *Fuck you, amigo*, he thought as he began making plans to desert. A few nights later he slipped out of the camp with his rifle and went looking for his brother Francisco.

The Baldivia brothers and a couple dozen followers spooked around the mountains of southern Jinotega, taking potshots at the Sandinistas and harassing them here and there. Eventually they went to Honduras, chasing rumors of the FDN. When they found the contra camps, they chose their noms de guerre; Encarnación became Tigrillo, and Francisco chose Dimas, the pseudonym of the fallen *Milpa* leader Pedro Joaquín González.

For months Tigrillo insisted that he could easily recruit thousands of campesinos if the FDN would just send him with a professional-looking force and the promise of guns. No one believed him. His whiny hillbilly accent, his grammatically fractured mountain Spanish, his backwoods manner, all seemed comical to the former National Guardsmen who made up the FDN's general staff and corps of commanders. Tigrillo's colorful exaggerations, which to campesinos were an ordinary way of making a point, made him seem like a bullshit artist to the Guardsmen. (When one of the former Guardsmen asked him how many Sandinista troops were based at Lake Apanás, Tigrillo replied: "There are so many *piricuacos* around there that if I shot my rifle up in the air three times, I'd hit two.") In American terms, it was something like Snuffy Smith trying to communicate with a roomful of West Point graduates.

But when Tigrillo and Mike Lima returned from their patrol through Zelaya, Jinotega, and Nueva Segovia departments in August, the general staff started taking Tigrillo more seriously. He might be a hick and a buffoon, but when it came to the campesinos Tigrillo knew what he was talking about. And his recruits idolized him; the same things that made him seem like a fool to the ex-Guardsmen—the tall tales, the braggadocio, the swaggering caricature of macho—made him larger than life in campesino eyes.

The Argentines believed Tigrillo could be an important weapon for the FDN: a campesino revolutionary commander, like Pancho Villa, who through his example would spark insurrection among the peasants. The Argentine colonel, Villegas, began doing little favors for Tigrillo, like giving him a special sniper's rifle. Bermúdez didn't share the wild optimism of the Argentines, but he knew that the FDN had to do something to deflect the criticism that it was nothing but a revived National Guard. He made Tigrillo the first campesino in the FDN with the rank of commander.

Not everyone on the general staff agreed. Those peasants are not soldiers, one officer protested, and they'll never be soldiers. They're nothing but a goddamned bunch of *comemonos*—monkey-eaters. They do all right when they're following an experienced military man. But you put a monkey-eater in charge of other monkey-eaters, and you'll be sorry.

It worried Bermúdez, too, a little bit. So when Tigrillo's unit was ready to go inside on its first patrol, he assigned Mike Lima to go along as a "coordinator," a sort of adviser. A year earlier Bermúdez might have scoffed at the idea of turning to a twenty-three-year-old former second lieutenant for a steady hand and sober advice. But right now, Mike Lima was the FDN's brightest star.

After he returned with the new recruits in August, Lima crossed right back into Nicaragua as soon as he could load up with fresh ammunition. In a bold dawn attack on October 21, he struck the strongest Sandinista military post in northern Jinotega, a two-hundred-man base at the junction of the Río Bocay and the Río Ayapa. Though the compound was heavily fortified, Lima used what passed for heavy artillery among the contras—60mm mortars, M-79 grenade launchers, and light antitank weapons—to reduce it to ruins.

Within an hour, Sandinista troops were arriving in helicopters from every direction. Eventually, Lima estimated, two thousand Sandinistas were chasing him, but his men escaped the dragnet and reached the Cordillera Isabelia, a rugged half-moon-shaped mountain range east of the Río Bocay where pursuit was nearly impossible. Enraged when they lost their prey, the Sandinistas turned on the Indians in the zone. Less than a month after Lima's attack, the government uprooted eight villages in Jinotega Department along the Río Coco and forced seven thousand members of the Miskito and Sumo tribes to march hundreds of miles south to government coffee farms in Matagalpa Department. In the middle of the relocation, a Sandinista army helicopter crashed, killing eighty-four Indian women and children.

Guerrilla war has its own brutal and perverse logic. The forced resettlement of the Indians by the government, cruel though it was, represented a major contra triumph. It was an admission by the Sandinistas that the contras were a militarily significant force that the government could not control; it was a propaganda debacle for the FSLN, both at home and abroad; and it fed contra recruiting by further alienating the local population.

In November, Lima, Tigrillo, and 120 contras stole across the Río Bocay. This unit included only 14 National Guardsmen; the rest were campesinos or former Sandinista soldiers. Their assignment: recruit. "We have to grow and grow and grow," Bermúdez told them. Once across the river, they split their force. Tigrillo would recruit, while Lima would seek out Tigrillo's brother Dimas, who had stayed inside Nicaragua with 60 men when the June patrol ended. Lima was uneasy about what Dimas might have been up to by himself. Dimas seemed a little too anxious to prove himself, to show that he was as great an *hombre* as his brother. A guy like that, Lima thought, might do something really crazy.

On November 23, Lima linked up with Dimas. The little campesino commander was aloof, but several of his men eagerly sought Lima out to tell him what had happened during the past three months. As they talked, Lima realized his fears had been well-founded.

In late August, as soon as he was on his own, Dimas marched his force to La Colonia, a village about six miles inside Nicaragua, to the small farm of a man there named Chilo Osorio. Osorio lived in a well-tended wooden house with several rooms. In Managua, it would have been nothing, but here among the simple campesino huts, the house was a conspicuous mark of success. In back there were perhaps twenty cattle. In Russia, they would have called Osorio a *kulak*, a successful peasant entrepreneur. Out here, hundreds of miles from Managua and a world away from its political intrigues, Chilo Osorio lived in peace with four sons and two pretty teenaged daughters.

Dimas ordered the men to kill him.

"He's been supplying the Sandinista army," Dimas explained after he gave the order. Some of the men were doubtful. Of course Osorio probably sold some cows to the Sandinistas when they came through La Colonia; but if the contras were going to execute everyone who did that, the bodies would be stacked to the peaks of the Cordillera Isabelia. This looked more like an old grudge between neighbors being settled under the guise of politics. The house, the cows, the daughters—no doubt a lot of people in La Colonia were fiercely jealous of Chilo Osorio.

A few of the men grumbled when Chilo Osorio and two of his sons were shot. Others were skeptical when Dimas said two of the other boys, who looked to be about thirteen and fourteen, had to join the contras—they couldn't fathom what good two kids so young and unwilling were going to be. And many of the men were openly critical when Dimas announced he was taking one of the daughters as his woman. The other was claimed by a contra named Israel Galeano—or Franklyn, his nom de guerre. Franklyn said she had been his girlfriend before the war; but Franklyn hadn't lived around here, and the look on the girl's face didn't suggest romance.

The muttering quieted, though, over the next two weeks as the men realized it had a high price. Dimas was ordering a man shot almost every night. Sandinista infiltrators, he called them. But he didn't seem to have any evidence. And at least one of the "infiltrators," the men noticed, had fallen under suspicion only after he flirted with Dimas's new woman. Soon the body count of "infiltrators" was up to twelve.

Lima seethed as he listened to the story. He wasn't tender-hearted—this was war, after all—but it was so **unprofessional,** especially killing your own troops. And during the next couple of weeks, as the patrol moved toward Honduras, Lima and Dimas didn't try to conceal their animosity for one another from the men. "*Guardia* son of a bitch!" Dimas would shout. "Monkey-eating piece of shit!" Lima screamed back. As they approached the Honduran border, Dimas seemed increasingly nervous. *He is afraid to explain all those executions*, Lima thought.

On December 5, when they were supposed to cross the Río Bocay into Honduras, Dimas told Lima he wasn't going. He was taking the men to rendezvous with Tigrillo instead.

"No, you're not," Lima insisted. "The men are going to Honduras with me, as we planned."

"You're not the commander here!" Dimas howled. He yanked his rifle up, finger on the trigger, at the exact instant Lima did the same. They stood there in a jungle clearing, guns trained on one another, while the men watched. The former National Guardsmen in the unit began edging toward Lima. "Calm down," Dimas, suddenly unnerved, urged Lima.

The rustle of movement came from the other side of the clearing. Like a stray plot line from a cheap novel, Tigrillo had blundered into their camp.

"Stay there," Lima ordered Dimas, and he hurried over to talk to Tigrillo, standing agape at the edge of the clearing. In a few brief sentences, Lima sketched out what had happened. "Don't worry," Tigrillo assured him. "I understand. I'll talk to Dimas; everything will be okay." Tigrillo turned to walk away—then whirled and jerked his rifle to his shoulder, aimed straight at Lima. "I'll kill you, you son of a bitch!" Tigrillo bellowed.

Lima stared back. *If I look scared, even a little bit, he'll shoot me*, he thought.

They stood there like that for a long time before Tigrillo lowered the rifle and walked away.

The remarkable thing was that, despite all the executions, despite all the screaming matches, despite the commanders holding one another at gunpoint, the patrol was a success. They brought back five hundred new recruits. The new men were immediately taken to the FDN training camp in a dusty Honduran village named La Fortuna. The camp was run by Walter Calderón—Toño, the National Guard lieutenant who escaped Nicaragua in a boat.

When Toño arrived in El Salvador, he had planned on making his life there. Surely, he reasoned, the Salvadoran army would have some use for men who had been fighting the Sandinistas and knew their tricks. After all, the Sandinistas didn't make any pretense about their next move: *Si Nicaragua venció, El Salvador vencerá,* they were always saying—if Nicaragua won, El Salvador will win. But his friends in the Salvadoran military didn't believe him, so Toño moved on to Guatemala and scuffled around at odd jobs.

In October 1979, some friends got hold of a Nicaraguan passport with a valid U.S. visa in it. Toño, his wife, Lua, and thirteen other people—men, women, and children—posed for a photo together. Then they pasted it inside the passport, and headed for the airport. The Guatemalan immigration people examined the passport curiously, then waved them aboard the plane. In Miami, they lined up at a checkpoint staffed by a pleasant-looking blonde lady whose face turned wild and red when she saw that passport. She took them to a little room in the back and shrieked at them for almost an hour, but since she didn't speak Spanish and they didn't speak English, it was relatively easy to endure. Finally somebody else came and turned them loose. Toño and Lua hit the streets with nothing but $10 and a vague idea that Miami was full of rich Nicaraguans who would help.

It wasn't that easy, of course, but they made it. Toño got a job in a gun factory ("Gee, you pick this up pretty quick," the assembly-line foreman said in surprise) and at night sold pots and pans door-to-door. They bought a car. They had a baby girl. And at night, Toño dreamed he was walking the streets of Managua with his daughter. His wife scoffed at that. "She won't care anything about Managua," Lua said one evening as she diapered the baby. "She's an American."

When Somoza was killed, Toño went to the funeral service out of curiosity. "I felt like I was in Nicaragua," he told Lua afterwards. "I saw all the old National Guard officers making an honor guard, bodyguards clearing everyone out of the way for Hope Somoza. It was very weird."

He didn't tell Lua what had happened at the end of the mass. El Chigüín, Somoza's son, stood near the altar, surveying the dozens of National Guardsmen in the church. "Lieutenant Palma!" he barked at an aide. "Get all the phone numbers and addresses. The war starts today!" Toño signed the sheet they passed around. Although he wouldn't fight for the Somozas again—only a fool would make that mistake twice—he was curious about what they might be planning. But no one ever called.

70

The funeral, however, started an itch that Toño found difficult to scratch. Somebody told him about Commander Juan Carlos, a crazy old Spaniard who was trying to raise an anti-Sandinista army, and Toño became his Miami representative for a while. Then, in the summer of 1982, an old National Guard friend came by the apartment. He showed Toño a picture of a group of men cradling weapons: FAL rifles, an M-79 grenade launcher, several RPG-7 rocket-propelled grenades. "Those are fancy weapons," Toño said, impressed. He had read newspaper stories that told of ragged bands roaming the border with hunting rifles. But this was a professionally equipped army.

"The Americans are behind us now," Toño's friend explained. "Look, the campesinos are willing to do all the dying. The least the *Guardia* can do is to give them some training. Why don't you come help us?"

Two weeks later, on July 22, Lua drove Toño to the airport to catch a plane to Tegucigalpa. They saved the most difficult conversation for the end.

"You are free to do the thing you think is right," Toño told his wife. "You're not obligated to wait. We are adults. And I would be glad if you wait for me, but if you can't, I understand. But please call me if you decide . . . the other thing."

"It's your decision," Lua replied. Her voice was soft, but her eyes were dry; all the tears had already been cried. "We've got a daughter. I will try to wait. But you know life in the United States is hard. If I do something wrong, please understand. You're making a decision that is hard for me."

Toño knew she wouldn't wait. American women are impatient, and Lua was an American now. But he didn't say anything. The war would take a long time, he knew, two or three years. But he didn't have any doubts about who would win. *With the Americans behind us, how can we lose?* he thought as he waved good-bye and boarded the plane.

In Honduras Bermúdez put Toño, once the youngest instructor in the history of the Nicaraguan military academy, in charge of training new recruits. Toño soon realized his experience at the academy had little relevance to this job. For one thing, military academies deliberately set forth to wash out as many men as possible. The idea was to keep only the very best, most dedicated cadets and to send the rest back to civilian life.

The FDN, however, was trying to do just the reverse: attract as many people as possible. Toño's job was to find a place for any able-bodied man (or woman—that was another thing that was different from the academy) who wanted to fight.[3] He was not only trying to find the best soldiers, but also to get the best out of all the recruits. Instead of kicking out a man who had trouble understanding the mechanics of his rifle, as the National Guard would have done, Toño had to work more closely with him. "These campesinos are not training to get an insignia," he reminded his staff. "They're training to save their lives."

Because so few of the campesinos had ever attended school, Toño modified the training so that almost all of the six-week course was in the field rather than the classroom. The toughest thing to teach them was map-reading—almost none of the recruits had ever seen a map before—and the easiest was shooting. And there were a few areas where Toño found he couldn't teach them anything at all. They were far better than any National Guardsman could ever hope to be at collecting intelligence in the field. They could tell old tracks from new tracks, how many men made them, and whether they were heavily or lightly equipped. They were expert in detecting noises and smells that were alien to the mountains: the sounds the jungle birds make when disturbed, the odor of weapons oils, the faint stench of a distant pile of human feces.

Toño went from camp to camp, training between one hundred and two hundred recruits at a time. But after a few months he felt frustrated. What good was it to train the men if their commanders just holed up in border camps? And teaching other men to fight the Sandinistas wasn't the same as doing it yourself.

When Tigrillo and Mike Lima brought in five hundred new recruits at the end of their patrol in December, Toño saw his chance. He went to Tegucigalpa to make a proposal to Bermúdez: He would take half the new recruits, fashion them into a unit, and go deep inside Nicaragua, to Matagalpa Department— eighty miles from the border, farther than any contra patrol had ever been. But this wouldn't be a patrol; the idea would be to establish a new theater of operations, with a unit not linked to any of the border base camps.

Bermúdez looked skeptical, but he okayed the plan. Then he asked a favor. They were trying to add some political elements to the war. So far all the contra units were just known by the name of their base camp. Since Toño wouldn't have a base camp, how about naming his unit after a popular politician the Sandinistas had murdered?

"So," Toño told his staff later, as he recounted the conversation, "we're going to be called the Jorge Salazar Task Force."

"Who is Jorge Salazar?" one of the men asked.

"I don't know," Toño replied, "but we're going to make him very famous."

It took almost two months to organize the Jorge Salazar Task Force. It was difficult to convince other contra officers that it would be possible for the unit to supply itself so far from the border or to stand up to the intense military pressure that the Sandinistas were sure to apply. In the end, Toño had a former National Guard sergeant, Juan Rivas—who called himself Commander Quiché, after a Guatemalan Indian tribe—as his executive officer. Almost all his other subcommanders were campesinos. One of them was Tirzo Moreno, the former cattleman, now known as Commander Rigoberto.

The Jorge Salazar Task Force was organized along the same lines as other contra units. Each task force was composed of two to five units of 60 troops apiece, known as groups. A group, in turn, was made up of three detachments of 20 men each. The Jorge Salazar had four groups; and traveling alongside it would be another unit, the 160-strong San Jacinto Task Force, under Commander Renato, an ex-National Guard lieutenant whose real name was Francisco Ruiz.

The contras started out with about three days' worth of food. And, learning from Mike Lima's summer reconnaissance patrol, they took money—about $60 in cordobas per man. The money, Toño calculated, should last two months. After that, they would have to rely on supplies captured from the Sandinistas. The plan was vague: Set up a base of operations; establish a net of civilian informants and messengers, or *correos*; send out patrols to harass the Sandinistas and to recruit new troops. There were no specific military targets, and there would be little guidance from headquarters. Contra radios transmitted on only a few easily intercepted frequencies, and their only code was a simple letter-for-letter cipher (where M substitutes for A, N substitutes for B, O substitutes for C, and so on) that any Boy Scout could crack in a few minutes. Secure communications were nonexistent, even within the Jorge Salazar itself; Toño had no walkie-talkies.

The Jorge Salazar crossed into Nicaragua on February 6, 1983. For the first few weeks Toño feared the expedition was a disaster. First there was the comic-opera ambush of the Sandinista pickup truck, when his two heaviest weapons were knocked out by his own troops and a quarter of his men forgot to fire at all. (To compound Toño's despair, his subcommander Fernando—who in civilian life was an evangelical preacher named Diógenes Hernández—turned loose the single prisoner they captured after a lecture about the meaning of God, but before any military interrogation.) Then, as the Jorge Salazar moved across Jinotega Department, the men began deserting. At first it was just a trickle, but as they approached Matagalpa Department it turned into a flood. One bleak morning Toño found thirty-seven packs and rifles neatly stacked, their owners vanished.

"It's not that the men don't want to fight," one of his commanders advised Toño. "But they're almost all from Jinotega. They don't want to go to unfamiliar territory to fight for a commander they don't know very well. They've gone home, to wait for another commander to pass through—someone who will stay in Jinotega, where they're comfortable."

Luckily, Toño's increasingly thin force was not tested again for another two weeks. It seemed that Sandinista troops were massed on the border to prevent infiltration; a commander who could maneuver past the front lines would have a clear path to the interior.

But Toño was no longer sure he would have a unit left to take advantage of that. When he reached Matagalpa and began his recruiting efforts, the campesinos were indifferent. Toño talked about all the things he knew they were angry about—rationing, Cuban teachers, mandatory political meetings, slights to the Catholic Church—and they just shrugged. Finally, a toothless old peasant on the west side of Matagalpa explained the problem. "No one believes you're contras," he said. A couple of months earlier, the Sandinistas dressed some of their own troops in captured contra uniforms and sent them through the area, claiming to be from the FDN. Anyone who demonstrated sympathy was immediately arrested.

"I know it seems crazy, but we have to prove we aren't Sandinistas," Toño told his men. They set up an ambush outside a village called El Martillo. When no Sandinista military vehicles passed, the contras began stopping vehicles from government ministries, burning them, and sending the drivers away on foot. In half a day, Toño torched two large trucks, a pickup, and a jeep.

The local campesinos were thrilled; when the contras marched off, dozens of peasants followed along for several hours, selling them food and filling them in on the local gossip. One man even gave them a cow as a present. Within days, five hundred volunteers joined the Jorge Salazar. Toño armed as many as he could and set up a camp in a mountain village called El Rosario. There he trained recruits, organized *correos*, and dispatched reconnaissance patrols.

The El Martillo ambush alerted the Sandinistas that a contra unit had penetrated deep into Nicaragua. To Toño's surprise, he began hearing references to his unit on government radio broadcasts as the FSLN tried to explain how such a thing was possible. The first announcements amused him: The Sandinistas said the Jorge Salazar was a small group of CIA-trained commandos who had parachuted into Matagalpa. But a few days later, another newscast enraged him. Now the radio was saying that the Jorge Salazar was surrounded, out of ammo, and on the verge of annihilation.

Toño summoned his commanders. "We're not going to let them get away with that bullshit," he said. "We're going to take the Waslala Road for twenty-four hours. Let them explain that on the radio."

The Waslala Road was the major east-west artery on Matagalpa Department's northern edge. Toño's men, split into five forces, seized a seven-mile stretch of the road and overran three small military garrisons in between. The attack began at 5 A.M. on March 8 and lasted until the next morning. Then the contras faded back into the mountains after getting word that a huge Sandinista force in Waslala was headed their way.

The Waslala Road operation was tactically successful—the contras suffered only eight dead and the Sandinistas lost perhaps six times that many—but as time passed Toño realized it was a strategic error. He used up more than half his ammunition and drew thousands of Sandinista troops into the area hunting him. For the rest of his stay in Matagalpa, he would be in a defensive position.

By the time Toño's reconnaissance patrols returned in late May—one made it all the way to Boaco Department, just fifty miles from Managua—the ammo shortage was critical. On May 31, most of the contras headed for Honduras. But part of the Jorge Salazar Task Force stayed behind. Commander Dumas—a former preacher and small cattle merchant named Antonio Chavarría, who joined the contras when the Sandinistas seized his church—remained in Matagalpa with twenty-five men. The Jorge Salazar, in one form or another, stayed inside Nicaragua for the next seven years.

Swollen with new recruits, hundreds of them unarmed, Toño's force made an inviting target on the way home. As they neared the Honduran border, the contras blundered into a Sandinista trap near a village called Golondrina. Everywhere they turned there were ambushes, and the unarmed recruits panicked; Toño was trampled by one of his own men fleeing on muleback. Because so many recruits bolted, the contras never learned the true extent of their casualties, but without a doubt they lost more men in that one day in Golondrina than they had during the entire four-month expedition.

Despite the sour ending, everyone in the FDN considered the operation a success. A group of contra politicians, headed for Europe to line up political support, took along a map with colored plastic overlays to show where the Jorge Salazar had roamed. In a meeting with Bermúdez, Toño went over the lessons he had learned: Sandinista military pressure was the strongest on the Honduran border, and campesinos deeper inside Nicaragua were just as sympathetic to the contras as those along the Río Bocay. What it added up to was that the FDN would be even more successful if it would just move off the border. But, Toño added—mindful of the desertions as he marched across Jinotega—they had to start educating the campesinos that the war must be fought all over Nicaragua, not just around their own villages.

There was one more thing, Toño said. He wasn't happy with the way some of the men treated civilians. Commander Renato in particular was too brutal, quick to shoot any campesino accused of helping the Sandinistas. The FDN should give some lectures on human rights, Toño suggested, and remind the men that they must win the peasants over, not terrorize them. "Because this could get out of control very easily," Toño warned. "Once a commander is out there in the jungle, he's on his own. He does what he wants."

Bermúdez nodded but didn't say anything. He was thinking of Commander Suicida.

7 | Growing Pains

Frank Arana shivered and fiddled with the shower knobs. You never seemed to be able to get enough hot water in Tegucigalpa, and the chilly mountain air oozed in through every crack and chink in the walls of the safe house in the early morning. Later, when he went to the Radio Fifteen studios to prepare the next broadcast, the day would warm up. But the mornings were always nippy.

"This is a Sandinista assault, you fascist son of a bitch!" a voice roared as the shower curtain jerked open and a fat .45-caliber automatic lodged against his head. Arana stood there like a statue in a rainstorm, afraid to turn his head, afraid to twitch a single muscle, afraid to think. Then he heard the high-pitched, wheedling laughter, and Arana's knees went limp as he slumped against the shower wall. "Good morning, Frank," said the man in the camouflage fatigues, his hooded Oriental eyes crinkling with mad humor as he pulled his gun back and wiped it on a towel. "Are you ready to go to work?" It was a moment before Arana could find his voice. "Suicida," he croaked, "you son of a bitch, you almost gave me a heart attack!" But Commander Suicida just kept drying his gun and laughing.

Throughout 1982 and 1983, the FDN general staff thought its army might expand to fifty thousand. The Sandinistas were slow to react to the contras and reluctant to commit their regular army to combat in the country-side. When the FSLN learned of a contra unit operating in the mountains in Nueva Segovia or the jungle of Zelaya, it usually responded with its poorly trained and underequipped militia. The militia troops were mostly campesino draftees, and many of them—if they had to fight at all—would have preferred to be wearing contra uniforms. They were anything but aggressive, and when forced into a battle by circumstances, they usually got clobbered. The contras referred to them as *carne de cañón*, cannon fodder. The Sandinista press gangs that roamed the small towns of the north searching for new militia recruits

76

touched off the flight of tens of thousands of peasants to Honduras in 1982 and 1983, and that further inflated the ranks of the FDN.[1]

The contras soon learned, however, why successful guerrilla armies take years to build. It was simple enough on the ground in Nicaragua: A commander planned an ambush, put his men in place, and, when he saw the Sandinistas, started shooting. It might work, and it might not. But there was no special complexity to it.

But behind the lines everything was ambivalent, enigmatic, ambiguous. There were egos to assuage, sensibilities to soothe. There were petty jealousies and grand ambitions. There were political tensions and personal sore spots. There were blundering fools and calculating charlatans and well-meaning idiots. There were sleeping grudges, awakening. There were political exigencies and moral urgencies. There were the traditional conspiracies of the Nicaraguans and the imperial demands of their tangled sponsors.

Some of the problems developed because the contras grew too fast. In December 1981, the FDN had 500 troops. A year later the number was 2,500. And by December 1983, contra ranks soared to more than 6,000. The explosive growth outstripped everything: their ability to move supplies, to collect and analyze intelligence, to set up communication networks.

Other problems developed because the contras grew at all. Any organization must balance competing philosophies, ambitions, and egos. Guerrilla armies are no exception. If anything, the problem is worse for them; they start from scratch, with no traditions or long-standing institutions to hem in the ambitious. And the men who run them are, by definition, outlaws: resisting civil authority, using guns to get their way. Guerrillas can easily turn erratic and vicious.

The FDN's growing pains weren't restricted to the men with guns. For that matter, they weren't restricted to Nicaraguans. The Americans and the Argentines, too, quarreled: among themselves and with each other.

The first signs of strain showed up on the FDN's political side. And perhaps it was not very surprising that Chicano Cardenal was right in the middle of it.

When the FDN was created in August 1981, out of the merger of the Fifteenth of September Legion and the UDN, Cardenal was the one man everybody agreed should play a key political role. He was well known; his anti-Somoza credentials were impeccable; and he had never collaborated with the Sandinistas when they were in power, not for a minute. Cardenal was a nearly unique phenomenon: a Nicaraguan who appealed to all exile factions and had committed sins unforgivable to none.

Everyone concurred that Cardenal would head the FDN's three-man political directorate, which would be the organization's ultimate authority. With civilians in charge, no one would be able to claim the FDN was under the control of the former National Guardsmen; that was the theory, anyway. A second seat went to Cardenal's buddy Mariano Mendoza, an affable anti-Somoza trade union leader.

The third seat went to the sullen Arístides Sánchez, whose lifework in prerevolutionary Nicaragua consisted of spending the vast real estate fortune he inherited from his father. Though Sánchez had never shown interest in nor aptitude for politics, he somehow convinced the military high command that he would represent its interests in the directorate.

Throughout late 1981 and early 1982, while Bermúdez organized the FDN army in Honduras, the directors lived in Miami and crisscrossed the United States trying to drum up support among exiles and American politicians. They even recruited former National Guard officers living in the United States. Despite their longtime opposition to Somoza, both Cardenal and Mendoza felt it was imperative to the success of the FDN to have the military expertise of the Guard. But they did have some strange moments. Once, at a meeting with exiles in San Francisco, a former Guardsman kept squinting at Mendoza. "I think I know you," the man said, puzzled. "Yes," acknowledged Mendoza, "you tortured me."

As long as Cardenal and Mendoza were in the United States and the rest of the FDN was in Honduras, everything went fine. In February 1982, however, the political directors moved to Honduras. And sparks began to fly.

Even in his younger days, before Nicaragua had disappointed him so many times, Chicano Cardenal was not the sort of guy that people called easygoing. As a college kid at Catholic University in Washington, D.C., Cardenal got into more than a few bar brawls. The passing years had tamed his fists, mostly, but sharpened his tongue. Rival politicians weren't just wrong, they were "fucking whores." Lefty economists weren't merely misguided, they were "thieving bastards." Government officials didn't simply make mistakes, they were "corrupt sons of bitches."

That Cardenal was nearly always right only made matters worse. He constantly had the air of a prophet spurned. When the Sandinistas started their literacy campaign, sending thousands of teachers out into the countryside to teach *campesinos* to read, Cardenal was the only member of the businessmen's group COSEP who wanted to publicly attack the idea. "Chicano, you're against everything," one COSEP official said dismissively.

"You stupid fuckers, what do you think they're going to be teaching out there?" Cardenal railed back. "A bunch of shit about Lenin and hand grenades." A few months later, when chastened COSEP officials admitted he was right, it just made Cardenal angrier.

For months after the revolution, when other politicians and businessmen were trying to find common ground with the FSLN, Cardenal insisted that the Sandinistas were communists and it was hopeless. (He had also warned for years that negotiations with Somoza were a waste of time. Everyone ignored him then, too.) Then the FSLN, breaking its promises about free elections, granted itself a majority on the Council of State—the interim legislative body—and made Cardenal the council's vice president without his consent. To be an unwilling officer of such a quisling sham was the final humiliation to Cardenal, and less than two weeks later he fled to Miami.

There are many lessons that might be learned from Nicaraguan history. What Chicano Cardenal drew from it was that his country's political culture was sick, rotted by personal ambition and *zancudismo*, parasitism. He could trust his own judgment; everyone else's was suspect. He would suffer fools and whores no longer. They had mismanaged the opposition to Somoza so badly that Nicaragua wound up in the hands of communists. He would not tolerate them in the FDN.

What seemed like no-nonsense management to Cardenal, however, often looked like authoritarian despotism to others. The first thing he did was to ban Argentine military advisers from the room when the FDN political directorate and general staff were holding discussions. The Argentine colonel Riveiro's jaw dropped the first time Cardenal kicked him out. "Get out of the room," Cardenal repeated. "It's not your concern." On other occasions, he refused to meet with Argentine advisers in Honduras and made them fly to Miami if they wanted to talk to him.

To Cardenal, his frequent clashes with the Argentines were just a matter of reminding them that they were advisers, not commanding generals. To the Argentines, it was rank insubordination. And to many of the other FDN officials, it was a case of needlessly offending a generous and valuable ally.

The Argentines were not alone in feeling the sting of Cardenal's tongue. He often gave Bermúdez names of men to be recruited and placed in command positions. To Cardenal, this was perfectly appropriate; the political directorate was the FDN's top authority. To Bermúdez, it was a case of a politician making purely military decisions well beyond his competence.

Even when he stuck to the political arena, Cardenal was heavy-handed. The FDN had a political executive committee in Miami with which, theoretically, the directors were supposed to confer. When the committee members complained that they weren't being consulted, Cardenal fired them. To Cardenal, the committee was just another embodiment of Nicaraguan political corruption, a bunch of people in Miami who had invested nothing in the FDN but thought they could connive their way into authority. To everyone else, dismissing the committee was the last piece of evidence that Cardenal was a power-mad *caudillo* who wouldn't listen to anyone.

The Argentines and the FDN general staff agreed that Cardenal and Mendoza had to go. A couple of days later, in early October 1982, the Argentines got the Hondurans to seize their passports to prevent Cardenal and Mendoza from making a political trip to Costa Rica. Meanwhile, the contra guards at the safe house where they lived were changed. It was all a psychological operation to frighten them into leaving, but the plan worked much better than anyone foresaw. Cardenal and Mendoza, afraid they were about to be assassinated, went into hiding, then called a CIA pal for help.

While they waited for the CIA man, Cardenal and Mendoza killed some time at the movies. They saw *Missing,* the paranoid Costa-Gavras thriller in which the CIA and the Chilean military junta kidnap and murder a young American. By the time the Agency officer arrived, Cardenal was in a frenzy. "That fucking movie, that's what's happening right here!" he yelled. "I can assure you, that's not the way we do things," the CIA man replied soothingly.

And it wasn't. Cardenal's dealings with the CIA, away from the Argentines and the FDN general staff, had been calm and intelligent. The Agency wanted

79

him to stay with the contras. But after a couple of weeks of trying to patch things up again, the CIA officers realized it was hopeless. Cardenal and Mendoza flew back to Miami. Everyone else began picking up the pieces.

With Cardenal and Mendoza gone, the FDN needed a new political directorate. And as the contras began putting a new one together, the CIA stepped out of the shadows.

For months the Agency had been increasing its direct involvement with the FDN. Originally, a single CIA officer coordinated delivery of supplies; then, a second began visiting Bermúdez to discuss strategy; and, eventually, about half a dozen officers were meeting regularly with the contras.

As the silent partner in the tripartite alliance became more vocal, the relationship between the Americans and the Argentines began to strain. That it had survived the 1982 Falklands War at all was a geopolitical miracle. The Argentines had expected the United States to remain neutral—perhaps even to counsel restraint to the British. After all, the Americans and the Argentines were partners in an anticommunist crusade in Central America, weren't they?

When Washington sided instead with the British, the Argentine government was enraged. For a time it appeared the contras' Argentine advisers might be called home. That didn't happen. But the Argentine president, Leopoldo Galtieri, was obviously going to fall, and it looked like the whole government might go with him. With the Argentine participation in the tripartite alliance looking shaky, the CIA began taking a more active role with the contras.

As the contact between the CIA and the Argentines increased, the CIA worries increased: not that the Argentines would leave, but that they would *stay*. Agency officers were appalled by the things they heard the Argentines say—that the "dirty war" they had fought against their own leftists should be the model for the war in Nicaragua; that there was nothing immoral about killing communists, uniformed or not; that generous use of brute force was the way to impress civilians. Their death-squad diatribes were not only lousy advice, but they would also touch off a political earthquake if they ever reached Washington.

The Americans were not alone in doubting the utility of Argentine advice. As contra commanders gained combat experience, many of them began questioning the relevance of the Argentines, who were intelligence officers without field experience. One day Mike Lima was chatting with one of the Argentines about the difficulty of fighting a Sandinista army that had so much more in the way of men and equipment. "No problem," the Argentine breezily instructed him. "You see a truck, you shoot the driver. With six bullets you can get six trucks and wipe out a whole company." *Gee, why didn't I think of that?* Lima wondered as he walked away.

It also seemed that some of the Argentines expected to get more out of this war than the thrill of a victory over communism. One officer, flying from Tegucigalpa to Buenos Aires by way of Miami, was detained by U.S. Customs agents who discovered he was carrying $40,000 in cash. They let him go after a few hours, to the disgust of CIA officers who read about it in the next morning's cable traffic. "*You* tell me where he got it," snapped one of the spooks who complained to me about it. "Do you think he opened his piggy bank?"

When he was still with the FDN, Chicano Cardenal went to Washington to confer with Dewey Clarridge's number two man, a dapper officer named Jerry Gruner.[2] Cardenal was perplexed by a series of questions from Gruner about the size of the directorate's safe house in Honduras. "How many people are in your house in Honduras?" the CIA man finally asked.

"Three bodyguards, a cook, and her child," Cardenal replied.

"The payroll is thirty-two persons," Gruner said grimly.

The Argentines, for their part, no longer saw the Americans as superhumans. "Johnnies," the Argentines called them. They blamed the Johnnies for the erratic flow of contra supplies (although many of the glitches stemmed from the rapid, unexpected growth of the FDN) and resented them butting into other aspects of the program when they couldn't manage their own responsibilities.

The Johnnies also lacked guts, as far as the Argentines were concerned; while they were sneaking around their safe houses and criticizing everyone else, the Argentines were hanging out there exposed. They didn't accompany the contras into Nicaragua, that was true, but they were nonetheless paying a price in blood. It wasn't in the newspapers, but everybody knew what had happened to Héctor Francés.

His real name was Estánislao Valdez, even though everyone called him by the phony Francés name listed on his documents. Although Francés was young— maybe in his late twenties—he was already a captain in Argentine military intelligence. That was a tribute, no doubt, to his enthusiasm; no one else spoke as frequently, or with as much relish, about the "dirty war." Chicano Cardenal told friends that any time he talked with Francés, he felt like he was drowning because there was so much blood in the conversation.

Francés, a wiry, brown-skinned little guy who was often mistaken for a Nicaraguan, was in charge of building a contra network in Costa Rica, and whenever FDN officials were in San José they would stop by to see him. He struck the contras as remarkably paranoid. As he talked, even inside his home, Francés was constantly jerking his head around, looking this way and that, watching for whatever might be sneaking up on him. Once, during a dinner with Cardenal and Mendoza at San José's plush Hotel Cariari, there was a power failure. When an emergency generator kicked the lights back on a couple of minutes later, Francés had disappeared. They found him under the table.

But a man in Francés's line of work had good reason to be paranoid. Perhaps he forgot that for a moment. On October 7, 1982, Francés met Frank Arana, the contra propagandist, for a cup of coffee in a corner snack bar near his home in San José's Los Yoses neighborhood. They talked about getting an exiled Nicaraguan bishop to come bless the contra troops in Honduras. The coffee shop had two doors, opening onto different streets. When they were finished, Arana left by one, hailed a taxi, and went back to his hotel. Francés left by the other—and walked into the waiting arms of a gang of Nicaraguan State Security agents.

Francés was never seen again. But two months later, the Sandinistas distributed a videotape of a seventy-minute interview in which Francés identified himself as a "defector" and then went on to expose details of his work with the FDN. As the contras watched the tape, they marveled. Here was the most gung ho of all the Argentine officers, nervously licking his lips and stammering while he denounced his superiors as "traitors to Argentina." The Sandinistas must have some amazing interrogation techniques, everyone agreed, to have reduced Francés to this.

As the contras went about setting up a new political directorate, the CIA flexed its muscles. In October, Clarridge flew to Buenos Aires to lay down the law. The Argentines would have no say about the new directorate, he warned, and there would be other changes they wouldn't like. Then he returned to Miami, where the executive committee that Chicano Cardenal had tried to fire was mulling over names to fill an expanded seven-member directorate. The theory was that with seven directors there would be less chance that one would turn into a *caudillo*. The committee had compiled a list of about forty candidates.

Clarridge and the four or five other Agency officers who met with the committee said the CIA would insist on two things: Arístides Sánchez, whom the Agency considered the most destructive person in the entire contra movement, could not be a director. And Enrique Bermúdez must be elevated from military chief of staff to the political directorate. Some of the contras resentfully assumed that the CIA intended to run the directorate through Bermúdez. They might have been even angrier if they had known the truth: Clarridge still nursed hopes of unifying the FDN with Edén Pastora's troops in the south and of making Pastora the military commander-in-chief. Bermúdez was being kicked upstairs to make the transition easier. Bermúdez himself didn't want to join the directorate and agreed only when Clarridge flatly told him the Americans would cut off the money if he refused.

Eventually the Nicaraguans settled on five other directors to go with Bermúdez. They included Indalecio Rodríguez, a veterinarian twice jailed by Somoza, then forced into exile for nearly twenty years, and Marco Zeledón, once the head of Quaker Oats in Managua and active in the business community's opposition to Somoza. Alfonso Callejas was a cotton farmer who had been vice president of Nicaragua from 1969 to 1972 and then resigned in a major public break with Somoza. The only woman chosen was Lucía Cardenal Salazar, the widow of the murdered coffee grower Jorge Salazar. The CIA had strongly backed Mrs. Salazar, even though she had no political experience. The idea was to make her a contra version of Violeta Chamorro. The final director was the eclectic Edgar Chamorro, who had pursued careers as a priest, an advertising man, and a commodities broker.

Its enemies would later claim that the FDN directorate was created top-to-bottom by the CIA. The accusation was based on a single source: an account published in the *New Republic* by Edgar Chamorro several years later, after he turned against the contras. According to Chamorro, he was sitting in his Miami brokerage when a CIA officer he had never met before called out of the blue to offer him the director's job. The rest of the directors were also chosen by the Agency, he wrote.[3]

But Chamorro's account is untrue. He was active in the contra movement from the very beginning; he was an official in Chicano Cardenal's UDN, and he was a member of the FDN executive committee that Cardenal tried to abolish. His name was on the list of forty nominees prepared by Nicaraguan exiles in Miami, and *they* chose him; the CIA didn't have any idea who he was. The other five directors were also on the exiles list.

The seventh seat was held for a politician still inside Nicaragua. A month later, he came out: Adolfo Calero, manager of the Coca-Cola bottling plant in Managua and a tough-talking member of the Conservative Party who was jailed twice by Somoza. Calero, a Notre Dame graduate, had worked with the CIA in Nicaragua for years. But it was Bermúdez—sending messages with American reporters traveling to Nicaragua—who recruited Calero to the contras, not the CIA.

With the addition of Calero, the contras believed they had finally assembled a set of political credentials beyond question. Of the seven directors, six had been well-known opponents of Somoza; the other, Bermúdez, had a spotless military record in the National Guard. Surely, the contras thought, this will stop people from calling us Somocistas. They were wrong.

The ouster of Chicano Cardenal, the fuss about creating a new political directorate, and the removal of Bermúdez as the top military officer in order to make room for Edén Pastora comprised the first chapter in what would become a long and repetitive story: the dysfunction of the contra political wing. Throughout the war, contra politicians jockeyed for position, usually worrying more about who would be the next president of Nicaragua than the success of the movement. Products of a political culture where conspiracy and intrigue meant everything and persuasion and teamwork meant nothing, where manipulation of powerful allies was the proven road to power, the contra politicians rarely sought an internal consensus. Instead, every time there was a dispute, they unveiled the heavy artillery: the Americans. The contra politicians ruthlessly pitted brigades of CIA officers, State Department diplomats, and congressional staffers against one another in a no-quarter-given struggle. The contras even had an expression for it: *Everybody has his own gringo.*

The Americans, with their own tangled political agenda, were only too happy to play. With congressional support for the contras always hanging by a few votes, the Americans were constantly trying to placate so-called swing voters by diddling with the movement's political structure. It would undergo three major political makeovers in five years, and each time the Americans would try to portray the result as a more "liberal" directorate purged of rightist and Somocista elements. That the political distinctions they drew were irrelevant to the Nicaraguans—for whom family connections, personal friendships, and the ability to dispense patronage were far more crucial than ideology—was not important to the Americans. They were playing to a Washington audience, by Washington rules.

Meanwhile, trouble was brewing on the military side. And the removal of Bermúdez turned up the temperature.

After Commander Toño's four-month stay in Matagalpa Department in early 1983 proved that a contra force could operate deep inside Nicaragua on a prolonged basis, the word came down from the general staff: Commanders should go inside and stay inside. Each commander was assigned a zone of operations. The idea was to establish a base of operations, set up a network of *correos,* and then send out patrols and launch ambushes. As the heightened military activity boosted recruiting, the contra unit would expand its operations. When the unit grew big enough, it would break in two, like an amoeba, and the new unit would go still deeper inside Nicaragua. In this fashion the FDN would gradually cover more and more ground, until the war raged throughout the countryside.

As the commanders moved inside, however, a distance that was more than geographical developed between the men in the field and the general staff in Tegucigalpa. Bermúdez modeled the general staff along the same lines as most conventional Western military forces. There were officers in charge of logistics, communications, personnel, psychological operations, intelligence, counterintelligence, and operations. The staff officers had been, for the most part, captains and majors in the National Guard; they were all in their forties and fifties, and several of them also had physical problems. Edgard Hernández, in charge of intelligence, weighed nearly three hundred pounds. El Diablo Morales, the logistical officer, was wounded in the leg during the revolution and could barely walk. None was fit enough to go inside Nicaragua for prolonged operations with the troops.

Tension between soldiers at the front and those in the rear echelons is at least as old as the Napoleonic Wars. In a conventional army, staff officers do not go into combat, either, but they usually have some field experience. Obviously, though, none of the contra staff officers had ever been guerrillas. They had never operated as an illegal, clandestine force hunted by a powerful, government-supported army. And as the contra field commanders moved inside Nicaragua, many of them bitterly objected to what they felt were ridiculous orders from the staff officers.

It wasn't like the old days, the field commanders complained. When a National Guardsman got shot, an officer called for an ambulance or a helicopter, and the soldier went to a hospital to be worked on by doctors. When a contra got shot, he was lucky to get an injection of antibiotics from a paramedic. Then he had to be carried out through the jungle by other soldiers—a trip that never took less than days, usually weeks, and sometimes months.

When a National Guard unit was low on food and ammo, an officer radioed for more. When a contra unit ran out of food, the hungry men could either steal some from the campesinos—hardly the way to win support from the civilian population—or march back to Honduras on empty stomachs. And a unit low on ammo had no choice but to leave Nicaragua. For the first thirteen months of the war, the FDN had no aerial resupply capacity at all, and the two wheezing

C-47s that the contras finally put in the air in April 1983 could supply only a fraction of the troops inside.

Everything else was different, too: the terrain, the tactics, the weapons, the troops. The general staff was trying to refight the last war, the field commanders argued, without understanding that the two sides had reversed. The Sandinistas were the army now, and the National Guardsmen were the guerrillas. You couldn't just tell a commander to go inside and stay inside, and make no allowances. It was like shrimp soup—you had to taste it to know what it was all about.

The staff officers, however, wouldn't even spend time in the base camps along the border, much less go into Nicaragua. They seemed reluctant to leave behind the restaurants, nightclubs, and whorehouses of Tegucigalpa. Whenever Toño tried to see El Diablo Morales, the logistical chief, by day, he found him playing chess; after dark, he was always in the bars.[4]

These resentments and frustrations existed before the CIA forced Bermúdez off the general staff and onto the directorate. But Bermúdez, with political skills honed during four years in Washington, was not so abrupt and confrontational with the field commanders. His replacement, Emilio Echaverry, had even less combat experience than Bermúdez (Echaverry, too, was an engineer), and he seemed to have taken advanced classes in arrogance when he studied at the Argentine military academy. Once, when Mike Lima's unit crossed into Honduras, Echaverry stormed up to him. "I thought I told you to stay on the Nicaraguan side of the river," Echaverry thundered. "What are you doing here?"

"We were out of food!" Lima barked back. While dozens of his men looked on, Lima yanked his pistol from its holster and handed it, butt-first, to Echaverry. "Here, take it, you shit-eating son of a whore!" Lima demanded. "I'll go home and take it easy." Echaverry declined, but it was not his last public confrontation with Lima.

Bermúdez knew the limitations of the general staff. But he had a limited number of officers trained in military administration; a disorganized logistical network was better than none at all. He did his best to make the staff spend more time in the FDN camps. Once, while Echaverry visited Argentina, Bermúdez rounded up the staff officers and drove them six hours to one of the mountainside camps. "Stay here and talk to the men and find out what's going on," he ordered them, then left in the only vehicle that could navigate the rutted, meandering mountain roads. When Echaverry returned to Tegucigalpa a week later, the officers sent him a plaintive radio message begging to be rescued.

Bermúdez also recognized that the friction among his officers was more complicated than it appeared to outsiders. It had to do with an ancient National Guard feud between the EEBI, the unit commanded by Tachito Somoza's son El Chigün, and the rest of the Guard.

After El Chigün graduated from Harvard and decided to follow his pop into the family military business, he demanded—and got—his own unit. The EEBI was dominated by young officers, handpicked by El Chigün, who were encouraged to regard themselves as the Guard's elite. They lived in an air-conditioned barracks, and their officers' mess had a menu. Even the enlisted men could choose from three entrées at dinner. Other Guard units spent about 60 cents per man per day on food; the EEBI budget was four times that.

The EEBI officers developed a sneering contempt for the rest of the Guard's officer corps, particularly the older, higher-ranking officers who made up the Guard's general staff. The Spanish term for general staff is *estado mayor*; EEBI officers referred to it as the *establo mayor,* the general stable. To them, other Guard officers were just a bunch of cattle.

The schism between the EEBI and the rest of the Guard spilled over into the contras. Many of the original members of the Fifteenth of September Legion (including nearly all the members of the criminal Special Operations unit) were former EEBI officers. When Bermúdez forced out some of the Special Operations men after their kidnapping of the young boy in Honduras went awry, most of the remaining EEBI officers held a grudge. And they were unanimous in their loathing for the contra general staff, which didn't contain a single EEBI veteran.

It wasn't just the EEBI officers who disdained the rest of the National Guard and mocked the contra general staff. The scornful elitism seeped down through the ranks of the EEBI enlisted men, including a peculiarly Chinese-looking sergeant named Pedro Pablo Ortiz. Of course, in the FDN, Ortiz was no longer a sergeant. For that matter, he was no longer Ortiz. Now he called himself Comandante Suicida.

Suicida and the band of men from his EEBI unit, los *Cascabeles*—the Rattlesnakes—never really quit fighting the Sandinistas. On the final day of the revolution they escaped the southern front in a hijacked tugboat. After landing in El Salvador, they made their way back through Honduras to the craggy mountains along the border with Nicaragua's Nueva Segovia Department. There they launched an enterprise that was equal parts guerrilla warfare and banditry. They murdered local Sandinista officials, sniped at an occasional militia patrol, and supported themselves by rustling cattle inside Nicaragua for resale in Honduras. They chose their targets out of personal vengeance as much as anything else; Suicida and several of the *Cascabeles* were from Nueva Segovia, and whenever a friend or relative reported some indignity at the hands of a Sandinista busybody, that man was marked.

Eventually Suicida's group hooked up with the Fifteenth of September Legion. And when the FDN was created, and the U.S. aid began to flow, Suicida's force grew faster than anyone's. He already had a core of trained men, his National Guard buddies. And he had *mística*, mystique, an almost occult ability to make men willing to die for him. Suicida was the first contra commander to break the seventy-five-man-per-unit ceiling imposed by the Americans. By early 1983 he had 1,200 troops.

Decades before, another guerrilla warrior with *mística*—Augusto Sandino— had ruled these mountains of Nueva Segovia. And very early in his contra career, Suicida began to think of himself as another Sandino. Perhaps it was his woman, La Negra, who put the idea into his head. La Negra, everyone agreed, was much smarter than Suicida. Back in Managua, she had been a nurse; she could read and write, even knew a little bit of basic accounting. Both Suicida and La Negra were tough and ambitious. It showed through in the name they chose for the old mountaintop farm that served as their base camp: Pino-I, as though soon there would be a Pino-II and a Pino-III. Suicida intended to be a warlord.

Suicida was by no means the only one trying to create his own little empire along the border. As the war moved inside Nicaragua, several commanders declared their operational zones private fiefdoms. They were known within the FDN as *caciques,* Indian chiefs. Other contra units violated the territorial rights of a *cacique* at their own risk. Once, when Mike Lima's men were returning from a long patrol, they crossed back into Honduras through Suicida's zone. Suicida's commanders swooped down on them and seized all their heavy weapons—at gunpoint.

All the *caciques* created problems, but Suicida was the worst. He was merciless with campesinos in his zone who were accused of collaboration, and none too demanding about evidence. The campesinos began to complain to other FDN commanders that Suicida's men left a trail of rapes and murders wherever they went. Prisoners were left outdoors naked overnight or tied to trees.

Even crazier than Suicida, many FDN commanders suspected, were the men around him. The most dangerous was a former Guard enlisted man named Julio César Herrera, whose nom de guerre was Krill. Krill enforced discipline among the men by killing them for trivial offenses like arriving late for drills. He always seemed to be looking for trouble. One day, Mike Lima was sitting in a bar frequented by the contras in Danlí, a flat, dusty Honduran town halfway between Tegucigalpa and the FDN border camps. As he drank his beer, a chocolate-skinned, curly-haired young contra in his early twenties walked in. As he strolled by Lima, the man paused to stare, then ran his fingers under Lima's chin, as though he were a pet cat.

"Who are you?" Lima asked in a mild voice. "Krill," the other contra answered. "Ahhh," Lima said, nodding. He knew the name. Lima walked to the nearby table where his gear was stacked, picked up his rifle, and ostentatiously clicked the safety off. Krill backed off that day, but a couple of weeks later in the same bar, he didn't. After an argument—it started with such a small thing that no one would later remember what it was—Krill pumped a popular commander named Jaguar full of bullets.

Suicida's unquestionable recruiting skills were not matched by his tactical ability. He never understood the paramount importance of the element of surprise. A contra attack usually had its greatest success in the first few hours; after that, the Sandinistas could use their superior capacity in communications and transportation to reinforce and resupply. Suicida, however, would lock into epic set-piece battles in which he hurled his men at the same target over and over without success.

The grand prize, for Suicida, was the weatherbeaten Nicaraguan town of Jalapa, a few miles from the Honduran border on Highway 20. Jalapa had an airstrip and could serve as a supply depot. But Suicida's ambitions for the town went well beyond that; he saw it as the capital of a liberated chunk of Nicaragua that might even ask the United States for diplomatic recognition. That was what he said, anyway. Other commanders thought his obsession had more to do with the fact that Suicida grew up near Jalapa. Seizing the town, for him, would be a sort of aberrant "local boy makes good" story.

Again and again Suicida assaulted Jalapa. The first time was in November 1982, when Bermúdez was still chief of staff. Bermúdez okayed the attack just before leaving for Miami to help piece together a new directorate. He had no idea that when the initial attack failed, Suicida would send wave after wave of men at Jalapa for ten days and use up a million rounds of ammunition. The general staff frantically tried to call it off by radio, but Suicida wouldn't listen. He was an EEBI and the modern Sandino; what right did a bunch of desk officers have to tell him anything?

When the FDN started out, Suicida had been one of the first commanders to launch attacks inside Nicaragua on a regular basis. Coupled with the rapid growth of his force, that made him the closest thing the contras had to a star.

By March 1983, that was no longer true. Other commanders, Mike Lima and Toño and Renato and Quiché, had gone deeper into Nicaragua and stayed longer. None of them had a fiasco like the Jalapa offensive on his record. But when the contras decided the time had come to publicize their war, the very weakness of Suicida—his obsession with Jalapa and his insistence on fighting around the border—became a strength. Reporters would not have to travel on foot for a month to reach him, as they would to interview the commanders of the Jorge Salazar Task Force in Matagalpa. Suicida was rarely more than two or three days from the border.

In retrospect, sending reporters inside Nicaragua with the rebellious and brutal Suicida seems like lunacy or worse. But his bloodlust, while no secret to his fellow commanders, was not known to the civilians in the FDN press office. So they arranged a rendezvous with Suicida inside Nueva Segovia for James LeMoyne of *Newsweek* and Christopher Dickey of the *Washington Post*.

The war itself was certainly no secret, and a number of stories had already disclosed the American backing for the FDN. But the contras wanted to personalize their side of the story, and the results were far better than they could have dreamed. Dickey's dramatic stories and photos splashed across the *Post* front page. He wrote that Suicida was a "guerrilla warlord" and described Krill directing a firefight "like a conductor searching out the notes of each instrument in an orchestra."[5] For months afterward, every time Dickey wrote a story about Nueva Segovia, he mentioned Suicida's name.

Stardom can be just as fatally intoxicating to guerrillas as it sometimes is to matinee idols or rock'n'roll singers. The very first issue of the FDN's propaganda magazine *Comandos* featured a striking photo of a burly Indian contra staring menacingly at the camera, a machine gun cradled in his arms, two bandoliers of ammo crisscrossed on his chest. The picture was so arresting that a wire service picked it up, and it was published in newspapers around the world. The young Indian began visiting Honduran bars, striking poses, telling war stories. Within a few weeks he was dead, the victim of a pointless brawl with a macho drunk.

Celebrity beguiled the young Indian into thinking he was the toughest man in all the bars of Honduras; it cost his life. Celebrity made Suicida imagine that he was the mightiest warlord in Central America; it cost many lives.

Again Suicida went after Jalapa, and again he was repulsed. He brushed aside the general staff's threats to cut off his supplies; Suicida and La Negra, who kept the books for him, had already anticipated something like that. For months he had been telling the supply officers in Tegucigalpa he had 2,200 troops, when the real number was only 1,200. Now Suicida had plenty of guns and ammo stashed, and if the general staff tried anything, he would give it a stark lesson in the differences between desk officers and real guerrilla commanders.

By May 1983 the stories from Suicida's Pino-I camp were getting too lurid for the general staff to ignore. La Negra was acting more and more like a commander, issuing orders and countermanding directives from Tegucigalpa. And not only was she having a clandestine affair with Krill, there were reports that she was ordering some of the troops to sleep with her when Suicida was away. Sexual adventurism was common in the FDN camps, and many of the commanders carried out personal vendettas by seducing the women of their rivals. But for a woman to be acting this way was utterly scandalous in macho Nicaraguan society. And if Suicida found out, the consequences would have been unthinkable.

Before the general staff could act, the Sandinistas took care of part of the problem. To get to Suicida's Pino-I camp, it was necessary to travel a twelve-mile stretch of road between the Honduran villages of Cifuentes and Las Trojes. The road was straight, flat, and narrow, and it lay only one hundred yards or so from the border. It was an ideal spot for an ambush; and one afternoon in mid-May, as La Negra and a car full of contras started down it, a Sandinista machine gun riddled their Toyota with bullets. There were no survivors.

La Negra's death pushed Suicida over the edge. He attacked Jalapa for the third time in six months, but by now the Sandinistas had a major garrison in the town. The general staff, trying to distract Suicida, told him to go after the Sandinista forces along the Honduran border, in the villages of El Porvenir and Teotecacinte, which surely included the troops who ambushed La Negra. Suicida, however, no longer even made a pretense of guerrilla warfare. His head-on assaults were decimated, and a Sandinista counterattack came so close to the border that the Honduran army had to use its own artillery to drive the Sandinistas off.

The chaos finally overwhelmed the general staff, which at last fulfilled its threat and cut off ammunition and weapons to Suicida's forces. Suicida responded by driving to Tegucigalpa with eight of his men, in uniform and carrying their rifles. Six of the men surrounded FDN headquarters. Suicida and the other two, rifles in hand, swaggered inside, going from office to office to harangue the staff officers.

At last Bermúdez and Echaverry agreed that something had to be done. Bermúdez had recently brought in four former National Guard colonels from Miami, hoping to upgrade the general staff. But the other officers resisted, so the new colonels were just sitting around, waiting for an assignment. Bermúdez and

Echaverry sent them to the border to conduct a formal court-martial investigation under the old National Guard procedures. Their job was to separate the truth from legend and rumor. Bermúdez and Echaverry wanted to know exactly what was going on at Pino-I without the coloration of personal jealousies, old National Guard feuds, or Sandinista propaganda.

The colonels returned with a stunningly detailed indictment of Suicida. Rapes, executions, abuse of his own men, the purloined arms stockpile, the open rebellion against the general staff—it was all there. Krill alone had killed more than thirty of his own men. The colonels unanimously agreed that there was only one suitable punishment: death. These were not normal excesses of war; they were the criminal acts of a psychotic gangster with 1,200 gunmen behind him. If Suicida, Krill, and a couple of the others were not executed, the colonels warned, this rot would spread.

There would be a formal hearing later—Suicida and the others would even have an officer assigned to argue their defense—but the real decision was made when the general staff agreed to have them arrested. Arresting the commander of 1,200 troops could very well touch off an armed mutiny. It was far too great a risk to run for anything less than a dead certainty.

Suicida made it easy by allowing his demented ego to overcome his judgment one last time. He sent a message to General Alvarez, asking for a meeting; he thought Alvarez, hearing the story of Suicida's feud with the general staff, would banish the staff and make Suicida commander in chief. Instead, Alvarez alerted Bermúdez and Echaverry. They sent one of Alvarez's aides in a helicopter to Suicida's border hideout to invite him to a meeting in Tegucigalpa with the general. When Suicida returned on the chopper, he was arrested. Krill and two others, Cara de Malo and Habakuk, were also picked up.

Bermúdez insisted that the entire general staff sign the death warrant. There could be no question later that this was some personal feud. There was no argument as the document went around the table. When it got to Manuel Antonio Caceres, the chief of psychological operations, he murmured: "It's a sad thing to do that." There was no argument to that, either.

Suicida and the other three were executed in mid-November, at the Nicarao base camp near the Honduran village of La Lodosa. They used a rope looping it around his throat and then putting men on each end to jerk it like a macabre game of tug-of-war. The first three died quietly, but not Krill his eyes bulged, and his lips turned blue, but he wouldn't die. For a long time he shrieked harrowing curses on his executioners.

News of Suicida's execution slowly made its way through the FDN's military ranks. But the civilians were never told. For months afterward, when the press office asked to send reporters in to visit Suicida, the reply was simply, "He's not available."

Eventually the news did leak out, but by then only a few reporters remembered Suicida. One who did, Christopher Dickey, wrote a book using Suicida as a metaphor for the whole contra movement.[6] But the only contra commander to be court-martialed and executed can hardly be considered typical, any more than William Calley was typical of American fighting men in Vietnam. What Suicida was, rather, was exactly what the contras understood him to be: a ghastly reminder that in guerrilla warfare, where ordinary military command and control are impossible, the potential exists for things to go terribly, terribly wrong.

The problems with Suicida, and the continuing complaints from the field commanders about the general staff, made it obvious that a stronger link had to be established between the staff and the troops. Bermúdez felt it was a matter of improving personnel; the Americans and the Hondurans believed a structural change was necessary. They said that the staff officer in charge of operations—the tactical chief—should be located inside Nicaragua.

Bermúdez was skeptical. He didn't see how the contras could possibly defend a big command post inside Nicaragua once the Sandinistas located it, as they would easily do by tracking its radio signals. But he was willing to listen to the proposal. In early September, a summit was convened at an old chicken farm outside Tegucigalpa where some contras trained. Duane Clarridge flew in from Washington, and Don Winters, the CIA's Tegucigalpa station chief, also attended.[7] So did General Alvarez and Col. Enrique Calderini, the chief of Honduran intelligence; the FDN political directorate; and the general staff. It was a mark of the fading fortunes of the Argentines that none of them was invited.

Clarridge ran through his ideas about a tactical commander: He had to be young, capable of clambering around mountains with the troops, and have combat experience. Clarridge was obviously excluding all the current members of the general staff. Then, he admitted, the CIA already had a name in mind: Justiniano Pérez. Bermúdez barely controlled his shock. The supervisor of the Fifteenth of September Legion's notorious Special Operations group, the advocate of kidnappings and bank robberies—the CIA wanted to put Pérez in charge of contra combat operations! *Is it possible the Americans don't know about this?* Bermúdez wondered. He certainly wasn't going to be the one to tell them. So instead Bermúdez argued that Pérez was unacceptable because he had left the FDN eighteen months ago, and this position had to be filled by someone the contra troops knew and trusted. Then he offered his own nominee: Hugo Villagra, the Legionnaire who led the dismally botched 1980 attack on the communist radio station in Costa Rica. The gringos reluctantly accepted.

Villagra himself was probably not going to win any trophies for scrupulous attention to international law. After his attack on the radio station flopped and the Costa Ricans jailed him along with the rest of his squad, Villagra relaxed and waited for the judicial machinery to do its work—Costa Rica usually dealt with foreigners accused of politically inspired crimes by expelling them. But after seven months, it was evident that political complications had muddled the picture. No charges had been filed, and it looked like Villagra and his men might stay in jail forever.

So he sent a coded letter to the Fifteenth of September Legion's headquarters in Guatemala, outlining a rescue mission. On October 29, 1981, almost a year after the attack on the radio station, it got under way. Five Legionnaires, three men and two women, smuggled some guns on board a Costa Rican commuter flight in a guitar case and used them to hijack the plane. Forcing it to land at the international airport in San José, they swapped the passengers—including an American—for Villagra and the other contras. The plan was to fly to a deserted airstrip in Guatemala, where a Legion plane would be waiting to carry them to safety.

But Villagra's second contra operation was no more successful than his first. First the chief hijacker decided that it had been so easy to bargain with the Costa Ricans that they should go for double or nothing. He ordered the crew to fly to Managua. "We'll land there and demand that they release some National Guardsmen from prison," he announced.

"Are you crazy?" Villagra shouted. "The Sandinistas don't give a shit about a Costa Rican flight crew being held hostage. They'll kill us all!" The hijacker relented, but then, for reasons known only to himself, decided they should land in El Salvador instead. The Salvadoran army picked them up in less than an hour, and they spent another year in jail.

In December 1982, two years after he left on a cream-puff mission that was supposed to take an hour, Villagra reported back to contra headquarters. He felt like a character he had read about in an American book, Rip van Winkle, who went to sleep and woke up a hundred years later. The Fifteenth of September Legion no longer existed; it was now the FDN, and almost all the men he knew were gone: Justiniano Pérez, Guillermo Mendieta, Eduardo Román, most of the men from the EEBI. Villagra was not sure how he felt about the new organization.

Not as confrontational as a lot of the men from the EEBI, Villagra nevertheless shared their disdain for the military abilities of regular Guard officers. He thought Bermúdez was too much politician and not enough soldier. But the FDN's delicate position required someone with both military and political skills to strike balances within the army, between the campesinos, the ex-Sandinistas, and the former National Guardsmen; and outside, among the Argentines, Hondurans, and Americans. The EEBI officers, right from the start, had shown no political sensibilities at all. They cuddled up to the lunatic right in Guatemala, staged kidnappings in Honduras, and stole cars in the United States. Now Villagra was going to be the tactical commander, and with some help from a bumbling CIA paramilitary specialist, his stunted political instincts would lead to a major calamity.

It started as Villagra was preparing to go inside Nicaragua in his new status. Several field commanders complained that they weren't getting enough money to buy food for their men while they were inside. Villagra made some oblique inquiries to Echaverry; he thought he understood Echaverry to say that the Americans had cut the aid. So he went to see *Coronel* Raymundo, the newly arrived CIA man.

Coronel Raymundo was actually Ray Doty. When Doty was a real military man—a paratrooper in the U.S. Army's 82nd Airborne—he had been a sergeant. But the contra leaders didn't feel comfortable taking advice from a sergeant, so they promoted Doty to colonel shortly after he set up shop in a Tegucigalpa safe house.[8] A gruff, tactless man who radiated tension, Doty, who had organized anticommunist guerrillas during the not-very-secret U.S. war in

Laos in the 1960s, was supposed to be advising the contras on military matters. His ability to do even that much was suspect—he spoke little Spanish—but that didn't stop Doty from sticking his finger into all kinds of pies.

When Villagra asked him if the flow of American money was slowing down, Doty's face reddened. "Here are the books," he growled, slamming a set of ledgers down on a desk. "You see how much money I'm giving you." Villagra glanced through the figures, which seemed to confirm that American aid hadn't wavered. Without bothering to ask Echaverry directly, both men concluded that he was pocketing money. As chief of staff, he handled all the funds.

"Look, you're the new tactical commander," Doty said. "We're going to take advantage of that. We can't get rid of Bermúdez and Echaverry right now; it would be counterproductive. There would be too much bad publicity. But I'm going to give you the money for the men in the field. And I'll give Echaverry only the money for the general staff." Doty also gave Villagra a radio that would permit him to communicate directly with the CIA without having to go through the regular contra communications network.

In effect, Doty was staging a barracks coup. By channeling both the CIA's money and the communications through Villagra, he was making Villagra commander in chief of the FDN. He had no authority for this scheme from his Agency superiors, much less the contra directorate. Besides sowing mistrust and encouraging conspiracies among the contras, Doty's plan was also unwieldy; if Villagra was going to be inside Nicaragua, obviously he couldn't distribute cash to the other commanders. That would require the creation of a "finance committee" completely outside the chain of command. In their own way, Doty's actions were as crazy and anarchic as anything Suicida ever did.

Then he made matters worse. Doty began meeting independently with individual field commanders, telling them the general staff was corrupt and inept and it would have to go. He felt encouraged; they all seemed to agree. Actually, however, the commanders were slightly awed by Doty—for most it was their first meeting with a CIA officer—and thought it prudent to agree with the man who controlled their supply pipeline. Although most of the field commanders shared Doty's assessment of the general staff, they didn't see any palatable alternative. Villagra was a smart man, they agreed, but he hadn't been tested in the field.

Doty launched his coup on November 25, 1983. He sent his assistant, a young Puerto Rican CIA officer who called himself Alex, to meet with the field commanders in Banco Grande, the Honduran village used as a jumping-off point for contra infiltration into Nicaragua. Most of the important FDN commanders were there, and a CIA helicopter went around picking up those at other bases. Toño attended, along with Mike Lima, Tigrillo, Dimas, and several others. From the general staff, only Villagra and Manuel Antonio Caceres were present.

As he stood before the commanders in an old farmhouse, Alex opened a briefcase. Bundles of paper money spilled out onto the table. Alex pulled some $100 bills out of a stack and waved them under Tigrillo's nose. "Do you know what this is?" Alex asked.

Tigrillo was transfixed. "No," he mumbled, eyes riveted on the bills.

"This belongs to you," Alex said. "You should be receiving five of these every month. How many of you were receiving this money?" There was an unearthly quiet in the room. "How long has he been stealing my money?" Tigrillo finally gasped, breaking the silence. Everyone understood who he was referring to: Echaverry. "Don't worry," Alex said. "From now on, you'll get your money from Villagra."

Alex's dramatic little show was a deliberate distortion of the facts. Bermúdez had recently begun paying $300 a month—not $500—to the families of men recruited from the United States. It was a simple matter of market economics; without the stipend, the men could not afford to leave their families. The "family support," as it was called, was not extended to men with families in Honduras; the FDN fed and clothed those families at the contra base camps. Bermúdez had deliberately not talked about the family-support payment because he knew it would become a source of jealousy and divisiveness, which, of course, was the very reason Doty had told Alex to reveal the payments.

Word of the Banco Grande Rebellion, as it was called, quickly spread through the FDN. No psychological warfare operation by the Sandinistas could have done as much to disrupt the contra army. The FDN's already-tenuous chain of command was near the snapping point. The CIA seemed to be saying that Villagra was now the commander in chief and that Echaverry and the general staff didn't matter. More subtly, the message was that the CIA, and not the Nicaraguans, had the right to hire and fire contra leaders. Besides encouraging the men to disregard their top officers, Alex's revelation of the family-support money set the field commanders against one another. It deepened the division between the campesinos and the ex-Guardsmen (since all the commanders who were getting family support were Guardsmen) and created a new schism between those who came from the United States and those who didn't.

Doty evidently launched the Banco Grande Rebellion in late November because he knew the contras were about to stage a major operation that would take all the field commanders inside Nicaragua, where they would be in close radio contact with Villagra, their new tactical commander, but outside the reach of Echaverry and the general staff. Perhaps if Doty had been paying more attention to his job—advising the contras on military operations—instead of trying to establish his credentials as a Machiavellian prince, he would have seen the obvious: the attack was a recipe for disaster.

Echaverry came to Banco Grande the next day, November 26, to brief the field commanders. As he stood in front of a large map, in the same farmhouse where the day before the CIA had told the commanders he was a thief, Echaverry seemed nervous. He was full of false heartiness and theatrical patriotism, as though he was on camera. It was obvious to the commanders that he knew about their meeting with Alex. What was not obvious was whether Echaverry sincerely believed in the preposterous strategy he was describing.

The plan (it had actually been designed by Villagra, although Echaverry didn't say that) was for 2,850 contras, split into five units, to take a crescent-shaped chunk of territory straddling the borders of Nueva Segovia and Jinotega departments. On the western edge of the crescent was the town of Quilalí; on the southern tip, the town of La Vigía; and on the eastern edge, the village of El Cuá. The crescent covered about 350 square miles; Echaverry told the commanders that if they could hold it for seventy-two hours, the FDN directorate would proclaim a provisional government and the armies of Honduras, Guatemala, El Salvador, and Panama would begin supporting the contras by air.

Not a single commander in the room believed that the plan had even a faint chance of success. It was obvious to all of them that it had been devised by a tenderfoot who hadn't actually been fighting inside Nicaragua. More than five thousand Sandinista troops were massed in and around the area Echaverry wanted them to take, and if the contras launched a threatening offensive, the FSLN would undoubtedly move in thousands more by helicopter. As Mike Lima listened to his assignment—to take the town of La Vigía with eight hundred men—he thought it might be barely possible, with the four new 82mm mortars the CIA had just given him, to hold it for twenty-four hours. After that it would be suicide. The Sandinistas would move their cannons and Soviet rocket launchers to the battlefield, stand back out of the range of Lima's mortars, and pound him.

Toño's objective sounded more feasible: to overrun the Sandinista garrison at Wanblan on the Río Coco, on the northern edge of the crescent. Toño had no doubt he could hold Wanblan for seventy-two hours—the Sandinistas would be concentrating on retaking Quilalí, Wiwilí, and some of the larger towns—but he was baffled by Echaverry's belief that the FDN could launch such a large and intricately coordinated attack. The contras were having a good deal of success in northern Nicaragua, it was true, but only when they stuck to small ambushes and quick raids managed by a single commander.

When elaborate communications or complicated logistics were required, it was a different story. Nearly all contra attempts at sophisticated attacks, particularly those that required coordination between several units, had been complete failures. It wasn't just Suicida's bloody, senseless pounding of Jalapa. In June and again in October, the FDN had tried to strike a Sandinista tank battalion in Chinandega Department, but both times failed to destroy a single tank. Even less auspicious was Operation Marathon in late September, an attack personally planned by Echaverry and closely resembling this new operation. In Operation Marathon, six contra units were supposed to descend on the city of Ocotal, where about one thousand Sandinista troops were based. The idea was to seize the town for seventy-two hours and use a government radio station there to broadcast FDN propaganda.

But almost everything that could go wrong did. Most of the contra units were late getting into position—one never left Honduras—and Villagra, who was supposed to be coordinating the operation on the radio, was nowhere to be found. The contras managed to take only part of the town for a few hours; Commander Venado, the only contra officer who was in position on time, became the target for the entire Sandinista army and was shot up so badly he never returned to combat.

If Echaverry remembered Operation Marathon or any of the other attacks that had gone awry in the past six months, he didn't mention them during his briefing. In fact, the longer he talked, the more confident Echaverry sounded.

Shit, Toño thought as the briefing broke up, *he's talking like we've already done it.*

After the briefing, the commanders wandered out of the farmhouse in groups of two and three, muttering. None of them trusted Echaverry any more, and none thought this crackpot plan would work.[9] But each commander accepted his assignment. Doty was handing out new weapons, radios, boots, and big caches of ammunition to everyone in preparation for the operation. Once this harebrained attack was over, the commanders would still have the new equipment to go after the Sandinistas in their own way. It was a price they were prepared to pay.

The only commander who didn't go on the attack was Mike Lima. On November 27, the day after the briefing, he was test-firing new mortars from the CIA. Doty had passed him several boxes of ammunition along with them, marked in perplexing Chinese characters that Lima couldn't read, except for the number eighty-two. It seemed obvious that they contained ammo for the new mortars.

But they wouldn't fire. Four times Lima's men dropped the rocket-like projectiles down the mortar tubes, and four times nothing happened. *Shitty Chinese ammo,* Lima thought. *Why can't the CIA buy American?* As he repacked the ammo to return it to Doty, one of his men interrupted. "Commander, maybe we just got one bad box," the soldier suggested. "Why don't we try a shell from another box?" Lima nodded and pried open a new carton. And for some reason, he didn't know why, he decided to try this one himself. "Stand back," he warned the men, and they moved off thirty feet or so. Lima himself leaned away from the tube as he dropped the round inside it.

What he didn't know was that the CIA had made a mistake; the ammo was for an 82mm recoilless rifle, not a mortar. A recoilless rifle round propels itself by a sudden, violent release of gases. In a recoilless rifle, they blow harmlessly out the open rear of the weapon's tube. But in a mortar, where the back end is closed, the gases can't escape. It was amazing good luck that the mortar's firing pin didn't trigger the first four shells. On the fifth, the luck ran out. The explosion turned the mortar tube into jagged, white-hot shrapnel that blew four contras to pieces. Most of the blast went over Lima's head, but he caught enough that his right leg was pulverized and his right arm dangled grotesquely by its tendons. As they loaded him onto the CIA helicopter to take him to the contra hospital at the air base at Aguacate, everyone thought Lima was dead.

Despite the practice-range disaster, the plan proceeded. All units had to leave for Nicaragua within forty-eight hours. There was a quick huddle; Toño would take over Lima's unit and attack La Vigía, it was decided, and Villagra himself would lead Toño's men against Wanblan.

While Villagra and Doty were busy preparing for the operation inside Nicaragua, Bermúdez set about undoing their political handiwork. He talked to Donald Winters, the CIA station chief in Tegucigalpa, and discovered that Winters had not approved the Banco Grande Rebellion. Winters quickly sent off cables to Washington. Meanwhile, General Alvarez was livid when he learned of the public humiliation of his old friend Echaverry. "I know him very well," Alvarez said during a meeting with the CIA people, "and Echaverry is no thief." There was an ominous tone in his voice suggesting that the fates of Echaverry and the FDN, as far as Alvarez was concerned, were linked.

Two days before the big attack was to begin, Villagra's radio crackled to life in his camp in the Jinotega jungle. Through the static he could hear the voice of the aide he left in charge of the money from the CIA.

"Bermúdez is here, and he says we have to give the money back," the aide said. "He says he has an order from Washington."

"He's lying," Villagra answered confidently. "Call *Coronel* Raymundo."

"I already did," the aide replied. "He says he can't do anything. He said to tell you, 'I also have superiors.'"

Villagra didn't say anything for a minute. He was stunned by the enormity of Doty's betrayal. The CIA man had lured him onto a limb, and now Villagra was left dangling, out here in the middle of the jungle surrounded by men who barely knew him and, he could tell after five days, didn't really trust him.

"Okay, give Bermúdez the money," Villagra sighed. "Get a receipt. And tell Raymundo I'm resigning as soon as this operation is over."

The attack failed more profoundly than anyone could have imagined. Just as in Operation Marathon, several of the units failed to reach their positions on time, and none of the commanders held their objectives for more than an hour or two.

One of the commanders who was late was Villagra himself. As he approached Wanblan, the men grew more and more jittery. They even pulled their guns on two campesinos walking along the road. "Let them go," Villagra ordered. "But they're Sandinista militia," protested one of his men. "Let them *go,*" Villagra insisted, the whole Suicida debacle weighing on his mind. His men lowered their guns, and the two campesinos went on their way—to Wanblan, where they were indeed members of the militia. When Villagra's force reached the town, the Sandinistas were waiting for him. They stationed small groups of troops in the hills outside town; as the contras were about to start their sunrise attack, they realized Sandinistas were behind them. The contras broke and ran in all directions without firing a shot. When Villagra limped back into Honduras a week later, only two of his eighty troops were with him.

He went to Doty's hut, and they stood there eyeing one other for a few minutes. "Raymundo, you're a big disappointment to me," Villagra finally said. "I'm sorry," Doty replied quietly. "What will you do now?"

"I'm going to Miami," Villagra said. His family was already there, with visas provided by the CIA. "I'm going to Miami," Villagra repeated. "If you won't give me a visa, I go wetback."

"No, no," Doty said. "You'll have it tomorrow." The visa arrived even faster than that; Villagra was on a plane to Miami that afternoon.

With Villagra gone and Doty chastened, the Banco Grande Rebellion collapsed. In the long run, however, it had results. Within six months, Bermúdez had replaced the entire general staff. El Diablo Morales went to Costa Rica to open an FDN office there and never came back. Edgard Hernández died of a heart attack. Manuel Antonio Caceres resigned to take a job with the Honduran state telecommunications agency.

Echaverry survived a CIA audit. The Agency accountants said they had seen better-kept books in fourth-grade Junior Achievement projects, but in the end they found all the money. A few months later, however, Echaverry's tarnished star fell with a thud. The Honduran armed forces deposed General Alvarez in a barracks coup, and Echaverry's friendship with the departed general became a political liability rather than an asset.[10] He moved to Argentina, and Bermúdez became commander in chief again.

Mike Lima was not dead. They amputated his right arm above the elbow, set the two breaks in his leg, and six weeks later, he was back at the camp learning to fire an automatic rifle with his left hand. He would lead men into Nicaragua again, several times.

In September 1990, I sat on the back porch of the small white house Lima was sharing with another family in Miami. He was laughing as he told me about some crazy thing that happened once on a patrol. And then I asked a question that, apparently, no one had ever asked before: What did he feel when the mortar exploded?

"What did I feel?" he repeated, his voice suddenly low and hoarse. "What did I feel? I felt pain. I felt confusion. I felt fear. I thought I was dying. I thought I was dead. I wanted to cry, but I was the commander. Commanders don't cry."

And then, seven years later, Mike Lima cried.

8 | Down South

Oh, no, Alvaro Jerez thought to himself queasily, *now we've done it. Pastora is in one of his moods.* Commander Zero was pacing the floor of the San José headquarters in tight zigzag patterns, his voice rising and falling in a quickening cadence. At irregular intervals he would abruptly halt and jerk his arms this way and that in melodramatic gestures. *We should never have tried to talk to him while he's like this,* Jerez lamented silently. The thing was, Pastora was like this almost all the time now.

Jerez and a few other members of the ARDE brain trust had made the mistake of telling Pastora they thought it was necessary to divide up the responsibilities of command, to create a general staff the same way other military forces did. "Betrayal! Betrayal!" Pastora was shrieking now. "They are trying to put aside El Hombre, that's what they are doing." He paused, then looked straight at his quailing aides. "There is only one solution!" Pastora shouted. "I am going to kill myself!" He reached for a pistol in the holster on his hip, and Guachán González lunged from behind, pinning Pastora's arms to his sides. "No, no, Hombre, we love you! We love you!" As the two men struggled, other aides grabbed Pastora in bear hugs, piling on until the whole struggling mass collapsed on the floor amid muffled shouts of "We love you!"

It was September 1983, just five months since Pastora had declared war on the Sandinistas, and already it was clear to the upper echelon of his advisers that something was gravely wrong. Pastora lurched from calamity to calamity: alienating allies, wrecking military operations, and throwing wild tantrums at the mildest criticism. Few of his aides had failed to witness at least one "suicide attempt."[1] Most of them thought he was unstable, even downright nuts. A few even suspected he was a Sandinista agent, wasting men and money on a deliberately ineffectual effort while preventing the more militarily competent FDN from opening a southern front.

The first few weeks of the war had been surprisingly easy. Only a few hundred Sandinista troops huddled along the Río San Juan, poorly armed border guards

99

who were accustomed to nothing more troublesome than an occasional smuggler. Within two weeks, seven hundred ARDE troops had crossed into Nicaragua and were launching ambushes and raids pretty much at will. Costa Rican immigration clerks sitting in their offices just across the river heard the crackle of automatic weapons every day. With startling speed, ARDE pushed the Sandinistas completely away from the eastern Río San Juan.

Pastora established camps on the Nicaraguan side of the river. The westernmost ARDE base, known as Tango, was located near El Castillo, the site of an old Spanish castle, halfway between the Atlantic and Lake Nicaragua. The base farthest east, appropriately called Delta, was in the river's delta just a few miles from the Atlantic Ocean. In between there were bases in the villages of La Penca, to the west, and Sarapiquí, to the east.

Even after Pastora established the bases, the Sandinistas didn't launch a counterattack. The territory along the Río San Juan is a hellish melange of malarial jungles and jagged mountains. There are no settlements farther than a few hundred feet from the river itself, and the jungle is impassable. It rains up to 250 inches per year; the creatures that flourish are snakes and mosquitoes.

Only one objective of military importance existed in the area: the route by which the Sandinistas received shipments of Soviet arms. The Soviet ships entered Nicaragua at the Atlantic port of Bluefields and moved inland 50 miles along the broad expanse of the Río Escondido to the town of Rama. There they were loaded onto trucks to travel 180 miles over a narrow highway, crisscrossed with bridges and culverts. Cutting the Rama Road, possibly even blocking the Río Escondido by sinking a ship in it, was precisely the objective the CIA had in mind for Pastora, and the Sandinista high command didn't have to read Clausewitz to guess that. But the route lay 80 brutal miles north of the Río San Juan, and the Sandinistas believed that the cruel terrain would help them stop Pastora without committing a major force.

Had Pastora threatened the border west of Lake Nicaragua—where a narrow corridor of plains opens to Managua and where most of the southern front combat took place during the war against Somoza—the FSLN's reaction probably would have been much different. But the Sandinistas had their hands full with the FDN in the north. And they were also reluctant to enhance Pastora's stature by making a public fuss about him. (Managua's progovernment newspapers, which on some days carried a dozen stories apiece railing about Somocistas in the FDN, were eerily silent on the subject of Pastora.) As long as Pastora flailed around in the jungle, the Sandinistas were content to ignore him.

Tito Chamorro, Popo's cousin, was given the assignment of hacking out trails that Pastora's troops could use to infiltrate north. He did it with forty men who swung machetes constantly from dawn to dusk. It took them a month to complete the first passage—a footpath barely wide enough for a mule—to the village of Atlanta on the Río Punta Gorda, forty miles north of the border. Even on the paths, a guerrilla carrying thirty pounds (little more than his weapon and ammo) could only hike about five miles during a thirteen-hour day.

The rugged terrain meant that ARDE's infrastructure—the military bureaucracy that handles supplies, medical evacuation, and communication—was critical. But Pastora now insisted that every single detail be cleared through him. The same was true of combat operations; even the smallest attack had to be okayed by Commander Zero. The result was pure chaos. As a commander, Pastora's strength had always been his skill as a rhetorician: "He is a man who is capable of inspiring people to go to their death," as one of his subordinates put it. The details of exactly how they would die—the logistical and organizational details that a good military commander must grasp—had always been left to someone else.

But few of Pastora's experienced commanders from the revolution had joined him in ARDE. Popo Chamorro was only on hand for the last two months of the revolution. Tito Chamorro spent most the war in Somoza's prisons. Wicho Rivas was "commander" of Pastora's artillery unit in 1979, but his only role was to provide a Nicaraguan face for an outfit that was almost completely composed of combat-hardened foreigners from Cuba, Argentina, Chile, and other countries. Guachán González had experience in logistics but not in combat or operational planning.

The single experienced commander who joined ARDE—José Valdivia, Pastora's second in command during the revolution and the man who really ran the southern front in 1978 and 1979—had left in disgust before the war even started. Pastora was not sorry to see him go. He had learned a lesson during the revolution, he told his aides. Within the Sandinistas there had been an epidemic of *comandante*-itis. Everybody wanted to be a commander. "In this war," Pastora lectured his staff, "we won't put up with that disease. There will only be one commander, and that commander will be me."

Aides soon noticed, however, that Pastora's cure for *comandante*-itis entailed much more than just doing away with the job of second in command. Pastora was actually anti-organization. He refused to delegate any authority or establish any command structure and was openly suspicious of anyone who advocated it. "Pastora, as all *caudillos* are, was terrified of organizations because organization means that you take power away from the personality, the *caudillo*," observed Arturo Cruz, Jr., some years later. "Organization means that you have to delegate power, you do not concentrate everything at the top. And that is the beginning of a conspiracy. He was afraid of a conspiracy being started, and so Pastora—instead of plotting against the Sandinistas—started plotting against his own people, keeping them divided."

The fallout was horrendous. Successful commanders found themselves transferred to new units in different regions. Supplies flowed erratically or not at all. Troops who moved deep inside Nicaragua, to a point where they might be able to threaten the Rama Road, found that most of the food and ammunition still wound up along the Río San Juan. Units that had the supplies to mount operations often found their plans derailed by Pastora. Time after time he approved attacks, only to get on the radio at the last minute to cancel them. When Harold Martínez, who had been with Pastora since the late 1950s, proposed an assault on the Sandinista border post at Peñas Blancas on the Pacific side of Nicaragua, Pastora authorized it. As Martínez got ready to leave San José to join his troops at the border, Popo Chamorro took him aside.

"If you really want this attack to take place," Popo warned him, "you have to cut communications with us 48 hours before it's scheduled." Martínez nodded. A week later, almost exactly 48 hours before the attack was set to go, Pastora told Popo to get on the radio and cancel it. Popo dutifully began calling Martínez's frequency, hoping he wouldn't answer. "I'm sorry, *Comandante*, but we have no radio contact with them right now," Popo reported a few minutes later. Pastora kicked a stool across the room.

A commander who seized a target of opportunity would quickly learn that initiative was not a quality Pastora rewarded. When Wicho Rivas called in one day to report that he had set an ambush along one of the small tributaries of the San Juan and killed two dozen Sandinista troops, Pastora ordered him back to Costa Rica. When Pastora did permit an attack, it often had less to do with troop strength and tactical advantage than with astrological signs or supernatural omens. Commander Zero had become a great believer in reincarnation and now fancied he was Augusto Sandino himself, reborn. He had adopted most of Sandino's wacky metaphysical beliefs.

Much worse than the attacks Pastora canceled were the ones he compromised. Every day at sundown, Pastora would begin working the big radio on the first floor of his San José headquarters, calling his various units. Sometimes Sandinista officers would come on the frequency by mistake, but Pastora, instead of breaking contact, engaged them in long debates. Popo ricocheted between horror and hilarity as he listened to these conversations. "Pastora, you're a son of a bitch!" a Sandinista officer shouted one night. "No, no," Pastora corrected him. "Humberto Ortega is a son of a bitch. And I'm going to prove it to you. Where are you, Punta Gorda? Well, I have five hundred men just north of there and tomorrow at sundown they're going to come and kick your ass!" Popo put his face in his hands—the attack really was scheduled. Sometimes Pastora would even go to the big wall map while he talked and scream coordinates at the Sandinista officers.

Anything Pastora himself didn't give away to the Sandinistas was passed along by the spies who honeycombed ARDE. At least a dozen Sandinista agents were eventually identified within Pastora's ranks, and ARDE leaders privately conceded that the real number was many times that. Several of them were Pastora's mistresses.

But Pastora's pernicious weakness for women was only one part of the spy problem. While the FDN commanders in the north were suspicious of defecting Sandinistas, Pastora welcomed them without even perfunctory security checks. In 1983, Popo Chamorro's sister Angelica Lugo, who was married to the head of the Sandinista marines and had been working with FSLN *comandante* Jaime Wheelock, showed up in San José unannounced.

"I'm here to work with you," she told Pastora. "Can you type?" he asked. When she said yes, Pastora made her chief of personnel. She had access to documents showing exactly how many men ARDE had, where they were, and what they were doing. Popo simply threw up his hands and stayed away from the situation. He was not going to denounce his own sister as a potential spy, but he couldn't believe that Pastora had given her such a sensitive post without even asking any questions.

Six months later, while Popo was in Pastora's office, Angelica walked in. "Tomorrow I'm going back to Managua," she calmly informed Pastora. "You are a piece of shit, you are a shit-eater, you are infiltrated by the CIA." As Popo and Pastora sat there, she picked up the telephone and dialed Jaime Wheelock's office in Managua to tell him she would be on the morning plane.

The higher a defector's connections to the Sandinistas went, the less likely Pastora was to have reservations. And the most honored defectors of all were the ones who ought to have been the most suspicious: those from Tomás Borge's Interior Ministry. When two of Borge's personal assistants, brothers named Guillén, came to ARDE, Pastora made one of them chief of intelligence. Every time an ARDE operation failed because of faulty intelligence, the other ARDE commanders wondered about the Guillén brothers. But Pastora never did.

Adding it all up—the canceled attacks, the compromising radio conversations, the flagrant disregard for internal security—some of Pastora's aides wondered if he might really be a Sandinista agent. A slightly milder variant of this suspicion was that Pastora had no real intention of defeating the Sandinistas, but only wanted to be welcomed back as the tenth FSLN *comandante*.

Certainly many of the politicians around Pastora said ARDE had gone to war in order to *reform* the Sandinistas rather than to oust them. Their view was that the Borge-led "prolonged popular war" faction of the FSLN should be ousted, and the *tercerista* faction led by the Ortega brothers should be strengthened by adding Pastora to the Sandinista directorate.

The three most prominent of the reformists were Arturo Cruz, Jr., the witty young intellectual who had fled the Sandinista Foreign Ministry; Alvaro Jerez, a neurosurgeon considered only slightly less erratic than Pastora himself by many ARDE officials; and Carlos Coronel, the coffee planter who was Pastora's closest adviser.

All three shared the dubious belief that Fidel Castro would salvage the situation by intervening on the behalf of the "real" Sandinistas, the noncommunist moderates. (That was also a favorite theory of Pastora, who consequently continued to praise Castro in speeches and interviews well into 1984.) Cruz Jr. flew to Washington to plead the reformists' case with the head of the Cuban Interests Section; Coronel and Jerez went to Havana, where they met with several high officials. They were also in regular contact with Jaime Wheelock in Managua.

None of the negotiations got anywhere, but they did raise suspicions about the loyalties of the negotiators—especially Coronel. Of all the factors that tainted the relationship between Pastora and the CIA, the single most poisonous was Coronel. But the gringos weren't the only skeptics; almost no one trusted him.

Coronel was a patrician Nicaraguan coffee planter who despite his family background (the Coronels were not only wealthy, but had also founded a pro-Fascist movement in pre–World War II Nicaragua) was an early Sandinista. He had been with Pastora almost from the beginning. Some cynics even referred to him as the brains behind Pastora.

The problem with Coronel was that no one knew, really, who he worked for.

Of all the Sandinista leaders, he had been Castro's favorite. He also had close contacts with the Soviets when he was with the Sandinistas, and he was Pastora's first liaison with the CIA. The Agency soon became convinced, however, that Coronel was a communist and a Castro agent, leaking secrets and intent on hijacking Pastora's army when the opportunity presented itself. Coronel's adamant refusal to take a lie-detector test did nothing to allay CIA fears.

The Coronel matter was not the only source of friction between Pastora and the CIA. Duane Clarridge could accept, however reluctantly, that Pastora would not unify with the FDN. But Pastora couldn't leave it at that. First he took out a series of newspaper advertisements in Costa Rica calling the FDN "criminals." Then he made a clandestine radio broadcast, urging the Sandinista army to leave his men alone and save its bullets for the FDN.[2] Horrified, CIA officers gave Pastora the first in a four-year series of stern lectures that had no effect. "It just wasn't in his personality," recalls one aide. "He could promise that he would behave and go to church . . . and then he would do it again the next day."

The CIA was also quarreling with Pastora over weapons. Pastora was angry that by late June 1983 he had received only about 3,500 rifles. The CIA countered that he had more than enough for his troops and was handing out weapons promiscuously, to anyone who asked. Some of them were actually surfacing in the hands of communist guerrillas in El Salvador, and the CIA was certain that others were going to Costa Rican leftist groups, which might provoke the government to suspend its hospitality to Pastora. Pastora retaliated for the sermons by firing his equivalent of a nuclear weapon: He pulled his troops out of the field. Within a week, the CIA caved in and promised another 1,000 rifles.

While he nagged the CIA for rifles, Pastora used an unexpected windfall to launch a more ambitious project. In December 1982, Francisco ("Paco") Fiallos, the stylish, Harvard-educated Sandinista ambassador to the United States, looted $668,000 from his embassy's bank accounts and disappeared. When Fiallos surfaced four months later in San José, he had $630,000 left. He donated $500,000 to Pastora and kept the rest—a "finder's fee," he and Pastora called it with straight faces.

Pastora used the money to launch his own air force. He purchased three twin-engine Beechcraft airplanes (one, with the registration number N-666-PF, became known as the "666 Paco Fiallos" in honor of the man who made it all possible), two Cessnas, and an $8,000 hang glider mounted with a toy motor.

The hang glider, Pastora proclaimed, would win the war. It was so small it would never show up on radar, he said; all they had to do was mount it with a rocket-launching pod, and the contras could zoom through Sandinista air defenses at will, terrorizing the enemy from the skies. But, weighted down with all the military hardware, the glider moved like an airborne slug, and it flew so low that the Sandinistas could have knocked it down throwing rocks. No ARDE pilot was willing to fly it into the combat zone.

Pastora, however, remained convinced that he could win the war in the air.

He had three other aircraft—an Islander, a Cessna, and a Hughes helicopter—from the CIA. He got the Cuban exile community in Miami to buy him two more helicopters, and he begged and borrowed other aircraft until his fleet numbered fifteen. Even a donated aircraft was expensive; it took a $20,000 bribe to Costa Rican customs officials to get the CIA-purchased helicopter into the country.

Unfortunately, Pastora's war in the air was just as disaster-prone as his war on the ground. His hot-rodding pilots crashed six aircraft. One of the helicopters donated by Cuban exiles was shot down by his own men as it approached an ARDE base, just four days after it arrived from Miami. And despite the impressive arsenal of aircraft, Pastora managed to launch only five aerial attacks in three years. One of them, designed to garner publicity, did just that, netting the worst headlines of Pastora's guerrilla career. And, remarkably, it could have been even worse.

It was code-named *Operación Voltaje del Sol*—Operation Solar Shock. As dawn was breaking, a Cessna and a Beechcraft would swoop out of the sun and pound Managua with high explosives. The idea was to pull a Latin version of "thirty seconds over Tokyo," the famous U.S. bomber raid on Tokyo in the early days of World War II that served notice that, even in a weakened state, the Americans could bring the war directly to Japan. Not only would a raid on Managua garner incredible international publicity, but the Sandinistas wouldn't be able to keep it a secret from ordinary Nicaraguans by censoring the news. Everyone in Managua would see that the contras were *real*.

The big question, of course, was what targets to hit. Pastora wanted to bomb the Bunker, Somoza's old command post that was now the Sandinista military nerve center. Because most of the buildings in the Bunker compound were heavily reinforced, Pastora insisted that the little Cessna designated for the attack carry five-hundred-pound bombs.

The pilot who would be at the controls of the Cessna, Augustín Román, was a former National Guard lieutenant who had learned to fly in American training programs. He had a very close relationship with the CIA. In fact, he had talked the Agency into giving Pastora the plane and picked it up himself at an Agency airfield in Virginia. Román was no coward, but he was no fool, either. He was sure the Bunker would be protected by thick concentrations of antiaircraft guns, and the heavy bombs would make the Cessna slow and unmaneuverable as it approached. This was a suicide mission.

He went to see an old friend, an American rancher and pilot named John Hull who managed several farms in northern Costa Rica. They were fly-boy buddies from years before, when Hull had owned land in Nicaragua. Now Hull was the CIA's border liaison with the contras. Román told Hull about the plan, and Hull agreed it was a stupid idea. "I saw a report on Managua air defenses last week," Hull told the pilot. "You're right. The Bunker is ringed with Soviet guns, the kind that lock onto a target with radar. You'll never even get close."

Román looked glum.

"Look, tell Pastora you think it's a great idea," Hull, who privately thought Pastora a blowhard fool, suggested. "But tell him the propaganda value will be a lot better if he flies along with you. Think of the headlines: 'Commander Zero personally bombs Managua.' Maybe he'll think twice if he's going along.''

What neither Hull, the pilot, Pastora, nor anyone else considered was that the Bunker was located less than one hundred yards from the Inter-Continental Hotel, where nearly every foreign journalist and visiting political dignitary (including U.S. congressmen) stayed during visits to Managua. On a hot news day, a couple hundred media and political celebrities might be housed at the Inter-Con. A five-hundred-pound bomb that landed squarely on the Bunker would still do serious damage to the hotel. And if the bomb missed the Bunker by a few yards, the carnage would be mind-boggling.

When Pastora heard Román's idea, his interest in the Bunker waned. Instead, he decided, the Cessna could carry a lighter load of two-hundred fifty-pound bombs and hit the Casa del Gobierno, the government building where Daniel Ortega and many other top Sandinista officials had offices. Meanwhile, the Beechcraft would attack a Soviet communications center that had been covertly installed in the Villa Fontana residential neighborhood. The raid was set for September 8, 1983.

Something, though, went badly awry. Instead of the Casa del Gobierno, Román attacked the passenger terminal at Sandino International Airport several miles away. The plane was caught in the shock wave from its own bombs and flung to the ground, killing Román and his copilot. An airport worker also died.

The fallout from the raid was horrendous. Attacking a civilian passenger terminal would have been a public-relations black eye in the best of circumstances. To make matters worse, two U.S. senators, William Cohen and Gary Hart, were due to speak at the airport a few minutes after the attack. When they arrived, they found the VIP lounge, where they were to appear, a smoking ruin.[3] On top of that, Román's briefcase—containing ID cards, phone numbers, and other documents linking him to the CIA—was found in the plane.

The other attack, on the Soviet communications center, went as planned. But back in Costa Rica, Pastora and his commanders were obsessed with Román's foray against the airport. Why did he change targets? Why didn't he tell anyone? Popo Chamorro thought he might have part of the answer when he saw the next morning's Managua newspapers. A North Vietnamese general had been departing the airport just about the time Román dropped his bombs. Could one of Román's CIA contacts, pursuing an ancient vendetta from Southeast Asia, have told him to hit the airport? Popo became more convinced when he learned that CIA officials were denying they knew when the air raid was scheduled. *What a bunch of bullshit,* he thought. *We loaded the bombs at their hangar at the Ilopango air base in El Salvador.*

Pastora's pilots launched three more air raids, against the ports in Corinto and Puerto Sandino on the Pacific, and on a sugar refinery near León. But the air war, like so much that happened on the southern front, never lived up to expectations.

The negative publicity over the airport raid was Pastora's first. Ever since he took over the National Palace, reporters had loved him. He was accessible, witty—his intricate Spanish puns, even if they couldn't be translated into English, delighted journalists—and he knew how to craft colorful quotes that make good newspaper copy. Pastora was particularly skillful in using interviews to needle the State Department and the CIA without coming across as anti-American; he managed to convince many reporters that the U.S. government was responsible for nearly everything that went wrong in ARDE.[4]

But Pastora's poor judgment, recklessness, and refusal to discipline his subordinates eventually strained his romance with the press. Although Pastora usually managed to avoid any personal damage, the southern front was at the center of most of the bad publicity about the contras between 1983 and 1987. Most of the stories were sideshows to the real issue—the war—but they provided no end of ammunition to opponents of the Reagan administration's aid to the contras.

The worst of the scandals centered on the tangential involvement of a few contras in drug trafficking. That there were some connections was hardly surprising. Latin American guerrillas have long smuggled drugs, or provided protection to those who do, to raise funds. Some groups, like Colombia's M-19 and Peru's Sendero Luminoso, have relied almost exclusively on drug profits to fund their operations; others—notably those in El Salvador, Argentina, Guatemala, and Uruguay—have searched for narco-dollars only during dry spells in their ordinary businesses, bank robbing and kidnapping.

Moreover, northern Costa Rica was already a busy supply depot for smugglers before the contras came on the scene. When the Sandinistas were fighting Somoza, they established a network of remote airstrips and refueling points in Costa Rica to aid their gunrunning flights. After the revolution, a number of pilots who had delivered weapons decided the network provided a perfect way station for planes carrying drugs from South America to the United States.

Add to that the fact that many of the aviation companies best suited to supplying a clandestine guerrilla force (those with fleets of durable planes capable of landing on primitive airfields) also dabble in smuggling, and it was almost inevitable that ARDE would have contact with narco-traffickers.[5]

The first links were established in 1983, when Pastora decided to build an air force with the $500,000 from Paco Fiallos. He assigned Karol Prado, one of his assistants, to assemble the planes. Prado was another of Pastora's dirty little Somocista secrets—a former Managua construction baron with deep business ties to several of Somoza's financial partners and cabinet ministers. He was one of Pastora's most trusted aides. Pastora even used Prado as his personal cash courier, toting large sums of money between Miami and Costa Rica. No one else in ARDE shared Pastora's confidence in Prado, and more than a few were afraid of him.

Prado bought five planes from a Miami company called DIACSA, headed by a Cuban exile named Alfredo Caballero, who had flown a B-26 during the Bay of Pigs invasion in 1961 and then lived in Nicaragua for many years. Caballero had a lucrative sideline: he supplied aircraft and facilities to a gang of smugglers moving thousands of pounds of cocaine from Colombia to the United States through Costa Rica. He was eventually convicted of importing cocaine to the

United States and sentenced to five years of probation. The conviction did not surprise anyone in ARDE's offices, and several of Pastora's aides wondered why Prado had elected to do business with Caballero.

When Congress stopped U.S. aid to the contras in 1984, the CIA's aerial supply of Pastora's troops inside Nicaragua ceased. The situation became desperate: none of Pastora's planes was capable of large-scale supply missions. In September, while trying to raise money in Miami, Popo Chamorro and another Pastora aide, Octaviano César, got a call from Popo's ex-wife. She had a wealthy friend, she said, who might be interested in making a substantial donation.

César was first to meet the man, a wealthy Colombian named George Morales. Morales owned a number of planes, he said, and he might be willing to donate one to ARDE. When Pastora saw pictures of the planes, he didn't hesitate: "The C-47, that's exactly what we need for supply flights." César, Popo, and Marcos Aguado—the head of Pastora's air force—returned to Miami to seal the deal.

All three of them say they had no suspicions about Morales. He was just another wealthy anticommunist exile who wanted to help out. In most American cities, their story might not wash. But in Miami, where the Cuban community was collecting rifles door-to-door to help the contras, the offer of a combat supply plane doesn't necessarily raise eyebrows.

Morales was indeed an ordinary Miami character, but of another sort. He was a drug merchant, importing vast quantities of cocaine and marijuana into the United States from the Bahamas. When he met with the contras, he was already under indictment for smuggling marijuana. Morales figured that if he scratched the CIA's back by helping out the contras, the Agency would scratch his by getting rid of that pesky indictment.

Morales would later testify before Congress that he put the deal to the contras just that baldly when he met César, Popo, and Aguado in late September. The three of them swear he said nothing of the kind.[6] But what happened next is not in dispute. "Your offer is a kind one," Popo told Morales, "but we don't have any money to move the plane." The C-47 was in Haiti, and ARDE would have to fly its pilots there by commercial jet and then purchase fuel to get the plane to ARDE's hangar in El Salvador. No problem, Morales said, I'll give you $10,000 to get organized.

After two weeks of paperwork, the plane was ready for pickup. But before he turned it over, Morales said, he wanted to see if Aguado could really fly. How about buzzing over to the Bahamas for an afternoon, with Aguado at the controls of Morales's private plane? They made the forty-five-minute flight to Nassau, had a hamburger, and returned. On the way back, Morales asked the men if they would carry $400,000 in cash and checks through customs for him. Even by Miami's unusual standards, that's not an ordinary request. But the contras insist that they still didn't suspect anything. They carried the money, dutifully declaring it on customs forms, and returned it to Morales after clearing immigration.

Morales and Popo returned to Costa Rica soon afterward. Aguado and another pilot, a Costa Rican named Gerardo Durán, went to Haiti with Morales to pick up the plane. During the trip, Morales took Durán aside and suggested they go into business together. Durán agreed and began hauling cocaine on the same flights that carried weapons to the contras.

Eventually the ARDE brain trust learned that Morales was a smuggler. There was some talk about returning the C-47, but Popo argued against it. "That makes no sense," he said. "If we return it, Morales will just use it to smuggle drugs." And the C-47 was a workhorse for ARDE, one of the few planes its pilots did not destroy. During the next sixteen months, the plane moved 156,000 pounds of supplies from El Salvador to Costa Rica, and made eleven supply drops inside Nicaragua.

The Americans never complained about the C-47. But they did warn Pastora repeatedly that Gerardo Durán was smuggling drugs. Pastora ignored their protests until Durán was indicted in both Costa Rica and the United States in 1986. Many ARDE aides thought Pastora and Prado must have known all along. Durán was Pastora's personal pilot. On all their flights together, did they never talk about the drugs? And why did Pastora and Prado loan Durán an ARDE airplane for a private flight in 1985? Durán never told anyone where he took the plane, but it evidently was an international flight; he ditched the Beechcraft in the Pacific and, after his rescue, paid Pastora $50,000 for the lost plane.

Durán was not the only Pastora intimate to get mixed up in drugs. But despite the best efforts of contra critics to prove it, no evidence has surfaced that ARDE was institutionally involved in the drug trade. In 1986, Senator John Kerry of Massachusetts, among the most vehement opponents of U.S. aid to the contras, launched a much-publicized investigation into alleged contra drug trafficking. After three years (during which his staff regularly leaked erroneous or distorted material to the Washington press), Kerry's subcommittee finally produced its report. "The subcommittee did not find evidence that the contra leadership participated directly in narcotics smuggling in support of their war against the Sandinistas," the report concluded. The most serious charge the committee could muster was that "individual contras accepted weapons, money and equipment from drug smugglers."[7] The same undoubtedly could be said about individual soldiers in the U.S. Army.

Robert Bermingham, an investigator for the congressional Iran-contra committee that held televised hearings in 1987, sifted the evidence turned up at the hearings. "Hundreds of persons, including U.S. government employees, contra leaders, representatives of foreign governments, U.S. and foreign law enforcement officials, military personnel, private pilots and crews involved in actual operations were questioned and their files and records examined," Bermingham reported back to the committee. "Despite numerous newspaper accounts to the contrary no evidence was developed indicating that contra leadership or contra organizations were actually involved in drug trafficking."[8] Representative Charles Rangel's House committee on narcotics also investigated the contras and came up empty-handed.

By the time all the congressmen concluded that the drug issue was spurious,

Popo Chamorro had a magisterial collection of subpoenas and a $70,000 legal bill. Several other contra leaders had similar debts. The single contra to come away happy was Marcos Aguado, chief of the ARDE air force. When George Morales donated the C-47 to ARDE, the technicalities of the law required him to draw up papers "selling" the plane for $1. Aguado was registered as the new owner, since ARDE itself wasn't incorporated in the United States. When the southern front disintegrated, Aguado sold "his" plane for $100,000.

9 | The García Family

I used to hear contras talk about the García family all the time. It seemed to be one of the most powerful and sinister clans in Nicaragua. So many of the conversations began, *los maldito García* . . . those damned Garcías. Finally one afternoon a slightly inebriated contra official told me his wife had just left him for a García.

"Who *are* these Garcías?" I demanded. "And why haven't I ever met one?"

"You really don't know?" the contra said in astonishment. "What are the last three letters of García?"

That was how I learned that "García family" was contraspeak for the CIA, an innocent phrase that could be shouted in drunken anger at a Tegucigalpa bar (and was, often) without panicking everyone in the room.

The CIA was certainly not the only part of the U.S. government that supported or worked with the contras. The State Department and the National Security Council also played important roles. But the CIA involvement was longer, deeper, and more intimate. State Department officials met contra politicians in Washington and occasionally ventured out to the border camps in Honduras by helicopter to visit for an hour or two. But dozens of CIA officers lived in the camps, day and night, for months at a time. Moreover, while State Department officials shuttled from one job to another, many of the same CIA personnel stayed with the contra project, in one capacity or another, throughout most of the war.

The difference in the way the two organizations interacted with the contras led to an odd paradox. The CIA, in the popular view, is a cold-blooded agency that unsentimentally manipulates those it finds useful, then ruthlessly casts them aside like worn-out parts. The State Department, by contrast, is supposed to be relatively humane.

When it came to the contras, however, the poles were reversed. To the State Department, the war was impersonal. The contras were not an independent, organic group with views and ambitions of their own; they were simply one aspect of U.S. policy toward Nicaragua, which could be cut and shaped in whatever fashion necessary to please the congressmen who held the federal purse strings.

But for most CIA officers—at least those on the ground in Central America— the contras were an authentic peasant army of brave men fighting to retrieve their country from communism. Many CIA men found it impossible to stay aloof. They were infuriated and anguished by the ebb and flow of congressional support for the war and the maze of restrictions and prohibitions that were imposed from Washington. Some lost all vestige of professional detachment and took sides in every petty contra quarrel. Others sacrificed their careers rather than obey rules that made some sense in the Washington offices where they were devised but had horrible human repercussions in the jungle.

In Washington, where the war was only an abstraction, this behavior was difficult to comprehend. In April 1987, the staffers of the congressional committee investigating the Iran-contra scandal came out of a closed-door hearing rolling their eyes. They had been listening to a CIA officer explain why he helped deliver arms to the contras during a time when Congress had ordered the Agency to stay away. The CIA man, trying to describe the massacre of a contra unit that went inside Nicaragua without adequate ammunition, had embarrassed the committee by crying.

But to say that the CIA had a better understanding of the human cost of the war is not to say that all of its officers were heroes and geniuses. Many were arrogant, and some were indisputably idiots and bunglers. Some of the worst mistakes were made at the top: if the State Department spent too much time pandering to domestic political considerations, the CIA assiduously ignored them. And when the CIA displayed its scorn for Congress, the lawmakers took it out on the contras.

Plenty of mistakes were also made at lower levels, which isn't surprising. By 1982, when the first CIA officers appeared in contra camps in Honduras, paramilitary specialists were an endangered species at the Agency. Not since the wars in Southeast Asia ended in 1975 had the CIA had been intimately involved with a guerrilla force. Shortly after that, President Jimmy Carter and his CIA director Stansfield Turner fired hundreds of officers in the Agency's operations directorate, which oversees clandestine activities. Many paramilitary specialists—relatively useless when there's no war going on—were among the victims.

One other factor contributed to the CIA's uneven performance with the contras: Comparatively few of the people who worked on the project were among the Agency's best and brightest. Most officers, offered the opportunity to join the contra effort, ran in the other direction as fast as they could. The Agency's paramilitary track record was anything but glorious; more often than not, these operations ended with a native guerrilla group abandoned on some lonely beach, mountaintop, or jungle clearing, and the career of an unlucky CIA officer ritually sacrificed. It happened again and again: to Sumatran rebels in Indonesia, to Kurdish mountain tribes in Iran, to Hmong tribesmen in Laos and Montagnards in Vietnam, and—most notoriously—to the Cuban exile army that perished at the Bay of Pigs.

A lot of people at the CIA's labyrinthine 1.4 million-square-foot headquarters in Langley, Virginia, thought from the beginning that the contra program had all the earmarks of one of these disasters. There was no evidence of congressional support for it; just to win congressional *tolerance*, the Agency had to lie about what was going on. In December 1982, a few days after President Reagan signed National Security Decision Directive 17, authorizing $19 million in CIA aid to the contras, Agency director William Casey met with the congressional committees that oversee intelligence operations. He told them the contras would be a five-hundred-man force that would disrupt the flow of arms from the Sandinistas to the communist guerrillas in El Salvador.

Casey's explanation was absurdly false. The Sandinistas were supplying weapons to the Salvadoran guerrillas, it was true—so many that, at one point, the Salvadorans complained they couldn't absorb them all. But the bulk of the supplies went by air, or by boat across the Gulf of Fonseca. The contras could do nothing about either of those supply lines; they could only disrupt shipments moving by land, the least important of the three channels. And Edén Pastora's forces in the south couldn't even do that; they were on the wrong side of the country, hundreds of miles away from the nearest supply route to El Salvador.

Why the congressional committees accepted such a patently fraudulent rationale is difficult to understand. And to pin down exactly what Casey really believed is even harder. Sometimes Casey told people he just wanted the Sandinistas to turn inwards, to quit supporting the Salvadoran guerrillas and mind their own business. Other times he suggested that the combination of contra pressure, popular discontent inside Nicaragua, and withdrawal of international support for the FSLN might ignite a national uprising against the Sandinistas. The State Department and the National Security Council had other, hazier goals. Ronald Reagan's explanation was the foggiest of all: The Sandinistas were supposed to "say uncle," whatever that meant.

But if Casey was equivocal about the results he hoped the contras would achieve, there was no doubt at all that he saw Sandinista Nicaragua as the newest and most vulnerable extension of the Soviet empire, a place where damage could be inflicted. And he wanted action, not alibis. He wanted men who could *get things done*. Casey was a veteran of the old Office of Strategic Services, the World War II predecessor of the CIA. One day William Donovan, the head of OSS, called him in. Get some guys into Germany, Donovan said. No explanations, no details: just do it. Within weeks Casey was parachuting spies behind Nazi lines. Now Casey the old man—he was in his late sixties—looked for officers like Casey the young man; can-do guys, or, in Langley parlance, cowboys.

The first one he found was Duane Clarridge, the man with the silk scarves, big cigars, and monocle. Clarridge, head of the CIA station in Rome, had no Latin American background. But during one of Casey's trips to Europe, CIA legend has it, Clarridge set up an elegant dinner for him, with lots of *très délicat* sauces and fastidious attention to detail. Clarridge was definitely the kind of guy who could *get things done*. Casey promptly signed him up for what was to become the CIA's second-most influential job.

The CIA is divided into four directorates. One manages administrative

113

details. Another, science and technology, is in charge of electronic information-gathering—spy satellites, signal intercepts, and the like. A third, intelligence, analyzes all the data that stream into the CIA.

The fourth directorate, operations, oversees covert actions—all the skullduggery that most people associate with the CIA: recruiting spies, planting propaganda, setting up clandestine radio stations, breaking into foreign government offices, and advising guerrilla groups. Within the operations directorate are more than a dozen separate divisions, including six set up along geographical lines. The divisions supervise all activities within their geographic zones—collecting intelligence, running agents, mounting operations.

Casey believed the operations directorate had become sluggish and timid after enduring the intelligence scandals of the Nixon and Ford administrations and the general retrenchment in intelligence operations under the Carter administration. In particular, Casey thought, the operations directorate was too skittish about covert action, activities designed to influence the course of events rather than merely collect information. One of the first things Casey did after he became CIA director was pitch out the 130-page book of guidelines that governed covert operations. He replaced it with a single memo that said, in essence, to use common sense.[1] But changing the rules, Casey believed, would not be enough. He had to turn loose some people who could *get things done.*

So Casey made Clarridge chief of the Latin American division. Then the two of them agreed to create a special task force, a step taken only when the CIA is planning activities of extraordinary intensity or complexity that require more attention than a division chief can afford to devote. The task force coordinates all the operations directed at a specific target, and it also cuts through several layers of CIA bureaucracy and makes it easier to obtain resources from around the Agency. During the 1980s, there were three CIA task forces: one for Angola, one for Afghanistan, and one for Central America. The Central American Task Force was by far the most muscular, with hundreds of employees crammed into a rabbit warren of offices on the third floor at Langley, hundreds more scattered around the five Central American countries, Panama, and Belize.

In theory, at least, the creation of the Central American Task Force should have allowed Clarridge to concentrate on the rest of Latin American while the task force chief took care of Central America. The reality was just the opposite. Clarridge completely ignored Mexico, South America, and the Caribbean, leaving them to his deputy. And Clarridge had unlimited access to Casey. In effect, the CIA had created a fifth directorate: anti-Sandinista activities.

As Clarridge created an unprecedented bureaucratic empire in Washington, he also began assembling a team on the ground in Honduras to aid the contras. His first recruit was the CIA's station chief in Asunción, Paraguay, the officer who called himself Joe. During the first week of 1982, Joe was at a dinner party when he was summoned to the embassy by the CIA's equivalent of an air-raid siren—a cable coded *"Night* Action, Eyes Only." It was the first such message to the Asunción station in years.

When Joe got in touch with headquarters, Clarridge told him he had a new assignment, so sensitive that it could only be discussed face to face. After a quick flight to Washington, Joe got his marching orders. Like nearly every other mid- and low-level officer who joined the contra project during the next seven years, Joe understood that the object was, unambiguously, to overthrow the Sandinista government.

In 1982, Tegucigalpa was a sleepy geopolitical backwater, off all known diplomatic and journalistic trade routes. The scruffy mountaintop city's collective pulse was so slow that it was the only capital in Central America without its own McDonald's. In short, Tegucigalpa was the polar opposite of wartime Casablanca. But Joe's arrival marked the first tiny sign of a transformation that left Tegucigalpa the looniest, most intrigue-ridden city in the hemisphere.

In the beginning, Joe was alone and almost entirely isolated; virtually no one at the U.S. embassy even knew of his existence, and those who did couldn't find him through the tangled thicket of false identities Agency headquarters created for him. Working with the Hondurans and the Argentines, Joe set up a CIA operations base that functioned independently of the regular Agency station.

To stay out of sight as much as possible, one of his offices was located just outside the city on a Honduran Special Forces base. The other was twenty miles west of Tegucigalpa in a nearly deserted village of mud shacks called Lepaterique, perched so high in the mountains on a road so bad that it might as well have been on the moon. The contras could even practice firing mortars there undetected. (As time passed and the contra war became less covert, the isolation of Lepaterique became less of an advantage and more of a hindrance. Eventually contra activities were moved to a more accessible site, and Lepaterique became an operations center for clandestine CIA programs in El Salvador.)

As the CIA began nudging the Argentines aside in the wake of the Falkland Islands war, Joe's seclusion eased. So many Agency officers flooded into Honduras that they practically took over the discreetly tucked-away Hotel Alameda. The new mix of Garcías was not always a happy one. The CIA has its own peculiar set of class distinctions, as sharply drawn as any Hindu caste system. At the top are the FIs, or foreign intelligence officers—the classical spies. Below them are the paramilitary specialists. And at the bottom are the officers from the technical directorate who build gadgets, forge documents, and break locks.

Ordinarily the three groups have only fleeting contact. An FI operating as station chief in a foreign country might bring in a paramilitary officer on temporary duty to train the local president's bodyguards, or he might ask for a technical officer to help install a wiretap. But they aren't required to work together on a long-term basis.

The contra program, however, needed the services of all three. FIs had to supervise the delicate political balancing act between the Hondurans, the Argentines, the Nicaraguans, and the Americans. Paramilitary specialists had to help teach the contras basic military skills and advise their commanders on military strategy and tactics. And technical officers were necessary for specialized training in communications and explosives.

In Vietnam, the last time the CIA's disparate wings were forced into close

115

contact, it had been an ugly scene. Now, as the Agency reinforcements rolled into Honduras, everyone remembered why. The FIs, most of them holding graduate degrees, were forever wondering out loud why they should take advice from the paramilitary "knuckledraggers." After all, weren't they the same guys who lost the Vietnam War?

For their part, the paramilitary men openly sneered at the "FI pukes," gutless college boys who had never pulled a trigger outside of an Agency firing range. (The paramilitary boys were fond of punctuating conversations with questions like, "How about if I just kick your fucking ass?") And everyone dumped on the techs, whose enlistment in the CIA did not alter their lifelong status as nerds. As the paramilitary officers began to predominate, their complaints about the FIs seeped back to headquarters. Slowly but steadily, reputations began to erode.

Even so, the first few CIA officers to work with the contras enjoyed a wild-and-woolly life-style. Virtually unsupervised, responsible to almost no one, they had a free hand; it was more like the free-swinging CIA of the 1950s than the lumbering bureaucracy of the 1980s. One García's landlady paid a surprise visit to his apartment one night and found him packing contra propaganda leaflets around a small explosive charge that would scatter them when it went off; bomb parts and beer bottles were strewn all over the living room floor. She shrugged, went upstairs to her own apartment for a bottle of Scotch, and came back to keep him company while he built more bombs.

It wasn't just Honduran civilians who were bemused by this new James Bond element moving into their sleepy society. The country's military men were feeling their way, too, anxious to help but not always sure what these strange gringos wanted. In October 1982, Joe and a group of Honduran army officers flew into Puerto Lempira, a remote port on the country's Atlantic Coast, to set up a contra supply station. As the helicopter descended, a Honduran colonel pointed at a couple of men standing one hundred yards away, snapping photos of the chopper through fish-eye lenses. "Those are journalists, I think from a French news agency," the colonel said. "Do you want me to take care of it?"

A glint in the colonel's eye made Joe fairly certain that "taking care" of the journalists would involve much more than calm persuasion. "No, thanks, just let them go," he replied. Two weeks later, a photo taken that day covered half a page of a special report in *Newsweek* titled "A Secret War for Nicaragua." Joe's face was clearly visible in the photo under the caption, "Some friendly visitors from the north."[2] Joe, visiting Costa Rica for the weekend, got a panicky cable from headquarters telling him not to return to Honduras. His job had already been in jeopardy, the cumulative effect of the complaints about him from the paramilitary knuckledraggers, and this photo had undone all Joe's deceptive tricks to cover his identity. A few days later he was reassigned to El Salvador. The contra project had claimed its first CIA victim.

With Joe gone, the Agency decided to put a knuckledragger in charge on the ground in Honduras. After all, U.S. money had been rolling in for almost a year, and the contras were still bunched along the border. Political sensitivity was fine, Clarridge decided, but it was time that the show was run by somebody who knew which end of a gun the bullets came from.

The man he chose was Ray Doty. Doty arrived around the end of 1982 and began an assignment that would last three tumultuous years. By the time he left Doty had seen the contras grow, sometimes with his help and sometimes despite him, from a disorganized band of cross-border raiding parties into a giant peasant army; alienated every single contra leader of any consequence; won the CIA's top medal for his management of the program; and presided over several calamitous endeavors that nearly doomed the whole thing.

Many of the contras he worked with saw Doty as the embodiment of both American virtue and vice. No one worked harder, or longer hours. And no one was less willing to listen to advice. He was a good man to have on your side, but a terror if he thought you had crossed him—and to Doty, it didn't take much to feel crossed. He was a generous man, who had thrown his soul into the contra program; at the same time, a single misplaced bullet could prompt Doty to rage like a battalion of GAO auditors. He hated communism and wanted to get rid of the Sandinistas, but he had little patience with any idea that didn't involve shooting at them. Putting the war in a political context, explaining what the contras were fighting for and against, was a waste of time to Doty.

He spent countless hours trying to impose form on the shapeless chaos that enveloped contra logistics. He got the supplies to flow more smoothly (though by no means perfectly) from the United States to Honduras, and when the contras complained that Washington was shipping them some weapon or bit of gear unsuited to the jungle, Doty was a more effective interlocutor than any of the FI officers had been. He got additional contra camps set up, he got training programs running. From semi-anarchy, he created semi-order.

At the same time, he operated by a military book so rigid that it seemed like dementia. He had a manual with resupply timetables—it specified, for instance, that a soldier ought to need new boots every six months—and its word was law. Once, when a CIA officer on temporary duty from Washington told Doty that a particular unit couldn't go back inside Nicaragua until it got new boots, Doty exploded. "That's bullshit!" he roared. "I gave them a thousand boots two months ago." The visiting García, perplexed, took a helicopter out to the contras' Nicarao base to see the unit for himself. "Ray, they're holding the soles onto those boots with twine and rawhide," he reported back a few hours later. Doty, grudgingly, coughed up some more.

One reason Doty was so unyielding was that he rarely visited the camps himself to actually see what was going on. The first thing he did when he arrived in Honduras was abandon the clandestine office Joe had set up on the Special Forces base and open a new headquarters right in the heart of one of Tegucigalpa's plush hillside neighborhoods. He arrived every morning at 4:30 A.M., barking for coffee, and conducted nearly all his business there. He didn't like the border camps, where he had to communicate in his pidgin Spanish—and where, worse yet, he had to travel in a helicopter. During those long years in Laos, Doty survived more than enough crash landings, thank you, and he wasn't nostalgic about it. If there was a cloud in the sky, he wouldn't fly.

Doty seemed to have little regard for Nicaraguans. Whenever one of his resupply timetables went wrong, whenever a unit ran out of ammo or food before the manual said it should, Doty believed that the fault must lie with the

117

contras, that they must be selling their supplies on the black market or running a scam. If a single pair of military boots turned up on the feet of a civilian in a village outside a contra camp, Doty would cut off boots to the entire camp. At one point in 1983, he was withholding ammunition from so many units that new trainees only got to fire eight rounds of ammunition on the practice range before going into combat.

Curiously, Doty got along much better with the Honduran and Argentine military men who were involved in the contra program. He met with them once a week or so in the Tegucigalpa safe house where the contra political directors lived. Mostly the meetings were administrative: the contras would ask for Honduran trucks to move men from one camp to another, or the Hondurans might complain that some contras had gotten drunk and rowdy in a Honduran border town and ask Bermúdez to put a lid on it.

But there was also some talk of military strategy at the meetings. The Hondurans and the Argentines, who had no experience at guerrilla warfare, constantly urged the contras to mass large forces and attack towns and major military bases. Doty, who supposedly knew guerrilla warfare inside out from his experience in Laos, did not contradict them.

Seizing a town had some propaganda value. But the objectives of such an attack had to be limited; it was one thing to take a town for a few hours for show, quite another to hold it against a massive Sandinista counterattack. And any attack that required more than a single contra task force was probably doomed; they simply weren't experienced enough yet to stage coordinated assaults. Yet that was exactly what the Hondurans and Argentines were telling them to do.

The contras, new to guerrilla warfare, were still feeling their way. Rejecting advice from their allies, their only source of beans and bullets, was difficult. So, with increasing frequency, they went head to head with the Sandinista army, a fight they could not possibly win.

Every new report of a set-piece battle, however, brought more consternation at Langley. The loudest complaints came from officials on the Special Activities Staff, the division of the Agency's operations directorate that specialized in paramilitary projects. Doty was their man, but the Special Activities people couldn't understand what he was doing down there. This was no way to fight a guerrilla war. Clarridge defended Doty's dedication and drive, but on the subject of tactics he was silent. Finally one day, late in 1983, he capitulated: "Let's send Adkins down there."

Jim Adkins, a former West Virginia cop starting his seventeenth year with the CIA, was the oddest of Agency ducks. He started as a paramilitary specialist working on an annual contract, but then moved over and became a full-fledged FI officer. And he had Latin American experience, too; he had been the CIA station chief in Bolivia (and, before that, Guyana, where he was the first person at the U.S. embassy to discover the Jonestown massacre).[3]

Like Doty, Adkins had been part of the secret American war in Laos. For three years he lived in a hooch a grenade's throw from the North Vietnamese border. For months at a time, he saw no one but the primitive Hmong tribesmen that he was supposed to mold into a modern army that could harass the North Vietnamese troops, tie down as many as possible so they couldn't go south and kill Americans. He was so good at it that he won a commendation, which, like all CIA awards, was immediately locked in a safe at Langley.

Adkins's unique blend of experience—paramilitary and FI, Laos and Latin America—made him an obvious choice to work with the contras. In fact, Clarridge had been trying to shanghai him into the program ever since Adkins returned from his tour of duty in Bolivia in May 1983. But their first conversation hadn't gone well. Before Clarridge could even explain what he wanted, Adkins was shouting at him. "You asshole, you've ruined my good name around here!" he yelled. "You didn't back me up worth a shit in Bolivia!"

This was an argument that had raged in the cable traffic between Langley and La Paz for more than six months. Clarridge had sent one of his young protégés, an officer named Bill Bosch, to Bolivia to try to subvert Soviet and Cuban diplomats. Adkins, within weeks, was trying to get rid of Bosch. The young officer, Adkins said, was a petty thief, he was conducting adulterous liaisons with foreigners in the CIA's secret safehouses, and he was such a crummy spy that the Soviets and Cubans were getting more information from him than the United States was.

Clarridge hadn't taken kindly to these attacks on his man. The real trouble, he retorted, was that Adkins didn't know how to work with young officers. In essence Clarridge was saying Adkins was a lousy station chief. Those would have been fighting words even if they had been confined to the cable traffic. But Clarridge repeated them, often, around the halls at Langley. A man's career could get destroyed that way, and Adkins had been seething for months.[4] When he finally had the opportunity to talk to Clarridge face-to-face, he unloaded.

Clarridge didn't back down, but he was uncharacteristically restrained in the face of the colorful insults Adkins hurled at him. When the volume subsided a bit, Clarridge spoke soothingly. "Look," he said, "I want to offer you a job."

"What are you talking about?" Adkins asked suspiciously.

"I'd like for you to go down to Central America and take our base in Honduras over," Clarridge said. "I want you to work with the contras."

"You've got to be fucking kidding," Adkins shot back. "Whoever takes that job is going to be screwed. Congress hates that program, and one of these days they're going to turn on it. You guys in headquarters will protect yourselves, and the guy in the field will be screwed." He walked out of Clarridge's office.

For months Clarridge kept up the pressure, but Adkins ignored it. His wife had just had a baby, and he had a new house out in the Virginia suburbs. He had been overseas for nearly all his sixteen years in the CIA, and he thought it was time to come home—particularly if the alternative was working with a guerrilla army that the U.S. government, sooner or later, would cast aside like an old toy. Instead, he took an opening in the CIA's paramilitary personnel office.

In late 1983, however, Clarridge tried again. This time he had Rudy Enders, the chief of all CIA paramilitary operations, ask Adkins to take the job.[5] When Adkins refused, Enders went to his fallback position: How about two months of temporary duty in Honduras, coaching the contras on infiltration and military tactics, with the title of "senior adviser"? Reluctantly, Adkins accepted.

When he arrived in Tegucigalpa in February 1984, Adkins couldn't decide

119

which was more appalling, the contras' military tactics or the CIA station's attitude. Doty, it seemed, was no more interested in taking advice from another American than he was from a Nicaraguan; this program was strictly a one-man show. For the first several days, he wouldn't even see Adkins. Don Winters, the station chief, did agree to a meeting—so he could tell Adkins to butt out. "I just want to get one thing straight," Winters instructed him. "There's only one senior adviser to the contras, and that's Ray Doty."

The contras were no happier to see Adkins than the CIA station was. Enrique Bermúdez listened politely, but it was obvious that he considered Adkins one more burden to bear, one more obnoxious gringo to humor. It didn't help that Adkins's message was so implicitly critical. He tried to phrase it as politely and as positively as he could, but the fact was that Adkins had found the state of contra military thinking to be even more primitive than headquarters imagined.

Most of the task forces simply wandered across the border, flung themselves in a frontal assault at the first town they ran into, and then rushed back to Honduras. Because the contra attacks were so unimaginative, and because they rarely got more than a few miles inside Nicaragua, the Sandinistas had been able to deploy twenty thousand troops along the high ground on the border. They were so tightly arrayed that in recent months the contras had difficulty even infiltrating.

Adkins began to seek out individual task force commanders. "Look, if you mass your forces, the Sandinistas are going to beat the shit out of you," he counseled them. "They've got artillery, they've got air support. You've got to break down into smaller groups and then hit them in ambushes." And, he added, it would be easier for the contras to live off the land if they traveled in smaller groups. A campesino village might be able to spare beans and rice for fifteen or twenty men, but not for two hundred. Some commanders were receptive; others were full of excuses.

After a couple of weeks, Adkins wrote a long cable to Langley with his assessment of contra strengths and weaknesses. On the plus side, he told headquarters, there was no shortage of men ready and willing to go inside Nicaragua and fight. Bermúdez might have inflated estimates of his manpower, but not by much. The contras were growing into a huge army.

On the downside were the reliance on large units, the difficulty in infiltration, and the abysmal security surrounding contra communications. The CIA had given them thousands of one-time code pads—simple ciphers that are used for a single day then discarded. Though each cipher is comparatively easy to break, by the time the enemy does it, the code has been abandoned. But, Adkins had discovered, the contras were reusing the pads ten or fifteen times apiece, and the Sandinistas were surely able to decipher the messages after two or three usages. "We're just trying to save paper," one of the commanders explained. "Fuck the paper!" Adkins screamed, the first time he had really lost his temper. "Those things are twenty-five cents apiece."

In his cable, Adkins told headquarters the contras would never learn to use the code pads properly; they needed new radios with voice scramblers instead. And he outlined a new infiltration plan he wanted to implement. After crossing the border into Nicaragua, instead of heading south or west—the ultimate theaters of operation—contra units would go east, into the empty jungles of Zelaya Department. Then they would circle back around to the west, get behind the Sandinista units massed along the border, and hit them from the rear. That would pull the Sandinistas off the border and make it easier for the next unit to infiltrate.

The cable, however, didn't leave Honduras. Every cable had to be okayed by either Winters or Doty, and they vetoed it. Adkins shrugged and waited. Sure enough, a searing rocket from Langley arrived forty-eight hours later: Where's Adkins? Why haven't we heard from him? What's his evaluation of contra military strategy? Reluctantly, Doty pulled Adkins's cable out of a drawer and sent it along. After that, Doty and Winters were more helpful to Adkins. His infiltration plan was implemented, and the contra traffic jam along the border eased as units moved deep inside. In April, Adkins returned to Langley, mission accomplished, happy to be gone from what he still saw as a doomed program.

But Doty and Winters continued to freeze out another officer who had been sent from headquarters to help the contras set up supply lines inside Nicaragua. The supply expert whiled away his two months in Honduras on a road-building project, driving a bulldozer.

Adkins had certainly been right about one thing: Bermúdez didn't trust him. By 1984, the contra commander's relations with the CIA were frosty. It seemed to Bermúdez that the contras were absorbing a lot more punishment from their putative amigos at Langley than from their sworn enemies in Managua.

From the beginning, the contras had been ambivalent about the CIA connection. Like nearly everyone else in Latin America, they had a highly exaggerated view of the Agency's capabilities. Latins, both friend and foe, believe firmly in a CIA that can decide to topple a government at breakfast and be gnawing its grisly bones by lunch. Confronted with the possibility of forming an alliance with this American juggernaut, the contras were excited but also leery. How could you be sure that the beast, in a hungry moment, wouldn't gnaw *your* bones?

In more than two years of working with the CIA, Bermúdez had learned that treachery was not the only thing to fear from the Agency. The CIA was certainly capable of double-dealing—the Banco Grande Rebellion incited by Doty had illustrated that—but more often it was arrogance rather than malice that led the Agency into trouble.

The greatest arrogance of all came at the very beginning, when the Agency sold its involvement with the contras as an effort to stop the weapons flow to El Salvador. In September 1983, with that thin cover falling apart, the CIA told Bermúdez he had to assuage congressional egos with some attacks on the Cosigüina Peninsula, a rectangular chunk of Chinandega Department that bulges into the Gulf of Fonseca. The tip of the peninsula, barely twenty miles from El Salvador, was the center of the FSLN's seaborne arms smuggling.

Fifteen commandos infiltrated Nicaragua by land for the first attack, slipping between Sandinista units and making their way to the Pacific Coast. On September 14, they took canoes to La Pelota, an island at the mouth of the

Padre Ramos Estuary at the base of the Cosigüina Peninsula. The contras blew up an empty arms warehouse and three of the fourteen boats that ran guns from the island.

Similar forays continued for the next four months, but blowing up a few canoes and huts didn't stop the arms traffic. Meanwhile, the raids diverted the FDN's attention and resources from the real war. Some attacks were quite ambitious, including an air raid on Radio Venceremos—the Salvadoran guerrillas' clandestine station, disguised as an "agricultural station" improbably located atop a dormant volcano on the Cosigüina Peninsula. "You'd think we were planning to invade Nicaragua, the amount of time we're putting into this thing," one disgusted CIA officer remarked to another as the date of the air raid approached. Five small contra planes mounted with rocket pods attacked the heavily fortified station from different directions, but some arrived late and were driven off by antiaircraft fire. The planes destroyed a few buildings but didn't manage to knock the station off the air.

The only target that might have put a serious crimp in the arms flow—the major weapons depot and smuggling fleet at the port of Potosí, just a few miles from the tip of the Cosigüina Peninsula—was also the most heavily guarded. Several times small groups of contras landed on the beach near Potosí, only to be fought off by the Sandinista garrison. The last time it happened, on January 4, 1984, the contras were caught in a vise. A crossfire, from the garrison on one side and a Sandinista patrol boat on the other, threatened to cut them to pieces. Two helicopters, one piloted by CIA contract agents and another by contras, had to come to the rescue, along with an Agency speedboat. The CIA chopper, since it was in the neighborhood, blasted a couple of warehouses on the ground to bits.

The helicopter attack prompted a bitter protest from the Sandinistas to the Honduran government. The Hondurans, sensitive about their international image, were already concerned about contra operations along the western part of their border with Nicaragua. Farther east the countryside was so rugged, mountainous, and isolated that the contra presence was difficult to prove. The populous western plains, however, were another matter. Anyone taking a casual Sunday drive through the southwestern town of Choluteca could see contras moving around in pickup trucks, rifles strapped to their backs.

The nervous Hondurans had already forced the contras to close one of their three western bases. Now they were even more dismayed; the attacks on the Cosigüina Peninsula might bring not just international embarrassment, but also financial catastrophe. If the Gulf of Fonseca became a war zone, it would destroy the fishing industry and interfere with commercial shipping.

If General Alvarez, the contras' patron saint, were still in command of the Honduran armed forces, perhaps the consequences would not have been so severe. But Alvarez was gone, deposed by Gen. Walter López, the head of the air force. Unlike Alvarez, López did not regard the contras as his country's first line of defense against the communist regime across the border. The Americans, he was certain, would never permit open Sandinista aggression against Honduras. López tolerated the contras only because he could use them to extract more aid from the United States; certainly he wasn't going to let them jeopardize the

Honduran economy. López immediately seized all the contras' boats and diving equipment and closed both their bases near Choluteca. His actions also spooked the Salvadoran military into canceling plans for contra bases in El Salvador.

Bermúdez could only shake his head in disbelief. From the bases around Choluteca, the contras had a direct route down the Pacific Coast into Managua. The Sandinistas had to anchor thousands of troops there to block the way. Now the westernmost contra base was Nicarao, across from western Nueva Segovia Department. Closing the Choluteca bases enabled the Sandinistas to leave 240 miles of the border unprotected. Several FSLN battalions moved east, making contra infiltration and supply even more difficult. The meaningless attacks in Cosigüina ordered by the CIA had cost Bermúdez half his theater of operations.

The Cosigüina attacks were, it seemed to Bermúdez, part of a pattern: the CIA entangled the contras in some misconceived and ruinous operation, then the contras paid the political price. That was exactly what happened when Casey and Clarridge decided to bring the Sandinistas to their knees by cutting off Nicaragua's supply of oil. Every drop of it arrived through four ports: Corinto, Puerto Sandino, San Juan del Sur on the Pacific Coast, and El Bluff (near the city of Bluefields) on the Atlantic. If the ports could be put out of commission, the entire Nicaraguan economy—not to mention the Sandinista military machine—would grind to a halt.[6]

And Casey and Clarridge thought some abrupt action was needed; Congress was beginning to balk at spending tens of millions of dollars on a contra program that seemed pretty damned big for something that was merely supposed to be shooting up mule trains headed for El Salvador. In the fall of 1983, Congress appropriated only $24 million for the contras in the next fiscal year, half of what Casey asked for. If he could just show that the Sandinistas were truly on the ropes, Casey thought he could get more money.

In October 1983, the Garcías invited Bermúdez to go along on a two-pronged attack on the ports in Corinto and Puerto Sandino. The operations would be staged from a mother ship, a chartered oil-field service ship that could launch speedboats and helicopters. While the mother ship stayed well offshore, safely out of sight, the speedboats, armed with cannons and rocket launchers (most of them had been confiscated from drug smugglers; the CIA called them "Q-boats") would carry divers and explosives close to the coast. At Puerto Sandino, the objective was to blow up the underwater intake pipe of the oil storage tank; at Corinto, to destroy the only bridge connecting the mainland and the small island where the oil storage tanks were located.

Taking the top contra military officer on a potentially hazardous mission made no more sense than General Eisenhower storming ashore with the first wave at Normandy, but the Agency was trying to send Bermúdez a message: This is how a professional operation is done. And Bermúdez was anxious to go; he was too old and out of shape to hump around the mountains with his troops, but this was a way of taking part in the action.

Bermúdez thought the mission would last a couple of days. But once aboard the mother ship, they waited . . . and waited . . . and waited . . . for the weather and moon and tides to be exactly right. The American in charge of the operation—a former U.S. Air Force major with no naval experience—was strung way too tight; he paced the deck madly, barking orders right and left at men who seemed to be looking for a place to hide.

Finally, all the conditions were right. Shortly after sundown, the crew loaded into the Q-boat: a pilot, a mechanic, four divers—three Ecuadorans and a Costa Rican—and Bermúdez, the only Nicaraguan, manning the boat's 25mm chain gun, capable of drilling a round through five inches of steel.

About thirty seconds into the operation, everything began going wrong. The pilot turned west instead of east, heading for Hawaii. It was a full hour before he realized his mistake. Then, when the Q-boat reached the spot where the frogmen were supposed to dive, the chief diver decided to stay aboard to "coordinate" the mission, instead of swimming to the bridge as planned. The other three frogmen reluctantly plunged into the water. But when they came ashore near the bridge, one of them had lost his package of explosives. They decided to hide their equipment ashore, abandon the mission, and return to the ship—but on the way back one of the frogmen got lost. All night the Q-boat cruised along the beach, looking for him, until daylight forced it to return to the mother ship.

The lost diver, it turned out, had made it back to shore, where he knocked on the door of a fisherman's hut, still carrying his flippers and oxygen tank, and asked if he could spend the night. The next evening he showed up at a prearranged emergency rendezvous point and a helicopter brought him back to the ship.

The mission commander wanted to try again, but word came from a CIA source that the Sandinistas had discovered the equipment that the frogmen left ashore. Another attempt would be suicide. The hell with subtlety, the commander said. I've got a contingency plan for this. On October 11, the Q-boat went out again, but this time neither Bermúdez nor the divers were aboard. A mercenary veteran of the French Foreign Legion manned the chain gun, and the rest of the crew was armed with grenade launchers and machine guns. They planned to slip the boat into the narrow channel between the mainland and the island, travel past the oil tanks a mile or so to a dock where Sandinista patrol boats tied up, and sink them with the chain gun. Then, as the Q-boat left the channel, it would shoot up the oil tanks as well.

For the second time, the plan went awry. The Q-boat got into the channel undetected, but as it pulled parallel with the oil storage tanks, an unexpected shift in the current dragged the boat onto a hidden sand bar. The pilot revved the engine furiously, trying to get loose, and the noise attracted the attention of Sandinista soldiers onshore. For a moment the crew froze, but the Sandinistas thought the Q-boat was one of their craft. They had obviously been through this before: "Pull this way! This way!" they shouted in unison. Their advice worked, and the Q-boat yanked free.

There was no use trying to go farther into the channel, the pilot advised the crew. The charts weren't right; they would just get stuck again. So the Foreign Legionnaire wheeled his gun around, and as the Sandinista soldiers gawked, he pumped a shot straight into the oil tanks.

It was like, the crew said later, a vision of hell. One after another the five tanks exploded, the flames shooting hundreds of feet into the air like a giant funeral pyre. When they were all ablaze, the gunner destroyed a giant crane used in unloading freighters. Then he began hurling the high-explosive shells into anything else he could see, including a South Korean ship docked nearby.

The soldiers on shore, who only moments before had unwittingly helped their enemies off the sandbar, now ran screaming in all directions. Most of them didn't even think to fire at the Q-boat as its crew lobbed grenades into their midst. When the crew couldn't see anything more to shoot at, the Q-boat headed back out to sea, the flaming oil lighting its way. The fire raged all night, burning up 3.4 million gallons of fuel, and the Sandinistas had to evacuate twenty thousand residents from Corinto. A few days later, a CIA team on the ground took pictures; the damage stunned even Agency officials.

Three days after the Corinto raid, the Ecuadoran frogmen tried another foray, this time against the oil pipeline in Puerto Sandino. They were only slightly more successful. Instead of attaching the explosives to the steel pipe, which would have taken months to repair, the divers blew up the flexible hose at the tip. It took only a few weeks to replace the part.

Bermúdez returned to Honduras after ten days at sea, anything but impressed with CIA efficiency. The mission's management had been erratic, he felt, and the planning even worse. Why were the Garcías using pilots and divers from other countries, people who didn't know the Nicaraguan tides or coastline— and were incompetent and cowardly to boot? Plenty of Nicaraguans could have done those jobs much better. When Don Winters, the Tegucigalpa station chief, asked how the mission had gone, Bermúdez said just what he was thinking.

Winters passed those thoughts back to Langley. And that was how Bermúdez learned the CIA's cardinal rule of covert action: Come what may, little brown natives do not criticize big white chiefs in Washington. Or, as some Agency officers liked to say, "That shit flows one way, pardner." Rudy Enders, the CIA's top paramilitary man, went completely bonkers when he read the cable recounting Bermúdez's observations. He sent back a sizzling message to Winters: Bermúdez would *not* discuss CIA operations any further. Bermúdez would *not* question the Agency's professionalism again. Bermúdez *would* apologize.

While Enders disciplined the rebellious natives, Casey and Clarridge discussed the operations with congressional oversight committees. The CIA men were ecstatic; they had learned that the Sandinistas had to put $100,000 down on repairs. The congressmen were less thrilled. Every time they got a briefing like this, it was harder to pretend that the contras were only interdicting arms traffic to El Salvador. The congressmen would have been even more upset if they had known some of the CIA plans that weren't carried out. For nearly a year, the Agency had pondered taking an old freighter into the narrow channel at Corinto and blowing it up. The idea was abandoned only because no one could figure out how to evacuate the crew. And the contingency plan that *was* used in Corinto—sending the Q-boat into the channel to shoot up the oil tanks—was originally part of a plan for a full-scale invasion of Nicaragua. The invasion plan called for a three-pronged assault: the Q-boat would attack the oil tanks as a diversion, while several hundred troops landed on a nearby beach, and frogmen blew up the bridge to prevent Sandinista reinforcements from reaching the area.

125

The CIA officer who drew up the plan in August 1983 was never clear on what was supposed to happen after that. Were the troops supposed to advance inland, or just hold their beachhead until a larger force arrived, or evacuate by sea after scaring the hell out of the Sandinistas, or what? He didn't know; his assignment was simply to map out the initial assault. And someone was definitely anxious to see it: the officer was ordered, at 5:30 one afternoon, to have an invasion plan ready by 8:30 the next morning. A few days later, he was told without explanation that the operation was canceled. But at Langley, as at the Pentagon, no plan is ever thrown out. Instead, it's filed away, against the day when a timid Ecuadoran frogman or some other regrettable surprise requires a quick change of strategy.

The attacks on Corinto came within a hair's breadth of disaster. If the lost Ecuadoran diver had been captured, or if the grounded Q-boat had not gotten off the sandbar, the Sandinistas would have had prisoners who could tell the whole world about the Agency's still-secret involvement in the war. More cautious men might have taken the near misses at Corinto as an omen to step back, to continue slowly but surely turning up the pressure on the Sandinistas through the contras themselves.

Casey and Clarridge, however, still wanted to go for a home run. Clarridge took credit for their next scheme: They would mine Nicaragua's four major ports. After a few explosions, oil tankers would refuse to enter Nicaraguan waters, and even if they wanted to, their insurance rates would go sky-high.

Clarridge bragged that he got the idea from his Columbia graduate studies of the Russo-Japanese War of 1905; the Russian fleet was virtually destroyed by Japanese mines. Clarridge, however, must have slept through a few lectures— he didn't seem aware that the Russo-Japanese conflict was a formally declared war rather than a covert action. And if his studies had touched on the second half of the century, Clarridge might have learned of the congressional furor that resulted when the Nixon administration mined North Vietnamese ports during an undeclared war in 1972.[7]

When the mining was announced at a CIA staff meeting, the officers hooted in disbelief. "The general reaction was, what the *fuck* are we doing down there?" a CIA officer told me later. "Then there were a few people who said, I don't want to *know* what we're doing down there." Nobody could believe Congress would swallow this. But Casey and Clarridge were undeterred, even when they learned the mines would have to be specially manufactured.

The idea was that the mines would be "firecrackers" that made a lot of noise without doing too much damage. Since all the mines in the U.S. arsenal were designed to sink warships, new ones had to be built. They were manufactured in the United States, then armed with three hundred pounds of explosives (a firecracker, it seems, is in the eye of the beholder) in Honduras. Some of the mines were magnetic, detonated by the steel in a ship's hull; others were activated by the noise of passing engines. Q-boats, again operating from a distant mother ship, would place the mines.

The CIA informed Bermúdez about the mining before it started. But no one asked for his opinion, and after Rudy Enders's frenzy over his earlier criticism,

Bermúdez didn't volunteer his thoughts. Mining the ports wasn't a bad military strategy, from his perspective, but he wondered about the seeming contradiction. For months the CIA had complained that the contras were recruiting too many men, making it difficult to persuade Congress they were just interdicting arms shipments to El Salvador. Now the Agency itself was doing something that couldn't have the remotest connection to arms interdiction since the Sandinistas did not send arms to El Salvador from deepwater ports. But, Bermúdez figured, the CIA understood Congress better than he did.

The mining began around New Year's Day 1984 and continued through early April, anything but quietly. More than a dozen times, Sandinista patrol boats chased the Q-boats and fired on them. The Sandinista boats, however, usually came out second best. The Q-boats were more heavily armed, and on the rare occasions when they got into trouble, a CIA helicopter came swooping in from the mother ship and blasted the Sandinista craft. During two days of mine-laying at El Bluff, on the Atlantic Coast, the CIA sank two pesky patrol boats and seriously damaged two others. In between laying mines, Agency Q-boats found time to shoot up oil storage tanks at San Juan del Sur, with results nearly as spectacular as those at Corinto.

The Q-boats placed about seventy-five mines in all. Dutch, Panamanian, Liberian, Japanese, and Soviet ships struck them, without incurring serious damage; several Nicaraguan fishing boats hit them and sank. But the strategy failed; oil kept flowing into Nicaragua. Mexico and Venezuela used the mining as an excuse to cut off their oil shipments (the Sandinistas owed the two countries hundreds of millions of dollars and obviously had no intention of paying the debt), but the Soviet Union quickly filled the void. And other shipping continued unabated. Clarridge, in staff meetings at Langley, worked himself into smoking rages over the stupidity of the international shipping industry. Didn't these idiots know that Nicaraguan harbors were full of *high explosives?* What could they be thinking of?

The mining came to an abrupt and bizarre halt in mid-April. On the evening of April 5, Senator Barry Goldwater, the Republican chairman of the Senate intelligence committee, was at his desk on the Senate floor when he was handed a classified memo prepared by the committee staff describing the mining. Goldwater abruptly took the floor and slurringly began reading the memo aloud until a staffer wrestled it away. But Goldwater continued to fume; four days later he wrote a letter to Casey: "I am pissed off. . . . This is an act violating international law. It is an act of war. For the life of me, I don't see how we are going to explain it."[8] Then he leaked copies to the capital press corps.

Goldwater's pyrotechnics set off a devastating chain reaction. The Senate and House both passed harsh condemnations of the mining. The Sandinistas filed suit against the United States in the World Court, and although the U.S. government was on sound legal ground in refusing to recognize the court's jurisdiction, it was a fearful propaganda black eye.[9] Worst of all, the mining solidified congressional resistance to aid for the contras. A Reagan administration request for $21 million in supplemental aid was turned down, and it was obvious that there would be no money in the regular October appropriations bill either.

It would be thirty-two months before official U.S. military aid began flowing to the contras again; meanwhile, Reagan administration officials went scurrying through back channels, trying to line up donations from private individuals and other governments. Eventually a National Security Council staffer named Oliver North would devise a clever way to extract money for the contras from the radical Iranian regime of the Ayatollah Khomeini in a ruse that would hopelessly cripple the Reagan presidency.

This whole line of tumbling dominoes proceeded directly from the CIA's mining, which surely makes it one of the most catastrophic covert actions in the history of U.S. intelligence. But the blame doesn't all belong at Langley. How could Casey and Clarridge have foreseen the wildly disproportionate and largely dishonest reaction from Congress? The CIA claimed to have briefed congressional intelligence committees and their staffs eleven times on the mining before Goldwater's tirade on the Senate floor. Hearing transcripts verify at least three of the briefings: to the House committee on January 31, 1984, and to the Senate committee on March 8 and 13. At least two senators who did not attend the committee sessions—Democrat Patrick Leahy of Vermont and Republican Claiborne Pell of Rhode Island, both opponents of Reagan administration policy in Central America—got private briefings from the CIA on the mining.[10] Some senators later claimed that the briefings were ambiguous about who was actually laying the mines. But did any of them really think that a Nicaraguan peasant army had its own mother ships, speedboats, and mine factories?

And when Barry Goldwater said mining harbors was an act of war—well, what did he think arming six thousand peasants with automatic rifles was? It struck a number of CIA officials as profoundly hypocritical that so many congressmen were perfectly willing to send peasants to kill one another in a guerrilla war that inevitably took a heavy toll of civilians, but professed horror and outrage when a few ships were damaged. It was Goldwater who most puzzled everyone at Langley. He had always supported both the contras and the CIA. (In the mid-1970s, when he was a member of the Senate committee that investigated CIA abuses, Goldwater had even refused to sign the report.) What could have caused this bizarre outburst? Simple, Casey told his staff: Goldwater was drunk the evening he began reading the classified memo to the Senate. And, having made a fool of himself, he couldn't back down. Casey thought there was no use in forcing a public confrontation with Goldwater, who was, after all, a friend to the CIA. And, he told the staff, Goldwater had already sent a sort of apology. It wasn't widely noted, but when the Senate cast ballots on a resolution condemning the mining, Goldwater voted against it.

That placated some of the aggrieved spooks. But it angered Bermúdez. The gringos in Washington whooped and hollered at each other like a pack of wild Indians, but the only scalps taken, Bermúdez noted, were Nicaraguan. The mining had been a CIA operation, start to finish, but none of the congressmen suggested firing anyone at the Agency or cutting its budget. Instead, they took it out on the contras.

* * *

On October 12, 1984, a congressional ban on CIA involvement with the contras went into effect. (This was the most famous of the so-called Boland Amendments, five restrictions attached to U.S. appropriations bills between 1982 and 1986 that restricted American aid to the contras. They were authored by Edward Boland, a Democratic congressman from Massachusetts who chaired the House Intelligence Committee.) But as the fifty Garcías attached to the program packed up their gear, they left behind one last public relations time bomb ticking away.

The seeds of this final fiasco were planted in June 1983, when Casey himself paid a secret visit to the CIA safe house in Honduras for a detailed briefing on the war. He was impressed with the military operation, so much so that he put in the paperwork for a medal for Ray Doty. But Casey thought more attention should be paid to the political context of the war. Somebody needed to instruct the contras on winning hearts and minds, not just ambushes. Of course, if all the contras were doing was interdicting arms shipments to El Salvador, there was no need for them to establish a political context, but Casey brushed that contradiction aside. Let's get a psychological operations expert in here, he directed, who can put together a training manual.

In a couple of weeks, a quirky, professorial-looking CIA contract employee floated into Tegucigalpa to write the manual. To the CIA station, he was known by his code name, Blackjack; to the contras, he introduced himself as John Kirkpatrick. Fiercely anticommunist, Kirkpatrick had a distinguished career; he was a former Special Forces major who had served in the wars in Korea and Southeast Asia. After the My Lai massacre, the Army chose Kirkpatrick to teach a course on the law of war at West Point, in hopes he could help avert another such ghastly mess. By now, though, the gaunt and ruddy-faced Kirkpatrick was in his fifties. And he was, well, odd. "He was too Irish to be American, if you know what I mean," one of the contras said later.

Kirkpatrick, every day, dressed head-to-toe in black. He was in the bars most nights until closing, and after a few drinks, he often began weeping. He called himself, in sonorous tones, The Priest of Death. The contras, behind his back, referred to him more prosaically as The Umpire and wondered if he wore black underwear, too.

After a couple of months, Kirkpatrick, working mostly from old U.S. Army training manuals, had stitched together an eighty-six-page psy-ops handbook for the contras.[11] Edgar Chamorro, the contra director in charge of propaganda, had it translated into Spanish and printed several thousand copies. But when he showed it to some of the other directors, they complained. One paragraph talked about provoking confrontations with the Sandinistas in order to "cause the death of one or more persons, who would become the martyrs" of the movement. Another suggested that "professional criminals" be hired to "carry out specific selective 'jobs.'" And the manual used the word "neutralize" in connection with removing Sandinista officials.

"Edgar," Adolfo Calero admonished, " 'neutralize' sounds real bad, even if you don't mean it that way." Calero told him to remove eight pages of the manual with razor blades and substitute new, rewritten material. Edgar had

129

four new pages typeset, deleting the suggestions about using criminals and creating martyrs. But, unimpressed with Calero's argument about the word "neutralize," he let it go.[12]

As a couple of young contras sat around the directorate's safe house, slicing out the pages with razor blades, John Kirkpatrick burst in. "You son of a bitch!" he roared at Edgar, "I want to talk to you!" At first, Edgar thought he was dealing with the worst case of writer's ego in the history of publishing. But as Kirkpatrick continued bellowing, it became apparent that he was angry over an insult to a young contra friend of his. "Come in the other room with me!" he shouted. His face flaming red, Kirkpatrick finally looked like a real Priest of Death.

Edgar, on the other hand, turned pale. "This animal is going to beat me," he whispered to Frank Arana, the contra propagandist. As they walked into the other room, Arana followed them. When Kirkpatrick turned around, he saw Arana switching on a tape recorder. "So that's the game," he snapped and walked back out of the office. When news of the scene reached the U.S. embassy, Kirkpatrick was whisked out of the country. None of the contras ever saw him again.

His legacy, however, proved harder to banish. The jargon-choked manual turned out to be almost completely useless. Most of the contras couldn't read at all, and only a handful could pick their way through Kirkpatrick's tangled thickets of verbiage. Stacks of the expurgated manuals sat in the FDN's Tegucigalpa offices, available to anyone who asked. Several journalists picked up copies and found it unexceptional.

But in mid-October 1984, with less than a month to go before the presidential election, someone leaked a copy of the original manual, with the language about criminals and martyrs intact, to an Associated Press reporter in Washington. On October 14, the AP ran a story on the manual that focused on the paragraph about "creating a martyr" without noting that it had been deleted before the manual was distributed.[13] Headline writers immediately dubbed the handbook "the CIA murder manual," and soon it became common wisdom that the Agency was back in the assassination business. And in this scenario, the contras were the moral and political equivalents of the Mafia buttonmen that the CIA hired to kill Fidel Castro two decades before. Once again, Casey was dragged up to Capitol Hill to explain himself. And once again, a bastard CIA project had landed the contras in hot water.

Of all the infamies heaped on the Agency in 1984, the "murder manual" controversy was the most contrived. First, U.S. Army manuals had been advocating much worse things for decades without so much as a whimper of congressional disapproval.[14] Second, nearly all the offensive material was edited out of the manual before it was distributed. All the complaints revolved around a single sentence: "It is possible to neutralize carefully selected and planned targets, such as court judges, justices of the peace, police and State Security officials, CDS [Sandinista vigilance groups] chiefs, etc."[15]

To an American public whose knowledge of the intelligence business came mostly from cynical Hollywood spies who speak in elliptical euphemisms, it was easy to decipher what the term "neutralize" meant: Kill. Murder. Assassinate. Knock off. In the real world, though, spies use dictionaries just like the rest of us, and the best definition of *neutralize* comes right out of *Webster's:* to make ineffective, to counterbalance. It means the same in Spanish. Neutralizing an enemy official can take many forms—friendly persuasion, bribery, physical restraint, blackmail. Assassination is included, but it's at the far end of the spectrum. Almost every how-to book on insurgency and guerrilla warfare makes use of the term. Humberto Ortega, in his guerrilla days, wrote an instructional tract for Sandinista cadres that included the exhortation to "go neutralizing the informants, enemies of the revolution."[16]

Just which definition did John Kirkpatrick have in mind? The evidence is ambiguous. The sentence about neutralizing Sandinista officials was in a section labeled "Selective Use of Violence for Propagandistic Effects," which seems to imply the worst. But elsewhere the manual suggests that the contras set up public tribunals where they can "shame, ridicule and humiliate the 'personal symbols' of the government of repression in the presence of the people." And, it adds, "the 'enemies of the people,' the officials or Sandinista agents, must not be mistreated in spite of their criminal acts."

Kirkpatrick can be faulted for writing on such a sensitive subject with a lack of clarity, particularly for a reading audience of unsophisticated peasant soldiers. But it is fairly obvious that he was not trying to feed contra bloodlust. Most of the rest of the manual was plainly aimed at making the contras more sensitive to the importance of human rights, making them pay more attention to the way they treated civilians. It acknowledged the obvious: "A guerrilla armed force always involves implicit terror because the population, without saying it aloud, feels terror that the weapons may be used against them." Then it added a warning: "The guerrillas should be careful not to become an explicit terror, because this would result in a loss of popular support. . . . The guerrillas should be persuasive through the word and not dictatorial with weapons."

The actual content of the manual, however, couldn't compete for congressional attention with alliterative headlines. Casey was forced to hand out written rebukes to five officers. The highest-ranking was Vincent Cannistraro, head of the Central American Task Force. Joe Fernández, chief of the task force's propaganda operations, was reprimanded, along with his deputy, a junior officer.[17] Don Winters, the Tegucigalpa station chief, got a reprimand, and so did the officer who was Kirkpatrick's handler.

Two other obvious candidates for censure, Clarridge and Doty, went untouched. Clarridge pled ignorance: he couldn't read Spanish. Doty, who could, skated free on the direct orders of Casey. That award Casey had suggested for Doty—the Distinguished Intelligence Medal, the CIA's highest—had finally come through just a few weeks earlier. It would have been difficult to explain reprimanding and decorating him for the very same actions. Anyway, the reprimands were pro forma. Winters was sent on to Panama, one of the Agency's most important stations; Cannistraro got a top position at the National Security Council; Fernández was named station chief in Costa Rica. Kirkpatrick himself was tenderly eased out of his CIA contract, but the Agency immediately got him another with the NSC.

For the contras, the casualties were more serious. Edgar Chamorro's relationship with the other contras had been deteriorating for a long time. Part of it was jealousy; a year earlier, the FDN directors had voted Adolfo Calero their president. "That's ridiculous," Edgar complained. "I'm the grandson of a president. I'm from the oldest political family in Nicaragua." Hostility between the two men grew steadily.

Edgar's other problem was only indirectly with the other contras. All the contra leaders worried that their movement might be, as they put it, Bay of Pigged: abandoned by the Americans. But for Edgar, it was an obsession. He bought dozens of copies of Peter Wyden's book *Bay of Pigs* and handed them out like party favors, always adding: "We can't let this happen to us."

Edgar's solution was for the contras to operate as publicly as possible. The less secret the program, he reasoned, the more difficult it would be for the gringos to walk away. Many other FDN officials didn't trust journalists and avoided them, but Edgar could be found at almost any hour of the day or night schmoozing at the Hotel Honduras Maya in Tegucigalpa where all the reporters stayed. Every story that was written, he felt, raised the public relations price the Americans would pay if they tried to sacrifice the contras in a backroom political deal.

His strategy worked; by 1984, the contras were the worst-kept secret in CIA history. But the Honduran military authorities detested Edgar. Every time they held a press conference to deny that the contras were in Honduras, the newspapers quoted "a high-ranking contra official" saying they were lying. The Hondurans knew exactly who that official was. When the CIA couldn't make him stop, the Hondurans took action themselves. In September, while Edgar was visiting Miami, General López informed the other directors that he would not be allowed to return to Honduras.

The Honduran ban was probably temporary, but a few weeks later news of the training manual broke. Calero and the other FDN directors were certain Edgar had leaked it. Who else would have had a copy of the unexpurgated manual? They expelled him from the directorate. Edgar, wounded, called them CIA puppets. The other directors began spreading stories that he was a homosexual, a child abuser, even a Sandinista mole. The State Department tried to deport him.

Looking for shelter, Edgar found it on the American Left, always eager for new ammunition to use against the contras. He wound up on the payroll of the Institute for Media Analysis, an outfit run by Ellen Ray and William Schaap, the publishers of *CovertAction Information Bulletin,* the journal in which CIA renegade Philip Agee unmasks Agency officers. Edgar's speeches and articles grew more and more distorted: The contras were mercenary butchers, their leaders so many CIA-trained dancing bears. Every quarrel in the history of the FDN was reduced to a contest between American-backed Somocista puppets on one hand and progressive Nicaraguan nationalists on the other. Edgar even testified for the Sandinistas in the World Court case.

In March 1990, when I met Edgar for an interview at a hotel on Key Biscayne, I gently suggested that some of the things he had written twisted the truth. He didn't disagree. "I was all alone when I left the contras, and the Left helped me out," Edgar explained haltingly. He looked sad, and lost.

* * *

When the Garcías pulled out of the contra camps in October 1984, most of the contras were sorry to see them go. It was true that the gringos butted in too much and had a lot of arrestingly stupid ideas. But they hated communists, which was good. And they were a visible symbol of U.S. support. Guerrilla warfare is a lonely affair, and it is comforting to know that someone is on your side, especially when that someone is the most powerful country on earth.

And the García family had been a source not only of inspiration but amusement. What the contras really loved was the way the CIA would lay all this superconspiratorial groundwork and then commit some egregious security blunder that ruined it all.

For instance, there was Chicano Cardenal's furtive Agency contact in Honduras, a slippery García who called himself John Perham. For their first meeting, Cardenal had to take the stairs—not the elevator—to room 303 at the La Ronda Hotel, knock on the door at exactly 7 P.M. and say "I have arrived early." The countersign was "No, you have arrived exactly on time," although Cardenal had no idea what he would do if it wasn't given.

Fortunately, he didn't have to come up with an alternative plan; the meeting came off as scheduled. But Perham insisted that he couldn't be seen by any other contras. If Cardenal was driving around town with Mariano Mendoza, one of the other FDN directors, when Perham summoned him to a meeting, then Mendoza would have to wait in the car or at a nearby restaurant. That rule absolutely could not be broken, Perham lectured Cardenal sternly, or their relationship was over. And Cardenal faithfully observed the edict for six months. Then Perham locked his keys inside his car, and had to flag Cardenal down for a ride. "Hi," he greeted Mendoza, sitting in the front seat. "I'm John Perham."

As sorry as the contras were to lose them, the Garcías were even sorrier to be going. They believed in the war, of course, but it hadn't hurt that helping the contras was a lucrative pastime. With the hazardous duty pay that accompanied the project, many of the paramilitary specialists were making $70,000 to $75,000 a year. CIA contract employees were doing even better. On top of their salaries, they got $105 a day in living expenses. But since they could live for free in the contra camps, some were clearing $3,000 a month in unused expense money alone.

Much more important than the money, for most Garcías, was the opportunity. The paramilitary specialists were mostly former Green Berets too young to have served in Vietnam, an everlasting source of lamentation for them. They were all walking booby traps: no actual combat experience, but lots of sexy training that filled their heads with crackpot schemes they were anxious to try out. They were constantly proposing loony-tune air raids or naval missions that the few veteran Garcías had to veto (though, in fairness, a lot of their ideas were only slightly nuttier than things Casey and Clarridge actually tried). A few of their plans, however, slipped though.

One day in 1983, a truck full of Garcías pulled into the FDN's Nicarao base and began unloading hundreds of big yellow balloons. As fascinated contras crowded around, the CIA men inflated each balloon, attached a small metal box to it, and launched it into the air. As the balloons lazily drifted toward Nicaragua, a García explained the plan. The boxes contained small explosive charges and contra leaflets. The charges were set to explode after the balloons had time to float a couple of hundred miles inside Nicaragua, scattering the propaganda leaflets deep inside the country. The Sandinistas would freak out.

"What happens," one contra asked his commander as they watched the last balloon bob away, "if a storm comes and the wind changes direction?" The commander replied that he was no balloon expert, but that the gringos undoubtedly considered that possibility. Well, not exactly. For the next ten days the U.S. embassy spent its time fielding phone calls from Belize and Guatemala, where contra pamphlets were suddenly raining down out of clear azure skies.

The younger officers, though, had no monopoly on dumb mistakes. Sometimes every García in the county seemed to have some weird brain disease. That was the conclusion of a CIA officer from Washington who was assigned temporary duty in Tegucigalpa in the early years of the war. He arrived on a Friday, and after several hours of briefings, a couple of other Garcías invited him out for a beer. "There's this really terrific bar down the street," one of the men explained. "You're not going to believe this place. It's full of beautiful women, really great looking, but there are never any men there except us." The visiting officer was pleased; what had looked like a grimy assignment in a drab backwater country was starting to sound good. With the other men, he bellied up to the bar and ordered a Port Royal beer, then turned around to check out the chicks. He promptly spit his beer on the floor. The women, every single one of them, were drag queens.

10 | The Last Hurrah of Commander Zero

Oh, was Edén Pastora preening! The reporters were waiting, and what a show he had for them! Sixty prisoners of war and a whole town captured! The new capital of Nicaragua Libre! Today he was Commander Zero again! But why was his older brother Felix taking him aside when there were cameras waiting? "Edén," Felix begged, "at least please rub some mud on your boots!" It wouldn't do for the reporters to guess that, while his troops were winning the battle of San Juan del Norte, Commander Zero had been sitting comfortably in his San José headquarters three hundred miles away.

San Juan del Norte was ARDE's single moment of military glory. Within days, the organization was spinning crazily toward its ignoble end.

Pastora first tried to take the town, a weatherbeaten little port at the southeastern tip of Nicaragua, in 1983. He laid siege to the town for five days in July before the Sandinistas drove him off. Ten months later, he tried again. In late March 1984, two hundred ARDE troops began slipping into a circle around the port. On April 12 they stormed the city, which was defended by about seventy Sandinista troops in a surprisingly fortified position. It took three days to overcome their resistance, plus the timely intervention of CIA speedboats armed with light artillery, which shelled the town—although more rounds fell among Pastora's own troops than within San Juan del Norte.

Those details notwithstanding, when the fighting ended ARDE held the town. The attack had been designed and executed by Tito Chamorro, but he knew better than to take any public credit. Pastora flew in on a helicopter from San José to strut before the cameras. That act of revolutionary polity wasn't enough to save Tito Chamorro from the catastrophic consequences of military success; a few days later, Pastora fired him.

To hold San Juan del Norte would have been a strategic triumph for Pastora. Although it was a good two weeks overland from the Rama Road, ARDE's strategic objective, the town had both port facilities and an airstrip capable of supporting a C-47. Pastora could have anchored his supply operation there and freed ARDE of the political vagaries of Costa Rica. But his plans were even grander: Pastora intended to christen San Juan del Norte the capital of Nicaragua Libre and ask the United States to recognize a provisional government. ARDE politicians were already squabbling over their posts in the new administration.

Those, of course, were the very same reasons the Sandinistas could not possibly allow him to hold the town. On April 17, five hundred Sandinista troops launched a coordinated assault, hitting San Juan del Norte by both sea and land. Dozens of contras were killed, and as the others fled they left behind encrypted CIA radio equipment. A few days later, the Sandinistas attacked Tango base, on ARDE's western flank; again the contras abandoned radio equipment as they retreated.

In the midst of the chaos, an ugly side of Pastora surfaced. Three times during the siege of San Juan del Norte and the long retreat, Pastora personally ordered an ARDE soldier named David Moreira to execute civilians—four people in all. Pastora's security chief, Miguel Urroz, ordered another eight executions that Moreira was certain were also okayed by Pastora. In each case, the pretext for the killings was that the civilians were FSLN sympathizers who would betray the contras to the Sandinista army. But Moreira doubted that, especially since one of the victims was his own brother-in-law, abducted from the Costa Rican village where he was living. All the "spies," Moreira noted, owned horses or cattle that Pastora and Urroz confiscated after the executions.[1]

When the disastrous chain of events that began in San Juan del Norte was finally over, Pastora was livid. It was the CIA's fault, he told his commanders. They promised me if we had the port, they would bring in enough ammo and supplies to defend it. Across San José, at the U.S. embassy, the same scene was going on in reverse. "The CIA people I talked to were tearing their hair out," Ambassador Curtin Winsor, Jr., would recall years later. "They knew he couldn't hold it." A meeting was arranged at Pastora's headquarters. It ended with him kicking four CIA officers out and banishing them from ARDE installations for good.

He kept in touch with the Americans, though. Winsor, who was fascinated by Pastora even though he was increasingly leery about whose side Commander Zero was really on, decided he wanted to meet this wild man whose misadventures seemed to occupy 90 percent of the embassy's time. Winsor threw all diplomatic caution and protocol out the window and invited Pastora to breakfast at the ambassador's official residence. When Pastora arrived, Winsor was amused to discover he was wearing a disguise—heavy black-rimmed glasses and a big hook nose, like a Groucho Marx Halloween mask. Pastora explained that he couldn't jeopardize his credibility by being seen with the U.S. ambassador.

Not all American officials, however, were as tickled by Pastora. Robert McFarlane, Reagan's new national security adviser, agreed to meet Pastora in Washington but insisted on absolute secrecy. Pastora's aides reminded their chief over and over again that the slightest leak would destroy any hope of a relationship with McFarlane. Pastora dutifully kept quiet until he arrived back in San José and ran into some reporters at the airport. Where have you been, *Comandante*? they asked. "Oh, I've been talking to this McDonald or whatever his name is," Pastora replied, "trying to get some cheese out of him." His aides could practically hear the White House doors slamming.

McFarlane had agreed to meet Pastora because the gringos, once again, were trying to coax the FDN and ARDE into a unity agreement. This time the idea was finding favor among other ARDE officials. Even Alfonso Robelo, the political chief, thought it made sense. But Pastora wouldn't come along, not unless he was made commander in chief of the whole organization. Given the military wreckage of the southern front, the CIA wouldn't entertain that idea for a minute.

So Pastora called a press conference for May 30, 1984, to announce that he was separating from ARDE. Because the Costa Rican government wouldn't permit the meeting in its territory, Pastora held it in one of his camps across the Río San Juan, just inside Nicaragua at a clutch of farm huts known as La Penca. (Typically, Pastora left his house in San José at 3 A.M. to arrive ahead of the reporters so he could pretend to them he had been there all along.) It was after dark when the twenty-one journalists arrived and climbed steps to the upper floor of the two-story wooden building where Pastora was waiting.

The journalists crowded around Pastora asking questions—all but one, a young man who called himself Per Anker Hansen and said he was a free-lance Danish photographer. Hansen had been trying to get an interview with Pastora for weeks, but now that he was here, he lost interest. He put down his metal camera case by the table where Pastora was standing and headed outside. He told ARDE soldiers he was "going to take a leak." Inside, a soldier bringing coffee to Pastora accidentally kicked over the suitcase, then leaned forward to hand him the cup. A moment later, an eerie blue light flashed through the room—no one recalls hearing the sound of the explosion, though it must have been fierce—and everyone was slipping around in pools of blood and severed limbs.

Pastora, with shrapnel in his legs and burns over much of his body, was whisked away in a motorized launch. The journalists stayed there for hours. Some of them didn't last that long; a Costa Rican television cameraman, who had inadvertently filmed his own murder, drowned in his own blood within minutes. Linda Frazier, a thirty-eight-year-old reporter for an English-language weekly in San José, lingered for hours, her legs blown off. For a long time, she whispered things to her friend Reid Miller of the Associated Press. But Miller couldn't hear a word. The explosion left him deaf.

In all, three journalists and five soldiers died. Pastora's injuries—the first combat wounds of his long career—kept him in and out of hospitals for several weeks, but were not serious. (Much of his convalescence was spent in a Caracas hospital, where a covey of Miss Venezuelas were on hand to cheer him up.) Pastora was glad he had shaved that morning, though, he told friends; if his long beard had caught fire, he would probably have died.

It was several days before the mysterious Per Anker Hansen's metal camera case was pinpointed as the origin of the explosion. By then he was long gone.

His photo agency turned out to be fictitious and his identity borrowed from a stolen passport. Police investigators learned that Hansen had been traveling around Latin America for four years; they found traces of him in Panama, Mexico, Honduras, and Peru. He had a female companion, also traveling with a stolen passport. She had visited Nicaragua and had a multiple-entry visa for that country.

Hansen's real identity has never been established. Neither has his employer. Conspiracy theories multiplied like shrapnel in the days after the bombing, but they all return to three sets of suspects: the CIA, the Sandinistas, or a rival contra group. There is no evidence at all that establishes a direct link to anyone. But circumstantial evidence seems to point to the Sandinistas, who routinely relied on political assassinations dating back to their guerrilla days. They were particularly obsessed with ARDE and Pastora; when Pastora made his 1982 speech breaking with the FSLN, Sandinista army chief of staff Joaquín Cuadra talked pointedly about "the long arm of revolutionary justice." And Sandinista television labeled Pastora "the Trotsky of our revolution," a chilling reference to the Bolshevik dissident who was exiled to Mexico and wound up with an ax buried in his head by Stalin's henchmen.[2]

The Sandinistas had already carried out several well-documented attempts to assassinate ARDE officials. In one of them, the FSLN exploited Pastora's infatuation with ex-Sandinistas. A Sandinista vice minister of commerce named Rodrigo Cuadra Clachar and a companion came to Costa Rica in June 1983, claiming to be defectors, and quickly won Pastora's trust. A few days later, on July 3, the two men were blown to bits on their way to see Pastora; a radio-controlled bomb in Cuadra Clachar's briefcase, which he apparently intended to leave in Pastora's headquarters, was accidentally detonated as they parked near the powerful radio transmitters at police headquarters. The La Penca bomber had also used a remote-control device triggered by radio waves.

Three months later, Gregorio Jiménez Morales, a member of the Basque terrorist group ETA, was arrested while drawing plans of Pastora's home. And in November 1984, another Sandinista who had infiltrated ARDE threw a grenade into Alfonso Robelo's car outside his San José home. Robelo wasn't touched; his fiancée spent six months in the hospital. There were also at least two Sandinista attempts on Robelo's life before he left Nicaragua. Finally, there is the fact that a Sandinista spy named Nancy, Pastora's mistress, abandoned her cover and returned to Managna two days before the La Penca bombing.

Conversely, circumstantial evidence seems to exonerate the CIA and rival contra groups. Certainly if either had wanted to kill Pastora, they wouldn't have needed to stalk him for weeks in the guise of a phony journalist. He could simply have been summoned to a meeting at a CIA safe house in San José and shot or drugged. Pastora himself, in the weeks after the bombing, blamed the Sandinistas. Only later, when the CIA cut him off, did he begin accusing the U.S. government.[3]

Nonetheless, the CIA theory has been a popular one with the American Left. The Christic Institute, a leftist "public interest" law firm, filed a $24 million lawsuit on behalf of Tony Avirgan, a free-lance television cameraman injured in the blast. The lawsuit said the La Penca bombing was the work of a vast twenty-year conspiracy of contras, Cuban-Americans, right-wing Libyans, National Security Council staffers, and current and former CIA officers. The suit was dismissed in June 1988; in February 1989, a federal judge ordered the Christic Institute to pay more than $1 million in legal costs to the defendants on the grounds that the suit was frivolous and without merit.

By the fall of 1984, the CIA, once so proud of recruiting Pastora, wanted nothing more to do with him. But the Agency hoped to preserve his army until a competent commander could take over. In the final week of September, a CIA officer called Popo Chamorro to ask for a meeting. Popo was properly impressed with the cloak-and-dagger arrangements; he would have to go to a roadside vegetable stand and wait for a car to pick him up.

Popo told Pastora about the call. Commander Zero paced the room furiously, hands clasped behind his back. "Why do they want to meet with you?" Pastora demanded. "I don't know," Popo shrugged. "Okay, you can go," Pastora decided, "but report back to me immediately." Popo left him there, still pacing like an overwound toy.

When Popo arrived at one of the Agency's suburban San José safe houses, the CIA officer got right to the point. "Congress has passed a new law, and our time is running out," the spook said. "We can give you 1 million pounds of arms and ammunition. But you have to be able to receive all of it at one time, in one week. A ship will deliver 300,000 pounds, and the rest will come by air. You must have five airfields ready to receive it, all of them in Costa Rican territory and not in Nicaragua. Can you do it?"

"Why only 1 million pounds?" Popo challenged. "We need more than that—we have been waiting for years. Why not 3 million, or 4 million? I can accept 4 million, not in a week but tomorrow." This was a ridiculous bluff—ARDE had never taken a delivery bigger than twenty thousand pounds. And Popo had no authority from Pastora to do anything but listen.

"What we have is 1 million pounds," the CIA officer repeated. "Take it or leave it." Popo took it.

Predictably, Pastora went crazy when he heard the news. "No, no, we can't accept it!" he shouted. "They want to bury us, they want to prove us incapable!"

"We need the weapons," Popo replied. "And I have a commitment. I'm going to keep it." For an hour he soothed Pastora's feelings, then let it slip that part of the shipment consisted of World War I–vintage Springfield rifles. Nothing made Pastora angrier than the feeling that he was getting gringo hand-me-downs. "No Springfields!" he screamed. "Tell them to send the Springfields to the bottom of the sea!"

A week later, Popo and the CIA officer traveled to Tortuguero, Costa Rica, about twenty-five miles south of the Nicaraguan border, to supervise the off-loading of the three hundred thousand pounds of supplies that arrived by ship. It was a wretchedly stormy night, with pounding rain and blustering winds that whipped the surf seven feet high. Even Popo's Miskito Indian boat crews, accustomed to the high Atlantic waves, were reluctant to take the small boats out to the CIA ship. But Popo finally bullied them into it. "We're ready," he shouted to the CIA officer over the wind.

139

"The batteries in my radio are dead," the CIA man shouted back.

"Well, put in your backups," Popo replied.

"What backups?" the CIA man asked. *Jesus Christ, I'm beginning to see why Pastora is so crazy all the time,* Popo thought. They had to climb a nearby hill and signal the ship with a flashlight. The next morning Popo learned that the airdrops were no smoother—more than half the parachutes had landed in the Río San Juan.

It shouldn't have surprised anyone; the CIA supply effort in the south was always plagued with weird mishaps and errors. Once, a CIA airdrop contained boots—but only left boots. Another time the agency dropped several thousand pounds of dry rice and beans—but they were mixed together, which made it impossible to cook. The most notorious snafu was the time a unit deep inside Nicaragua broke open the crates from a supply drop and found tens of thousands of sanitary napkins, "many more sanitary napkins than the female comrades needed," one aide noted dryly.[4] The sanitary napkin airdrop was so bizarre that several of the commanders concluded that the CIA was offering a commentary on their masculinity and courage.

The last-ditch supply effort allowed Pastora to keep his army more or less in the field. In the days after La Penca, a Sandinista offensive had pushed his troops out of several of their camps, but the swampy jungles posed just as many supply problems to the FSLN as they had to the contras. Sandinista troops soon withdrew, and ARDE once more inched north.

But Pastora's spell over his troops was waning. They were tired of his tantrums and his megalomania (since the attempt on his life at La Penca, Pastora was convinced he was not only the reincarnation of Sandino, but Napoleon too, and he often hinted that he and Jesus Christ had a good deal in common). They had lost all confidence in his ability as a strategist, and they were sick of fighting with him about supplies. Even the massive million-pound infusion from the CIA was reserved mostly for units along the river. As usual, commanders who moved deep inside Nicaragua got little or nothing. Pastora's one unquestionable skill—his ability to inspire men to go to their death—was no longer of any use, since he wouldn't go inside Nicaragua where his troops were. In July, when Alfonso Robelo left ARDE, most of Pastora's pilots went with him, and they took their aircraft. Pastora's mighty air force was reduced to a single twin-engine Beechcraft.

In September 1984, the field commanders gathered on the Río San Juan to talk over the situation. They decided, on their own, to make Popo Chamorro the chief of combat operations and the second in command of ARDE. Several times before the commanders had pled with Pastora to organize a staff and designate a chief of operations, but this time they were demanding it. Facing open rebellion, Pastora accepted their plan. But it was clear to Popo that his friendship with Pastora had never been more delicate.

In early 1985, Pastora came to Washington trying to repair his relationship with the Americans. When no one would meet with him, he tried an old tactic: shaming them through the press. The CIA had cut him off to retaliate for his independence, he whined. He didn't mention that since October it had been illegal for the CIA to give him anything, and, of course, he didn't mention the 1 million pounds of supplies he got as a going-away present. ARDE's bank account was only $63, Pastora told everyone, and he was going to have to hock his gold Rolex watch to pay for his medical bills from the La Penca bombing. He didn't mention that he had a collection of at least four Rolexes—each one a gold President model, which retails for about $10,000—and that every time he pawned one, a wealthy supporter immediately got it out of hock and returned it.[5] Again and again he sounded his chorus: "The CIA is a son of a bitch . . . the CIA with its black hands that, if you touch them, you wind up with manure."[6]

This time it wasn't working. When we met one evening, Pastora told me he had to learn to be more of a diplomat. "I'm always getting into trouble," he sighed. "A U.S. citizen [he winked and rolled his eyes—*a CIA officer, I'm confiding an intelligence secret to you*] told me this. He said they couldn't give me help because if I got help I would overthrow the Nicaraguan government. And the laws of the United States forbid this, he said. So I asked, 'In that case, how did you overthrow Allende?' He said to me, 'See, that's what's the matter with you. That's why we don't like you.' "

When Pastora returned to San José empty-handed, a surprise awaited him. Popo Chamorro had been invited to Washington. He met there with Adolfo Calero of the FDN and Arturo Cruz, Sr., the former member of the Sandinista-controlled junta who had been one of Pastora's closest advisers at the beginning of the contra war. The Americans were pushing again for unity, and Calero and Cruz did not believe that Congress would approve any more money unless all the contra factions could get together. They wanted Popo to join the new group—to be called the United Nicaraguan Opposition, or UNO—bringing ARDE's troops with him. If he agreed, Calero would immediately give him $200,000 to buy supplies for the men, and more would follow on a regular basis.[7]

The negotiations were confusing because, as Popo quickly realized, UNO was not a Nicaraguan project; it was being imposed by the gringos. In his talks with Calero and Cruz, Popo got the impression Pastora would be welcome in UNO as a member of the political directorate. But later, when Popo met with National Security Council aides, they said there was no place for Pastora. Popo was furious. He was willing to ask Pastora to change jobs, but to simply hijack the army from under him would look like Popo had been bought off. He turned to his fiancée, María Elena Martínez, who was translating. "Tell them to roll that $200,000 up and stick it up their asses! I don't believe in Pastora anymore, but I'm not going to betray him." Pale and speaking in a wavering voice, María Elena repeated his words in English. "You are a very proud man," one of the Americans said coolly. His tone did nothing to reassure María Elena.

Later, however, Popo met the gringos again and thought they reached an agreement that Pastora could join UNO. The $200,000 was to be delivered in Costa Rica. But when the money arrived, conditions were attached, most notably the exclusion of Pastora. "Forget it," Popo told Calero in an angry phone call. "This is not the original agreement."

Popo immediately told Pastora exactly what had happened. But Pastora didn't believe a word of it; as far as he was concerned, Popo was conspiring against him with the Americans. Later, at home, Popo considered his life: He was chief of combat operations for a penniless army that was forbidden to fight and was run by a madman. As crazy as Pastora had grown, Popo was no longer even sure it would be a good thing for ARDE to win the war. More and more often he found himself thinking that Pastora had the potential to be the worst dictator in Nicaraguan history.

The next day Popo resigned. "I don't want to fight with you any more," he told Pastora. He moved to Miami, married María Elena, and continued raising money for various groups on the southern front. But Popo's war was over.

And so, really, was Pastora's. In June 1985, the Sandinistas sent 1,700 men to storm his flanks: 200 assaulted the lightly defended Delta base from the Atlantic, and the rest came down the river to Tango base from a Sandinista garrison on Lake Nicaragua in San Carlos. Another 100 Sandinistas were dropped by helicopter in between the two pincers of the attack.

It would have been easy enough for ARDE to blunt the offensive. Several hundred contras who had penetrated north toward the Rama Road could have turned around and struck the Sandinistas from their blind side. Popo's last task as chief of combat operations was to call the commanders to order them to fall back and protect the river camps. Ganso, Leonel, Navigante—Popo radioed them one by one. And they all said no. "These are my men, and I don't have faith in Pastora anymore," one of the commanders explained. The Sandinistas rampaged down the Río San Juan, and by the end of June, Pastora no longer had a base in Nicaragua.

There was one brief final chapter to write in the saga of Commander Zero. Its author was a man the contras knew as Tomás Castillo. Joe Fernández—his real name—was a rotund, olive-skinned Cuban-American in his eighteenth year with the CIA. Fernández was no stranger to ticklish assignments; as a Miami cop, years before, one of his jobs was to help the FBI plant bugs on Martin Luther King, Jr., whenever he came to town. Fernández knew the contras inside out. In 1982, working in the Miami station, he had helped set up the FDN; in July 1984, he became the chief of station in Costa Rica. Fernández had always thought Pastora was on the flaky side, even when Duane Clarridge was crowing about his new recruit. After Fernández got to Costa Rica, his attitude hardened further.

It wasn't just that Pastora was an inept commander, or even that he refused to unite with the FDN. To Fernández, Pastora was a virulent disease that infected everything around him with paranoia and mistrust. When Fernández began talking to some of the young ARDE commanders, he was floored by their open apprehension. Pastora, it seemed, was telling everyone that the CIA had made an unholy pact with the KGB to destroy the contras. The young campesino commanders believed it, since they could not imagine why Pastora would lie about a thing like that. Neither could Fernández.

The final straw came on August 7, 1985, when Pastora ordered his men to kidnap a boatload of American leftists from the anticontra group Witness for Peace (and about twenty reporters covering the trip) as they floated down the Río San Juan. Fernández learned about the abduction in a phone call from

National Security Council aides, who said their counterterrorist group was going into emergency session on the kidnapping.

"Let me get back to you," Fernández said and dialed ARDE's headquarters. "Are you out of your mind?" he shouted when Pastora got on the phone. "Do you realize you are going to be labeled an international terrorist bandit?"[8] Six hours later, the Americans were released, seemingly none the worse for wear, but Pastora was a marked man as far as Fernández was concerned.

Of course, that was much easier to decide than to accomplish. The CIA often referred to guerrilla groups under its sponsorship as "clients," implying a cozy, civilized business relationship. But Fernández had learned that dealing with the contras, particularly Pastora, was more like trying to negotiate with a wildcat labor union. "To say there was any control on our part would be inaccurate, even, at times, ludicrous," Fernández would testify years later to a disbelieving Congress.[9]

In November 1985, Fernández saw an opening. He learned that a couple of Pastora's field commanders had accidentally bumped into some FDN units inside Nicaragua. Without any prompting from politicians or gringos, the young commanders worked out an impromptu agreement to share supplies and intelligence. This seemingly simple understanding reached in the middle of the jungle was a great breakthrough; it was the first time commanders of the two forces had met each other, and it seemed to prove the hypothesis that if Pastora were out of the picture everyone would get along better. A month later, a couple of the same commanders came to Costa Rica and made a similar arrangement with El Negro Chamorro, who commanded a small independent contra force on the border.[10]

Now Fernández made his move. In late January, he was able to get six of Pastora's eight commanders to Costa Rica to meet El Negro Chamorro and Robelo. Fernández actively participated in the meeting, steering the conversation, but he was careful that any promises came from Robelo and El Negro. And come they did. There would be regular supply drops to the commanders, and a little bonus—$5,000 apiece for each one who agreed to break with Pastora and sign an agreement with El Negro. All six of the commanders agreed. When Pastora found out, he shrieked, he ranted, he threatened, he made dark prophecies about the KGB. No one listened. To add insult to injury, one commander used part of his $5,000 to buy one of Pastora's daughters a gold chain.

That Fernández would steer the commanders toward El Negro Chamorro was a sign that the CIA's exasperation with Pastora had surpassed all rational bounds. Chamorro was a brave man who had fought Somoza from boyhood. But El Negro's best days as a commander were behind him. His single combat foray inside Nicaragua had been in 1983, when he was allied with the FDN. As part of a larger FDN offensive, El Negro and his thirty men were assigned to cut a section of highway near a Nicaraguan border town called El Espino, in Madriz Department, and prevent Sandinista reinforcements from moving down the road.

Instead, El Negro got carried away and attacked the customs post in El Espino. When the Sandinistas counterattacked in force, El Negro galloped back across the border to a Honduran pay phone and called CIA headquarters in Langley, Virginia, collect, to ask for artillery support.[11] The battle eventually spilled over into Honduras, provoking the government to expel El Negro. Now he spent his days on the Costa Rican border, hung over so much of the time that his own men called him Commander Johnny Walker.

No one seriously believed El Negro was going to lead an effective southern front. He fulfilled only one purpose—to undo Pastora. That role he played well, although Fernández's careful handiwork was almost upset by a gringo interloper: John Singlaub, a retired U.S. army general who was raising private funds for the contras. Singlaub understood the CIA's complaints about Pastora but found him personally engaging and thought there ought to be a place for him in the war against the Sandinistas. "His only asset was this great name recognition, this myth, and we ought to get him doing the things he did well—talking to socialist politicians in Europe," Singlaub explained later. "I just really like him. He's a great guy, but he has no military sense. And he can't select people who can do it for him."

In March 1986, just as Pastora was about to throw in the towel, Singlaub flew to Costa Rica to talk with him. They hammered out an agreement: Pastora would take his men inside Nicaragua, get military operations started, and then depart for lobbying trips to Europe and South America. In return, Singlaub would provide boots, food, ammo, medicine, maps, and new encrypted radios.

Pastora had promised all this before and never lived up to it. But even more troubling was the way the agreement was written. It said, "The *United States* will provide . . . ," which seemed to imply the U.S. government, rather than Singlaub, was making the agreement.

Before Singlaub left Costa Rica, he dropped off a copy of the agreement to the new U.S. ambassador, Lewis Tambs, who cabled a copy to Washington. When Fernández saw the text later, he lost his mind. It was "incredible" that Tambs hadn't put a stop to this, Fernández said. Tambs knew that the whole thing "was contradictory to strategy, policy, and legality, because to support the private effort of this American, Singlaub, who was, you know, a private citizen, contravened the Boland Amendment . . . to say nothing of the fact that we didn't want to give Pastora any encouragement whatsoever." Fernández ended his tirade only when a vicious cable arrived for Tambs from Elliott Abrams at the State Department in Washington repeating pretty much the same message, only more so. The tone of the cable was so brutal, Fernández thought, that the ambassador was certainly going to be fired. (Tambs resigned six months later.)[12]

Scrambling behind the scenes, the CIA derailed the agreement. The supplies Singlaub promised to deliver were stored in an FDN warehouse, so it was a simple matter to stop the delivery. By early May, with only 150 men left and no supplies in sight, Pastora knew the game was over. He announced one more time that he was quitting and then, media-conscious to the end, slipped back to Nicaragua while aides drove thirteen jeeploads of reporters to the border to see him emerge from the jungle on May 16, 1986. "We have been shot down by the CIA, but never defeated," he said as the cameras clicked and whirred.

All that morning, Elliott Abrams had been trying to get a telephone patch by radio into the jungle camp. The gringos had changed their minds one last time. Couldn't something be worked out? Couldn't Pastora be a roving ambassador for the contras? "I'd look like a clown if I went back now after making the announcement," Pastora sniffed when Abrams finally got through. As usual, Commander Zero had had the last word.

Pastora was held in a police barracks in Cartago, Costa Rica, for a few weeks while the government decided whether to grant him political asylum. Technically, Pastora was a fugitive from Costa Rican justice on a host of minor violations, stemming not only from his military activities but also his amatory ones—he had failed to answer a summons in a child-support lawsuit, among other things.

On June 2, I stopped to visit him. It was by no means certain that Pastora was going to get asylum—Oscar Arias, the new Costa Rican president, didn't much like him—and he was glum. But the sight of a reporter cheered him up. I asked him if there were anything he would change if he could go back in time. "Yeah," he said. "I would be born a communist. The communists have friends, they're never left alone."

Then he offered me his prescription for peace in Central America.

"The solution is that the Pentagon stage a coup against Ronald Reagan," he explained in mock-professorial tones. "They could take out the State Department and just help the Nicaraguan people to fight their own war and make their own policies. This, which seems like a sacrilege to American democracy, is the only way to stop communism. If the Americans don't make this sacrilege to democracy, every democrat will be dead." As I jotted notes, Pastora turned to an aide. "Now the Americans are going to send a gringo general to kill me for saying this," he said. Just then, a Costa Rican policeman gestured for Pastora to come to the phone. He put the receiver to his ear and listened intently for several minutes. Then his face crackled into a broad smile. He put the phone down. "They're giving me asylum," he said and began packing his bags.

11 | The Dry Years

The big house on the hill, with its gleaming marble staircases and glass-enclosed wing overlooking the city lights, seemed slightly unreal to the contra commanders. A few of them had been in houses this grand before—Commander Aureliano came from a well-to-do family, and Commander Quiché's father-in-law in Guatemala had some money—but for most of the contras, the U.S. ambassador's residence in Tegucigalpa was from an alternate universe that they could scarcely imagine.

But the spookily silent waiters kept the Scotch flowing freely, and the party began to loosen up. The ambassador even made a little joke, that Congress said he couldn't give them guns, but the law didn't mention Johnny Walker Black Label. He was a friendly man, this new ambassador. His name was Ted Briggs, and he had invited them to Tegucigalpa for a small party, to assure them that the gringos were still their pals even though there hadn't been any military aid for more than two years.

"Don't worry," Briggs was saying to the commanders. "The white elephant will wake up in the future. You need to keep your courage up; when the white elephant wakes up, we'll smash the Sandinistas."

The image of the United States as a drowsy white elephant was too much for Mike Lima. "Great," he told the ambassador, tipsily waving the clawlike prosthesis the doctors had attached where his right arm used to be. "But by the time the white elephant wakes up, all of us will be dead."

The 1984 cutoff of American aid provoked by the CIA's disastrous mining came just as the contras were establishing themselves inside Nicaragua. Finally rid of the problems that dogged them in late 1983—the murderous rampages of Suicida, the gringo-induced mutiny against the general staff, the dubious military advice of the Argentines—the contras concentrated on infiltration. By midyear they had six thousand troops inside; the contra army

146

was so big that a new organizational unit—the regional command—had to be created to designate clusters of two or more task forces.

With few exceptions the contras avoided the big set-piece battles that they lost on such a regular basis the year before. Instead, they concentrated on small ambushes and hit-and-run raids. The Sandinistas were slow to adjust to the new tactics. The contras shot up so many convoys on a single stretch of highway running through a gorge in western Jinotega Department, near the village of Zompopero, that the commanders joked that they had to reserve ambush sites weeks in advance.

There were so many contra task forces operating so deep inside Nicaragua that the Sandinistas all but abandoned the border region. A swath of territory ten or twelve miles wide along the frontier in Nueva Segovia and Jinotega departments was so totally under FDN control that contra troops listened to boombox radios as they marched through it. Bermúdez sometimes swam in the rivers in the border zone; on one occasion, the contras took old Huber Matos—a key commander in Castro's revolution, later sentenced to twenty years in prison for his outspoken anticommunism—into a Nicaraguan village to give a speech to the campesinos.

As the contras steadily expanded their area of operations, however, an invisible noose was tightening around their necks. And, once it was in place, they would struggle for the remainder of the war to loosen it.

The problem was supply lines, which grew ever more precarious as the war moved deeper inside Nicaragua. In popular mythology, guerrilla forces don't have to worry about supply lines—they live off the land. To some extent that may be true when it comes to food, but "the land" can't provide bullets, grenades, spare radio parts, or rifles for new recruits.

And in Nicaragua the equation was complicated by both the deprivation brought on by Sandinista economic mismanagement and the FSLN's ubiquitous State Security apparatus. When the communist guerrillas in El Salvador, for instance, wore out their boots, they simply robbed a bank, then sent a man into the nearest town to buy some. For the contras that was impossible. In Nicaragua, where nearly everything was rationed, a request to purchase fifty pairs of boots would bring a laugh from the merchant and a series of probing questions from the Interior Ministry cop who would be on the scene within minutes.

If contra units were going to stay deep inside Nicaragua, some method of getting supplies to them had to be devised. And that was what prompted The Great Ho Chi Minh Trail Debate, one of the longest running arguments between the CIA and the contras.

The Ho Chi Minh Trail was the complex network North Vietnam used to supply its regular army and the Viet Cong guerrillas during its long war to conquer the South. Initially the trail was just a network of jungle footpaths running from North Vietnam through Laos, Cambodia, and finally into South Vietnam. But by the war's end it was no longer a trail so much as a freeway: a six-hundred-mile-long web of widened roads, reinforced bridges, and underground fuel dumps that delivered sixty thousand tons of supplies a day to communist forces in the South.[1]

If the Viet Cong could do it, the CIA argued to Bermúdez, then the contras could do it. They would create their own Ho Chi Minh Trail, starting somewhere around Banco Grande on the Honduran side of the border, running east through the jungle fifty miles or so, then hooking back west toward Matagalpa Department, essentially the same route contra troops were using to infiltrate. Supplies would be carried in to the troops by contra family members: women, children, men too infirm to fight.

Bermúdez found the suggestion insulting. "Our families are not a bunch of Chinese coolies," he snapped to one CIA officer who brought the plan up. But Bermúdez also had other, more practical objections. The Ho Chi Minh Trail was almost entirely in the neutral countries of Laos and Cambodia, where American and South Vietnamese troops couldn't get at it. The Americans bombed it constantly, but that was like throwing rocks at ants.

This new version of the trail being proposed by the CIA, however, would be completely inside Nicaragua. What would prevent the Sandinista army from moving a battalion right onto the middle of it and sitting there? Much better, Bermúdez argued, would be an aerial supply system. The Sandinista air force had no modern fighter planes, and the army had no sophisticated antiaircraft weapons. Why not just drop supplies by parachute to contra troops? It would be much quicker and much easier than developing the intricate ground networks that a Ho Chi Minh Trail would require.

The debate raged, off and on, for years. But it was particularly intense in 1983 and 1984 as the contras penetrated farther and farther into Nicaragua. The man who was often caught in the middle was Mario Sacasa, the chief contra supply officer.

Sacasa, a Georgetown-educated banker in his early thirties, fled Nicaragua shortly after the Sandinistas took over. He had no military background at all, but often Sacasa felt that gave him an advantage over the former National Guardsmen who dominated the contra general staff. The Guardsmen, in making the switch from a conventional army to a guerrilla force, had to unlearn a lifetime of military doctrine. Sacasa, to whom everything was new, found it much easier to adapt to the unique conditions of guerrilla warfare.

To Sacasa, the Ho Chi Minh Trail arguments made a good deal of sense, at least on paper. So he began calculating how far, how fast, supplies could move on the ground. The CIA plan, he discovered, called for one thousand mules that could carry three hundred pounds apiece.

"You guys are crazy," Sacasa declared to Ray Doty. "There aren't that many mules in all of Honduras and Nicaragua put together. And even if there were, they can't carry half that load. Bring me some mules from Kentucky, and we'll try it."

Sacasa didn't know it, but the United States had already tried Kentucky mules in Nicaragua. In 1929, the U.S. Marines chasing Augusto Sandino imported sixty-five of the animals to haul supplies through the very same territory where the contras were now fighting. But the strapping American mules couldn't subsist on jungle foliage, so a steamer full of U.S. oats and hay was dispatched to Nicaragua, where 225 oxcarts were required to haul it to Matagalpa.[2] The mules wound up consuming more supplies than they delivered.

148

As soon as Sacasa uttered the words "Kentucky mules," the CIA backed off. Sacasa thought that was just as well. Creating ground networks would have required a fundamental reorientation of the FDN. Most armies have eight to ten support personnel for every soldier. In the contras, the ratio was reversed. Where, Sacasa wondered, among the illiterate campesinos who made up the great bulk of the FDN forces, could he find enough people to build the infrastructure to support a Ho Chi Minh Trail?

        In a semicapitulation to the contras, the CIA bought them two ancient C-47 cargo planes, capable of carrying six-thousand-pound payloads. But maintenance problems frequently grounded them (one plane was so old the contras called it the Rusty Pelican, after a restaurant on Key Biscayne where CIA men liked to have working dinners), and even when they flew there were inexplicable glitches.

In October 1983, Toño and Tigrillo called for a supply drop. They were stuck in an out-of-the-way patch of jungle in western Jinotega Department with large concentrations of Sandinistas on three sides of them. They had 1,100 new recruits, but only 80 armed men. If the Sandinistas caught them, it would be a massacre.

Every day headquarters promised a supply drop, and every day it failed to arrive. Toño was frantic; in five and one-half years of fighting the Sandinistas, as a National Guardsman and now as a contra, he had never felt so helpless. Then one morning just before dawn, headquarters called. The plane was on its way; Toño should get his signal fires ready.

Less than an hour later, they heard the monotonous drone of the C-47. Toño barked a confirmation code into his radio to let the pilot know he had reached the drop zone and then turned to his officers. "We have to get the guns out of the crates quickly, and then get out of here," he warned them. "If the Sandinistas see the plane dropping parachutes, they'll be after us right away."

The men watched nervously as the parachutes sprouted from the plane's side like camouflage-colored mushrooms. While the 'chutes drifted lazily down, the men crouched at the edge of a clearing that now seemed preternaturally quiet. Everyone strained their ears for the sound of advancing boots that would signal that the Sandinistas were on their way.

At last the first wooden crate hit the ground. Toño sprinted into the clearing and frantically pried at the top with his knife. Finally he jerked it open and plunged his hands into the . . . dinner plates. DINNER PLATES! Thousands of metal dinner plates, enough for the biggest dinner party in the history of Nicaragua. *Maybe when the Sandinistas get here,* Toño mused, *I'm supposed to invite them to dinner and reason with them.*

The next day Toño gave up on aerial resupply and sent the unarmed recruits sneaking through FSLN lines while he stayed with his eighty armed men, preparing a suicidal last stand in case the Sandinistas discovered the evacuation. They didn't, but it had been an insanely close call. "We've got to do something about getting supplies inside," Toño said at a meeting of commanders in Honduras a few weeks later. "If the Sandinistas know that we have to come back here every two or three months, they'll just wait at the border for us."

Early in 1984, he got his chance. After the smoldering discontent among the field commanders that preoccupied the FDN during the final months of 1983—the anger at Echaverry and the general staff, the Banco Grande Rebellion, and the disastrous CIA attempt to put Hugo Villagra in charge of the troops—Bermúdez wanted peace in the ranks. He gave Toño the job Villagra had quit: tactical commander. Toño would set up a command post inside Nicaragua and coordinate all military operations. The other men would no longer complain that they were being directed by an officer unfamiliar with battleground conditions. And Toño was one of the few National Guardsmen who could give orders to the campesino commanders without causing resentment.

Within weeks Toño realized the job wasn't going to work. Communications with the other commanders were too sporadic. Knowing where they were at a given moment was nearly impossible, never mind coordinating their operations. Nor was it easy to assert authority over the other field commanders. To them, he was just another disembodied voice in the ether. He couldn't enforce his radioed orders, had no way of knowing if a commander had even tried to carry them out.

But there was one thing Toño could do. Using Tigrillo's men, he effectively fenced off a vast chunk of mountainous territory on the far western fringes of Jinotega Department for use as a supply depot. Small contra planes shuttled back and forth to it several times a week, dropping equipment; task forces that were out of supplies could make their way to the mountains to pick them up. It wasn't ideal, but it was better than trekking all the way back to Honduras.

Meanwhile, when the C-47s could get into the air, they flew supply missions to units deep inside. The pilots often had to match wits with their own forces on the ground as much as with the Sandinistas. One pilot flew to Matagalpa Department to make a drop to a unit that had been begging for resupply for several days. When he made radio contact, the commander on the ground greeted him happily. "I've got a full load for you," the pilot said. "It will take three passes." He dropped the plane down to five hundred feet and got ready for the first drop.

Down below, the contra troops settled back to wait for this tedious operation —and then they saw, hovering several thousand feet above the supply plane, two Soviet-made An-2 biplanes. The Sandinistas, so high above the C-47 that its pilot couldn't see them, were coming in for the kill. The field commander started to get on the radio to alert the pilot of the C-47, but another officer stopped him. "If you say anything," the second officer warned, "the plane will leave and we won't get the supplies."

The commander called the pilot. "Listen, *primo*, we're in kind of a hurry down here," he said. "Maybe you could step on it."

"Why, is there a problem?" the pilot asked.

"No, no, we're just anxious to get back to the war," the ground commander lied.

The C-47 finished its first pass and came around for a second. "Really, we'd like to get out of here," the ground commander urged over the radio. "Keep your shirt on, the war isn't going anywhere," the pilot snapped. Finally he made a third pass, and the last parachutes popped out of the hatch. "Okay, see you later," he said, and tilted the C-47 upward for the first time. A moment later, the radio crackled to life again: *"Son of a BEEEEEEECH!"* The pilot kept saying it over and over as he dipsy-doodled his way across the horizon, trying to get away from the Sandinista planes. The contras on the ground calculated that it was 192 son of a bitches back to the safety of Honduran airspace.

But too many commanders, too many times, asked the pilots to fly into the lion's mouth. In October 1983, Roberto Amador—the former National Guard pilot who was chased away from the U.S. embassy in Guatemala three years earlier—was shot down in Matagalpa Department after the Sandinistas captured a contra radio operator and used him to lure a supply flight into their gunsights. And in September 1984, another ex-Guard pilot named José Luis Gutiérrez was shot down in Jinotega Department after a field commander lied and told him there were no Sandinista units in the area.

One reason Toño was promoted to tactical commander was the hope that he could deal with the pint-sized commander who was the FDN's biggest headache: Tigrillo. Tigrillo's unrivaled skills as a recruiter made him indispensable to the contras. But at the same time, his insubordination, his egomania, and his ruthlessness were intolerable. Scarcely a month went by without complaints that Tigrillo had carried off some young *chica* who caught his eye. And he treated northwestern Jinotega Department as his imperial fiefdom; rumors circulated that he was even opening warehouses to start his own grain purchasing agency.

Toño's assignment was to convince Tigrillo to move his burgeoning regional command from his edge-of-the-world domain in Jinotega toward central Nicaragua. The FDN couldn't afford to keep 1,200 troops out in a distant jungle enclave that no one wanted anyway.

All the campesino commanders disliked fighting outside the districts where they grew up. One major difficulty was that so few of them could read maps, which made it much tougher to adapt to new terrain. But eventually most of them adjusted. Tigrillo's problem was not so much learning new geography, Toño thought, but moving to a new place where no one knew him, where he wasn't automatically ceded the right to the fattest cow and the prettiest girl.

"Just try it," Toño urged during one of his many arguments with Tigrillo. "You can be a hero all over Nicaragua, not just in Jinotega."

So in October 1984, Tigrillo set off for populous southern Estelí Department, one hundred miles away by airplane but many times that if you were walking up and down mountains. The march betrayed Tigrillo's weaknesses as a commander. He had no idea how to break his 1,200 men into different groups and yet coordinate their movements over such a great distance. So the whole command stayed together, moving in a single long line that took two to three hours to snake past a given point. Tigrillo got away with it as long as they were moving through the lonely stretches of northern Jinotega, but an ambush was inevitable as they approached the population centers in the western half of the country.

When Tigrillo's forces drew near Lake Apanas, they skirmished with the Sandinistas for two days. On the third day, they had to break cover to cross

Route 3, the highway between Jinotega and San Rafael del Norte. It was a vulnerable spot, outside the jungle canopy, open to aircraft as well as artillery. Tigrillo stayed there at the road, shooing the men across in twos and threes, and when the Sandinista attack came he was the easiest target of all. A rocket-propelled grenade flung him into a roadside ravine, shattering his left kneecap.

Perhaps his knee could have been saved if his men, carrying him in a hammock, had evacuated due north through Nueva Segovia Department. An open route ran through there, and he could have reached a contra hospital in Honduras in three days.

But Tigrillo wasn't from Nueva Segovia. "We go back through our old territory," he told his men, "through the places we know." It took fifteen days, and by the time Tigrillo could be treated his knee was a writhing mass of pus and infection. The contra doctors did what they could, but Tigrillo spent most of the next year in New Orleans hospitals having chunks of bone and cartilage removed. When they were finished, Tigrillo was left with a circus-fun-house knee that he could bend backwards or forwards with his hand. At the age of thirty-four, he hobbled like an old man.

A few days after Tigrillo crossed back into Honduras, his old enemy Mike Lima did the same. Lima walked, he wasn't carried, but his body bore so many scars that it looked like a road map. And some of his worst wounds were invisible.

It was a full year now since the mortar accident that took Lima's right arm. Just six weeks after the explosion, he was back in the Nicarao base camp, learning to shoot left-handed. And three months after that, he led his men back into Nicaragua. "Are you sure you want to do this?" Bermúdez asked. "You don't have to prove anything to anybody. You already fought in this war." Lima just shook his head. Three weeks he came back in a hammock: During an ambush, a grenade landed barely three feet away from him. A pack mule absorbed most of the blast, which saved Lima's life, but his left arm and leg were broken.

After his limbs healed, Lima went inside again on several brief trips. Something, however, wasn't the same. He heard things at night; he worried about Sandinista ambushes even in the heart of contra enclaves. And then in November, as Lima chatted with one of his men, he heard the sputtering hiss of an incoming mortar round. "Get down!" he screamed, flinging himself to the ground. The shell exploded—a half mile away. When Lima looked up, he saw the other soldier still standing, gaping at him in bewilderment. "I think it's time for me to go back to Honduras," he muttered, climbing slowly to his feet.

Neither Tigrillo nor Lima would ever fight inside Nicaragua again. Within a few short days at the end of October 1984, the contras lost their best recruiter and one of their best fighters.

In November, Toño left his command post in Nicaragua and returned to Honduras. The U.S. aid had begun to run out in July, and there were fewer and fewer supplies for him to distribute from his secure area in Jinotega. When Congress outlawed aid altogether in October, the supply flights stopped completely. "Helping with logistics was the only part of the tactical commander's job that was worthwhile," Toño told Bermúdez. "Now even that's gone. I want to raise a new task force and go back inside as a field commander."

But, Toño noticed, contra troops were starting to flow back out of Nicaragua. So far it was only a trickle, but as supplies dried up, Toño knew, the number of retreating contras would grow. It hurt to see the FDN's operational zone shrink by even an inch of uninhabitable jungle; all that territory had been paid for in blood.

As the Sandinistas sensed the contras' collective pulse slowing, they pressed their advantage. In February 1985, the FSLN began a buildup along the Honduran border that eventually numbered forty thousand troops. The Sandinistas clearly intended to crush the contras before the Americans had a chance to rethink their position on aid. They started by tightening the noose that was already in place: the supply lines.

Because the contras had refused to set up a Ho Chi Minh Trail, their units inside had three basic sources of supply. They could march back to Honduras and pick up new equipment. They could get airdrops. And they could obtain some aid from sympathetic campesinos inside Nicaragua. Most task forces did all three, using campesino food and small drops of ammo and boots to prolong their stays inside, returning to Honduras only when their packs were absolutely empty.

But when the Hondurans closed down the contra bases on the western side of the country after the CIA-ordered attacks on the Cosigüina Peninsula, it was harder for FDN units to march out for supplies. And after the two C-47s were shot down, the aerial supply program went from feeble to comatose. Now the Sandinistas moved against the final leg of the triangle: the campesinos. In early March, Sandinista troops began shutting down entire villages in Nueva Segovia and Jinotega departments, sending the peasants to relocation camps farther south, where they couldn't help the contras. In many cases, their homes were burned and livestock slaughtered to prevent their return. Some seventy-five thousand campesinos were uprooted, leaving a vast free-fire zone across northern Nicaragua where anything that moved was presumed a military target.

Creeping stealthily through the empty territory, the Sandinistas massed at the border across from the FDN's headquarters camp. On the night of April 26, they showered the base with Soviet-made Katyusha rockets, followed by a major infantry assault. About forty contras were killed, along with two Honduran soldiers from a squad stationed in the nearby village of Las Vegas. Within days, the Hondurans ordered the base closed. Once more the contras shifted east, farther from the urban corridor along Nicaragua's Pacific Coast. *If we go any farther east*, Toño mused, *we'll have to learn to speak Chinese.*

Toño and Mike Lima, old friends from the military academy, talked often of the perplexities of commanding an orphan guerrilla army that, it seemed, was forgotten to the world. They watched their troops coming in with toes jutting through worn-out boots, no more than a handful of ammunition in their pockets. Don't worry, they told their men, Ronald Reagan will fix it. But at night, drinking beer together, their talk was gloomy. What if the Americans didn't change their minds? How could the contras, without help, ever hope to fight an army equipped by the Soviet Union?

153

"We've got to do something to convince people that we can't be killed off so easily," Toño said one night. "We have to do something so big and so public that no one can deny that we are alive."

What Toño had in mind was seizing a chunk of Route 1—the Pan-American Highway, which corkscrews all the way from Brownsville, Texas, to the jungles of southern Panama. Although the highway is Central America's principal commercial artery, in three years of full-scale war, the contras had never managed to hit a single target on Route 1. "If we do something over there, everyone will know about it," Toño reasoned. "The Sandinistas can't hide it like they usually do. All the journalists will be writing about it."

Together Toño and Lima designed an operation that would require almost three thousand men. Their plan was to seize a forty-five-mile stretch of Route 1, from just above Estelí to the northern outskirts of Sébaco, just sixty miles northeast of Managua.

At the heart of the plan was the capture of two towns along the border of Matagalpa and Jinotega departments—La Trinidad, a collection of muddy roads and wooden houses that was home to eight thousand people, and smaller San Isidro a few miles south. Meanwhile, other contra units would seize bridges at the north and south ends of the targeted length of highway, blow them up, and ambush any Sandinista reinforcements. The objective was limited: to take the towns early in the morning, hold them until dusk, and then slip away in the darkness. There really wasn't enough ammunition to do much else. Two other units would take positions northeast of Route 1 to cover the withdrawal.

Eight different units would participate; Toño would be the senior commander on the scene, and Lima would coordinate the different units by radio from Honduras. They went over the order of battle—the list of which commanders would attack which targets—without disagreement, until Toño said he wanted to use Commanders Tiro al Blanco and Iván to cover the retreat to Honduras. Both of them were campesinos, friends of Tigrillo. And like Tigrillo, they were in a more or less perpetual state of alienation from the National Guard commanders.

"They won't do it, Toño," Lima argued. "They'll change their minds, they'll decide to do something else at the last minute. The only way you can count on them is if you travel with them, if you stay with them at all times."

"They'll do it," Toño predicted confidently. "I'll talk to them—you know I get along with them better than anyone else."

"Even if they show up where they're supposed to, they don't have the military capacity for this kind of a job," Lima warned. But Toño wouldn't budge.

The La Trinidad operation was the most ambitious attack the contras had attempted since the cataclysmic 1983 attempt to carve out a liberated zone in northern Nicaragua. Toño had been part of that attack and remembered well its humiliating failure. But this operation had a much better chance of success, he thought, even though FDN resources were far more limited now. The contras would have the element of surprise; every day they listened to Sandinista officials boasting on the radio that the contras were "strategically defeated." No one would expect a large attack in the middle of the country. By the time the Sandinistas recovered and counterattacked, the contras would be gone.

The attack was tentatively scheduled for July 31, but Toño was to finalize the date by radio once all the commanders arrived at their positions inside Nicaragua. Because it would take weeks for all the commanders to move into place, infiltration began early in the month. Toño's unit was one of the smallest, with just sixty men, and he deliberately called attention to himself as he crossed into Nicaragua, hoping to divert Sandinista attention while some of the bigger units slipped inside unnoticed. But he was much too successful; the Sandinistas latched onto him and attacked ceaselessly for three days and four nights. Toño's men had to move constantly to stay ahead of them, humping through the jungle in the dark.

By the time he linked up with another small unit in the Kilambé Mountains of central Jinotega, Toño was exhausted and his men were low on ammunition. He decided to wait for a couple of days and link up with the two commanders assigned to protect the escape route, Tiro al Blanco and Iván. But two days later, when they were due to arrive, the commanders radioed that they hadn't been able to get enough boots and ammo to outfit their 650 men. They weren't coming.

The plan that looked so good on paper when Toño and Lima drew it up in Honduras was beginning to fray at the edges. Commander Dimas Negro's unit, on its way to a point just north of Estelí, bumped into some Sandinista troop trucks by mistake on July 25, about seven miles short of its destination. Although the accidental combat resulted in a spectacular contra victory—at least twenty-nine Sandinistas were killed—it seemed that the element of surprise was lost. To make matters worse, Commander Douglas radioed that he would be at least a day late to his jumping-off point; he wouldn't be ready to attack until August 1. And then, worried that he didn't have enough men, Douglas radioed Commander Denis, who was supposed to capture San Isidro. He convinced Denis to abandon the attack on San Isidro and join him in La Trinidad instead. Commander Coral, assigned to seal off the southern end of the operation by blowing up a bridge just outside Sébaco, had the opposite problem: he reached the area on July 25, and he wanted to launch the attack before the Sandinistas detected his presence.

These were precisely the kind of problems Toño was supposed to take care of as the senior commander on the scene. But on July 27, bad weather around Kilambé knocked his radio off the air, and he was out of touch for the next seventy-two hours. Lima tried to hold everything together from the headquarters in Honduras, but he was too far away and communications were too tenuous.

So instead of all the attacks going off together in one big confusing bang, they erupted consecutively, like a string of firecrackers. The first assault was launched on July 27 by Dimas Negro, a rugged former private in the National Guard's EEBI. His assignment was the toughest of the whole operation—diversionary attacks on the periphery of Estelí. Any action around Estelí, a city of forty thousand and the most fervent stronghold of FSLN support in the country, would be the focus of Sandinista attention.

Dimas Negro would have been under heavy pressure even if all the contra attacks began at the same time as scheduled. Out there by himself, he was

155

frightfully exposed. He took two bridges on Route 1 and tried to blow them up, but the explosives only damaged them. Before he could try again, the Sandinistas counterattacked and forced him off the bridges. He went for his secondary target, a radar station, and the Sandinistas sent tanks after him.

On July 28, Coral decided he couldn't wait any longer and seized the bridge over the Río Viejo just north of Sébaco. "I don't understand it," Coral complained by radio just before the Sandinistas counterattacked. "We packed sixteen dynamite charges on the bridge, and we blew sixteen big holes in it, but the goddamn thing is still standing." Like Dimas Negro, he had no time for a second attempt.

On August 1, the attack on La Trinidad finally began when the contras blew a passing Interior Ministry jeep to bits with a rocket-propelled grenade. Then they swarmed into La Trinidad, where the townspeople directed them around sentry posts so they could hit the militia headquarters by surprise. In less than an hour Douglas had complete control of the city.

A subcommander named Fernando Negro was the first to see the helicopters racing toward his unit at 150 miles an hour. Some of them peeled away from the formation to land and disgorge hundreds of Sandinista troops. Others kept coming, their nose-mounted Gatling guns roaring. And then spidery vapor trails popped out from the pods on their sides as the helicopters fired their rockets. In seconds seven of Fernando Negro's men were dead, the rest madly scattering across the rocky ground in a hopeless search for cover.

The contras had seen Sandinista aircraft before—mostly the old An-2 biplanes and creaky T-33 jet training planes, reoutfitted as fighters, that the National Guard left behind in 1979. Occasionally, the Sandinistas would rush troops to the site of a contra attack in the Mi-8 transport helicopters they got from the Soviets.

But these were something new: Mi-24 gunships, heavily armed killing machines that the boys at the Pentagon called flying tanks. With a range of 99 miles and a top speed of 199 miles an hour, the Mi-24s could follow the contras anywhere, firing freely from their load of 130 rockets. And, unlike most helicopters—fragile machines that can sometimes be knocked down by a lucky rifle shot—the Mi-24s were armored, invulnerable to anything but an antiaircraft missile.

When the Mi-24s were unloaded from Soviet freighters in El Bluff nine months earlier, the contras had learned of it within hours. They had even kicked around the idea of borrowing a T-33 trainer from the Hondurans, repainting it with the insignia of the Sandinista Air Force, and bombing the helicopters on the ground. Afterward they would put out the story that the raid was carried out by a defecting Sandinista pilot. The risky plan had been abandoned, however, because no one thought the Sandinistas had pilots with the sophisticated training necessary to fly the Mi-24s. Nobody had anticipated that the Sandinistas would borrow Cubans to pilot the helicopters into combat.

By noon, the twenty helicopters based at an Estelí airfield had broken the back of the La Trinidad offensive. Six of the choppers were Mi-24s, which relentlessly pounded the contras as they tried to get away. Most of the rest were new Mi-17 transports, which for the most part shuttled Sandinista troops back and forth through the combat zone, but sometimes joined the gunships in attack formations. The contra withdrawal turned into a rout, even more disorganized because Iván and Tiro al Blanco weren't there covering the rear. The contras lost two hundred dead, four hundred wounded, and sixty captured—about a third of the troops that participated. (The Sandinistas admitted to about fifty dead, although the contras thought the real total was probably much higher.)

Toño returned to Honduras to a fuming contra officer corps demanding an explanation. Along with Tiro al Blanco and Iván, he was summoned to a meeting of commanders in a building at the new contra military headquarters near the village of Yamales. It lasted three days. Tiro al Blanco and Iván were openly fearful, but most of the venom was directed at Toño. He listened as commander after commander denounced him as a coward for staying in Kilambé through the whole operation and as an irresponsible derelict for not ensuring that the contra retreat was covered.

Some commanders even accused him of stopping in Kilambé not because his men were exhausted but because his girlfriend—a contra soldier named Judith—needed an abortion. After that accusation was hurled around for a while, Commander Johnson stood up. "I don't believe that this had anything to do with an abortion," Johnson told the others. "Everyone here knows Judith is a virgin—how could a man without any balls fuck her?" Less insulting but just as harsh was Toño's old friend Mike Lima. "Where were you for the last three days of the operation?" Lima demanded. "Why didn't you make radio contact? How could you disappear at such a crucial moment?"

Toño couldn't comprehend their anger. The operation didn't go exactly according to plan, that was true enough, but no operation ever did. Most of the problems were caused by the unexpected appearance of the new helicopters, and that was hardly Toño's fault. And what difference would it have made if Iván and Tiro al Blanco had been there? They would have had to run from the Mi-24s or be slaughtered, just like everyone else.

The other commanders, however, brushed aside Toño's defense. And when he realized they were on the verge of stripping him of his command, Toño was stunned. He had given up his family for this war, had abandoned a promising new life in the United States to join the FDN. Being a contra was *everything* to him. "Don't do this," Toño begged. "I promise you I can do better." As he pleaded, tears trickled down his cheeks. The other commanders, embarrassed, adjourned the meeting without taking any action.

At dinner that night, the commanders sat in small groups, murmuring about the day's events. "Maybe we were too hard on Toño," one commander said. "Maybe we should have been more confrontational with Iván and Tiro al Blanco. After all, they were the ones who failed to guard the retreat."

"No," Mike Lima replied thoughtfully, his fury spent. "It's Toño's fault they weren't there. If *I* had given them the order, they would have been there, because they know I would have them executed if they didn't show up. That's the difference between Toño and me. When people don't obey my orders, I punish them. Toño talks and talks to them, tries to explain to them what they did wrong, tries to be persuasive. I'm an authoritarian. Toño relies on his intelligence."

Toño sat alone, humiliated and bitter. No matter what anyone said, no matter how many casualties they suffered, he considered La Trinidad a success. The objective was to show that the contras weren't dead. And that had been achieved, never mind the helicopters.

On that much, at least, Toño was correct. The capture of La Trinidad generated big news throughout Latin America and the United States. The *Washington Post* called it "the rebels' most effective week in more than three years of fighting." FSLN officials admitted they were taken aback at the way the citizens of La Trinidad flocked to the contras, fed them information on Sandinista troop movements, and even served them coffee during breaks in the fighting.[3] Neither the Sandinistas nor the international press knew of the glitches, the things that didn't go as planned. They only saw what *did* happen: Without U.S. aid or advice, the contras launched an impressive, coordinated assault in central Nicaragua, and the local population greeted them as liberators.

The image of contra military competence was bolstered considerably by a lucky coincidence. The day after the attack on La Trinidad, Commander Dumas and a small band of troops from the Jorge Salazar Regional Command, one of the few units that didn't leave Nicaragua when the U.S. aid was cut off, raided the militia headquarters in Cuapa, a village in Chontales Department. Not only did his troops kill nineteen militiamen, virtually the entire local detachment, but when the Sandinistas rushed a convoy of elite counterinsurgency troops to reinforce the town, Dumas ambushed them and killed thirty-two. Dumas, so deep inside Nicaragua he was hardly in contact with the rest of the FDN at all, didn't know anything about the La Trinidad operation. But his attack made it appear the contras had launched a synchronized offensive that ran virtually the length of the country.

Little public note was made of the use of the Mi-24 gunships at La Trinidad, except by the Sandinistas, who observed how effectively the helicopters routed the contras.

The Mi-24s were not the first high-tech weapons the Soviets had supplied to the FSLN. From their first days in Managua, the Sandinistas had regarded the arsenal they inherited from Somoza as hopelessly old-fashioned. In 1980, with their only military threat a few cattle-rustling bands of former National Guardsmen on the Honduran border, the Sandinistas nonetheless coaxed 850 metric tons of military supplies out of Soviet bloc countries. The total rose every year until they were receiving 18,000 metric tons in 1984, including some of the most sleekly efficient killing devices on the isthmus. There were BM-21 rocket launchers, the "Stalin's Organ" that can fling a barrage of 40 rockets more than 12 miles through the air. And the AGS-17, which can spit out 100 grenades a minute. And tanks!—more armored vehicles than all four other Central American countries combined.[4]

As the guns poured in, the Sandinista military reproduced itself like an amoeba gone mad, doubling and redoubling at a frantic pace. When the FSLN guerrillas became the new Sandinista Popular Army in July 1979, they numbered about five thousand. By 1985, Sandinista active-duty forces totaled sixty-two thousand, with fifty-seven thousand more in the reserves.

Military skills did not, at first, keep pace with the numbers. The Sandinistas had plenty of experience fighting *as* guerrillas, but not fighting *with* them. Their first real innovation, in 1983, was to create the Batallón de Lucha Irregular (BLI), a counterinsurgency battalion of 750 to 1,500 men specially trained for rapid deployment. When militia or reserve units encountered the contras, BLIs were quickly dispatched to fight them. By 1985, there were about a dozen BLIs; they were more effective than regular army units, but by no means decisive.

In the weeks after La Trinidad, the Sandinistas took an even bigger leap forward: they married their powerful new helicopters with the BLIs. When contras were spotted—by units on the ground or a Soviet An-30 spy plane patrolling from the air base in Managua—the Mi-24s immediately flew to the scene and pinned them down with rockets and machine-gun fire. Meanwhile, Mi-17s ferried BLI troops into the area within minutes to surround the contras and finish them off.

The new tactics made it impossible for the contras to move by daylight or light fires at night, much less mount large attacks. Commanders who hadn't heard about La Trinidad soon learned the lesson on their own. In September a contra unit from the Jorge Salazar Regional Command assaulted a militia headquarters in Santo Domingo, in western Chontales Department. The contras were on the verge of taking the town when the Mi-24s appeared and, in a few agonizing moments, killed twenty-five men. That was the last significant attack by the Jorge Salazar for more than a year.

To the north, the Sandinistas organized the Tactical Operations Group, made up of five BLIs and twelve helicopters. The new group systematically cleared northern Nicaragua of contras, pushing them across the border into Honduras or west into the trackless jungles of Zelaya Department. The helicopters patrolled the southern slopes of the mountains along the Honduran border, blasting anything that moved; new infiltration was virtually out of the question. By the beginning of 1986, the few contras left inside Nicaragua were little more than vagabonds, huddled in out-of-the-way camps, trying to stay out of sight.

The Afghan mujahideen fighting the Soviet occupation of their country had faced these same problems a few years earlier. They were easily solved when the CIA provided shoulder-fired Stinger antiaircraft missiles that lock in on a chopper's engine heat and blow it to bits. But in early 1986, the CIA was still nowhere to be found.

12 | Not-Too-Private Enterprise

Alfonso Robelo moved along the receiving line, shaking hands and murmuring greetings. Robelo was no stranger to top-level gatherings; during his nine months on the junta that governed Nicaragua after the revolution, he met Jimmy Carter and Walter Mondale in the White House, Fidel Castro in Havana. Nonetheless, he was impressed with the amount of political and intellectual firepower concentrated in this one room. The Kissinger Commission—the blue-ribbon panel convened by the Reagan administration to study the problems of Central America—was visiting Costa Rica, and Robelo had been invited to this reception. He shook hands with Henry Kissinger, Jeane Kirkpatrick . . . and then a young man Robelo didn't recognize. He was wearing a suit, but something in his close-cropped hair and intense blue eyes suggested the military.

"Hello, how are you?" the man said in a hearty voice, firmly grasping Robelo's hand. When the handshake broke, Robelo gaped in astonishment. A small, folded piece of paper had appeared in his palm. Robelo fumbled the paper, dropping it twice, and finally shoved it in his pocket. Other guests eyed him curiously, and as Robelo resumed moving down the receiving line, he ricocheted wildly between mortification and amazement. When he reached the end of the line, Robelo hurried to a corner of the room and opened the paper. There was a phone number on it, followed by a message: *Next time you're in Washington, please contact me, my name is Oliver North.*

While Soviet bloc military aid flowed steadily to the Sandinistas—a total of perhaps $500 million by 1985—U.S. help to the contras zigzagged crazily. In 1982 and 1983, the United States provided about $48 million, part of it specifically earmarked in the secret intelligence budget approved by Congress, and part of it taken from the CIA's sizable contingency fund. For 1984 Congress openly voted $24 million to the contras, but also barred further aid from the contingency fund. Then, in October 1984, retaliat-

160

ing for the CIA's mining of the harbors, Congress cut off all aid. In August 1985, Congress changed course again, appropriating $27 million in "nonlethal" aid—food, uniforms, and the like.

The erratic behavior in Congress was partly due to the confusion brought on by the Reagan administration's foggy statements about just what the contras were up to. (Interdicting arms? Toppling the Sandinistas? Making them cry uncle?) But congressional equivocation was also caused, in part, by the desire to have a hand in managing policy without expending the time and energy to understand it.

Sometimes the intellectual sloth of Congress was merely silly—for instance, in 1982, when it approved an intelligence budget that included $19 million for the contras but then primly added that the money couldn't be used "for the purpose of overthrowing the government of Nicaragua." Sometimes it was smarmily hypocritical—for instance, in 1984, when after funding two years of a bloody war that killed thousands of peasant soldiers on both sides, Congress recoiled in horror from CIA mines that damaged a few ships, and cut off all money to the contras.

And sometimes it was downright daffy. On April 24, 1985, the House of Representatives voted down a Reagan administration proposal for $14 million in nonlethal assistance to the contras. The next morning, Daniel Ortega announced he was traveling to Moscow in three days to search for new economic aid. Congressmen went bananas at the news. "Daniel Ortega is a swine," bellowed one Democrat who had voted against the aid. But the Sandinista *comandantes* had been traveling to Moscow regularly since August 1979. "Do you think Congress is aware that professional wrestling is fake?" a contra politician asked me a few days later. Nonetheless, this time congressional ingenuousness worked for the contras instead of against them. The House reversed its vote, and in August, Congress approved $27 million in nonlethal aid to the rebels.

The nonlethal aid began arriving in contra camps in September 1985. The last significant amounts of CIA aid had come in July 1984. In between, the contras had survived on a trickle of off-the-books money obtained by a small group of overachieving military officers at the National Security Council, the main point of contact between the contras and the U.S. government after Congress cut off aid in 1984. The legislation terminating the aid prohibited contact between the contras and "any agency or entity of the United States involved in intelligence activities." NSC officials thought that left a loophole they could easily climb through; with a staff of only forty, the NSC had historically been in the business of advising presidents, not collecting intelligence or staging operations.

NSC officials began contacting, directly or indirectly, other governments, asking them for contributions. Israel, China, and South Korea declined. Saudi Arabia gave $32 million between June 1984 and March 1985; Taiwan contributed $2 million between late 1985 and early 1986. Meanwhile, the NSC also cooperated closely with a private fund-raising program directed at wealthy Americans that provided another $3.2 million to the contras.[1]

At the center of the effort was a nimble Marine lieutenant colonel named

161

Oliver North who coupled Boy Scout enthusiasm with Spartan dedication in the pursuit of his pet causes, which were many. He helped plan both the 1983 invasion of Grenada and the 1985 midair capture of several Palestinian terrorists who hijacked a cruise ship and murdered an American tourist, and he was constantly scheming to spring the American hostages held in Beirut.

But nothing was closer to North's heart than the contras. After he graduated from the Naval Academy and the Marine Corps' Basic School, North went to Vietnam in 1968. He left a year later with Bronze and Silver stars for bravery, and a conviction that Washington was selling out the fighting men on the ground. Later, as the North Vietnamese engulfed the South while the war-weary United States discreetly looked away, North broadened the indictment: Washington had sold out an entire *country* to the communists. As he became the NSC's dominant player on Central America, North swore that it would never happen to the contras.

North's first minor involvement with the anti-Sandinista campaign came in 1982. By 1984, it was his obsession. In May of that year, when the CIA began to sense that Congress was going to write the Agency out of the program, Duane Clarridge took North to a meeting of the FDN directorate in Tegucigalpa. Come what may, Clarridge told the contras, North would be their lifeline to the United States. Then, afraid he sounded too negative, Clarridge hastily added: "Don't worry. The United States will never desert you." The contras never saw Clarridge again.

Later in the year, as it became obvious that Congress was not going to appropriate another penny to the anti-Sandinista cause, Robert McFarlane, the president's national security adviser, assigned North to keep the contras together "in body and in soul." To North that meant much more than just scraping up some cash for them. He tried to become their cheerleader, their lead logistical planner, and their chief tactician as well.

He was more successful in some of those roles than others. His ideas about tactics tended to the grandiose. He wanted to hijack a ship carrying arms to the Sandinistas from North Korea. He wanted to seize Puerto Cabezas, in northeast Nicaragua, and declare it the capital of a liberated zone. He wanted to infiltrate commandos into Sandinista airfields and blow up Soviet helicopters on the ground. To help implement his schemes, North sometimes obtained intelligence from the CIA and the Pentagon and then passed it along to contras, skating along the ragged edge of even the most liberal interpretation of the laws regulating U.S. government contact with the rebels.

North's ideas struck most of the CIA officers who heard them as completely crackpot. They dismissed him as a bullshit artist, an amateur trying to play in their professional game. Perhaps a good deal of their discomfort with North was due to self-recognition—he was an NSC clone of the can-do, perpetual-motion, CIA officers with whom William Casey had stocked his Central American Task Force. Like many of the CIA men, North had only a superficial knowledge of Latin America—in briefings, he referred to satellite photos of baseball fields on Sandinista military bases as evidence of a Cuban presence, evidently unaware that baseball is Nicaragua's national sport—which he papered over with rabid anticommunism.

In any event, the CIA's attitude toward North was not shared by the contra leaders. They loved his supercharged approach and his unremitting optimism. When the contras met with North, they always came away with the feeling that it didn't matter how many helicopters and tanks the Sandinistas had—that they could win through sheer willpower. Of course, North usually had something more practical to offer as well: money. NSC fund-raising efforts channeled $41 million in cash, goods, and services to the contra northern and southern fronts between June 1984 and November 1986, more than the U.S. government dispensed through legitimate conduits during the same period.

North did not tell the contras where the money came from. In that, the contras were on equal footing with much of the U.S. government. Relatively few American officials knew anything about the NSC's efforts. And almost none was aware that North was using one of his covert accounts to fund another. In August 1985, in an attempt to win the release of American hostages held by Islamic fundamentalists in Lebanon, the Reagan administration began secretly selling arms to the radical Muslim government in Iran. North, who was deeply involved in the arms-for-hostages operation, hit on the idea of over-charging the Iranians for the weapons and then using the profits to help the contras. Although he didn't know it, the Ayatollah Khomeini sent $3.8 million to the contras with North's help between November 1985 and November 1986.[2]

One of the little-understood side effects of the congressional ban on CIA assistance to the contras was that when the Agency officers left, they took most of the contras' technical and logistical expertise with them. The contras had no one who could teach campesino soldiers to repair their radios in the field, no one who knew what to look for when purchasing an airplane, no one who knew how to forge the necessary documents to buy machine guns from Portuguese arms dealers.

Most of the contra political leaders had been chosen because they were fairly well known inside Nicaragua and could also help sell the program to other governments. But now, instead of moving in polite parliamentary circles, they had to go into the no-quarter netherworld of international arms traffickers and money-launderers. Much of the burden fell on Adolfo Calero, who since joining the FDN in early 1983 had become the most dexterous of the contra politicians, working comfortably with the CIA, Bermúdez, and the Honduran military and forging solid ties with conservatives in Congress.

Now in his mid-fifties, Calero had been a successful businessman before going into exile. He had been general manager of Managua's Coca-Cola bottling company and owned pieces of an automobile distributorship, a hotel, a ceramics plant, and a refrigerator factory.

But none of his business experience had prepared him for this strange new world where the most bizarre obstacles could surface without warning. Some of the problems were inexplicable. After Calero went to a good deal of trouble to open a Panamanian bank account to receive money raised by Oliver North, the account number somehow fell into the hands of an American contra supporter in Chicago, who sent a $30 check directly to the bank with a note wishing the rebels Godspeed in killing communists. The bank, which had thought it was dealing with a Panamanian merchant, promptly closed the account.

Other difficulties were more easily traceable. When money began to arrive, Calero delegated much of the buying to his younger brother Mario, who proved a singularly untalented purchasing agent. Mario Calero spent $125,000 on a speedy PV II, a World War II-era antisubmarine plane, thinking its velocity made it the perfect plane for supply drops. But the plane was so unstable when loaded that contra pilots were afraid to fly it. Told the troops needed packs, Mario bought thousands of duffel bags instead—strapless, so they couldn't be used in the field. (They wound up as expensive sandbags.) And the South Korean–made boots and canteen belts he purchased fell apart so quickly that some suspicious contra officials sent samples to the FBI, thinking kickbacks must be involved. No one ever proved that Mario Calero was stealing from the contras—though many people tried—but at the very least he was in way over his head.

Adolfo Calero handled most of the arms purchases himself. The first lesson he learned was that ideological sympathies counted for nothing in the bottom-line cosmos of the arms traffickers. Before the money began flowing in from NSC fund-raising efforts, when the contras were still penniless, Calero visited the Israeli military attaché in Washington to ask for help. The man promised he would be in touch.

A couple of months later the attaché called back. "I'm retiring, and I'm setting up a company with offices in New York, Israel, and London," he said crisply. "I'm ready to be of service. What equipment, exactly, do you need?"

"That depends on how much credit you can give us," Calero replied. The only response was a loud click, then the sound of a dial tone.

Later, when Calero did have some money for weapons, he found the best bargains were offered by the communist governments in Poland and China, which seemed perfectly willing to sacrifice socialist solidarity with the Sandinistas for the right price. The Chinese were so anxious to do business, in fact, that they didn't even ask for end-user certificates—the paperwork that vouches that weapons are being sold to a legitimate government, ordinarily required in every arms deal. It reminded Calero of the *comancheros*, the white merchants who sold guns to the Indians in the old American West.

Between 1984 and 1986 Calero was able to buy $19 million worth of guns and ammo. And each purchase dragged him deeper into a brass-knuckle quarrel between three sets of arms dealers, a conflict that often seemed more irreconcilable than the fight between the contras and the Sandinistas. At stake was not just the money flowing into contra bank accounts from NSC fund raising, but the much bigger sums that would be available if Congress ever approved more U.S. aid.

The first group surfaced even before the American aid ran out, early in 1984. James McCoy, the military attaché at the U.S. embassy in Managua when the Somoza government fell in 1979, had retired to work for an arms company. McCoy knew Calero from the old days, and he stopped in Tegucigalpa to suggest that if the contras ever needed weapons, he was the man for the job. A few months later, after U.S. support was cut off, Calero called McCoy and arranged to purchase $2 million worth of weapons and ammo on credit.

He discovered that McCoy and his partner, a former Marine named Ron Martin, were merely brokers; the weapons would come from a company called Gretch World. The ultimate source of the weapons, however, made no difference to Calero. Besides, whoever was behind Gretch World seemed enthusiastic. Not only did McCoy extend credit for the purchase, he announced that Gretch World would open a $14 million arms supermarket in Honduras—sort of a "Bayonets R Us," where the contras would have an unlimited charge account. McCoy and Martin were gambling that the U.S. government would be funding the contras again some day, and they would be ideally positioned to hit the jackpot in arms sales.

The seemingly perfect match between the contras and Gretch World, however, didn't last long. The CIA, North reported to Calero, thought the money behind Gretch World was suspicious. It was coming from Panama—the brother of Panamanian vice president Eric Delvalle was apparently involved—and the Agency was worried that the funds came from drug trafficking, stolen U.S. foreign aid funds, or both. The contras would need to find a new source for arms, and North had just the man: Richard Secord, a brusque, rotund, former U.S. Air Force general who could also help the contras set up an aerial delivery system.

Secord's life story was an eccentric mixture of bravery, brilliance, and ingenuousness. A West Point graduate commissioned into the Air Force, Secord won a Distinguished Flying Cross for a rescue mission in the Congo, flew two hundred secret fighter missions in South Vietnam in the early sixties, and masterminded Air Force involvement in the secret U.S. war in Laos. By all accounts Secord did a magnificent job, although reviews were mixed on the time he bombed the Ho Chi Minh Trail with Calgonite dishwasher detergent—to make it slippery, he said.[3] Secord rose to the rank of major general, frequently handling sensitive assignments (he set up the secret desert air base used in the unsuccessful 1980 attempt to rescue American hostages in Iran) and in 1981 became deputy assistant secretary of defense.

Everyone who worked with Secord noted both his acute intelligence and his prickly arrogance. It was the latter quality that caused him to maintain his friendship, and his financial entanglements, with a former CIA contract employee named Edwin Wilson, even after it was obvious to everyone else that Wilson had turned renegade, smuggling weapons and recruiting assassins for Libya's Muammar Qaddafi. When Wilson was finally arrested and sent to prison for fifty-two years, the fallout from the investigation wrecked Secord's career, although he was never charged with any wrongdoing. In May 1983, Secord took early retirement from the Air Force and went into business exporting electronics and security systems.

In November 1984, Secord arranged the first of four arms shipments for the contras, who would pay $11.3 million all told for the weapons he obtained. Calero was never very happy with the arrangement. Secord's deliveries were slow; the first shipload of arms, purchased from China, took six months to

165

arrive and was dubbed "the slow boat from China" by the contras. They also seemed expensive. (The price, although Calero didn't know it, included $1.9 million in profits for Secord and his business associates.) And the quality was not dependable. When Secord purchased a dozen Chinese-made SAM-7 antiaircraft missiles for $40,000 apiece, their electronic circuitry was rusty, and most of them wouldn't fire. One of the few that worked went off only after the contra triggerman gave up on it and lowered the weapon from his shoulder. The missile promptly discharged, nearly taking another contra's head off.

Calero didn't voice his complaints, though, until early 1985, when the third group of arms dealers entered the picture. This one was led by another retired U.S. general, John K. Singlaub. Singlaub had not only spent more than three decades in the U.S. Army, but he also knew a thing or two about clandestine operations and unconventional warfare, going clear back to World War II when he organized guerrilla units behind Japanese lines in southern China. Since leaving the Army in a public dispute with Jimmy Carter over the need for U.S. troops in South Korea, Singlaub had hopscotched the world, working with anticommunist guerrilla groups.

When he met with Bermúdez to offer the services of retired American military men as advisers, Singlaub learned some of the prices Secord was charging. He was appalled. "It looks to me like Secord is making a nice profit off you guys," Singlaub said. He showed the contras a dramatically lower price list for weapons he could buy through Poland. Calero couldn't believe the difference; Singlaub could get AK-47s for $135 apiece, and Secord was charging the contras $250 apiece. For the same money, the contras would be able to buy nearly twice as many weapons from Singlaub. Calero gave him the last $5 million in the contra bank account.

Calero never imagined that a simple act of thrift could have so many nasty repercussions. Secord, shown the list of prices that Singlaub offered, dismissed it. "He'll never be able to deliver on that," Secord predicted. North was even more upset. "To get these prices, Singlaub must be dealing with a crook," he told Calero. North wanted to call the deal off, but it was too late—the money was committed.

The other competitors for the contra arms business—McCoy, Martin, and their Honduran arms supermarket—took more direct action. The arms supermarket group was already deeply unhappy that the contras were buying from Secord and suspected that some kind of political fix was in. Yet another rival was simply intolerable. The supermarket's representative on the ground in Honduras, an excitable Cuban-American named Mario Delamico, used his connections in the Honduran military to obtain the shipping manifest for Singlaub's delivery. Then he flew to Washington, marched into the Polish embassy, and demanded the right to buy arms at the same prices Singlaub got. Within hours, Singlaub's European contacts were summoned to various Polish embassies around the world to be bawled out. The Poles had already had problems over the sale—the crew of one freighter quit when they learned where the weapons were headed.

The arms purchase from Singlaub was the last one Calero ever made. Shortly after it arrived, North announced he would no longer funnel cash to the contras.

Instead, whatever money the NSC raised would go into bank accounts controlled by Secord, who was going to set up an aerial supply operation for the contras.

As his involvement with the contras grew, Secord recruited a wide circle of business associates, Air Force buddies, and ex-spooks to help him (including several from the bunch that ran with Edwin Wilson). The Enterprise, as Secord called his blossoming organization, was involved in much more than just contra business. Any time Oliver North had a brush with covert action, The Enterprise was sure to follow: the secret American dealings with Iran, anti-Qaddafi propaganda broadcasts, shadowy Caribbean intrigues. The Enterprise owned half a dozen dummy corporations to disguise its activities and controlled bank accounts scattered through Switzerland, Liberia, and Panama.

But the heart of The Enterprise was the contra aerial supply system that Secord set up in late 1985 with the proceeds from NSC fund raising. He bought seven aircraft: two big C-123 transports, capable of carrying 14,000 pounds apiece, two smaller C-7 cargo planes, and three Maules for use as air taxis. The original idea was to supply the FDN troops on the northern front from the contra airstrip at El Aguacate in Honduras, and to help build a genuine southern front out of the tattered remnants of Edén Pastora's forces by supplying them out of a new airfield on Cape Santa Elena, a desolate Costa Rican peninsula. The Enterprise put $125,000 down on the purchase of a $5 million tract of land on Cape Santa Elena, then spent another $192,000 building an airstrip and a barracks on it.[4]

The aerial supply program, however, was snafu-ridden from the start. The Costa Rican airstrip was never usable because of improper drainage and wind erosion; the only loaded cargo plane to land there got stuck in the mud. (In May 1986, a new president who was hostile to the contras, Oscar Arias, took office in Costa Rica, rendering repair of the strip a moot point.) And the Hondurans, who often squeezed the contras to milk more foreign aid from the United States, banned supply flights from their territory just about the time Secord was setting up The Enterprise.

The Honduran ban was lifted a few months later, but by then The Enterprise supply operation had found a new home: Ilopango Air Force Base, in El Salvador. North, a year earlier, had helped cut Washington red tape so that a retired CIA officer named Felix Rodriguez could work with the Salvadoran air force on a counterinsurgency program. Rodriguez's ideas for the program had been hugely successful, and now he had enormous clout with the Salvadoran air force. North asked Rodriguez to use his influence to obtain hangar and warehouse space for The Enterprise at Ilopango.[5]

Even in an operation studded with colorful characters, the Cuban-American Rodriguez was one of a kind. Three times he had tried, with CIA help, to assassinate Fidel Castro. He was part of a sabotage team that infiltrated Cuba before the Bay of Pigs; when the invasion went awry, he took refuge in the Venezuela embassy in Havana and smuggled intelligence back to the United States. (One bit of information he passed along: reports that the Soviets were building missile bases on the island.) He spent another twelve years working as a

CIA paramilitary specialist in Cuba, Vietnam, and Bolivia, where he helped to capture Castro henchman Che Guevara. Guevara, minutes before his execution, gave Rodriguez his wristwatch.

During the purge of its paramilitary ranks in the mid-1970s, the CIA attempted to mold Rodriguez into a foreign intelligence officer: a case officer, a real spy, instead of a paramilitary knuckledragger. But there was a saying around the halls at Langley—when you tell one Cuban something, you've told them all—and it was not altogether stereotype. On Rodriguez's first undercover assignment in the Caribbean, while having a drink with an official of the local communist party, he blurted out the story of how he captured Che Guevara. Soon the CIA, citing a back injury Rodriguez suffered in a helicopter crash in Vietnam, eased him into a medical retirement.

Rodriguez was delighted to help the contras; to him, the Sandinistas were nothing but Fidel's goons. But as Enterprise planes began landing at Ilopango, Rodriguez wondered what he had gotten into. The first aircraft to arrive was a grizzled C-7 that lost an engine over Honduras. It began losing altitude, slowly at first and then sinking like a stone. The panicky crew started pitching out cargo: a $40,000 replacement engine for a crippled contra aircraft, $10,000 worth of parachutes and cargo-rigging equipment, a brand new Sears refrigerator. In the last desperate moments the crew threw away literally everything that wasn't attached to the plane, right down to the flight manuals, but it wasn't enough. The C-7 crash-landed at an emergency strip in Alcahutla, El Salvador. The phone was already ringing off the hook at Salvadoran air force headquarters; some peasants reported that a giant engine had landed in their village square and asked if this was a weird new war tactic they didn't know about.

The other aircraft were in only slightly better shape. They had no nighttime navigational equipment, and half the cockpit gauges didn't work. Many planes didn't even have altimeters. Engines conked out in the air with distressing regularity. There were no parachutes for the crewmen, and no radar detectors to warn of Sandinista antiaircraft weapons until Rodriguez bought a couple of Fuzzbusters at a hardware store in the States.

The crewmen were a mixed bag. Many of them were good, veterans of Air America, the private airline owned and operated by the CIA during the secret war in Laos. A few were head cases. But they all shared a certain confusion about what was going on. Some had been told they were going to be delivering food to refugees. "In dropping all this humanitarian equipment, you may have sealed cardboard boxes," one recruit was cautioned. "There is no need for you to look inside boxes."[6] Another, told he would be flying an executive jet, arrived for his first flight in a stylish blue captain's suit trimmed with gold braid.

When the crewmen went out to pick up one new mechanic arriving on a commercial flight at the San Salvador airport, they passed right by him—the man was so old and feeble he looked like he belonged in a nursing home. He was hearty enough, however, to swill a case of beer the first night and loudly announce that he specialized in fixing drug-smuggling aircraft at $5,000 a day. When he escalated his beer intake to a case and a half on the second day, Rodriguez bundled him onto a flight back to Miami. He eventually did the same with three British crewmen who spent several months in El Salvador—at a cost of $110,000—without ever flying a single mission. They didn't know how to pilot multi-engine planes, the only kind The Enterprise owned. So they spent their time drinking and running up $1,000-a-month phone bills to Europe.

The airmen's task was not an easy one. The original plans called for flying at night to nullify FSLN antiaircraft weapons. But The Enteprise's planes weren't properly equipped for night flying. On one of the first nighttime missions, a C-123 veered off course and grazed a mountaintop. The crew had no idea what had happened until they landed back at Ilopango and found tree branches jammed in the left engine.

The pilots tried starting the missions shortly before dawn to minimize their daylight time in hostile territory, but were thwarted by early-morning fog that hid the contras on the ground. They tried flying at sunset, but learned that rainy-season thunderstorms were common at that time of day.

The worst missions were also the ones that North and Secord insisted were the most important: those to Edén Pastora's old troops on the southern front. Even in daylight, the pilots rarely were able to locate the troops on the southern front. The pilots had map coordinates provided by the southern front commanders and relayed to The Enterprise by Joe Fernández, the CIA station chief in Costa Rica. But almost none of the southern front troops could read maps, so the coordinates were nearly always wrong. Mission after mission to the south was aborted.

The more Rodriguez saw of The Enterprise, the less he liked it. He was certain that it was being run by profiteers rather than patriots, particularly after he discovered that the operation was managed by Secord and his buddies from the Edwin Wilson gang rather than North. Those guys, Rodriguez believed, were little more than mercenaries. And there was corruption everywhere. The pilots were actually being paid $3,000 a month, but Rodriguez saw vouchers where their salaries were inflated to $16,000 per month. Someone was pocketing the difference.

By August 1986, Rodriguez had learned something else. Secord, North, and other Enterprise figures were trying to persuade the CIA to buy the aerial supply operation. It was only a matter of weeks, everyone was certain, until Congress approved new aid to the contras. And the managers of The Enterprise thought that a supply operation that was up and running ought to be worth at least $4 million to the CIA.

The reason the picture looked so bright for contra funding was another ghastly error of timing by the Sandinistas. On March 20, 1986, the House voted against resuming military aid to the contras. As the vote approached, both the contras and the CIA were aware that the Sandinistas had massed nine BLIs—about twenty thousand troops—along the Honduran border. Everyone assumed the Sandinistas were taking precautions against a burst of contra infiltration if Congress voted to restore aid. But everyone was wrong.

It all began with a CIA helicopter. In August 1985, Congress had quietly amended the law cutting off all contact between the CIA and the contras to permit the Agency to share intelligence with the rebels. It also allowed the CIA to set up a $13 million communications program for the contras, including training and equipment.

The first part of the program was teaching the contras to intercept Sandinista communications. In January 1986, the CIA began setting up listening posts on Honduran mountaintops just a few hundred yards from the Nicaraguan border, where teams of contras and Honduran soldiers—eighteen to twenty per post—methodically stole Sandinista radio signals.

On March 20, the very day Congress was voting against military aid, a CIA helicopter was carrying radio gear to one of the new listening posts in the Las Vegas Salient, a rugged patchwork of perpendicular mountains and dense jungle that juts into Nicaragua's Jinotega Department. Hovering over the post, the chopper began its descent—and suddenly there was gunfire from every side. In a matter of seconds, more than forty-five jagged bullet holes opened in the helicopter's sides and floor. The listening post was under Sandinista attack.

The pilot, a personable Rhodesian veteran known as Cocky, was fighting for his life. One Sandinista bullet smashed a bone in his leg, another tore an artery. The helicopter wasn't in much better shape, hemorrhaging fuel and hydraulic fluid. Cocky, tearing at the controls with all his strength, got the chopper back up in the air and turned it toward the headquarters at Yamales where the contras maintained a hospital. He didn't bother to use the radio. If he couldn't coax the chopper back to the base, he would to bleed to death before anyone could mount a rescue mission. It was a grim race to see who would give out first, him or the helicopter, and either way Cocky lost.

Coughing and sputtering, the chopper limped northwest toward the base. But with two mountains remaining between him and Yamales, the engine gave a final hack, then cut off; Cocky barely managed to put the craft down on a bare patch of hillside. Then he sat back in his seat and waited to die.

At Yamales, though, a contra pilot had heard the faint whine of an approaching chopper and then abrupt silence. Alarmed, he jumped in his own helicopter and flew toward the contra training camp, assuming that the other aircraft must have come from there. It was a wrong guess, but a lucky one just the same; the route took him right over Cocky's chopper. The wounded Rhodesian was rushed to the contra hospital, where he was in surgery almost continuously for twenty-four hours but survived to fly contra helicopters again.

The attack on Cocky's helicopter was the first warning that anyone—the contras, the CIA, or the Hondurans—had about Sandinista infiltration. There were nearly two thousand Sandinista troops from three BLIs inside the dense Honduran jungle, creeping toward the Military Instruction Center, a contra training base known as the CIM, its Spanish initials. The Sandinistas intended to annihilate the CIM with a surprise attack then decapitate the contra command structure by overrunning the Yamales headquarters a few miles away.

The Hondurans, although unhappy about the presence of the Sandinistas—particularly in numbers more than four times bigger than any previous border incursion—had neither the inclination nor the logistical ability to get involved. It was one thing to let the contras use bases in Honduran territory, quite another to send Honduran troops to defend them. The contras were on their own.

The closest contra force belonged to Rigoberto, the one-time cattle merchant.

After two years as one of Toño's subcommanders, Rigoberto had been given one of the Jorge Salazar Regional Commands as his own. Just three weeks earlier, he had returned with 2,800 troops after a year inside Nicaragua. They had no boots and no ammo, and many of the new recruits didn't even have guns. Bermúdez told him to round up the 900 men who were equipped and march them overnight to Papaleo, a mountain the Sandinistas would have to pass to reach the CIM.

The news caused a good deal of grumbling in the ranks. "Why should we have to defend Honduras?" one of the men asked Rigoberto while dozens of others nodded in approval. "We just got here. Let some other unit do it."

"We're going to do it because they're *piricuacos,* and our job is to kill *piricuacos,* whether they're in Nicaragua or Honduras," Rigoberto replied. The complaints subsided. By 2 A.M. on March 21, Rigoberto's men were on their way. At 5 P.M. the next day, they had their first contact with the Sandinistas.

For the next forty-eight hours, there was near-continuous fighting near the CIM. Rigoberto's troops were outnumbered and outgunned, but they knew the terrain much better. They hit the Sandinistas hard anywhere they had a small advantage, inched backward in search of better conditions when they didn't. Poor weather kept Sandinista helicopters on the ground, but their Stalin's Organ rocket launchers had the range to pound away at Rigoberto even from inside Nicaraguan territory. By March 23, the fighting had edged so close to the CIM that 250 new trainees who barely knew how to fire rifles were rushed into Rigoberto's lines.

Just when it seemed Rigoberto's men had been stretched to the breaking point, Commander Johnson came to the rescue. His unit had been camped at Banco Grande, getting ready to infiltrate into Nicaragua when the Sandinista attack began. On March 23, after a three-day march, his men hit the west flank in a thrust so savage and unexpected that the Sandinista troops buckled and ran. The entire offensive collapsed with such astonishing speed that Rigoberto's men slowed their pursuit, afraid they were being lured into a trap.

But late in the week, as he approached the border, Rigoberto realized just how completely the Sandinistas were routed. His men walked into a jungle clearing where a makeshift FSLN field hospital had been set up. Under the trees were two dozen bodies, their arms still connected to rubber tubes running up into empty plastic packages of plasma and antibiotics suspended overhead in the branches. The Sandinista army had left its wounded behind to die.[7]

The March 1986 incursion embarrassed Congress even more than Ortega's 1985 visit to Moscow, and in late June the House reversed itself and voted $100 million in assistance to the contras, including $30 million in military aid. The bill also allowed the CIA back into the war. Because the House bill differed slightly from the Senate version, liberal Democrats would be able to stall the aid for a few more months while the measures were reconciled in committee. But it was obvious that there would be more aid, and CIA involvement would make North and Secord's Enterprise an anachronism.

On the face of it, the approaching reentry of the CIA into the war effort should have been a cause for joy at The Enterprise. The makeshift aerial supply program based at Ilopango, always dependent for its existence on the whimsical charity of the Salvadoran air force, could be shut down. The aircraft and remaining supplies could be turned over to the contras themselves; after all, The Enterprise was set up with contributions intended for the contras.

But North, Secord, and the other Enterprise managers had a different idea: the CIA would *buy* the aerial supply program or at least subcontract with The Enterprise to keep running it. Secord had a prospectus prepared to tout the supply operation to the CIA—a remarkable document that listed the unusable Costa Rican airfield as an asset worth $1 million. It also set a price for subcontracting at $311,000 a month, which would have generated a cool $160,000 a month in profits to The Enterprise.[8]

North's motivation in trying to sell the supply program to the CIA appears to have been innocent enough. The nonlethal aid that Congress appropriated in 1985 was about to run out, and it would be several months before the new $100 million package of aid was finalized. North estimated it would cost $2 million to keep the contras supplied with food during the gap between the two U.S. aid programs. The way to cover it, North suggested to the CIA, was for The Enterprise to borrow $2 million to buy food. Then, when the $100 million aid package passed, the CIA could buy the aerial supply program for $2 million and The Enterprise would use the money to repay the loan.[9]

The motives of Secord and his business associates are far more questionable. From the beginning, they viewed the contras as their personal cash cow. When they sold arms to the contras, they marked up prices an average of 38 percent. Although they netted $16.1 million in profits on the secret arms sales to Iran, only $3.8 million went to the contras. The rest was divided up in commissions, or put in Enterprise bank accounts, and kept secret from both North and the contras. At the very moment that North—truthfully, as far as he knew—was telling the CIA that The Enterprise would have to borrow money to keep shipping food to the contras, The Enterprise had $5.5 million in the bank.

As far as Secord and the other Enterprise managers were concerned, the contras were little more than welfare clients, who didn't have the right to one thin dime of Enterprise assets. The Enterprise was even willing to take the contras hostage to wring money out of a reluctant CIA. In early August, when the Agency said it wouldn't buy the aerial supply operation—the CIA feared that Congress would assume it had been running the operation all along—Enterprise managers retaliated by grounding all supply flights, including a plane on the runway in Miami loaded with medicine the contras needed to treat an epidemic of mountain leprosy. When Felix Rodriguez, visiting Miami at the time, went to the airport and ordered the plane to leave anyway, The Enterprise threatened him with hijacking charges.

Secord always claimed that he didn't take any of the profits from The Enterprise. But his share was placed in a Swiss bank account from which he took undocumented, interest-free "loans" to pay for an airplane, a Porsche, and a stay at a fat farm. His partners didn't try to disguise their profits: they made about $2.4 million in less than two years from The Enterprise.[10]

* * *

In mid-August, the dispute between Rodriguez and The Enterprise cooled slightly, and the flights resumed. But Rodriguez expected that, sooner or later, Secord and his people would try again to make off with the aircraft. Rodriguez made sure that a contra soldier, armed with an AK-47, was on every supply flight to prevent hijackings.

For all the time, trouble, and heartache expended on the aerial supply operation, it had yielded few results. On paper, it appeared to be a success in the north, with more than fifty completed flights. But much of that was simply shuttling supplies from warehouses in El Salvador to warehouses in Honduras, rather than dropping them to units inside Nicaragua. And some flights carried as little as 350 pounds of supplies.

Much more effort was devoted to the few hundred bedraggled contras in the south. But so many missions were aborted after the contras misidentified their position that by mid-September there had been fewer than ten successful flights south. A new plan was developed: The pilots would pick out three drop zones in the south that were easily identifiable both from the air and on the ground—near the junction of two rivers, for instance—and deliver the supplies there. Units that needed supplies would go to one of the designated drop zones instead of trying to guide a plane to their own position.

The new system was much easier for the pilots, and they flew seven successful missions to the south in a little more than two weeks during the second half of September. But it also made it easier for the Sandinistas to predict where the supply flights might go and to station troops with antiaircraft missiles nearby.

On October 5, a C-123 loaded with ten thousand pounds of ammo, rockets, rifles, and boots took off from Ilopango at 8 A.M. for a drop zone in Chontales Department, in south-central Nicaragua. Four men were on board. Three were Air America veterans—the pilot, the copilot, and the kicker, who rigs the cargo and then pushes it out of the plane over the drop zone. The fourth crewman was a contra soldier with an AK-47, Rodriguez's insurance policy that the plane would return.

The pilot, William Cooper, was one of the best, having logged thousands of hours of flight time in Laos under harrowing conditions. Many of the crewmen, nonetheless, were reluctant to fly with him. Cooper had an agonizing case of psoriasis, a skin disease that turned his body into a angry red mass of scabs from the shoulders down. Doctors couldn't help him, and Cooper was in terrible pain almost all the time; even his bowel movements were torment. Cooper told some of the men that his wife left him because of the disease. He was growing more and more depressed, and his flying had become careless. Several of the men thought he had a death wish.

The C-123 flew out over the Pacific Ocean, then east across Costa Rica, and finally north into Nicaragua, up the east coast of Lake Nicaragua. When it was about thirty miles inside Nicaragua, a team of three Sandinista soldiers on the ground fired a SAM-7 antiaircraft missile that locked onto the engine exhaust. At 12:38 P.M. an explosion rocked the plane. In the back of the aircraft, kicker Eugene Hasenfus strapped on his personal parachute, the only one on board, and jumped. A contra patrol on the ground heard the plane crash and learned from campesinos that a crewman had parachuted. But before the patrol could find Hasenfus, he surrendered to the Sandinistas.

The supply operation shut down at once, its aircraft flown to Aguacate and turned over to the Honduran air force. But it was too late. For all the ostentatious cloak-and-dagger about The Enterprise's bank accounts and financial affairs, no one paid the slightest attention to operational security. The C-123 was a flying file cabinet of flight logs, address books, and identification cards that busted the program wide open when the Sandinistas recovered them.

The calls for congressional investigations, grand juries, and special Justice Department prosecutors multiplied daily after the C-123 went down. In November, the Reagan administration's secret arms deals with Iran were exposed. And late in the month, the Justice Department linked the two operations. Attorney General Edwin Meese announced that "between $10 million and $30 million" from the Iranian arms sales had been "deposited in bank accounts which were under the control of representatives of the forces in Central America." That wasn't true—the money was diverted to Secord and The Enterprise, not the contras themselves, and only $3.8 million was used for them. But the truth would not emerge for another year. Meanwhile Meese's words reinforced the stereotype of the contras as a crew of thieving Latin American plutocrats who idled their days away around the pools of their Miami condominiums.

Contra leaders seemed curiously unconcerned by this. I stopped to see Calero and Robelo on Thanksgiving Day and found them laughing uproariously over a cartoon of the Ayatollah Khomeini wearing a T-shirt emblazoned *I'm a contra too.* You guys certainly are cheerful, I observed. "When you have $30 million in a Swiss bank account," Robelo retorted, "you have to have good humor." They collapsed in guffaws. Later, more seriously, Calero explained that he was certain the contras would be exonerated. "In this whole Iranian deal, we are innocent bystanders," he insisted. "You will see that the people who criticize us for this have not been friends of the Reagan administration policy in this area anyway. . . . We will continue to receive aid from democratic nations and democratic peoples."

Calero was right about at least one thing: For a while, anyway, the contras would still be getting money. On October 17, Congress finally finished tinkering with the budget, which included $100 million for the contras. And when we spoke on Thanksgiving Day, the first aid was two weeks away. The war was about to heat up again.

13 | Spies and Lovers

The men were edgy as they took their seats around the big table. Confronting Commander Pastora was never easy, but this—telling a man his mistress is a communist spy—only God knew what might happen. As Pastora walked into the conference room and pulled out his own chair, more than a few of the men were wondering about the pygmy .22-caliber derringer that he always carried, even here in San José.

"*Comandante*, it's Nancy," one of the men said, plunging right into the deep water. "She listens too much, pries into too many things. Her story just doesn't add up. She's got to be working for the Sandinistas, spying on us." There was silence around the table as they waited for the black storm that was surely about to break.

But the commander's expression remained sunny. "No, no, you're wrong," Pastora insisted, waving his hand breezily. "She *was* a spy. But since I have been making love to her, she has abandoned the Sandinistas." Pastora had craftily deprogrammed her with his superadvanced libidinous technique.

The men were silent, their carefully marshaled arguments collapsing before Pastora's audacious new theory of counterespionage. They filed back out of the room. It would be another year before Nancy fled back to her Sandinista spy masters in Managua, rattling off radio codes and safe house addresses like an overwound talking doll. Pastora, it seemed, should have studied *The Joy of Sex* a little harder.

When it came to the spy wars, the contras unequivocally took a beating. In eight years of war, they never successfully penetrated the cities along Nicaragua's Pacific coast. There was no urban insurrection, not even occasional acts of sabotage or propaganda to bring the war home to the 60 percent of the populace that lives in the cities. As an American ambassador was fond of saying, it wasn't just that the contras didn't blow up Daniel Ortega's house, they didn't even spray-paint slogans about his mother wearing army boots.

175

The failure to move into the cities was costly, in both political and military terms. It kept the urban population sitting on the fence, unwilling to take up active opposition to the Sandinistas on behalf of a counterrevolution that wasn't a visible success. It allowed the Sandinistas to shape the image of the contras for the international press corps in Managua, which had limited access to the rural combat zone. And it meant that Nicaragua's fragile industrial infrastructure, teetering on the verge of collapse from Sandinista mismanagement, stayed functional.

A contra internal front could have crippled the Sandinistas with a single blow to the country's most inviting target: Nicaragua's only oil refinery. Owned, ironically, by Exxon, the refinery was more than two decades old; the antiquated equipment frequently broke down, and spare parts for the machinery were difficult to come by (all the more so because of the government's chronic shortage of hard currency). Even so, it refined about ten thousand barrels a day of crude oil from the Soviet bloc—including nearly every drop of the fuel required to keep the Sandinistas' fleet of helicopter gunships in the air. A well-placed bomb at the refinery, a lightly guarded and easily accessible facility just off a highway on the northern outskirts of Managua, would have thrown Nicaragua into economic catatonia within days. But not once in the course of the war did the contras even try.

As guerrillas, the contras were the exact opposites of the Sandinistas. The contras, when they were supplied, roamed much of the Nicaraguan countryside at will and enjoyed the support of most of the rural population. The Sandinistas, by contrast, suffered continuous betrayal and defeat during the years they tried to organize the peasants. It was only when they moved the war into the cities that they tasted success. The Sandinistas, for all their attempts to posture as the political voice of the campesinos, were essentially a movement of upper- and upper-middle-class students, the children of Nicaragua's aristocracy. The contras were an authentic peasant army.

The composition of the contra army, however, was a significant disadvantage when it came to setting up clandestine cells in the cities. Few contra soldiers had ever set foot in Managua, much less lived there. In the capital they would have been about as obvious, and as effective, as the Beverly Hillbillies.

The contras did attempt to set up some urban networks, but the Sandinistas quickly rolled up every one of them. Tomás Borge's State Security, closely coached by its Cuban counterpart and unfettered by the niceties of a democratic judicial system, worked relentlessly to prevent a contra foothold in the cities. Borge was anything but subtle. When he caught a whiff of counterrevolutionary sentiment in the Río Coco de Matagalpa region in early 1986, State Security made 1,500 arrests in less than two weeks.

At Borge's disposal were not only ten thousand State Security personnel,[1] but a vast network of informers. One of the first things the FSLN did upon seizing power was to organize the Sandinista Defense Committees (known by their Spanish initials, CDS) to be the "eyes, ears, and voice" of the revolution. The committees not only performed "revolutionary vigilance" for authorities, but they were also a powerful force for ideological conformity. Approval by the neighborhood CDS was necessary for a ration card, a license plate, a visa; if that wasn't enough, the CDS could summon *turbas divinas*—literally, divine mobs—of FSLN thugs to trash the homes of the politically suspect.[2]

The Sandinistas' ability to pounce on fledgling contra operations in the cities, however, stemmed from more than the reports of its domestic informers. Every contra organization was riddled with Sandinista spies who, when they weren't passing information back to Managua, were sabotaging equipment and disrupting operations with Stakhanovite zeal.

FSLN agents began penetrating anti-Sandinista organizations even before the war began. The very first was the embryonic internal front group that coffee grower Jorge Salazar was organizing when Borge's police shot him to death in November 1980. Two Sandinista military officers who Salazar thought were cooperating with him were actually FSLN provocateurs.

The Miami exile groups had scoffed at Salazar, said he was naive to think that he could organize without being infiltrated. Yet they were no more skillful. In August 1981, around the time the Fifteenth of September Legion's ex-National Guardsmen were merging with Chicano Cardenal's UDN, the UDN tried to set up an internal front. With $50,000 from the Argentines to get started and a promise from the Venezuelan government that its embassy in Managua would help, the UDN sent one of its officials to Nicaragua.

William Baltodano, who drew the assignment, was a former construction engineer who worked with the Sandinistas during the revolution but turned against them soon after. His engineering background would come in handy in the attacks the UDN planned to make on Nicaraguan industries. The first target: Nicaragua's only cement factory, twenty miles west of Managua in San Rafael del Sur. By blowing up the factory's kilns, the UDN high command believed it could shut down the factory for six months, and with no cement, the entire construction industry would grind to a halt. Baltodano spent several days in Costa Rica with Chicano Cardenal's brother-in-law, who had been the maintenance engineer at the factory and knew its layout.

Baltodano arrived in Managua on December 31, 1981. Three days later, before the plan got off the ground, he was arrested. The Sandinistas obviously knew he was coming.

If the Nicaraguan civil war had a master spy—a James Bond or a George Smiley—it was probably a loquacious young agricultural technician named Pedro Espinoza Sánchez. For at least four years, Sánchez wrecked network after network of clandestine contra operatives inside Nicaragua and stole thousands of their dollars. He used many code names: Napoleón, José Moreno, Halcón, Hernán. But most everyone, on both sides of the war, knew him as El Pez, the fish. In part it was a play on his initials, and in part it was because he was so hard to catch.

The first contact between El Pez and the contras came in 1980 when the Fifteenth of September Legion was tentatively recruiting for an internal front. El Pez, who was working at a Sandinista sugar mill, managed to infiltrate the group. It was a pattern that would be repeated many times: The contras were impressed with his enthusiasm, his imagination, and his evident familiarity with the necessities of covert operations. El Pez always seemed to know what

177

false identification documents would be necessary and how to get them; he always had ideas about how to find weapons and explosives; he was always the most effective recruiter. No one ever stopped to ask how he learned all these things working at a sugar mill.

El Pez perhaps had nothing to do with the misfortune of that first group, buried in its infancy by the political upheavals surrounding the Legion's merger with the UDN. But afterward, he stayed in touch with the new FDN. In 1982, he convinced FDN leaders in Honduras to put him in charge of unifying several small anti-Sandinista groups in the countryside around Matagalpa and to provide some money for the effort. He organized them into a military unit—and then led it into a Sandinista encirclement. Mysteriously, only El Pez and three others escaped.

After the Matagalpa debacle, El Pez made his way to Costa Rica and got in touch with Chicano Cardenal. Cardenal had split with the FDN, but his relations with the CIA were still good. With the Agency's help, Cardenal planned to organize an internal front. And El Pez volunteered his services. Cardenal—who remembered El Pez from the FDN but didn't know he had marched his military unit into a trap—welcomed an experienced hand. Within a few days, Cardenal made him the operational chief.

The Cardenal plan was the most ambitious of all the contra attempts to set up clandestine operations. It was to be organized around Nicaragua's opposition political parties. The parties would send about twenty recruits to Costa Rica for a few weeks for training in bombbuilding and other sabotage techniques. Cardenal, with the assistance of two wealthy anticommunist Costa Ricans— Oscar Saborío, the head of a big supermarket chain, and Rodrigo Crespo, who owned the Hotel Cariari resort—had arranged for the use of an isolated farm for the training. The CIA agreed to fund the operation and make small airdrops of explosives to the saboteurs inside Nicaragua.

Four times Cardenal flew to Costa Rica to meet with opposition party officials at the Hotel Cariari. Several agreed to help; the most prominent was Myriam Argüello, the head of a large Conservative Party faction. Only two or three people knew of the Argüello visit. One, naturally, was El Pez, the operational chief.

After two weeks of meetings, El Pez announced he was returning to Nicaragua to start laying the groundwork for the internal front, even though Cardenal didn't have any funds to support it yet. "Fine," Cardenal agreed, delighted at the dedication of his chief spook. "We'll raise some money here in Costa Rica and send a man inside with it next week." The courier, code-named Alarcón, left on schedule.

A few weeks later, El Pez smuggled a message out of Nicaragua. Bad news; it seemed that Alarcón was dead—it wasn't clear of what—and the money was lost. Cardenal sent back some bad news of his own. The CIA, angered that Cardenal had given a newspaper interview saying he was organizing an internal front, had broken relations with him. Cardenal was not optimistic that he could find another patron.

For a few more months, El Pez continued sending messages, asking about more funds. After several negative replies from Cardenal, the messages stopped.

178

And shortly afterward, Myriam Argüello was arrested. Several weeks later, international pressure forced her release, and she flew to Miami. "Chicano, what's going on?" she demanded. "Tomás Borge himself came to question me. And all he asked, over and over, was, 'What did you and Cardenal talk about in Costa Rica?' "

Now Cardenal began to wonder about Alarcón, the courier whose health had seemed so good when he left Costa Rica and had deteriorated so abruptly after he linked up with El Pez. But what could be done now? El Pez had disappeared and the internal front was dead anyway for lack of money. And after a lifetime of opposing Somoza and then the Sandinistas, Chicano Cardenal was worn out. He apologized to Myriam Argüello and got a job selling insurance in Miami.

El Pez, meanwhile, had shifted his attention north again. He got in touch with the FDN and wangled an invitation to Honduras to talk with Emilio Echaverry. In Honduras, El Pez skillfully played on the enmity between contra leaders. I've been training covert operatives for Chicano Cardenal in Costa Rica, El Pez confided to Echaverry, but that jerk couldn't come through with money or supplies. Why don't I go to work for you guys instead?

Echaverry, who hated Cardenal worse than cancer, was completely charmed by the idea that he was ripping off his old adversary, and in his glee didn't ask a single question about the FDN military unit that El Pez led to its tomb the year before. When El Pez left for Managua a couple of weeks later, he had a carload of FDN weapons, $1,500 of its cash, a map of its secret routes between Honduras and Nicaragua, and a list of the codes used to pass messages to units in the field on Radio Fifteen broadcasts.

The FDN command dispatched a steady stream of assignments to El Pez, who sent back detailed explanations of why every single one was impossible. Did Echaverry think it was so damn easy to just go blow up a television transmitter? What the FDN needed to be doing right now was organizing, not planting bombs. El Pez argued he could be more useful by helping supervise the network of agents set up by a controversial contra doctor who called himself Aureliano.

Aureliano was the nom de guerre of Manuel Rugama, a military academy washout who later got a medical degree. In January 1981, he gave up his medical practice in Mexico to join the contras. Because there were only two or three doctors, and because contra units rarely strayed far from the border, the physicians stayed inside Honduras. As contra troops moved deeper inside, and as more medical personnel joined the FDN, Aureliano argued passionately that some doctors had to start traveling inside with the men. That was where they could save the most lives. Intense and single-minded, Aureliano soon got his way. Leading fifteen pack mules loaded with medicine, bandages, and surgical equipment, he accompanied a contra unit bound for central Jinotega Department.

Unfortunately the unit was ambushed along the Río Cuá with such ferocity that it disintegrated. Aureliano, preoccupied with the wounded, was left behind. He tried moving north, to catch up with the remnants of his unit. But the Sandinistas were going north, too, trying to wipe out stragglers. So instead, Aureliano made his way to the nearest highway and caught a bus to Managua.

179

Contacting friends and relatives, he began stringing together a network of saboteurs.

After several weeks of clandestine organizing, Aureliano proudly contacted FDN headquarters in Tegucigalpa. The reaction was not quite what he expected; everyone thought his story was preposterous. Who ever heard of retreating from combat *toward* enemy lines instead of *away*? And on a bus, no less. Aureliano didn't help his credibility with the wild claim that his agents numbered in the hundreds. His tale provoked a rare moment of total unity among FDN commanders and CIA officers: To a man, they agreed he must be a Sandinista agent. Aureliano was ordered to return to Honduras. He left a relative, Carlos Acevedo, in charge of his spy ring and went back.

The gringos had recently introduced a new technique for ferreting out Sandinista spies, a polygraph machine. Aureliano was one of the first contras to take the lie detector test and one of the first to fail it. His expulsion was all but certain when Dr. Tomás, the head of the contra medical corps, stepped in.

Once a pediatrician in the National Guard medical corps with the rank of colonel, Dr. Tomás's real name was Ernesto Matamoros. He was perhaps the most widely respected figure in the FDN for the countless hours he put in patching up the Sandinista army's lethal handiwork. For nearly two years, Dr. Tomás had been working side by side with Aureliano in muggy, underlit contra operating rooms, and it was impossible for him to believe that Aureliano was a Sandinista. "This isn't fair," Dr. Tomás told Bermúdez. "You've got to give him a chance to prove that the lie detector is wrong."

A compromise was reached: Aureliano could return to his medical duties, under careful scrutiny, but his spook career was over. The ring of agents he left behind—which numbered more like eighty than eight hundred, Aureliano confessed—would stay under the command of Carlos Acevedo. Acevedo was a labor organizer, which gave him a wide array of contacts, and he was a pharmaceutical salesman who frequently traveled outside Nicaragua, which enabled him to keep in touch with FDN headquarters more easily. And to help the novice spy master Acevedo with the unfamiliar details of covert operations, the FDN provided a veteran cloak-and-dagger man: El Pez.

Acevedo was new to the spy business, but it was still obvious to him that there was something very peculiar about the way El Pez acted. He vetoed every proposed operation, and he was constantly demanding to know the real identities of all the agents. Acevedo's attitude toward the demands progressed from mild resistance to open hostility. One day in a safe house Acevedo and El Pez came within eyelash of shooting one another. Tempers cooled, but Acevedo began secretly recording his conversations with El Pez and sending the tapes to FDN headquarters.

At headquarters, there was an deepening sense that his nom de guerre wasn't the only fishy thing about El Pez. Echaverry, who was dazzled by El Pez's bombastic tales and glib explanations, was no longer chief of staff. And Bermúdez and the other officers, reviewing the record of botched and canceled operations, began to believe that their suspicions had focused on the wrong man. Aureliano's internal front group was genuine; it was El Pez who seemed to be playing a double game. They summoned him to Honduras.

El Pez realized he was in trouble from the moment he arrived at Tegucigalpa's Toncontin Airport. Honduran police instantly grabbed him and handed him over to the contras at a nearby safe house. There the questions went on for weeks. What happened to all the money that the FDN sent to El Pez? Where were all the agents he had supposedly recruited? What were their names? Why did he butt into Acevedo's affairs so often? El Pez deftly parried every thrust—not enough to erase the suspicions, but enough to deflect them. He was assigned to empty bedpans in a contra hospital just outside Tegucigalpa while the FDN tried to puzzle out what was going on. At the first opportunity, El Pez escaped, and the Nicaraguan embassy spirited him back to Managua.

As long as El Pez was able to keep them informed about what the internal front was doing—and thwart any really serious operations—the Sandinistas were content to let it putter along. The front's recruitment efforts, in fact, were a great convenience to the Sandinistas, alerting them to counterrevolutionary elements in Managua that they might not otherwise have spotted. Now that the contras were suspicious of El Pez, however, State Security had to move. In June 1984, the Sandinistas swept up about twenty members of the internal front, including Acevedo and Manuel Rugama, Aureliano's brother.

The Sandinistas made one last valiant attempt to reestablish their agent's cover story. El Pez was arrested along with the others and made a public "confession" of his activities. He was convicted of espionage and sentenced to eighteen years in prison. He gave a long interview to two FSLN sympathizers preparing a book of anticontra propaganda, portraying himself as a dedicated member of the FDN who was so tough that it took ten Sandinistas to capture him.[3] A few months after the arrests, the government granted humanitarian pardons to two of the convicted contras. One was a Catholic priest. The other was El Pez. The trick didn't work; after the notoriety of the spy trials, El Pez was burned, useless for undercover operations.

The contras made a careful assessment of the damage after the arrests decapitated their network of agents. Everyone that El Pez knew, it appeared, had been arrested. There was no reason they couldn't reactivate the rest of the network.

The inexperience of Aureliano and Carlos Acevedo, however, had already sown the seeds of the internal front's destruction. They hadn't compartmentalized their organization; almost everyone in the network knew everyone else. And now, after interrogating twenty prisoners at length, the Sandinistas knew everyone, too. For the next eighteen months, every time the FSLN felt that citizens needed another reminder that State Security was all-seeing and all-knowing, a few more members of the network were arrested. As for El Pez, he stayed in the business, recruiting new spies and helping them penetrate weak spots in the contra defenses.

In 1985, a lithe, cinnamon-skinned young woman from Managua showed up in Honduras, cursing the Sandinistas and asking for a job with the contras. For her nom de guerre, she chose La Garza, the heron, which seemed perfectly suited to her long, slim legs. The contras had plenty of female recruits, but most of them were campesino women, short and stocky and built for the hard life of the fields. The blow-dried La Garza was built more for fashion magazines. Within weeks, she had the run of the main contra hospital in Yamales, where the patients worshipped her and the doctors tried to pretend that they didn't.

One day La Garza told the doctors she wanted to confess something: She had come to Yamales as a spy. She was supposed to be collecting information and sending it back to Managua, but she didn't want to do that any more. She would never have agreed to it in the first place, La Garza added, except that her damn former boyfriend, who could talk an Eskimo into buying snow, had convinced her. His name was Pedro, but like everyone else she called him by his nickname, El Pez.[4]

La Garza was not the only alluring young woman who joined the contras with a hidden agenda. At the entrance to CIA headquarters in Langley, there's a statue of Nathan Hale. If the Interior Ministry in Managua had a statue, it would probably be of Mata Hari. In Nicaragua's civil war, "pillow talk" acquired a new and sinister meaning.

The first time the Sandinistas linked sex and spying was in 1978, when they were still guerrillas. One of their covert agents in Managua, a statuesque attorney named Nora Astorga, lured a Somoza general to her bedroom to be tortured and killed.[5] Perhaps anti-Sandinista politics are linked to some kind of hormonal imbalance, because the contras, time and again, fell victim to the same ploy. The first victim was the National Guard's top officer—Pablo Emilio Salazar, known as Commander Bravo—whose liaison with an old girlfriend in October 1979 led to his murder by State Security assassins. Bravo, who was in Honduras trying to organize the remnants of the National Guard into a force that could challenge the Sandinistas, didn't know his girlfriend had been recruited into FSLN service by her new lover, Edén Pastora.

Pastora's role in the operation against Bravo makes it all the more amazing that, later, he would be such a sap with Nancy.

Pastora had known Nancy for a long time. Her real name was Marielos Serrano; she grew up in Rivas, in the cattle country on the west side of Lake Nicaragua. She was small, with fair skin and dark hair. Men, asked to describe her, almost always used the word *mona*—cute. She took Nancy as her nom de guerre when she joined the Sandinistas during the revolution in 1978 and went to work in Pastora's logistical operation on the southern front. There she had a storybook romance with Popo Chamorro's brother William, who at nineteen was one of the youngest FSLN commanders. When William wasn't at the front, he could be found with Nancy in the camps in Costa Rica, holding hands, whispering. In May 1979, they were married in a ceremony conducted by another *comandante*. Two weeks later, in an attack on the border town of Peñas Blancas, one of the Sandinistas' own mortar rounds fell short, and William was killed.

After that, Nancy became a sort of spiritual figure for the southern front. Pastora often brought her to meetings of the high command, not to participate really, but more as an embodiment of Nicaraguan sacrifice, a reminder that young men were dying out there every day. Pastora was very tender with her then. After the revolution, Nancy moved into a house in Managua just down the street from Popo's, and he often saw Pastora's car parked over there. People whispered that Pastora's tenderness had turned to something else, but Popo ignored the talk. Life, he knew, goes on.

In 1982, as Pastora prepared a new war against his old Sandinista compañeros, Nancy showed up in Costa Rica. At first she didn't intend to stay; Popo had the impression she was just carrying a message to Pastora from someone in the FSLN. But Pastora wouldn't hear of her leaving. Within days she was installed as Commander Zero's official mistress. She even traveled inside Nicaragua to ARDE base camps alongside him, a contra soldier trotting behind them with a dainty bag of shampoo and cosmetics.

It was not unusual for Pastora to have a mistress; he had twenty-two children by God-knows-how-many women. Even among Pastora's men, steeped in Latin machismo, his behavior seemed excessive. Some whispered that Pastora was trying to compensate for his diminutive penis, so small it was known to his troops as el frijole—the bean. Such was Pastora's ego that he knew about the whispers and was delighted.

But Nancy was different than the starry-eyed revolutionary groupies Pastora usually shacked up with. Before long, she controlled Pastora's appointments: who he would see, what favors he would grant, what initiatives he would undertake. Nancy reviewed promotions, demotions, and dismissals, and her approval was crucial. "It was very feudal," recalls one of his aides. As she had in 1979, Nancy attended all the important meetings. But the men who remembered her from those days felt it was different. It wasn't just that Nancy was no longer shy about offering her opinions. She also seemed to be absorbing everything, asking questions about every minute aspect of ARDE. Any detail she didn't learn by day in staff meetings, she found out at night as Pastora blathered every secret thing he knew.

Nancy stayed in ARDE's San José headquarters for two years. Almost everyone there warned Pastora, at one time or another, that she was a spy. Popo Chamorro mistrusted Nancy so much that he would hardly say a word in her presence. The CIA went half-mad arguing with Pastora. Usually Pastora unleashed his political-reeducation-through-sexual-therapy defense. Sometimes he agreed Nancy was probably a spy but insisted he was only feeding her disinformation. Occasionally, he just stared blankly without saying a word.

By May 1984, the pressure was taking a heavy toll on Nancy. Weight loss turned her slim frame positively skeletal; she was visibly nervous all the time. On May 28, she simply disappeared. A few days later—after Pastora was nearly killed by the bombing at La Penca—she resurfaced in the headlines of the Sandinista newspapers in Managua. She had everything: the safe houses, the radio codes, the amount of CIA cash delivered to Pastora every month, and the name of every opposition figure who had secretly visited him in the past two years. She was the star witness at a series of spy trials.

And many of Pastora's advisers wondered if Nancy had managed to tip the Sandinistas off earlier about several ARDE operations that mysteriously failed, particularly a sabotage ring that the contras and the CIA had labored mightily to set up. The ring, equipped with an impressive arsenal of the CIA's top-of-the-line espionage tools—firebombs, tape players and megaphones to broadcast recorded firefights and panic neighborhoods, and even an FM radio transmitter that could interrupt government programming with a prerecorded Pastora speech—was busted without warning in February 1983.

Pastora, however, wasn't concerned. Long after she returned to Managua, he kept calling Nancy regularly, begging her to come back. Nancy was the one, Pastora said, that he truly loved.

Pastora wasn't the only contra who let true love, or perhaps true lust, blind him to the unlovely realities of Sandinista espionage. The FDN had its share of romantics. And none paid a more dramatic price than José Efrén Mondragón, the first contra war hero, whose affair with a Sandinista spy ended when his body turned up, stabbed and shot so many times that the wounds were difficult to count.

Mondragón, a former EEBI sergeant, was only twenty-one when he led the patrol that destroyed the Somotillo bridge in 1982 and launched the war against the Sandinistas. For a few months it made him the contra version of MacArthur. As a reward, the FDN gave Mondragón command of a task force operating in the same flatlands along the western border of Honduras and Nicaragua where he blew up the bridge.

Mondragón was a popular man there, with a lot of admirers. And none was quite as aggressively worshipful as the chestnut-skinned Nicaraguan named Norma Corrales, a regular visitor to the contra camps in western Honduras. She thought Mondragón must be the bravest guerrilla commander in Latin America to have snuck in right under the noses of the Sandinistas. That was what she told him, often. Mondragón, when he wasn't out on patrol, began spending most of his time with her.

The thing was, Corrales had said pretty much the same thing to several other contra commanders. Something about her put them off, though. She was too intense, almost theatrical, in her devotion. And then there were her frequent trips to Nicaragua, where she was often seen with Sandinista army officers. Corrales explained that she was merely bribing the officers to ignore her lucrative smuggling trade between Honduras and Nicaragua. The contra commanders suspected the real explanation was just the reverse, that the smuggling was merely a cover story for her close relations with the Sandinista military.

When other commanders warned Mondragón that Corrales was probably a spy, she told him that they were only jealous. Mondragón was too smart, and too brave, for this crummy army. Away from the contras, the sky would be the limit.

Caught in a tug-of-war between his woman and his army, Mondragón grew more and more confused. Confusion turned to chaos after an auto accident left him in a coma for a week. When he regained consciousness, he couldn't concentrate. Sometimes his thoughts scattered in mid-sentence. And sometimes a searing pain, deep inside his head, blotted out everything. He led a couple of patrols back inside Nicaragua, but Mondragón was in no shape to command troops. Bermúdez moved him over to Radio Fifteen for a rest.

Later Mondragón would tell friends that he never intended to defect from the contras. He just wanted to be away for a while, clear his mind, get his life in order. But Corrales warned that the other contras would kill him. They're always saying I'm a Sandinista, she reminded Mondragón. They'll think you're going to go back to Nicaragua, and they'll slit your throat. Her solution: we could ask for political asylum in the Mexican embassy in Tegucigalpa. In March 1985, they did.

But when Mondragón was permitted to fly to Mexico City, Mexican authorities turned him over to the Sandinistas, who bundled him onto a plane for Managua. There he was jailed until Lenín Cerna—Tomás Borge's right-hand man—paid a visit. There were only two options, Cerna said. One was to publicly accept the amnesty the Sandinistas offered to returning contras and cooperate with FSLN propagandists. The other was to stay in jail, where the rest of Mondragón's family might be coming to keep him company. Mondragón took the amnesty.

The amnesty gave Mondragón, at twenty-five, his second brush with fame. He was the only contra commander of any significance to return to Nicaragua, and the Sandinistas made the most of it. They printed thousands of leaflets with a picture of Mondragón hugging his mother. "He gave himself up, and he saved his life," the leaflet said. "The future of the contra is death." In the north, where the FDN operated, the Sandinistas pasted the leaflets to walls, nailed them to trees, dropped them from airplanes. Mondragón appeared on television, signed dozens of letters urging other contra commanders to defect, and cooperated on a lurid "autobiography."[6] The Sandinistas, in turn, gave him money and a small coffee farm near Jinotepe, southeast of Managua. They warned him never to travel north to the contra country except on FSLN-sponsored trips.

Mondragón's public performances, however, diverged significantly from his private thoughts. Norma Corrales had long since disappeared—he knew, now, that the other commanders had been right about her—and the mists in his brain from the auto accident were evaporating at last. The more clearly he focused on the world around him, the more he was appalled. It seemed to Mondragón that his entire life had been hijacked. He had never wanted to come back to Nicaragua, never wanted to shill for the Sandinistas. And he was haunted by the possibility that his appeals to defect might have been successful —that some contras might have returned to an uncertain fate after hearing him on the radio or reading his letters. He lost weight; he couldn't sleep; his face went slack and haggard. He made plans to leave Nicaragua.

The Sandinistas, sensing something was amiss, jailed Mondragón for several days. Lenín Cerna came to see him again. The Sandinistas were watching him closely, Cerna said. If he stepped out of line, the consequences would be serious.

When Mondragón was released from jail a few days later, in January 1988, he felt trapped. The Sandinistas would never let their prize-trophy defector get away. On the other hand, Mondragón couldn't bear to continue his life the way it was. In desperation, he sent a message to Bermúdez—part explanation, part apology. He'd been confused, under pressure. He hadn't intended to do these things. And to prove he was sorry, Mondragón added, he wanted to organize secret contra cells in Managua for sabotage and propaganda.

Mondragón's message looked, for all the world, like a setup, like another El

Pez. But there was a tortured quality to it that Bermúdez thought was beyond pretending. Intrigued, Bermúdez sent him some money and told him to go ahead. If Mondragón was pulling some kind of trick, the contras would lose nothing but a few thousand dollars. If he was serious, it could be a tremendous boon to the war effort.

As Mondragón prepared to put the money to use, he could feel the Sandinistas shadowing him. One afternoon in March 1988, he went to the offices of the independent human rights commission in Managua. Mondragón wanted to make sure that if he died, the Sandinistas couldn't turn it into one final act of treason against the contras. If he was killed, Mondragón told the human rights officials, they could be certain that State Security was behind it. He even hinted that death might be a relief. "If they think I'm guilty of something," he said, "I wish they'd carry out the sentence and get it over with."

Then he did the one thing the Sandinistas had warned him never to do: he went north, to the contra country of Chinandega Department. The Sandinistas tracked him. And on March 18, a State Security officer arrested Mondragón as he met with a cousin, another former contra. Their bodies were found the next morning in the Somotillo town plaza, just a few miles from the remains of the bridge Mondragón blew up six years earlier. He had been shot and stabbed more than 20 times, and there were marks where his wrists had been bound.

Mondragón's death brought him his last headline: *A Short, Agitated Life, A Tragic Finale,* the title of his obituary in Managua's anti-Sandinista daily *La Prensa.* The story made fleeting mention that Mondragón was once enamored of "a young lady that he met on the border, and of whom it was said that she did illegal business." The name Norma Corrales did not appear.

The Sandinista female spy corps didn't always use just sex to cast spells over the contras. Sometimes the figure of speech became disconcertingly literal. Playing on the superstitions of the peasant contras, the Sandinistas sent *hechiceras*—witches—into the camps posing as refugees. When the witches began laying down curses and using love potions to steal men from the other women, the camps dissolved into pure hysteria.

The single greatest outburst of sorcery was in 1989, when the Sandinistas managed to infiltrate six *hechiceras* at once into the headquarters camp at Yamales. For several weeks, the contras kept mum about the problem, but it came out into the open during a visit by Cresencio Arcos, one of the State Department's contra honchos. Several nervous commanders took him to a hut where the six *hechiceras* were confined.

"They're putting spells on the men, making them vomit up those insects," one of the commanders complained, gesturing at a pile of hellish-looking dead bugs in a corner of the room. "What are we going to do with them?"

Arcos, in one role or another, had been working with the contras for seven years. He had been asked for help with nearly every conceivable problem, from finding medicine for mountain leprosy to obtaining extra tickets to George Bush's inaugural ball. But this was the first time anyone had mentioned witches. They had to be pulling his leg. "I think," he said, with a perfectly straight face, "that the medieval ways are best."

When he saw the glances the commanders exchanged, Arcos realized he had made a horrible miscalculation. "That's just a joke," he hurriedly added, managing to keep most of the panic out of his voice. "The U.S. government does not countenance burning anyone at the stake. . . . Why don't you just send them over to the UN refugee camp at Jacaleapa?"

"We tried that," a commander replied gloomily. "When the UN people found out they were *hechiceras*, they sent them right back."

After a few hours of intense negotiation, Arcos persuaded the International Red Cross to take the *hechiceras,* and order was restored at Yamales. Not every Sandinista witch was so lucky. In 1982, a State Department official saw the corpse of another *hechicera* in one of the camps. The contras drowned her, then cut her head off so that her evil spirit couldn't reanimate the body.

Weakness of the flesh was not limited to the contras; U.S. officials proved vulnerable, a couple of times, to espionage concealed under thick layers of sexual magnetism. At one point during the war, both the CIA and the State Department's Office of Diplomatic Security learned that the U.S. ambassador to Nicaragua was having an affair with a Sandinista named Indiana Pérez, the sister of model and international FSLN fundraiser Bianca Jagger. The news of the liaison, though closely held, set off a minor earthquake in Washington. Even if the ambassador's conversations with Pérez stuck to purely amatory subjects, he was a married man, easily subject to blackmail. Around the time the affair was discovered, the ambassador's scheduled stay in Nicaragua was over. He asked for another tour, but his request was denied and his new assignment was a trivial one.

Even the CIA itself was not immune. In 1987, a "boff report"—the reports Agency personnel are required to file every three months on their sexual partners—revealed that a Honduran counterintelligence officer was sleeping with a CIA secretary. His interest was believed to be more than carnal.

The secretary's dalliance with the Honduran was dismaying enough to the Agency, but about a year later, Tomás Borge boasted of an even more startling counterintelligence operation. In May 1988, Borge was speaking to Miskito Indians in Yulú, a village deep in the jungles of the Atlantic coast, apparently unaware that foreign reporters were present. Borge was bragging that not a leaf fell from a Nicaraguan tree without Interior Ministry agents observing it (confirming, undoubtedly, the worst fears of his Indian audience). Why, he exclaimed, the Interior Ministry could even outspy the gringos. "We happen to have one of those agents right here with us today," Borge continued. "Maria Lourdes Pallais"—he gestured at a tall, striking brunette—"has carried out missions on behalf of the security agencies of the Interior Ministry in the heart of the CIA."

Pallais, a thirty-four-year-old reporter for the FSLN's official station Radio Sandino, was sitting with her husband John Carlin, a British newspaper correspondent. Carlin turned to her in surprise. Pallais silently nodded *yes.*

That her own husband only learned of Pallais's intelligence activities from a Tomás Borge speech indicates just how good her cover was. Until she took the Radio Sandino job, barely a month before Borge's impetuous revelation, few of her acquaintances suspected that she had any fondness for the FSLN. She was a second cousin of Tachito Somoza; her father was Somoza's private secretary, her uncle president of the Somoza-dominated congress. Pallais sat out most of the war in the United States getting a graduate degree in journalism from Columbia, then working for the Associated Press in New York.

In the early 1980s, she returned to Central America as a free-lance journalist, working occasionally for the Long Island newspaper *Newsday* and the CBS television news program *60 Minutes.* In 1982, she turned up in Costa Rica, where Edén Pastora was preparing to go to war against the Sandinistas. She claimed to be a contra supporter—not implausible, given her family connections to Somoza—and told Pastora her credentials as a journalist would make her useful as a courier. She shuttled back and forth, carrying messages from Costa Rica to Pastora's supporters inside Nicaragua. Sometimes she traveled with Pastora as his interpreter. Predictably, their relations became more than friendly.

Borge's claim that Pallais wormed her way into "the heart of the CIA" is a wild exaggeration. But she met a few times with Agency officers to offer information and perhaps could have helped the Sandinistas identify some of the people in the CIA's Costa Rica station. Mostly, however, she was spying on Pastora rather than the CIA, keeping an eye on him during his travels to the United States, where he was outside the reach of most of the other Sandinista agents planted in ARDE.

After Borge blew her cover, Pallais admitted to her friends that the story was true and instructed her New York attorney to confirm it to American reporters. But her confession didn't deter Cable News Network from hiring her as a part-time correspondent in Managua, despite angry complaints from the Nicaraguan exile community in Miami.

What might have been expected to be the busiest nest of spies in Central America—the CIA station in Managua—was a much quieter place than everyone believed. In Soviet bloc countries, because the risk of being tricked and exposed by the local intelligence service is so much greater, CIA officers are usually little more than mail clerks. Their most important job is servicing dead drops, the locations where agents pick up and drop off messages. The agents—the members of the host government who are passing information to the United States—are usually recruited when they're traveling outside the country. They almost never deal face-to-face with the CIA officers at the embassy.[7]

After the U.S. economic embargo of 1985 curtailed travel between the two countries, the Managua CIA station was forced to become more active in recruiting agents. But by then, the station was down to about a dozen officers, compared with more than one hundred in Honduras, and the station chief was a Middle East specialist who spoke no Spanish.

The Managua station had never really recovered from the twin hits it took in 1979 and 1981. As the revolution ended in 1979, the National Guard's intelligence service bolted from the country without destroying its files. The Sandinistas were able to sweep up nearly all of Somoza's agents, many of whom worked for the CIA as well. Two years later, a West German journalist released a catalog of CIA personnel assigned to Central America and the Caribbean, a list that burned thirteen Agency people in Managua. Afterward, the Sandinistas continued bouncing Agency officers from the embassy, either through outright expulsion or by publicly naming them, which forced their removal. Of nine embassy officials the Sandinistas publicly fingered as CIA officers between 1983 and 1986, at least four were indeed with the Agency—two of them station chiefs.

What covert work the Managua station undertook did not always get rave reviews. In August 1986, State Security arrested Guillermo Quant, the owner of a large Managua trucking company and vice president of the Nicaraguan Chamber of Commerce, on espionage charges. Throughout Managua the reaction was skeptical. Quant was such an outspoken anti-Sandinista that he seemed a poor choice as a spy. And the equipment that the State Security agents supposedly seized from his house, including a hollowed-out bathroom scale stuffed with secret codes, seemed so absurdly cloak-and-dagger that it almost had to have been planted.

But when the U.S. embassy had its regular Monday staff meeting a few days later, Ambassador Harry Berghold seemed to endorse the charges. And he wasn't pleased. "Can you believe those bungling assholes recruited that guy?" he growled. "Have you ever heard of anything so stupid? What did they think they were going to get out of him that they couldn't get by reading the newspapers?" Afterward, the staff was equally divided over which was more shocking: Berghold's open contempt for the CIA or his blunt confirmation of the identity of an American-recruited spy.

Of course, how many spies the Agency managed to recruit in high Sandinista circles is unknown. There appears to have been at least one. In late 1986 and early 1987, the Tegucigalpa CIA station was ordered to plan a lightning rescue from Managua. The officers who worked on the plan had no idea whom they were supposed to extricate, but it was obviously someone considered to be of dramatic importance. The plan was never put into effect, so the identity remained secret.

One possible name: Maj. Róger Miranda, literally the right hand of Sandinista Defense Minister Humberto Ortega (Ortega's right arm was withered from an old gunshot wound, and Miranda accompanied him to all meetings to take notes), who defected to the United States in November 1987. A contra official who worked intimately with the CIA assured me that Miranda was not a defector but a spy, recruited much earlier by the Agency. Miranda, the contra official said, bolted because he believed the Sandinistas were on the verge of discovering his treachery. Miranda, however, has publicly denied that he was a spy. It is known that, upon defecting, he brought with him details of the Sandinistas' long-range agreements with the Soviets on weapons, their plans to build a six-hundred-thousand-man army, and the number of Humberto Ortega's secret Swiss bank account.

To the north, in Honduras, the CIA had its hands full advising, training, and supplying the contra army, at the same time it finessed a delicate

189

political situation with the Hondurans. To the extent anyone paid attention to espionage, it was mainly counterintelligence—trying to stop Sandinista infiltration of the contras.

One thing that made it slightly easier was that the Honduran intelligence agency had bugged the Nicaraguan embassy in Tegucigalpa top to bottom, and CIA officials got daily transcripts of what the microphones picked up. They helped squelch several attempted penetrations of the contras. One telephone tap confirmed the CIA's worst suspicions about the international news media. A foreign wire service reporter called the Nicaraguan ambassador with an offer to arrange the defection of a contra soldier. The conversation also strongly suggested that relations between the reporter and the ambassador went far beyond the cordial.[8]

Even when the Honduran bugs disclosed the presence of a Sandinista spy in the contra ranks, it was not always easy to get the contras to act. The case that drove the CIA craziest involved a contra base commander named Armando López, a former National Guard lieutenant whose nom de guerre was Policía. Policía stubbornly refused to believe his girlfriend Estrella was a Sandinista spy. Even when the Americans showed him transcripts of the phone taps where Estrella was giving detailed descriptions of troop movements to a former boyfriend who worked at the Nicaraguan embassy, Policía insisted there was some other explanation.

Finally the CIA got the contras to transfer Policía up to El Salvador, where he acted as the liaison with Richard Secord's private air supply network. But, unknown to the CIA, he took Estrella along. No one realized she was there until October 1986, when one of the supply planes was shot down and crew member Eugene Hasenfus captured. Nobody could understand how the Sandinistas got so much information out of Hasenfus so fast, until it was discovered that Estrella had been providing them with material for months. This time, the CIA got Policía transferred to Swan Island, the remote coral reef 150 miles offshore in the Atlantic where its own supply planes were headquartered. And the only way Estrella could visit, the Agency added, was if she could swim to it.[9]

Estrella's background—she was a former National Guardsman herself, from the police division—offered perfect camouflage for a spy. In truth, however, Sandinista agents didn't need many false credentials. Almost anyone who could make his or her way to a contra camp would be welcomed with open arms. The contras had neither the time, capacity, nor inclination to do detailed background checks on every new recruit. Some commanders thought that as many 10 percent of the volunteers were Sandinistas. Even if that estimate is high, hundreds of penetrations unquestionably took place.[10]

But encouraging the contras to improve their counterintelligence capacity was an awkward matter for the CIA. From the very beginning, the counterintelligence office had been one of the principal sources of the contras' reputation as thugs. The first head of counterintelligence was Ricardo Lau, a Chinese-Nicaraguan whose eyes were so empty that even CIA officers shuddered when they saw him. "I believe if you ever met Chino Lau, you'd know that you were in the presence of someone special," a retired Agency officer once told me.

Lau was an excellent counterintelligence officer. He had an acute sensitivity to evasion, a good eye for details that didn't quite add up. And ruthlessness—which Lau possessed in abundance—is an important asset for counterintelligence officers, who must tear apart elaborate cover stories that have been carefully designed to ingratiate. But the ruthlessness has to be controlled within an institutional framework; tearing apart cover stories is one thing, tearing apart people is another. It was not clear that Lau knew the difference.

Lau was a colonel in the National Guard, a veteran of Somoza's Office of Security, which functioned as both Nicaragua's FBI and CIA. Those foolish or unlucky enough to fall into the office's hands were not treated gently. When he took over the same chores for the contras, Lau saw no need to change his work practices. He had, after all, even less accountability: in a guerrilla army, where recruits were under no obligation to stay and there was no central personnel registry, a suspect summoned to Lau's office could disappear without attracting undue attention. Some did.

The CIA began pressuring Bermúdez to get rid of Lau in early 1982 after hearing complaints about him, some from within the FDN, some from Edén Pastora, whom the agency was courting at the time. Bermúdez resisted for months. Lau was doing good work—nearly everyone he accused of spying for the Sandinistas proved guilty. And, Bermúdez believed, most of the complaints against him were politically motivated, a product of the old feud between the EEBI and the regular National Guard. In late 1982, the CIA got tough. "There won't be one more penny for your organization," Duane Clarridge told Bermúdez, "unless you dismiss Chino Lau from the general staff."

Complying in a technical sense, Bermúdez took away Lau's intelligence responsibilities and demoted him from the general staff. But he kept Lau on as chief of counterintelligence until 1985, when a series of scandals broke. First, the Honduran army blamed Lau for the murders of one hundred leftists—eighteen Hondurans and eighty-two Salvadorans—between 1982 and 1984. The army was using Lau as a scapegoat; most of the murders, in fact, had been committed by General Alvarez and his Military Intelligence Battalion 316. But Lau worked closely with Alvarez and had a hand in some of the killings.

The other charge was even more scandalous and had even less foundation. The former chief of Salvadoran military intelligence, Roberto Santivañez, accused Lau of arranging the murder of El Salvador's Archbishop Oscar Romero in 1980 in return for $120,000. Santivañez had been in the United States for more than a year talking about the activities of El Salvador's bloodthirsty right-wing death squads. But, oddly enough, he never mentioned Lau until the 1985 congressional vote on U.S. aid to the contras was approaching. (And he never explained why the Salvadoran death squads, which efficiently murdered thousands of their countrymen between 1979 and 1982, would need to turn to outside consultants.) His story has never been corroborated, and Salvadoran police who have investigated the murder do not believe it.

The truth of the charges, though, was secondary to the publicity surrounding them. Bermúdez told Lau he had to leave.

No contra counterintelligence officer who followed was ever as effective. And the CIA, fearing another Lau, shied away from pushing the issue too hard. Instead, the Agency brought in a polygraph operator and—unconcerned that he didn't speak Spanish—put him to work testing commanders, new recruits, and anyone else who seemed suspicious.

When the CIA demanded polygraph tests of ARDE leaders in the south, a wailing chorus of complaints arose over gringo arrogance and wounded national pride, primarily from the contras most likely to fail. In the north, however, the contras treated the tests mostly as a curiosity. They knew the lie detector didn't work. Several loyal commanders, like Aureliano, failed, and several supposed defectors from State Security passed, only to sneak back to Managua later. They wondered why the CIA had such faith in it.[11]

The polygraph did help in a few cases, including the biggest single contra roundup of Sandinista infiltrators in mid-1987. American military aid had just begun to flow again, after a layoff of more than two years, but the contras were having serious problems with sabotage in the Yamales headquarters camp and at the Aguacate air base.

Units headed back into Nicaragua were discovering that their new machine guns, mortars, and radios were missing key parts. Three contra planes were sabotaged. One, a C-47, crashed after a saboteur dropped a fountain-pen cap inside the gas tank; a few minutes after the plane took off, the cap was sucked into the fuel line, where it cut off the flow of gas. The best contra plane, a DC-6 that could carry twenty thousand pounds, crashed on takeoff after running over nails. And one of the smaller planes was wrecked as it landed when a horse released by a Sandinista agent galloped onto the runway, straight into the propellers.

Perhaps worst of all were the incidents at the main contra hospital in Yamales. Patients who appeared to be in good condition were dying without warning in the middle of the night: men who survived being shot by the Sandinistas or stepping on one of their land mines, who survived the long trip back out of Nicaragua by stretcher, who survived difficult surgery, only to die in their sleep. Much of the medical staff was depressed; a few members, like Dr. Tomás, were alarmed.

The mystery began to unravel when guards killed an intruder trying to slip into one of the border camps at night. On his body was found a piece of paper with the name of a contra soldier stationed at Yamales. Through interrogations and lie-detector tests, contra counterintelligence officers began rolling up the FSLN network, one name at a time. Eventually there were twelve, but their ringleader—apparently located in the nearby town of Catacamas, with a direct radio link back to Nicaragua—was never caught.

Some contras, when they learned they'd been working shoulder to shoulder for months or even years with Sandinista agents, felt a volcanic rage. It was at the hospital, where three paramedics turned out to be Sandinistas, that emotions ran highest. The paramedics had killed at least five wounded contras, and perhaps many more, by adding potassium chloride to the medications dripping into the patients through intravenous tubes. The drug upset the men's electrolyte balances, throwing their heartbeats into wildly irregular patterns and finally stopping them altogether. Without autopsies, the deaths looked completely natural.

Almost everyone at the hospital wanted to kill the paramedics, but Dr. Tomás locked them in his office for protection. Four months later, when the paramedics were part of a group of eighty Sandinista POWs who were released in Costa Rica, Dr. Tomás was sorry he saved them. "It wasn't fair that they got off so easily for that," he told one of the Americans. "What they did was cold-blooded murder."

The Sandinistas were more successful at sabotage and spying, but there was one small corner of the clandestine war where the contras had the edge: propaganda broadcasting. With the aid of CIA money but relying, for the most part, on their own ideas and expertise, the contras built the most sophisticated clandestine broadcast operation in the history of guerrilla warfare.

For most Nicaraguans, radio was by far the most important news medium. Fewer than half the country's homes had televisions, and illiteracy was high, despite Sandinista claims to have wiped it out. But nearly everyone had a cheap portable radio. The Sandinistas, recognizing the importance of radio, moved early to establish their control over it by closing down newscasts. At the end of the Somoza dynasty, there were forty-three different radio news programs in Nicaragua. After four years of Sandinista rule, there were only thirteen.[12]

Several of the contra politicians who joined the Fifteenth of September Legion were former Nicaraguan broadcasters who viewed radio as an important weapon against the FSLN. Long before the CIA got involved in the anti-Sandinista effort, the contras were beaming shortwave radio broadcasts into Nicaragua on Radio Fifteenth of September, a primitive station set up with $5,000 raised from the Miami exile community. Radio Fifteen began with an hour of programming a day and eventually expanded to two and a half hours, broadcast three times daily. To prevent jamming, it had five transmitters with five frequencies each.

As the Sandinistas closed down more independent news programs, Radio Fifteen grew in popularity. In November 1986, when Radio Fifteen broadcast a report suggesting that the FSLN was kidnapping children to steal their blood for transfusions to wounded soldiers, an angry mob numbering more than two thousand attacked a Managua police station with rocks and sticks.[13]

The CIA not only funded the expansion of Radio Fifteen, but it also bought a commercial station in Costa Rica and dedicated it to the contra cause. Radio Impacto was purchased with CIA money routed through Venezuela, and although it tried to retain the facade of an ordinary commercial station, the changes were anything but subtle. Radio Impacto's powerful AM signal was redirected north until it could be heard throughout much of Nicaragua at night. And it was augmented with simultaneous broadcasting on four different shortwave frequencies, making it nearly impossible to jam.

By day, the all-news station carried an unusually high number of stories about Nicaragua—economic shortages, government corruption, public hostility toward the Sandinistas—and by night, probably 98 percent of its programming related to Nicaragua. Although the contras did not directly operate Radio Impacto, the station appeared on their propaganda department's secret table of organization.

Radio Impacto was not the only anti-Sandinista station in Costa Rica. ARDE operated a low-powered AM station known as Radio Southern Front. In the early days, the ARDE broadcasts were made from three small, jeep-mounted transmitters along Costa Rica's western border with Nicaragua; the signal could reach barely the southern outskirts of Managua. Later, a more powerful transmitter was located in San José and the programming was increased to four or five hours a night. Like Radio Fifteen, Radio Southern Front was a mixture of military exhortations and crude political satire.

ARDE's most novel propaganda tool was a World War II–era antenna mounted on the side of the towering Orosi volcano south of San José. Technicians modified it to transmit on the same frequency used by Sandinista television. One night in October 1982, Popo Chamorro went to the antenna with a portable TV capable of picking up the Sandinista television signal. When the evening news began running video footage of a Daniel Ortega speech, Popo flipped a switch, and the ARDE antenna beamed a signal to the television repeater in Managua. Instantly the picture of Ortega flickered with distortion, and his speech was drowned out by the voice of Edén Pastora: "This is ARDE, calling to the people of Nicaragua! We are the true revolutionaries!" ARDE used the Orosi antenna more than one hundred times between 1982 and 1985 to disrupt Sandinista television signals in southern Nicaragua.

The contras also got into the newspaper and magazine business, with mixed success. The first FDN publishing venture was a small photo magazine, *Comandos,* aimed at Nicaraguan peasants. But it was difficult to distribute inside Nicaragua. Far more successful was *Nicaragua Hoy,* a four-page weekly supplement inserted into daily newspapers in seven Latin American countries with a total circulation of 624,000. Although the supplement was aggressively pro-contra, it was crisply written and didn't carry any identification as a contra publication; many readers simply assumed it was produced by their local paper.

The CIA's budget for *Nicaragua Hoy* (which was written, for the most part, by former *La Prensa* editor Pedro Joaquín Chamorro, Jr., and his wife, Marta Lucía) was a closely held secret. But in terms of bang for the buck, it was surely a better deal than the tiny intellectual digest *Resistencia. Resistencia,* with a circulation of barely five thousand, cost $33,000 per issue just for printing and distribution. *Resistencia* existed mainly as a makework project for Arturo Cruz, Jr., and several other liberal contra politicians with good connections at the State Department.

Contra propaganda efforts reached their peak with Radio Liberación, a 50,000-watt AM station that went on the air in 1987 and lasted more than two years. Although the CIA funded it, at a cost of $60,000 per month, it was one of the few contra projects the gringos never interfered in. Both technically and editorially, Radio Liberación was contra designed and contra operated.

The station was deliberately designed to make it difficult for the Sandinistas to apply political pressure to neighboring governments to shut it down. The studios were in Miami, at the contra political offices near the international airport. Thirteen hours a day of live programming were beamed via satellite to an AM transmitter in El Salvador, as well as shortwave transmitters in El Salvador, Honduras, and Costa Rica. But at various times throughout the day, totaling two hours, the live signal from Miami left the air, and each of the local transmitters would broadcast a different package of taped programs with "localized" news for northern, southern, and western Nicaragua. The idea was to confuse the Sandinistas about Radio Liberación's location, and it succeeded. Although the FSLN pinpointed the AM transmitter in El Salvador and got it closed down after about a year, the Sandinistas were never able to zero in on the shortwave antennas.

Radio Liberación's content was a radical departure from Radio Fifteen and Radio Southern Front. The latter two were military radio stations, designed to recruit new troops and help maintain the discipline and morale of contra units inside Nicaragua. They maintained a steady patter about contra military victories, even when there weren't any.

Radio Liberación, on the other hand, was a broadly political station that rarely mentioned armies or battles. It offered interviews with anti-Sandinista politicians of all ideological stripes, including many who weren't affiliated with the contras. Its newscasts maintained a pretense of evenhandedness. Radio Liberación also included sportscasts, music, and other entertainment programs.

Radio Liberación's success attracted many imitations. Radio Venceremos, the clandestine station of the Salvadoran guerrillas, started spicing up its hours of Marxist dialectics with music and sports shows. And Panamanian opponents of Gen. Manuel Noriega, who had closed all the country's opposition news media, came to Miami several times to consult the contras about setting up a radio station.

The Panamanians didn't reveal their plans. But in 1989, as the war in Nicaragua slowed to a crawl, Nicaraguans noticed that Radio Impacto was getting difficult to hear. Its signal seemed to have been redirected south, toward Panama. Nicaraguan news slowly disappeared from its broadcasts, and at night its announcers talked about almost nothing but Panama. On December 20, 1989, a few minutes past midnight, Radio Impacto's regular news show left the air. Instead a man with a clipped voice came on the air, reciting terse, nonsensical sentences: *Tango force, tango force, to point alpha. Delta force, delta force, to position five.* He continued for more than two hours, but by then most casual listeners had tuned to other stations. And by morning, in all the excitement over the U.S. invasion of Panama, everyone forgot all about it.

14 | 1987

Everywhere Mike Lima looked, the Yamales camp was a study in schizophrenia, packing and unpacking, bustle and solitude, boomtown and ghost town. Around one nearby cluster of huts, men were prying lids from wooden crates, pulling out clumps of rifles and radios. Across the dirt parade ground, other troops were loading duffel bags of medical equipment onto mules, minutes from beginning the long trek into Nicaragua. Broad sections of the camp were vacant except for a few stray dogs, sniffing uncertainly at the empty bamboo huts topped by sheets of blue-green plastic that rippled delicately in the morning breeze.

Lima gazed at his own men, gathered for his final words before they, too, moved out to the war. Never had the unit looked so good; it bristled with new weapons, gleamed with fresh bandoliers of ammo. Lima could see the spiky tips of rocket-propelled grenade launchers and the smooth cylinders of the Redeye missiles that, the gringos promised, would turn the Sandinista helicopters into a dim memory. Boots and packs had a virgin shine that the jungle, he knew, would soon rub off.

As he studied his troops, it occurred to Lima that the equipment wasn't the only thing that was new. So were the men. Here he saw the son of one of his first soldiers, there a cousin or a nephew. But Lima didn't see a single one of the fifty-nine men who marched to Nicaragua with him in 1982. Five years later they were all burned out, shot up, or dead. *The only one left,* Lima realized, *is me.*

The year 1987 was the military high-water mark for the contras. For the first and only time during the war, the United States funded them fully for an entire year. And for the first and only time during the war, the Sandinistas possessed no significant technological advantages. The contras had antiaircraft missiles to free them from the torment of the Soviet helicopters. They had encrypted radios, so the Sandinistas couldn't listen in on their

196

communications. And they had a professionally run aerial delivery system, so they didn't have to go running back to the border every month or two for new supplies.

The result was a white-hot war that took a staggering toll on the Sandinistas, on the contras, on the Nicaraguan economy. By July, the Sandinistas were reporting more than fifteen armed encounters with the contras per day, and they admitted to nearly eight hundred dead. In his New Year's Day address, Daniel Ortega jeered that the contras were "in the process of decomposition . . . The millions for the mercenary forces have produced nothing." Seven months later he was publicly calling for an "emergency response" from foreign governments to stem the economic hemorrhage of the war.

Throughout 1985 and 1986, as they languished without significant aid from the United States, the contras endured a ceaseless stream of abuse: They were lazy, they were cowards, they were inept, they were an empty husk whose real fighting was done by the CIA. By the end of 1987, they disproved every one of those charges. They infiltrated between ten thousand and twelve thousand troops into Nicaragua around a massive wall of men and weapons that the Sandinistas spent sixteen months creating. They penetrated virtually every part of the country outside the Pacific coast and demonstrated widespread support among the peasant population. They inflicted heavy casualties on the Sandinista army and crippled its transportation network. They showed they could move in small groups, mass for a big attack, and then disperse to avoid retaliation. And they successfully withstood a cunning FSLN political challenge aimed at splintering their military unity.

It wasn't enough to win over their detractors in the United States, but less than a year after the American aid began arriving, the contras had convinced a much tougher set of critics. Once Tomás Borge had sworn that the stars would fall and the rivers run uphill before the FSLN agreed to negotiations with the contras; but in November 1987, the Sandinistas did just that.

"Contras Fail to Make Field Gains," said a headline in the *Washington Post* on December 28, 1986. It reflected a question on the minds of many Americans and Nicaraguans alike: Where were the contras? It seemed like months since the U.S. Congress had approved $100 million in new military aid. Yet nothing was happening in Nicaragua. In the comic strip "Doonesbury," a couple of contra commanders named Homicida and Less-Than-Zero were using the money to buy bayside condos in Miami. That seemed, more or less, to sum it up.

In fact, on the day of the *Washington Post* headline, it was barely six weeks since the first bullet purchased with the new aid arrived at Yamales. Most of the delay was due to Congress. After the June vote in the House approved the $100 million, the CIA moved crates of weapons and ammunition to an airfield in Texas and told the Air Force to put several planes and crews on standby. When the technical differences in the House and Senate versions of the aid bill were resolved, the Agency would begin shipping supplies in a matter of hours. But anticontra Democrats in Congress managed to stall the aid package in conference committee for three and a half months before it became law on October 18.

Several weeks passed before any of the aid arrived in Honduras. Even then, it moved in crazy fits and starts. The contra supply officials who kept inventory as the giant C-130 supply planes unloaded began to suspect that someone at Langley had a truly deranged sense of humor or perhaps a hopelessly twisted obsession with personal hygiene. Some planes arrived with four cartons of Redeye antiaircraft missiles and sixty cartons of foot powder. One contained one hundred machine guns and eight hundred thousand tubes of toothpaste. The most perplexing shipment consisted of nothing but five thousand plastic spittoons. It took the contras more than a month to figure out what they were. The spittoons were finally sent to the medical corps for use as bedpans.

The contra field commanders were not at all amused; when they learned that William Casey was coming to Yamales for a secret visit on November 19, they planned a confrontation.

The Yamales visit was, quite literally, Casey's last hurrah. He shakily climbed atop a wooden reviewing stand, although his voice was firm and strong as he shouted into a small microphone. "It's a great privilege for me and my country and President Reagan to stand side by side with you in this struggle," he told an assembly of 3,500 troops. "This is a moving experience for me. . . . We rejoice today that we can join actively in the fight. I can assure you that this commitment is a solid one from the president and the Congress of the United States and the people."

There was a brief pause while his words were translated into Spanish, then a roar from the men below. The gringos were with them again! How could they lose?

Afterward Casey had lunch with his entourage, the local CIA men, and a few of the contra commanders. While Casey wolfed down his food—the contras were impressed by how much he seemed to like beans and rice—Commander Toño stood up and read a list of complaints prepared by the field commanders. Foot powder, spittoons, toothpaste—it was all in there. By the time Toño was halfway through it, the local CIA men had gone ballistic. Jim Adkins, the chief Agency adviser to the contras, stormed out of the mess hall, knocking his chair over as he left. The Tegucigalpa station chief stayed, but his face was tomato red. Alan Fiers, the head of the Central American Task Force, kept nervously turning to Casey and confiding, sotto voce, "I think what the commander is actually trying to say, Mr. Casey . . ."

The only one who remained calm was Casey. He brushed aside Fiers's explanations, thanked the commanders for their frankness, and promised that the CIA would do better. Then it was time to take the helicopter back to Tegucigalpa, where Casey's plane would return him to Washington. Only Casey knew what awaited him there. The previous night, on a secure satellite telephone, he had gotten a call from John Poindexter, the president's national security adviser. The Iran-contra scandal was about to break wide open, Poindexter warned, and Casey would have to testify before Congress in a matter of days. A CIA courier was already en route to Honduras with briefing books. Next to that, foot powder problems looked benign indeed.

As he boarded the helicopter, several of the CIA officers thought Casey looked tired. Most of them would never see him again. Within a week the scandal went public; within a month, a brain seizure put Casey in the hospital; and within six months, he was dead.

As the chopper lifted off, Jim Adkins turned to a small group of commanders that included Toño and Mike Lima. "How could you do that?" he demanded. "We're working night and day for you people. We're busting our *balls* for you. How could you stab us in the back like that? I'm telling you, *it's not our fault!*"

The contras had heard that before, so often that some of them thought "it's not our fault" must be the U.S. national slogan. But this time it was the truth. The source of the confusion lay not in Langley but in Honduras, in the arms supermarket that Miami weapons brokers Ron Martin and James McCoy set up in 1985 in anticipation that the U.S. government would one day resume funding the contras. There were $14 million worth of guns and ammunition sitting in Honduran warehouses, just waiting for the tidal wave of U.S. money that everyone knew was coming.

The arms supermarket group knew that when the contras had money to spend in 1985 and 1986, they purchased their weapons elsewhere. Martin and McCoy assumed that Richard Secord, their principal competitor for the contra account, had simply used his friendship with Oliver North to ace them out. Once the U.S. government was officially involved again, the supermarket group believed, Secord's high prices and slow delivery times would put him out of the picture. CIA officers on the ground in Honduras seemed to confirm that; they told Mario Delamico, the supermarket's representative in Honduras, that they expected to buy his stockpiled weapons with part of the $100 million aid package.

What the CIA officers didn't know was that the upper echelons of the Agency and the State Department believed the money behind the arms supermarket came from drugs and stolen U.S. foreign aid. The Agency would ship the contras arms from its U.S. warehouses rather than purchase them from the arms supermarket.

But when the first CIA planes got ready to take off from the United States, the Honduran army refused them permission to land. Within hours, Adkins, who ran the contra project in Honduras, had arrived at military headquarters to inquire if there had been some mistake.

No mistake, explained Gen. Humberto Regalado, the head of the armed forces. There was no need for the CIA to ship weapons to the contras from the United States when the arms supermarket had so many weapons on hand. The Hondurans would not permit the import of anything available at the supermarket.

Adkins had witnessed a thousand petty acts of extortion by the Honduran military, but this was staggering. It meant that almost all the Agency's arms shipments would be blocked. AK-47s, mortars, grenade launchers, rocket-propelled grenades—the supermarket had them all. It was bad enough when the Hondurans squeezed the contra program to get additional foreign aid, a frequent occurrence, but this was nothing but a personal rip-off. Regalado and the other senior officers obviously had a financial interest in the arms supermarket.

"General, how do we do this?" Adkins demanded, not bothering to hide the anger in his voice. "This is a decision in Washington that goes way beyond me. . . . You've sabotaged this whole thing."

"That's it," Regalado replied, smirking. "You either buy it, or the war doesn't go on."

"Goddamn it, maybe you'd rather have the Honduran army fighting the Sandinistas!" Adkins shouted. "This program benefits you a lot more than it does us. It's just a goddamn shame when a military officer puts personal profit ahead of his own country."

The only result of the meeting was a warning to the CIA station that if Adkins was ever seen at Honduran military headquarters again he'd be kicked out of the country. The ban on importing arms available at the supermarket stood. That excluded almost every weapon the contras used, except for Soviet-made heavy 12.7mm machine guns and the Redeye missiles. It also demolished the Agency's careful preparation for getting arms to the contras immediately. The supply loads waiting in Texas were arranged in lots of one hundred manpacks— that is, all the supplies that a unit of one hundred men would need. CIA freight handlers frantically tore apart crates and repacked them, removing most of the arms and ammunition and substituting whatever was at hand—foot powder, toothpaste, spittoons—so the flights could get under way.

It was two months before the Hondurans modified their ban on importing weapons; even then they retained restrictions that hobbled CIA efforts to arm the contras for months. The squabble wasn't resolved until Elliott Abrams, the assistant secretary of state for Latin America, and Alan Fiers came to Honduras to provide them a thorough briefing on the arms supermarket's financial backing.

The first load of CIA supplies arrived at Aguacate in mid-November. Combining the new boots, uniforms, machine guns, and Redeyes with ammo from their own meager reserves, the contras were able to outfit eight hundred men from the Jorge Salazar Regional Command I.[1] On November 30, Commander Rigoberto led them off to Nicaragua, crossing the frontier farther to the east than the contras had ever done before. He went over the border at an abandoned village called San Andrés de Bocay, where the Río Bocay and the Río Coco converged, so far east it was almost in Zelaya Department. Nonetheless, within days he was under heavy attack from the twenty thousand Sandinista troops massed along the border.

Rigoberto's infiltration alerted the Sandinistas that U.S. aid was at long last arriving. They repeated their thrust of the March 1986 Easter Egg War, sending 2,500 troops into Honduras to overrun Yamales and destroy the new military equipment on the ground. But the contras blunted the attack even more effectively than before, and Honduran A-37 jets flew into Nicaragua on December 7 and bombed FSLN airstrips in Nueva Segovia Department. The Sandinista offensive quickly subsided.

Contra infiltration resumed, this time in hard-to-detect groups of one hundred men. Well inside Nicaragua, they regrouped and hit the Sandinistas from behind. The FSLN border force dissolved, and by the end of January,

200

several thousand contras were inside Nicaragua, heading for their assigned operational areas.

Mike Lima watched the infiltration in secret surprise. He never admitted it to anyone, but by the end of 1986, Lima was no longer certain the contras had the ability to make war. Some units had been inside Honduras nearly three years. Those with more recent combat experience had suffered frightful poundings from the Mi-24 helicopters. By October 1986, less than 2,500 contra troops were left inside Nicaragua; their most important weapons were small antipersonnel mines designed to maim rather than kill. A contra unit with Sandinistas on its tail would leave two or three of the mines behind, hoping that when Sandinista soldiers were injured by the explosions, the others would stop to aid the wounded and let the contras run off into the jungle. In 1986, the contras never attacked, only retreated.

The CIA, Lima noted, was sensitive to the problem. Instead of expecting the contras to rush headlong into battle, the Agency took a step-by-step approach. First, about 130 contras were flown to a secret CIA training camp near Eglin Air Force Base in the Florida panhandle to learn specialties: demolition, communications, paramedical skills, psychological operations, human rights. Ultimately, about six hundred contras would be trained at the Florida camp.

Then the CIA introduced something new to the contras: a written strategy and timetable. When the war began, Enrique Bermúdez relied on *foquismo,* a theory of guerrilla warfare devised by Fidel Castro's lieutenant Che Guevara. In *foquismo,* guerrillas ignore political organizing. Instead, they focus military operations on a remote rural area where the government is weak. Winning battles, in *foquismo* theory, is the most effective form of political propaganda, and the more victories a guerrilla movement achieves, the more peasants will flock to its side. Eventually, the government topples.

Foquismo was popular among Latin revolutionaries (including the Sandinistas) in the mid-1960s, largely because it was a bold counterpoint to the stodgy caution of the traditional Latin communist parties. It failed everywhere, though, and when Guevara went to Bolivia to prove its viability, the army quickly cornered and killed him. As an all-encompassing military theory, it is mostly fantasy.

In small doses, however, *foquismo* can be useful. It was a helpful model for the contras when they were starting out in 1982. So much hostility to the Sandinistas already existed in rural areas that political proselytizing was unnecessary. Yet Nicaraguans were skeptical of armed insurgencies, having seen more than two dozen against the Somozas fail. Few would work with an anti-Sandinista organization, even clandestinely, before receiving assurances— in the form of military victories—that it had some prospect of success.

But the contras had long since outgrown *foquismo.* A comprehensive blueprint that laid out military goals and the specific tactics necessary to attain them was overdue. And the CIA, after extensive interviews with Bermúdez and many of the field commanders, drew one up.

It was a ten-page document that set out four phases of contra warfare over the next two years. The first phase, three months long, was reinfiltration. In the second, also three months, the contras would consolidate their positions in central Zelaya, forcing the Sandinistas to fight in unfriendly territory. The FSLN's supply lines would be stretched so thin that its helicopters would be vulnerable to Redeyes, its East German truck convoys to ambushes. Meanwhile, the contras' own aerial supply program would get into high gear, dropping a surplus of supplies to be cached in strategic locations.

During the third phase, six months long, the contras would move west into areas where they operated in 1983 and 1984 in Chontales, Boaco, Matagalpa, and Estelí departments. The contras would link up with the handful of combatants on the southern front remaining from Pastora's army and cut the Rama Road. They would set up training centers inside Nicaragua, and the Yamales headquarters would be moved to San Andrés de Bocay, eliminating an embarrassing problem for Honduras.

In the fourth phase, a year long, the contras would steadily increase the pace of their attacks and push farther west, assaulting departmental capitals in Estelí, Matagalpa, and the other provinces on the eastern side of Nicaragua's big lakes. At the conclusion, they would be poised to jump into León, Chinandega, and other population centers at the north end of the Pacific coast. The plan didn't spell it out, but the CIA officers who worked most closely with the contras envisioned that a fifth, final phase—moving the war into Managua and the other urban centers of the Pacific coast—would take eighteen to twenty-four months. Neither the Agency officers nor the contras themselves foresaw the contra army winning a conventional one-on-one slugging match. Rather, as the war approached the cities, the contras would provide the kindling for a national uprising against the Sandinistas, in much the same way Sandinista guerrillas touched off a broad rebellion against Somoza.

The CIA plan was ambitious but not implausible. If it contained an unduly starry-eyed assumption, it was that U.S. support would continue, uninterrupted, for three or four more years. The Reagan administration, in its robust youth, had only been able to win congressional votes on contra funding by sparse margins. Now, with the cancer of the Iran-contra scandal eating away at Reagan's power and prestige, even one more year of aid was a dubious proposition.

No one knew that better than Adkins, the CIA officer who shaped the strategy and timetable. After spending two months in Honduras coaching the contras on infiltration and military tactics in 1984, Adkins went back to Langley muttering a prayer of thanksgiving that he had escaped. Viewing the contra program from close up, he was more certain than ever that some day it would go down like a covert *Titanic,* with only enough lifeboats for the headquarters brass. But back at headquarters, the pressure on him to join the program started again, stronger than ever.

Adkins was no stranger to telling the Agency to flake off. His first assignment when he finished training in 1967 was to go to India and give sniper training to guerrillas who were fighting the Chinese in Tibet. Adkins knew nothing about sniping, and he couldn't tell the Dalai Lama from Dolly Parton. He argued and bitched and cajoled until he got his assignment changed to Laos.

Never during his career in the Agency, though, had Adkins felt pressure like this. To get away from it he bolted the CIA's Latin American division altogether and took a job in the Agency's Counterterrorism Group. But the seventh floor was not deterred. An old friend walked into the Counterterrorism Group's offices one day in September 1985 to find him emptying his desk. "Where are you going?" the friend asked in surprise. "To Central America," Adkins answered. "To be the next sacrificial lamb."

Adkins arrived at the end of September, just a month after Congress softened the Boland Amendment to permit CIA intelligence-sharing with the contras, the first legal contact between the two since 1984. (The contras immediately assigned Adkins the same rank they bestowed his predecessor: he became *Coronel* Jaime, although he never made it past private during his two years in the army.) After a week, Adkins offered his professional analysis to the Tegucigalpa station chief: "This is the most fucked-up thing I've ever worked on."

Adkins had strained under some goofball rules when he was advising Hmong tribesmen in Laos, but the contra program was such a maze of prohibitions, restrictions, and constraints that Adkins felt he ought to surround his safe house headquarters with a battalion of lawyers. In Washington, Congress and the Reagan administration were using the contra program as a club to beat each other senseless; it was the CIA officers on the ground in Honduras who had to make some sense out of the debris.

To start with, there was the narrow definition of intelligence-sharing. Adkins could fly out to the border and count refugees who were dying of dysentery or from the gangrene that set in after their toes were blown off by Sandinista land mines. That was okay, that was gathering intelligence. But he couldn't load the helicopter with food or medicine, or carry dying refugees back to hospitals; then he would be actively participating in the war. If the contras were planning to attack a target and asked if there were a machine-gun nest next to it, Adkins could confirm that. That was intelligence-sharing. But he couldn't add that there was also a rocket launcher, not unless they asked. That would be taking the initiative.

It seemed to Adkins, however, that all these rules could be suspended if a congressman wanted a favor. In January 1986, Russell Means and two other militant American Indian leaders, touring the Nicaraguan bush with Indian contras, were trapped by a Sandinista offensive. A cable from Langley arrived in Tegucigalpa: Plan a rescue mission to get Means and the other activists out. The CIA men in Honduras were dumbfounded. They weren't allowed to evacuate wounded contras from Nicaragua—they weren't allowed to evacuate *dying refugee babies*—but they were supposed to send helicopters deep inside, into the middle of a combat zone, to rescue a burnt-out 1960s radical whose political joyride had gotten a little bumpy? Damn right, headquarters said, he has friends in Congress.

After an exchange of vicious cables, Adkins prepared a rescue plan. Two Agency helicopters would fly down the Atlantic coast to Means's hideout, seventy-five miles inside Nicaragua. The helicopters would carry extra fuel tanks, but even so, the distance was so great that the CIA would have to infiltrate a refueling team by sea. And to make space for the fuel tanks, the choppers would have to fly "naked"—unarmed. The plan would work, Adkins thought, but there was a good chance that some CIA people would die. Luckily, just as they were about to launch the operation, Means and the other activists escaped on their own.

Whenever Adkins complained that all these rules made it impossible to run a coherent program, headquarters counseled patience. When the $100 million aid package passed through Congress, most of the restrictions would be chucked out the window. Meanwhile, Langley wasn't interested in excuses, just results.

Headquarters was wrong. When the $100 million was approved, the rules, if anything, got worse, thanks to an unnoticed amendment tacked on to a military construction bill by Robert Mrazek, a Democratic congressman from New York. The Mrazek Amendment got little public attention, but inside the walls of CIA headquarters it was a far more infamous bit of legislation than its more publicized cousin, the Boland Amendment. The amendment made it illegal for any U.S. official to provide training or assistance to the contras within twenty miles of the Nicaraguan-Honduran border, which made every single contra camp off-limits. It essentially barred CIA officers from the camps except when they were gathering intelligence or accompanying American politicians.

The Mrazek Amendment created a crazy quilt of confusing and paradoxical rules. CIA planes could fly for hours deep inside Nicaragua, braving Sandinista antiaircraft missiles, to drop supplies. But they couldn't make the quick and comparatively safe hop inside Honduras from Aguacate (just outside the twenty-mile limit) to the contra bases at the border, where thousands of men were waiting for equipment.[2] And although CIA officers were expected to fly out to the border camps so that congressmen could get pictures taken for constituent newsletters, they weren't allowed to carry food or medicine for the hordes of sickly refugees who arrived every week.[3]

The Mrazek Amendment produced yet another bottleneck in delivering aid from the $100 million package. CIA aircraft were not permitted to ferry supplies into camps, and the contras themselves had no planes large enough to carry supplies yet small enough to land on the short border airstrips. The only alternative was to haul the equipment in trucks, but that was more easily said than done.

Nearly all of the contra camps were in the Las Vegas Salient, the bleak, triangular chunk of Honduras that protrudes into Nicaragua's Jinotega Department. Only one dirt road led into the Salient, and in December, when the aid was ready to go, unseasonably late rains had turned it into an impassible morass of floods and mud slides. Even when vehicles could get through, they had to cross the twelve deadliest miles in Central America—the straight, flat stretch of road between the towns of Cifuentes and Las Trojes, only one hundred yards or so from the Nicaraguan border. The underbrush on the Nicaraguan side of the road was alive with Sandinista snipers and sappers, and FSLN artillery was dug in on hilltops a few hundred yards away. Scattered along the roadside was the macabre evidence of their handiwork: shattered huts, the burned-out hulks of vehicles, the grisly corpses of animals. Outside the sandbagged bunkers that dotted their rim of the road, the Hondurans posted dummies dressed in helmets and uniforms, staring blankly into Nicaragua. Whether the dummies were intended as decoys, morbid jokes, or simply as totems to whatever savage war god had cosmic charge of the road was never clear.

The road was routinely the target of Sandinista mining, sniping, and artillery barrages, all intended to stop the flow of contra supplies. (The Sandinistas, however, were none too discriminatory, and their victims included two American journalists—reporter Dial Torgerson of the *Los Angeles Times* and free-lance photographer Richard Cross—whose rented Toyota hit an antitank mine in 1983, as well as countless Honduran civilians.) They were effective: La Negra, Commander Suicida's girlfriend, was killed on the road, and many contra supply trucks were blown up there.

But the Mrazek Amendment left no alternative to using the road. A contra supply official known as El Hermitaño set out from Aguacate with a truckload of food during the first week of December. He managed to coax the vehicle up and down the twisting mud road through the mountains to Cifuentes, where it flattened out, and then started the twelve-mile run to Las Trojes. The Honduran soldiers watching from their bunker said later that the Sandinista sniper deserved a marksmanship award. His rocket went through the back window and out the windshield and didn't cause any damage to the truck except broken glass. The only thing the rocket hit inside the cab was El Hermitaño's head.

Finding Hondurans willing to rent their trucks for a trip along the Cifuentes-Las Trojes road, and finding contras willing to drive them, fell into the lap of Mario Sacasa, the supply chief. When Sacasa joined the contras in late 1983, there were only twenty-three people working in the supply section. In those days, buying and distributing 250,000 rounds of ammo was an assignment that could occupy the whole section for weeks. Now Sacasa was in charge of more than five hundred people and routinely handled consignments of millions of rounds of ammo.

Sacasa was often the man who had to explain to a commander leaving on patrol that, while there were no grenades for his men, they could have as much foot powder as they wanted. But Sacasa didn't mind; he was delighted to be dealing with the CIA again, screwups and all, after the nightmare of the $27 million package of nonlethal aid that the contras received in late 1985 and early 1986.

The $27 million was administered by the State Department through a specially created Nicaraguan Humanitarian Assistance Office (NHAO), which had four different sets of auditors approve every single item the contras purchased. The auditors pored over each request, pondering endlessly what was truly "humanitarian" and what was not.

Cigarettes, the auditors determined, were not; smoking was a filthy, unhygienic habit that was bad for the contras' health. ("I wonder," a contra mused as he told me about the conversation, "if it will occur to them to warn us that setting ambushes and attacking Sandinista military bases are also dangerous practices that could lead to acute lead poisoning.") Then the auditors also cut off money for matches. If the contras weren't going to be lighting cigarettes, NHAO reasoned, they didn't need matches. Of course, they wouldn't be lighting cooking fires either.

The NHAO auditors were also the most paranoid people Sacasa had ever met. They suspected a trick behind every contra purchase. One day they ruled that nonlethal aid could not be used to buy suspenders. The befuddled Sacasa asked why not.

"Because they could be used to clip ammunition and hand grenades to," one of the NHAO men replied primly.

"They could also be used to keep our pants from falling down in the middle of a battle," Sacasa retorted, to no avail.

Now, not only were the NHAO schoolmarms gone, but with the $100 million, the contras for the first time could come close to fulfilling their own supply formula. Each soldier heading into Nicaragua, for instance, was supposed to get five hundred rounds of ammunition, two hand grenades, and three days' worth of rations. In the past those numbers were largely a joke, but by mid-1987, when the U.S. aid was finally flowing smoothly, Sacasa found he was telling commanders "yes" more often than "no" for the first time since he joined the contras.

Another thing that helped was that by the end of January, the CIA's aerial supply system was rolling. Three Spanish-built CASA C-212s, flown by Rhodesian crews, shuttled back and forth between Nicaragua and Swan Island, a Honduran archipelago 150 miles offshore in the Atlantic. The planes were averaging three successful airdrops—about twelve thousand pounds of supplies—every two days. In addition, the contras themselves were using a rented DC-6 to make big drops of twenty thousand pounds apiece.

The planes, equipped with top-of-the-line navigational gear, flew much too high for the FSLN to shoot them down. And in the first seven months of the supply program, the Sandinistas managed to seize only five loads on the ground. (Their failure to capture many loads was all the more surprising because the Sandinistas had the Costa Rican pilot who flew the contras' rented DC-6 under observation in San José. Every time he was ordered to Honduras, the pilot went on a bender, roaring through San José bars like a Pamplona bull. Whenever it happened, CIA wiretaps picked up an excited phone call to Managua: *El Tico está saliendo*—the Costa Rican is leaving.) Most of the success was due to the contra training the CIA provided in Florida. Every unit had men who could read maps—so the contras could correctly advise the aircrews of their position—and operate radio beacons that the planes homed in on.

A commander could call for a supply flight on the new, secure communications gear the CIA provided. Every unit had an encrypted portable computer terminal for communicating with headquarters, and several commanders also had short-range radios with voice scramblers for tactical communication with other units. Because a commander could now divulge his position without giving it away to the Sandinistas, the contra situation room at Yamales, for the first time in the war, had up-to-the-minute maps showing the location of every unit.

Despite the new radio equipment, inside Nicaragua each commander was essentially his own master, staging attacks where and when he saw fit. Headquarters gave him only an assigned zone of operations and a list of suggested targets: Sandinista command posts, electronic intercept centers, power stations, bridges—sometimes with blueprints or charts supplied by the Pentagon office in charge of contingency planning for Nicaragua. Occasionally there might even be overhead photos taken from a satellite or a spy plane, although the Pentagon concentrated aerial reconnaissance on larger targets of potential concern in case of an American invasion.

The contras were delighted that the CIA was not resurrecting an old, acrimonious, tactical dispute over economic targets. Soon after the attacks on the bridges on Ocotal and Somotillo, Duane Clarridge and other CIA officials demanded a halt to purely economic sabotage. Bridges, power lines, telephone cables, and grain silos were all off-limits. To enforce the ban, the Agency refused to give the contras explosives. General Alvarez, the chief of the Honduran military who ordinarily saluted any blow against the Sandinistas, was as adamant as the Americans on this subject.

Bermúdez had some of his worst fights with Clarridge and Doty over the no-economic-targets rule. "You should be trying to defeat the Sandinista army, not ruin the country's economy," Doty explained. "Then why was the United States bombing all those German factories during World War II?" Bermúdez retorted. His allies, Bermúdez felt, were tying his hands because of political concerns that had nothing to do with winning the war. The Hondurans, who sold their excess electricity to Nicaragua, didn't want any damage to the country's power grid; they enthusiastically encouraged Nicaraguans to kill each other but didn't want it to cost Honduras any revenue. As for the Americans, they were trying to stir up an international fuss about the way the Salvadoran guerrillas were demolishing their country's economy. It would be hard for the United States to complain about the Salvadorans if the contras were doing the same thing in Nicaragua.

Bermúdez thought the whole thing was crazy; no war was ever won without crippling the enemy's economy. Whenever he could scrounge some explosives, Bermúdez kept ordering sabotage attacks. Several times contra units tried to blow up a bridge on the Pan-American Highway between El Espino and Somoto, every time drawing a stern reprimand from the CIA.

Now the Agency was not only providing blueprints and explosives, it was training two hundred contra saboteurs to use parachutes so they could be dropped near their targets. The payoff was quick. On February 16, saboteurs destroyed a power station near La Trinidad and blacked out much of northern Nicaragua for four days. In mid-March, several demolition teams parachuted onto the Pacific coast; they struck ten times in two weeks, plunging both borders into darkness. At the same time, the contras pulled off one of their few successful internal front operations. A courier smuggled a package of plastic explosives into Managua, where a civilian sympathizer—trained in demolitions in Honduras—used it to set off an explosion at the foot of an electrical tower. The tower didn't fall, though its base was blackened and twisted. But the knowledge that the contras had penetrated the capital rocked Managua.

The pace of the war doubled and redoubled. In January and February, combat was frequent—the Sandinistas recorded 680 armed engagements—but mostly fleeting as the contras broke contact to continue their infiltration. In March, as many units reached their operational areas, brief encounters gave way to planned assaults. Small Sandinista military outposts were under constant attack; two, in Zelaya and Jinotega departments, were completely overrun, and the contras captured forty-five thousand rounds of ammunition. The Sandinistas reported 426 battles during the month.

In April, the situation deteriorated so much that the FSLN quit talking about it. Military briefings to reporters ceased, and photographers who snapped pictures of the results of contra sabotage had their film confiscated. The war virtually vanished from the pages of the Sandinista press, which instead offered elaborately detailed accounts of battles in El Salvador. When the contras captured a garrison manned by one hundred FSLN troops near San Pedro del Norte in central Zelaya Department on April 28, the Sandinistas refused to confirm it for nearly two weeks.

Just four months earlier, an attack like the one at San Pedro del Norte would have brought swift retaliation from the Mi-24 helicopters. But the Sandinistas were learning to be more cautious with their choppers. In February, the contras hit an Mi-8 transport helicopter with an antiaircraft missile; in March, they hit two Mi-24s.

The CIA had supplied more than two hundred Redeyes, and they proved far more effective than the few SAM-7s the contras had purchased on the black market. Both missiles were shoulder-fired weapons that locked on to the heat in an aircraft's exhaust trail. But the SAM-7's electronic circuitry didn't stand up to the jungle humidity, and its two-stage propulsion system caused the missile's trajectory to dip in midflight, which, in the mountains, often led to the warhead slamming harmlessly into a hillside. The Redeyes were more durable and more accurate, and as the word spread, the contras lost their fear of the helicopters.

The choppers all but vanished from combat after another was shot down in May—an Mi-17, part of a phalanx of fifteen helicopters that accompanied 3,600 Sandinista troops on an offensive to push the contras out of San Andrés de Bocay. It took five days of heavy fighting to secure the area (which the FSLN quietly abandoned a month later), and while the Sandinistas were preoccupied with the offensive, the contras launched a surprise attack on Arlen Siu, near the eastern edge of the Rama Road, and blew up a natural gas storage depot.

Toward the end of May, as the rainy season turned rural Nicaragua into a clammy sea of muck and slime, the tempo of the war slowed. By the time it reached full speed again in late September, the landscape would be much different. The Sandinistas, worried by military developments, would try to move the war into the political arena. And the CIA would be quietly folding its tent.

In the eighteen months since it was allowed back in the ball game, the CIA had built a small empire around the contras. The Honduran station was the largest in Central America, with eighty officers working on the contra program alone. And although some people at Langley scorned it as nothing more than a Wild West pageant for the paramilitary knuckledraggers, the station was also a motherlode of intelligence collection. The contra program generated more than two hundred intelligence reports to Langley every month, many culled from electronic intercepts of FSLN communications. Honduran troops and contras at mountaintop listening posts on the border stole the signals; then they were logged, decoded, and analyzed by a squad of contra technicians manning rows of Radio Shack computers in a room at Yamales. As many as one thousand Sandinista messages a day fell into the hands of their enemies.

As impressive as it was, the CIA effort had weaknesses. One was numbers, or lack of them. Under the terms of an informal agreement between Langley and the congressional intelligence oversight committees, only fifty of the eighty officers working with the contras could be in the camps at a given moment. The Agency was trying to run a division-sized army with a battalion-sized staff. Even with the presence of two Army colonels from the U.S. Southern Command to help with administrative details, it was a near-impossible assignment.

The quality of the CIA people in Honduras varied wildly. The shortage of experienced paramilitary officers, and the resistance of many to a doomed program, meant that a lot of singularly unqualified officers wound up with the contras. One of the most notorious was a twenty-three-year-old assigned to work with the Miskito Indians on the Atlantic coast who spoke neither Spanish nor any of the Indian dialects. He delivered long sets of instructions to Indian soldiers in English; when they stared at him, uncomprehending, he banged their heads against the nearest tree.

No one was aware of it until U.S. Ambassador Ted Briggs, visiting the Atlantic coast, asked Indian leaders if there was anything he could do for them. They would appreciate a small favor, one Indian replied. "Please take that man out of here," the Indian said politely, nodding toward the young CIA officer. "Otherwise, we'll be obliged to kill him." Another Agency man on the Atlantic coast, who went by the name JP, was even more unpopular. One day an embassy plane landed on a Miskito airstrip, and the Indians, as usual, came running to greet it. When the hatch opened and JP stepped out, half a dozen Indians turned around and raced back to their huts. They returned with automatic rifles. JP got back on the plane.

Besides keeping his own knuckledraggers in line, the CIA's Adkins had to fend off the budding General Pattons at the State Department. During the two years when the Agency's contact with the contras was curtailed, the State Department got deeply involved in the program for the first time. And now State was reluctant to give up its new toy.

Mostly this took the form of tinkering with the contra political structure, showering money and titles on the contra politicians who entered the movement through Edén Pastora's movement in the south and then stayed on when Pastora self-destructed. They proclaimed themselves the "liberal" wing of the contras (although in Nicaraguan politics, liberalism had always been equated with the free-market economics these politicians opposed), and they boasted that they were the only true nationalists in the movement (although they owed their positions in it to the U.S. State Department). They included both the elder and younger Arturo Cruzes; Alfonso Robelo; and the César brothers, Alfredo and Octaviano.

Adkins didn't much care if the State Department wanted to jet the politicians around the world and show them off to Congress. But he fumed when the politicians tried to plot military strategy. Their pet concept was seizing a port on the Atlantic coast, declaring it the capital of Free Nicaragua, and asking for U.S. diplomatic recognition. The theory was that the Indians and Creoles on the Atlantic coast were so utterly alienated from the Sandinistas that they would, almost without exception, support the provisional government. Then U.S. military aid could be shipped directly to the contras without the cajolery and corruption necessary to send it through Honduras or Costa Rica.

The plan, Adkins thought, owed more to Custer than Patton. Guerrilla forces are not supposed to hold territory; they are supposed to hit and run. If the contras seized an Atlantic port, the Sandinistas would concentrate all their military might, every helicopter and tank, on taking it back. In fact, that was the plan's whole point. Once the United States extended diplomatic recognition to the contras as a government, the politicians assumed, it would rush armed forces to their aid rather than let the Sandinistas annihilate them. The Free Nicaragua plan was a Trojan horse with the U.S. Marines inside. The self-proclaimed contra "nationalists" wanted the gringos to win the war for them.

From a U.S. standpoint, of course, that was crazy. The very idea of aiding the contras was to keep U.S. troops out of a direct confrontation with the Sandinistas. And as far as Adkins was concerned, even if the contras somehow held on to an Atlantic coast port without U.S. intervention, it was still a rotten idea. It sent contra troops in the opposite direction from Managua and the Pacific coast, where the war would have to be won, which made about as much sense as it would have for the Viet Cong to move north toward Hanoi.

The State Department, however, persisted in seeing the Atlantic coast as the key to the war. The State people didn't necessarily insist on liberating a port, but they did argue that the CIA was not paying enough attention to the contra forces from the Atlantic's Creoles and three Indian tribes.

The belief that the Atlantic coast population was ready to rise in open rebellion against the Sandinistas had logical enough origins. The ties binding the Atlantic coast to the rest of Nicaragua have always been tenuous. It was colonized by England rather than Spain, and to this day the Indians and Creoles there refer to Nicaraguans from the Pacific coast as "the Spanish." Because the British wanted little more than safe harbor for their ships, they imposed few of their customs on the local population (the most notable exception being their language), and the Indian tribal structure remained generally intact. Even when the British disappeared, the humid, swampy lowlands of the Atlantic coast never attracted much interest from Managua. The Rama Road, the first land link between the two Nicaraguan coasts, was not completed until 1967.

The isolation ended abruptly when the Sandinistas took power and imposed their social blueprint on the Atlantic population. Soldiers arrived first—many more than the Somozas ever stationed there—and soon after came Cuban teachers and doctors, pushing out the American and European missionaries who filled those roles before. The Cubans, who championed both atheism and the Spanish language, were wildly unpopular. Tensions increased, and there were several confrontations with Sandinista troops in which unarmed civilians were killed.

On December 14, 1981, the local people struck back. Armed Miskito Indians captured a Sandinista border patrol, marched the six men to Honduras, and killed them. Several other attacks on Sandinistas followed in the next few days. The Sandinistas retaliated by arresting about thirty-five Miskito civilians and killing at least half of them, some by burying them alive. The war was on.

The Indians' armed resistance to the Sandinistas was spontaneous and effective. But the minute the CIA offered help, it fell apart. The modest amount of weapons and money the Agency sent the Indians led to unfathomable greed, corruption, and lust for power. The two principal Miskito leaders, Steadman Fagoth and Brooklyn Rivera, quickly turned against one another. Eventually a third faction, led by Moravian pastor Wycliffe Diego, surfaced. When the Indian contras weren't fighting with each other, they were trying to cut separate deals with the Sandinistas. None of the many highly publicized sets of peace talks ever came to anything, but they underscored the unreliability of the Indians as allies. They were always willing to sign a separate truce if it contained guarantees of autonomy for the Atlantic coast. The composition of the government sitting in Managua didn't matter to the Indians; it was just Spanish business.

No one at the CIA was too sympathetic to the Indians anymore, least of all Adkins, who mistrusted everything about the Atlantic coast. It had too few people and too many malarial mosquitoes to be of strategic importance. An active Indian army would have been valuable for tying up Sandinista resources. But the small Indian force—it numbered perhaps one thousand, although it was so loosely organized that no one really knew—fought less and committed more atrocities than any other contra unit.

But the State Department kept insisting that the Indians were a potentially effective force that the CIA was misusing. In April 1987, listening to the same old arguments from Elliott Abrams's assistant William Walker, Adkins threw up his hands. "Look, if you people think we're mishandling the Indians, why don't you just take it over?" he snapped. That was exactly what the State Department was hoping to hear. A few weeks later, Commander Chickenkiller came to Honduras.

His real name was Rick Chidester. But soon after his arrival in Honduras, as he argued with a group of Indians in a Miskito villages on the Atlantic coast, the six-foot, four-inch Chidester stomped his foot for emphasis, with inauspicious results for a passing baby chick. Ever after, he was *Comandante* Matapollo to the Indians. The other contras, who viewed his surreal struggles with the Indians with amusement and sympathy, called him El Rey Miskito, the Miskito King. It was a dry reference to Old Man, an ancient Miskito crowned king by the British in 1670 so they would have a negotiating partner. Old Man, taken to Jamaica for his coronation, had no idea what was going on. Observing the scaffolds being built for his coronation, he concluded he was about to be hung. Old Man promptly climbed to the top of a coconut tree and refused to come down.

Chidester often wished for a tall tree, too. The CIA's complaints about the Indians, he soon learned, had more truth in them than anyone at the State Department realized. One of Chidester's first projects was to set up a clandes-

211

tine radio station for the Indians. The State Department spent a good deal of money on equipment and a house trailer to use as a studio. But after several weeks, the station was still not operating. "It's too hot to work in that trailer," explained Charlie Morales, the Sumo Indian who was supposed to manage the station. So Chidester gave him $500 for an air conditioner. Still the station did not go on the air. "I told you, the trailer is too hot," Morales replied irritably when he was asked about it.

"But Charlie," Chidester reminded him, "I gave you money for an air conditioner."

"I didn't buy it," Morales admitted. "Rick, my people have hunger. I had to use the money to buy them food."

"Charlie, we're supplying plenty of food out there," Chidester said reprovingly. "Nobody is going hungry."

"All right," Morales conceded, "*I* had hunger. You hadn't paid me in a couple of weeks, so I used the money to buy myself food."

Chidester wordlessly held up the last receipt for Morales's salary as station manager.

"Okay, okay," Morales confessed. "I just took the money. But I don't want to hear any more about it. I don't want you rubbing my nose in it." Chidester sent a cable to Washington, explaining why the radio station wasn't on the air. He titled it "Charlie Eats the Air Conditioner."

The two Indian leaders with the most support were Fagoth and Rivera, both former student activists with a good deal of charisma. But each had hordes of enemies. Fagoth had done more fighting, but he was also a borderline psychopath who once kidnapped the Miskito council of elders—the tribal chieftains—and threatened to kill them all if he didn't get his way in a dispute. Many Miskitos claimed that Fagoth had once cut a captured Sandinista's ears off and forced him to eat them. Chidester wasn't sure that story was true, but he was impressed that so many Indians believed it. Once, as Fagoth was delivering a speech in a Miskito village demanding that the Indians make him their undisputed leader, black storm clouds materialized from a clear blue sky and lightning pierced the air. As Fagoth raged on above the noise of the storm, the Indians in the audience exchanged knowing looks.

No one feared Rivera, but almost no one trusted him, either. He was always quick to accept any offer of negotiations from the Sandinistas, even when it was obvious to everyone else that the FSLN was using the talks as a divide-and-conquer ploy. His "army" was mostly mythical. Rivera's Washington lobbyist, a smooth talker named Armstrong Wiggins, was an expert at playing on American guilt about Indians, and he got Senator Nancy Kassebaum of Kansas to insist that $5 million of the $100 million aid package be reserved for Rivera. A year after the money was appropriated, nearly all the supplies were still stacked in a Honduran warehouse. Rivera didn't have enough men to carry them away.

The State Department decided to strengthen the hand of the third Indian leader, the Moravian pastor Wycliffe Diego. Diego was a serious alcoholic with the smallest following of the three, but perhaps he could mediate between Rivera and Fagoth. When Chidester asked Diego how State could help, Diego replied that he needed a stockpile of gifts to help cement political alliances. "That's how we work," Diego explained. "If I go talk to someone, I have to give him a present first."

So Chidester flew with Diego to Miami and drove him around to shopping malls, helping him buy thousands of dollars worth of cameras, wristwatches, and calculators. Then they returned to Honduras. A week later Chidester saw Diego among a crowd of street vendors in downtown Tegucigalpa, doing a brisk trade in cameras, wristwatches, and calculators. Nonetheless, the State Department gave Diego a $10,000 monthly budget for "political activities," which vanished without a trace.

The unity agreement among the three leaders was supposed to be forged at a mammoth assembly of Indians on the Atlantic coast. At the last minute, the chief of the village where the assembly was to be held told Chidester it would have to be canceled unless the gringos provided some cows. It would be too humiliating to have guests, the chief said, and not serve them meat.

Chidester hopped into an embassy helicopter and told the pilot to cruise around looking for cattle. A few minutes later, they spotted a scrawny, emaciated cow, and the chopper landed. Chidester trotted over to the farmer. "How much for your cow?" he asked, prepared to pay as much as 200 lempiras, $100. The farmer eyed the helicopter. "For my cow," he announced, "I want 1,000 lempiras."

Swearing under his breath, Chidester counted out the bills, and they strapped the cow into a harness under the helicopter and returned to the village. There Chidester grabbed Fagoth. "You've got to come with me and buy cows," Chidester informed him. "You'll know how to bargain." Fagoth nodded and directed the chopper to a field where a large herd grazed. Before they got out to talk to the farmer, Chidester slipped Fagoth a wad of bills.

"How much for ten of your cows?" Fagoth asked the craggy old farmer as Chidester stood silently by. "The price is 1,200 lempiras a cow," the farmer answered, staring at the helicopter. "Okay," said Fagoth, equably. Chidester tackled him before he could count out the money.

The unity conference was held, and Fagoth, Rivera, and Diego sullenly agreed to form a single organization. (Only the cynical believed that their decision was influenced by the Honduran army, which—when two days had gone by with no agreement—surrounded the village.) Within three months they were publicly threatening to kill each other again.

Jim Adkins was not there to witness Commander Chickenkiller's performance. As Congress prepared for the Iran-contra hearings, investigators came sniffing around Honduras. And in May, Adkins was summoned back to Washington to talk to the CIA's inspector general, the Agency's internal investigative arm. The question was blunt: Did you obey the congressional restrictions? And Adkins' answer was blunter: No.

He had tried, for a time. For four months he stuck to the letter of the law, didn't do a damn thing for the contras but answer their intelligence questions. Then, on a visit to the contra camp in Capire, in the Las Vegas Salient, he noticed four dozen freshly dug tiny graves. A plague of measles was sweeping through the refugee families clustered around the camp, and on some mornings they buried the babies three to a grave. The contras had measles vaccine in Tegucigalpa, but no working aircraft to get it to the camps.

That night, as he lay in bed, Adkins thought about the graves and his own two babies asleep in the next room. He thought about how, just a few weeks before, the congressional restrictions hadn't stopped Langley from ordering him to plan a rescue mission for Russell Means. The next morning he sent the measles vaccine to Capire on a CIA helicopter.

After that, Agency helicopters flying to the border on (legal) intelligence-gathering missions often carried (illegal) cargoes of medicine and food. And when they came back out, the choppers usually carried several (illegal) ill or malnourished refugees. Once, when a mission to San Andrés de Bocay kept an officer busy on the ground for several hours, the chopper continued to shuttle back and forth on the same cycle: food and medicine out, people in.

Many times Adkins stuffed CIA helicopters full of contraband: measles vaccine, penicillin, starving eight-year-old girls. Only one of the illegal loads contained military supplies. It was in November 1986, when U.S. military aid had just resumed. Congressmen, anxious to see what they were getting for their money, were flocking to Honduras like tourists to Disneyland, and the CIA was flying them out to Yamales on a daily basis.

The Sandinistas infiltrated small teams of troops into the area, and in the communications center at Yamales, Adkins eavesdropped on their radio conversations as they tried to get one of the helicopters full of congressmen in the sights of their surface-to-air missiles. He cabled headquarters to stop the congressional visits. The visits will continue, Langley replied, and the contras will send out patrols to ensure the safety of the congressmen.

Adkins went to visit Bermúdez. "I need you to send out patrols," he said.

"You told us to concentrate on infiltration," Bermúdez protested. "You told us you didn't even want us to keep this base."

"Look, Enrique, you gotta do it," Adkins said wearily.

Bermúdez smacked a table angrily. "If you want it done, you give us help," he said. "You've got to supply the patrols by helicopter. We've got enough problems supplying the men who are going back to Nicaragua."

Adkins had been in Guyana in 1979, when religious cultist Jim Jones ran amok, shooting up a plane carrying a San Francisco congressman and then ordering a mass suicide. Adkins remembered the price the U.S. embassy paid for letting a congressman go in harm's way. So he broke the rules again.

About the same time he sent Agency helicopters to Yamales to pick up 130 contras who were being sent to Florida for training, another clear violation of the rules. But the only alternative was marching the men out along the Cifuentes-Las Trojes road, where Sandinista artillery would have cut them to pieces in a matter of minutes.

When the inspector general had heard the whole story, he was livid. "These were acts of disloyalty," he stormed. "You've jeopardized this entire program."

"I don't regret one goddamn bit of it," Adkins replied coldly. "I did what I had to do to protect my people and save some lives."

For seven months, Adkins languished on administrative leave while the

Agency decided what to do with him. Sometimes he went to ball games with Joe Fernández, the Costa Rican station chief, who wandered into the twilight zone of the Boland Amendment during his efforts to help out Oliver North's supply operation. Lewis Tambs, the U.S. ambassador to Costa Rica while Fernández was serving there, testified before Congress that he knew and approved of everything Fernández had done. It didn't seem to matter.

Adkins and Fernández were middle-level officers who were ordered to blaze a trail through the legal and political rubble of the fight between the Reagan administration and Congress over Nicaraguan policy, but no one came to their aid: not the Reagan administration, which refused to confront the congressional restrictions openly; not their Agency superiors, who wanted to hear about results and not obstacles. Adkins and Fernández had become part of the "disposal problem," a polite term the CIA coined after the Bay of Pigs invasion to describe what happens when the U.S. government walks away from the messy human debris of its foreign policy failures.[4]

(Late in 1991, the investigation of Iran-contra independent counsel Lawrence Walsh began to topple other CIA dominoes. Former Central American Task Force chief Alan Fiers pled guilty to a charge of withholding information from Congress, and former director of operations Clair George was indicted on ten similar charges.)

Five days before Christmas 1987, they were fired. "Our big mistake was not calling up the Soviet embassy and offering to defect," Adkins joked bitterly to Fernández. When the CIA suspects one of its officers is crazy, crooked, or potentially disloyal, it eases him out: severance pay, free psychiatric care, job placement help, a red carpet back into the world. Adkins and Fernández, fired for loyalty to the CIA, didn't even get a handshake.

At Langley, the fallout was immediate. An officer who had just spent six months learning Portuguese in order to work with the U.S.-backed insurgents of Jonas Savimbi in Angola announced that he wouldn't take the assignment. His refusal, his superior officers warned, would be an indelible black mark on his career. "I'd rather have a black mark," the officer retorted, "than wind up like Adkins and Fernández."

In Honduras, the CIA station was paralyzed. So many officers were running back and forth to Washington for questioning by congressional committees, the Iran-contra special prosecutor's office, or the Agency's inspector general that continuity and consistency were impossible. Adkins's replacement, an officer who called himself John Connally, was the most cautious CIA man the contras had ever encountered. "Why did they send us that guy?" Mike Lima asked Bermúdez. "He's just a bureaucrat. No matter what we say, all he says is, 'the law, the law, the law.'" No one called Connally *coronel*; he was just plain *señor*.

The rules on using CIA aircraft for humanitarian missions at the border changed, sort of. The Agency's lawyers decided it was not illegal for a CIA helicopter to carry a critically wounded contra to a hospital—as long as Langley gave specific permission. An officer visiting Washington from Tegucigalpa stopped by Adkins's home in suburban Virginia one day and told him about the new rule.

"Of course, by the time we can get permission from headquarters, the guy is liable to die anyway," the officer noted. "One of the pilots, a couple of weeks ago, just said, 'Fuck this; this guy's gonna die if we don't move him right now.' So they put him in the chopper and flew him in. Headquarters went crazy: 'How do we know he was really that seriously injured? How can we be sure?' The contra died a few days later. And I'm ashamed to say it, but we were all relieved. Because that was the only way headquarters was going to get off our backs."

On August 7 in Guatemala City, Daniel Ortega stunned everyone by signing a peace plan with the four other Central American presidents. "You're really going to sign it?" Salvadoran president José Napoleón Duarte blurted in disbelief as Ortega picked up his pen.

When the plan was introduced by Costa Rican president Oscar Arias in February, the Sandinistas denounced it as a Reaganite ploy. For that matter, enthusiasm among the other three presidents was limited. The vague plan contained no provisions for enforcement; and it equated Ortega's government with the other four, a comparison not well received by Duarte or José Azcona of Honduras. And as a recipe for peace for three countries with armed insurgencies—Nicaragua, El Salvador, and Guatemala—the plan had a spectacular weakness: it was produced without any input from the guerrillas and did not address their concerns.

In the end, though, each president had his own motive for signing the plan. Vinicio Cerezo of Guatemala and Arias were openly campaigning for the Nobel Peace Prize. Duarte believed the plan would delegitimize the guerrillas in his country, who lately had been beating him at public relations. Azcona, weary of his image as an American stooge, refused to stand alone against the plan. And Ortega was concerned about an alternate peace plan, much tougher, proposed jointly by the White House and Jim Wright, the Democratic speaker of the House of Representatives.

The Reagan-Wright plan called for three immediate and simultaneous actions in Nicaragua: an in-place cease-fire, restoration of all civil liberties, and a halt to both U.S. aid to the contras and Soviet bloc military aid to the Sandinistas. Meanwhile, the FSLN would have to schedule early elections and draw up plans to slash its military forces. If the Sandinistas did not comply within sixty days, U.S. aid to the contras would resume, and the implicit threat was that congressional Democrats would pass an aid package without protest.

Containing very little wiggle room, the Reagan-Wright plan was clearly unacceptable to the Sandinistas. Yet FSLN anxiety over the consequences of another year of war was growing. The contras were operating openly along the eastern side of Matagalpa, Boaco, and Chontales departments, less than fifty miles from Managua. Ferrying Sandinista troops all over the country, and keeping them supplied, was draining the government's fuel reserves; Ortega, in a desperate international plea for more oil, said Nicaragua would suffer a 20 percent shortfall of petroleum by the end of the year.

When the Sandinistas learned privately from Wright that he considered the Arias plan an acceptable substitute for the one he and the White House were sponsoring, they decided to take their chances with Arias.[5] Essentially, the Arias plan required all the governments in the region to stop arming or sheltering guerrilla groups, grant general amnesties, and lift nearly all restrictions on civil liberties. Each government was supposed to "take all necessary steps . . . to bring about a genuine ceasefire." And the plan also committed them all to asking for an end to support for guerrillas from governments outside Central America. The deadline for compliance with all the plan's provisions was November 5.

So in theory, the Sandinistas would have to lift their five-year-old state of emergency, reopen all the closed opposition news media, pardon approximately two thousand prisoners held on politically related charges, and halt aid to the Salvadoran guerrillas. Whether the plan required the FSLN to negotiate with the contras was unclear from the cryptic language about cease-fires. The return on the Sandinista investment: Honduras would have to eject the contras from its territory, and the other four presidents would have to ask the United States to quit arming the contras.

The Sandinistas clearly believed that many of their obligations could be finessed. It would be difficult to prove that they were still aiding the Salvadoran guerrillas. The definition of political prisoners obviously was open to argument. And while the Sandinistas did not relish reopening the opposition newspaper *La Prensa*, closed since June 1986, they could live with it, at least for a while.[6]

On September 23, the Sandinistas announced their cease-fire plan. They declared a unilateral cease-fire in three small enclaves in Jinotega, Nueva Segovia, and Río San Juan departments. Sandinista troops would withdraw from the zones, and FSLN "peace commissions" would go inside to urge contra commanders to accept amnesty and lay down their arms. It was, explicitly, an attempt to drive a wedge between contra field commanders and the movement's top leadership. "We'll talk to the guys with rifles behind trees in the jungle," said Alejandro Bendaña, Ortega's spokesman. "But we will never talk with the people in Tegucigalpa or Miami."

The cease-fire began on October 6. Within days it was apparent that it had backfired badly on the FSLN. The field commanders refused to talk to the peace commissions, often threatening to burn their vehicles if they returned. Meanwhile, the contras for the first time could leisurely mingle with the local population without fear of Sandinista attack. The only wedges being driven in the cease-fire zones were the ones the contras were pounding between the government and the civilians.

On October 15, after five years of trying, the contras finally closed the Rama Road. About 2,500 troops, from all five Jorge Salazar Regional Commands, launched attacks along a sixty-mile stretch of the road. They took four towns, including Santo Tomás and San Pedro de Lóvago in Chontales Department, two relatively large settlements that were both home to big Sandinista garrisons.

In San Pedro de Lóvago the contras methodically burned the garrison, mayor's office, courthouse, phone company, and government grain silos. At Santo Tomás they blew up a fuel depot. Along the length of the road, they destroyed twenty-five troop trucks and demolished five bridges. The only target that did not fall was the five-hundred-foot bridge over the Río Mico in the village of Muelle de Los Bueyes, near the eastern end of the road, where four hundred Sandinista defenders barely drove the contras off.

Their successful defense of the Muelle de Los Bueyes bridge led the Sandinistas to claim victory. No one believed them. The Rama Road was closed for two days, and when it reopened, reporters saw burned-out trucks, many of them still full of dead bodies, scattered every few miles. The Sandinistas said they lost 44 men—the most casualties they ever admitted to in a single engagement—and the actual number was probably closer to 150.

Bermúdez was frustrated that the Muelle de Los Bueyes bridge survived; its destruction would have disrupted the flow of Sandinista supplies for months. But he had learned something from the operation: The Sandinista army was stretched near its limit. FSLN patrols detected large numbers of contra troops moving toward the Rama Road several days before the attack. Yet they didn't react. No reinforcements or heavy weapons moved into the area. Since no target outside the Pacific coast was more strategic than the Rama Road, the only possible explanation was that the Sandinistas had nothing left to commit.

Bermúdez told his headquarters staff to start work on a new operation. They would call it Olivero, in honor of a commander killed earlier in the year near the Zelaya Department mining town of Siuna. The Sandinista troops who had ambushed him were about to pay the price.

For more than a year, off and on, the contras had been discussing an attack on the mining region in northeastern Zelaya Department. The rough triangle formed by the towns of Bonanza, Siuna, and Rosita was tempting for several reasons. The Bulgarian-operated gold and silver mines brought the Sandinistas millions of dollars in foreign exchange each year. A long-range Soviet radar station in Siuna enabled the Sandinistas to track contra supply flights, project their probable path across Nicaragua, and alert antiaircraft units. And the Bonanza-Siuna-Rosita triangle was also the weakest, most isolated link in the defensive cordon that the Sandinistas had constructed across northern Nicaragua to block contra infiltration routes. Only three roads, easily cut, were available to bring reinforcements.

At the same time, Las Minas, as the area was known, would be no pushover. Two Sandinista brigades, armed with heavy artillery, were headquartered there. The contras would face more than two thousand defenders.

Operation Olivero was the most difficult attack the contras had ever planned, not only because of its military complexity, but because the atmosphere at Yamales was growing poisonous. The Americans were making noises about cutting off the funding again, and the field commanders could barely fend off their despair. How many times could this happen? Many of the commanders had been at war for five years now. They had lost their families; their friends; some, like Mike Lima, even their arms or legs. It was beginning to seem that the war could go on like this forever.

As the commanders grew weary, old wounds reopened. The eternal feud between the ex-Guardsmen and the campesinos flared again, fanned in part by the State Department officials who were flexing their muscles now that the CIA was in disarray. Bermúdez's management style of seeking compromise and avoiding confrontation was less and less effective as the anger built up on each side.

In this climate, Mike Lima and the others who were planning Operation Olivero had to go from commander to commander, pleading for troops. At first they encountered mostly skepticism. But when the CIA came up with a bumper crop of supplies and a crackerjack set of aerial photos of Las Minas, the commanders grew more interested. And finally the very ambitiousness of the plan intrigued them.

The idea was to launch a twelve-pronged attack on the three towns. Outlying contra units would cut highways, and dozens of Redeye teams would encircle the region to make sure no helicopters got through. Altogether, 4,500 contras would take part.

Meanwhile, the Sandinistas' attention would be drawn elsewhere through an elaborate deception. Paratroopers jumped into the Jorge Salazar Regional Commands III and V with instructions for the commanders to radio Yamales and—using a code the contras knew the Sandinistas had broken—discuss a phony plan to attack the Rama Road. Other units to the south were instructed to hit any target they could find on December 18 and 19, to create the impression of a major push toward the road. And, finally, every contra unit changed its radio operators. The Sandinistas had been monitoring contra communications for so long they knew which operators belonged to which units; the massive switch would make it impossible for them to tell who was mobilizing.

Thirty-one units began moving toward Las Minas during the first week in December. Their specific assignments were delivered by paratroopers who jumped at night in the final few days before the operation. The orders were in writing, so even if a paratrooper didn't survive the jump, the unit would still get its instructions without having to use the radio.

The tight security was the idea of a CIA officer who called himself, improbably, Don Johnson. Johnson, a West Point graduate, was one of the few remaining Agency people who was interested in focusing on operations rather the legislative history of the Boland Amendment. The contras thought he was a useful adviser, if a little pushy—like all the other West Point graduates they had ever dealt with. The contras called West Point men "ringknockers," because whenever there was an argument about strategy, they began ostentatiously tapping their gargantuan class rings on the table. Johnson was the loudest ringknocker of all; he kept demanding more and more practice jumps of the contra paratroopers, until one—a quiet campesino who hardly ever talked—suddenly spoke up. "Look, *Señor* Johnson," he said, "if I break my legs, I want to do it in Nicaragua, not Honduras."

The attack began at 5 A.M. on December 20. The easiest target turned out to be Bonanza, where 200 Sandinista troops had just left after getting word that the contras were advancing on Rosita. That left only 250 Sandinistas to defend against 600 contras led by Commanders Renato and Poffi. When the contras captured a hilltop artillery position in the first minutes of the attack, the rest of the town's defense collapsed; by 7 A.M. Bonanza was under contra control.

Because of the Soviet radar station, the contras expected Siuna to be the scene of the fiercest fighting. More than 1,300 contra troops joined the attack. But through sheer luck, they struck the morning after the 366th Brigade's Christmas party, and most of the 600 Sandinista soldiers in Siuna were either drunk or passed out. Rigoberto and Mack, the chief contra commanders, held the town by 9 A.M.

It was in Rosita, the smallest and least significant target, that the Sandinistas resisted the most successfully. On December 18, as Commander Fernando's 1,200 men crossed a highway south of town, a Sandinista troop truck approached. The contras had no choice but to ambush it, alerting FSLN troops in Rosita. After six hours of combat, when the contras still held only part of the town, Fernando broke off the attack and withdrew.

The damage the contras inflicted during and after their attacks was spectacular. They destroyed the radar station, a hydroelectric plant, two airfield fuel dumps, a construction depot, three bridges, and several government buildings. They took more than fifty tons of food from government warehouses and gave it away to the local people. They wrecked the mineworks in Bonanza, but spared the older, barely functioning mine in Siuna after town residents pled with them not to harm it. The sweetest moment was when Rigoberto, as Sandinista prisoners gaped in surprise, went directly to a secret warehouse complex hidden just south of Siuna pinpointed by the CIA's aerial photography. After looting it of more than one thousand rifles and thirty antiaircraft missiles, he blew it up.

Rigoberto abandoned Siuna at the end of the day; Renato held Bonanza through the night before departing. No Sandinista reinforcements arrived until after the contras left. The contras lost forty-seven men in Operation Olivero, two-thirds of them in Rosita, and another two hundred were wounded. Sandinista casualties, the contras estimated, were more than double that.

Back at Yamales, Lima asked Bermúdez if Operation Olivero would make any difference to the Americans. "I think they have to take us seriously now," Bermúdez replied. But Lima couldn't tell if he really believed it. Maybe Bermúdez wasn't sure himself.

On November 5, Daniel Ortega, acknowledging that his attempt to negotiate with individual commanders had failed, agreed to peace talks. The first round was held in Santo Domingo on December 3 and 4, a second on December 21 and 22, while Operation Olivero was in progress. The Sandinistas refused to meet the contras face to face, so Nicaragua's Roman Catholic Cardinal Miguel Obando y Bravo worked as a mediator, talking with first one side and then the other. Serious negotiations were impossible under the circumstances, and nothing happened at either meeting.

Even meaningless talks, however, were a sign of how far the contras had pushed the FSLN in 1987. The Sandinistas admitted to losing 2,039 troops during the year. They claimed to have lost ten helicopters, and the U.S. embassy put the number closer to twenty. To pay for the war, the Sandinistas printed money; the annual inflation rate was 1,800 percent. In the countryside, campesinos selling goods to visitors from Managua asked for payment in soap or toilet paper rather cordobas. In the cities, the Sandinistas tripled the price of gasoline, then had to ration it anyway.

When Tomás Borge said that the stars would fall and the rivers flow uphill before the Sandinistas negotiated with the contras, he exaggerated. All it took was the roof falling in.

15 | Self-Destruction

Under the tin roof of the old customs shed, it was pandemonium, like an anthill kicked over. Two hundred fifty reporters ran in all directions, shouting questions, screaming dictation into phones, battering the keyboards of ancient telex machines. It was nearly midnight, and most of the journalists had only a few minutes before final deadline to file the biggest story out of Nicaragua in nine years: a cease-fire agreement between the Sandinistas and the contras, hammered out in the closing minutes of a three-day negotiation in the dusty border post of Sapoá. European reporters, whose deadlines had passed hours ago, clustered around the negotiators, barking questions in a bizarre polyglot of languages.

A hundred yards away, four commanders—the military delegates on the contra negotiating team—sat unnoticed in a darkened bus. The customs shed had no walls, and they watched the bedlam inside, thrown into harsh relief by the glare from the lights of a dozen television crews. It looked like an overexposed movie or a bad dream. Inside the bus, no one spoke. Tears trickled down Commander Fernando's cheeks; Toño chewed his lip to keep from crying.

Frank Arana, the chief contra propagandist, sat with them. He, too, was quiet, until Arístides Sánchez, one of the contra political directors, climbed onto the bus. "This is not what we fought for," Arana told Sánchez quietly. "We are going to be perceived as totally defeated. We are going to be perceived as surrendering."

"What do you want me to do?" Sánchez screamed, shattering the deathly silence of the bus. "We had to sign something! It was the only way the gringos would give us any more food for the troops!" He pushed past Arana and threw himself down in the back corner of the bus. Only ten minutes old, the Sapoá peace treaty was already tearing the contras apart.

The cease-fire negotiated in Sapoá from March 21 to March 23, 1988, should have been a triumph for the contras. Not only had they forced

221

top FSLN leaders to talk with them face-to-face, they had wrung major concessions from the Sandinistas and won the right to take part in writing a new constitution. And they achieved it all virtually without sacrifice.

But instead of inspiring the contras, Sapoá sent them reeling down the road to self-destruction. It touched off an orgy of conspiracy and treachery among their politicians and a landslide of blind recriminations and revenge among their commanders. It was a total systems failure; nearly every important contra official, political and military, deserved a share of the blame.

Even as Sapoá demonstrated the weaknesses and vulnerabilities at the top of the contra organization, however, it certified the authenticity at the bottom. As their leaders betrayed them or mindlessly flailed away at one another, frittering away their political capital with the Americans and ending any possibility of renewed U.S. aid, the contra troops stolidly refused to disband. If they were mere mercenaries or American finger puppets, as they were so often described, the contras surely would have melted away during 1988. Instead, they stayed together, an army poised to return to war as soon as it had bullets. Their solidarity would eventually force the Sandinistas to take desperate gambles in the hope of forcing their dismantlement.

The Sapoá peace talks were the first high-level negotiations between the Sandinistas and the contras, but they were hardly the first attempt to sort out Nicaragua's problems through diplomacy. Between 1983 and 1986, the five Central American governments met sporadically for regional peace talks sponsored by Mexico, Colombia, Panama, and Venezuela—the so-called Contadora Group, named for the Panamanian island where the first meeting took place. The talks went nowhere; the Contadora Group, more interested in image than reality, never proposed a real mechanism for verifying any of the democratic or military reforms the talks were supposed to achieve. Even less successful were the direct talks between the Sandinistas and the U.S. government in Manzanillo, Mexico, in 1984. In four months of meetings, the two sides never even resolved an agenda for the negotiations.[1] The contras themselves periodically proposed peace talks with the Sandinistas, beginning in January 1983, to no avail.

The Sandinistas agreed to negotiate indirectly with the contras in November 1987 as part of the Arias peace plan. They clearly intended the talks as a measure to defuse the Reagan administration's push for new military aid to the contras rather than as a bona fide search for a settlement. At first, the FSLN didn't even plan to send Nicaraguan representatives to the talks—the Sandinista negotiators were to be Paul Reichler, the American attorney who represented the FSLN in the World Court lawsuit against the United States, and Hans-Jürgen Wischnewski, a Social Democratic Party member of the West German Parliament who barely spoke Spanish. When the contras refused to negotiate with foreigners, the Sandinistas added their vice foreign minister, Victor Hugo Tinoco, to the delegation. They continued to insist, however, that the negotiations take place outside Nicaragua.

To foster the illusion of seriousness, the Sandinistas prevailed upon Miguel Obando y Bravo, Nicaragua's Roman Catholic cardinal, to mediate the talks. Without a doubt, Obando was the most widely admired man in Nicaragua. His opposition to the Somoza dynasty led Tachito Somoza to refer to Obando as Commander Miguel, the tenth Sandinista *comandante*. Yet after the Sandinistas came to power, Obando remained a tough critic of the government; his scorching Sunday sermons, broadcast live over the church radio station, were for years among the few public challenges that the FSLN couldn't censor.

If the Sandinistas hoped that refereeing the peace talks would silence Obando, they were disappointed. From the beginning, he was an activist mediator who tilted toward the contra position. Like the contras, he believed that the negotiators had to discuss political reforms as well as technical military details. And he put his weight behind another contra demand, threatening to quit mediating unless the Sandinistas agreed to face-to-face negotiations.

Early in the new year, the cardinal got his way. Direct talks were scheduled for February 18, 19, and 20 in Guatemala City. The first night, after several hours of fruitless discussion, Obando offered his own proposal. To jump start cease-fire negotiations, the Sandinistas would grant a general amnesty, lift all restrictions on freedom of expression, open talks on constitutional reform with opposition political parties, and "reconsider" the military draft. Obando's plan contained one concession to the Sandinistas: The contras would move their troops into designated enclaves, as the FSLN had been demanding, for thirty days while the details of a permanent cease-fire were worked out.

Although they had always rejected the idea of enclaves as a trap, the contras accepted the plan. The Sandinistas stalled. At noon the next day, when they still hadn't given him an answer, Obando abruptly walked out of the talks and told reporters that the Sandinistas couldn't make up their minds. "The mediator believes there is no reason at this time to continue these conversations," Obando, stiff with anger, announced. Within minutes he was on a plane for Managua, a day ahead of schedule.

The FSLN attempt to use the cardinal as a fig leaf for phony talks had boomeranged catastrophically, and on March 2, Daniel Ortega fired him, issuing a terse statement that Obando's services "are no longer necessary." But to lure the contras back to the talks, Ortega added two concessions. His brother Humberto would head the Sandinista delegation; and the talks could take place in Nicaragua—in Sapoá, a few hundred feet inside the country's southern border. After five years of war, the leaders of the two sides would finally sit down together at a table in their own country.

The breakthrough in negotiations, however, came as the sociopolitical fault lines through the contras were starting to heave. All the accumulated jealousies, rivalries, personal animosities, and political grudges were uncoiling at once in the wake of the new cutoff of U.S. aid.

On February 3, the House of Representatives voted down the military aid package, 219–211, a remarkably close vote after fifteen months of nonstop Iran-contra scandal, including twelve weeks of televised congressional hearings.

The contras, however, couldn't eat moral victories or shoot them at the Sandinistas. And as the dimensions of their loss became clearer, their anger flared. They knew the CIA supply planes based on Swan Island would disappear. But on February 28, when legal authority for U.S. aid ran out, the contras learned that their entire delivery capacity would vanish with the gringos. Their only functioning airplane, an old C-47, turned out to be rented. So did most of their trucks. Practically the only vehicle that the CIA actually purchased for them out of the $100 million aid package, a DC-6 supply plane, had been shot down the month before, the first aircraft downed by the Sandinistas since the Eugene Hasenfus flight fifteen months earlier.[2]

Without trucks or planes, it was impossible to supply contras inside Nicaragua, difficult even to move material to their border camps where thousands of refugees depended on them for food and medicine. It was as though 1987 was just a long, pleasant dream from which the contras awakened to find themselves back in 1985, hands tied again, facing an enemy whose supply lines from Cuba and the Soviet Union never dwindled.

Losing their supply pipeline would have been a bitter pill for the contras under any circumstances, but after the brutal fighting of 1987, it was doubly hard to swallow. They did everything the gringos asked, proved that their will to fight had survived the long layoff in 1985 and 1986, showed that they weren't afraid of the Soviet helicopters, and pushed the Sandinistas relentlessly. And it still wasn't enough for the Americans, who seemed to think their money entitled them to play God. The contras were grateful for the millions of dollars, but they wished the gringos would remember who was doing all the dying. More than one thousand contras died in 1987, and about three thousand were wounded. That scarcely seemed to have been noticed in Washington.

Many commanders, in fact, concluded that the way the Americans played ping-pong with contra aid—now they get it, now they don't—was due not to indecision but to malice. The Americans didn't *want* the contras to win the war. That was why, every time the contras had a run of military success, the aid got cut off. In the paranoid style of Nicaraguan politics, it made eminent sense that the Americans would spend hundreds of millions of dollars on a war in order to lose it. The truth—that the Reagan administration could not always get what it wanted from a Congress where both houses were dominated by hostile Democratic majorities—was incomprehensible to Nicaraguans, whose legislative bodies had never functioned as anything but rubber stamps for whichever *caudillo* was sitting in the presidential palace.

The amorphous anger of the commanders floated through the camps like a dark cloud, clinging to anything it touched. One of the main targets, incongruously, was Bermúdez himself. He was the commander in chief; he had more contact with the gringos than anyone. If aid stopped, many of the commanders reasoned, Bermúdez had failed.

The bitterest criticism came from campesinos and former Sandinistas. The animosity between the former National Guardsmen and the other commanders had not faded away, as both Bermúdez and the Americans had hoped it would. The National Guardsmen still considered the campesinos as amateurs in the military game; the campesinos still regarded every slight, real or imagined, as a form of class warfare. The acrimony submerged when U.S. aid was flowing and most of the contras were inside Nicaragua. But when the aid was cut, and the commanders spent too much time in Honduras, it resurfaced.

Every time the rancor between the ex-Guardsmen and the campesinos bubbled to the surface, both sides blamed Bermúdez for playing favorites. The campesinos claimed that Bermúdez gave the ex-Guardsmen the bulk of the supplies and headquarters jobs. And the ex-Guardsmen accused him of coddling the campesinos, permitting acts of wild indiscipline.

Neither side recognized, as Bermúdez did, that the contras were a delicate balance of competing interests that was always on the verge of flying apart. Professional military men fighting to avenge the last war, illiterate peasants demanding the return of their old parish priest, disgruntled ex-Sandinistas trying to punish their old *compañeros* for some snub, alienated Indians insisting that the Atlantic coast secede from Nicaragua, sleek politicians with their eye on the presidency: Bermúdez had to reconcile their contradictory agendas with those of the Hondurans, who wanted the Sandinistas pushed off their border at any cost; the U.S. State Department, which wanted a glossy product it could show off to Congress, regardless of whether it worked; and the CIA, which wasn't always sure what it wanted, but whatever it was, wanted it done the CIA way.

Every other contra organization had been torn to shreds by the struggle to resolve all these conflicting claims. Edén Pastora's ARDE, Negro Chamorro's UDN, the various Indian organizations—the gringos lavished money on them all, sometimes more per soldier than Bermúdez was getting, and yet every one dissolved into internal contradiction and chaos. Only one army grew, produced military results, and remained intact through lean times: the one Bermúdez put together. If Bermúdez had a historical analogue, it was not General Patton devising lightning thrusts against the enemy's underbelly, but General Eisenhower, stroking the sensitive egos of the French and British generals to hold a fragile alliance together while others planned the battles.

There was, for instance, the matter of Commander Coral. Coral (his real name was Freddy Gadea) was a former Sandinista who was one of the original *Milpas*, the peasant guerrillas who turned against the FSLN soon after the revolution. Inside Nicaragua, Coral was a skilled commander, popular with his men. Outside, in the Honduran base camps, he drank too much. And on the day in February 1987 that he asked Bermúdez for permission to take a pickup truck from the Yamales motor pool for a weekend in Danlí, Coral had already had a few beers.

Bermúdez authorized the trip. But when Coral went to the motor pool—after a couple more beers—Commander Machete, the ex-Guardsmen in charge of the vehicles, said all the trucks were reserved for official business.

"Look, you *Guardia* son of a bitch, I want a truck and I want it now," Coral snarled. Machete responded in equally colorful, and adamant, terms. As their voices rose, a passing ex-Guardsman, Commander Atila, stopped and tried to calm the two men down. "I can kick both your asses," Coral announced. His shouted threats drew a third ex-Guardsman, Mike Lima. "Look, why don't you and I go see Bermúdez?" Lima suggested. "We can get this straightened out."

What Lima intended as mediation, Coral saw as intimidation. "I don't have to go anywhere with a *Guardia*!" he shouted, drawing his pistol. "I'm a commander, just like you! You can't order me around." As Coral pointed the pistol, Lima dived behind a pile of sandbags. Three motor pool security guards fired their AK-47s at Coral in unison; he went down, his right leg shattered and bloody. The doctors had to amputate it.

The facts seemed clear: Coral was drunk, Coral was behaving aggressively, Coral pulled his weapon and pointed it at Lima. If anyone was guilty of anything, it was Coral—an open-and-shut case. But Bermúdez knew he couldn't let it go so easily. If he did, the shooting would pass into contra legend as the time three ex-Guardsmen ganged up on a campesino commander, blew his leg off, and got away with it because the ex-Guard commander in chief wouldn't permit an inquiry.

So, to the outrage of the ex-Guard commanders, Bermúdez convened a tribunal to hear charges against Lima. But he made certain that two of his most loyal commanders, Mack and Aureliano, sat on the three-member tribunal. Before the hearing began, Bermúdez instructed them privately to vote for acquittal. Lima was found innocent, the campesino commanders had the satisfaction of seeing a trial, and a potentially cataclysmic situation was defused. Hardly a day went by without Bermúdez performing some similar political sleight-of-hand.

With the cutoff of the American aid, it was getting more difficult to keep all these balls in the air. As the date of the Sapoá peace talks approached, the campesino commanders were once again holding meetings and issuing challenges to Bermúdez. As they often did, the campesinos cloaked the real source of their disgruntlement—their suspicion that they were assigned proportionally fewer pickup trucks than the ex-Guardsmen—in a loftier argument. They called for Bermúdez to appoint a second in command. And they announced they would press the issue at the end of February when all the commanders were scheduled to meet and, for the first time, elect their own general staff.

Bermúdez hadn't had an executive officer since Emilio Echaverry left the contras in 1984. Appointing a second in command, it seemed to him, would provoke needless tensions. The position would have to be filled by an ex-Guardsman. None of the campesinos had any experience or training in overseeing the support side of an army. And the Honduran military (which was, for most practical purposes involving the contras, the Honduran government) would certainly never deal with a campesino as an equal.

Yet appointing an ex-Guardsman would give the campesinos another grievance, not to mention riling up the State Department, which liked to pretend that no Guardsmen were among the contras. Bermúdez felt that during his infrequent absences from Honduras, the general staff worked well enough on a collegial basis without setting up a formal chain of command.

The commanders, including the former Guardsmen, disagreed. If something happened to Bermúdez, they feared, they would be left with a gringo-imposed leader or, worse yet, be torn apart by a devastating internal power struggle. For years, the commanders had nagged Bermúdez about naming an executive officer; now, with a general malaise creeping through the ranks, they decided to force the issue.

The meeting began February 29 in San Andrés de Bocay, where the contra headquarters had been moved from Yamales a few months earlier. As the commanders streamed in for the gathering, Bermúdez sprang a surprise: He was creating a new position, chief of staff, and that officer would also be second in command. He wanted Commander Quiché elected to the post.

Quiché was a former National Guard sergeant, but it was difficult for even the most stubborn campesino commander to oppose him. Quiché was Toño's executive officer on the first deep contra penetration to Matagalpa Department in 1983 and had since taken charge of all five Jorge Salazar Regional Commands, more than five thousand troops. He was a skillful military planner—he designed the operation that closed the Rama Road in 1987—but he was no Honduras-bound military bureaucrat. He spent months at a time inside Nicaragua, emerging only for a few weeks and then quickly returning.

Just a few of the men knew that more than anti-Sandinista passion kept Quiché inside Nicaragua. He was a fugitive from international justice, wanted for escaping from a Colombian prison where he was doing time on narcotics-trafficking charges.

After the fall of Somoza, Quiché wound up in Guatemala, where he married a Cuban-American woman whose family was involved in narco-trafficking and all the various unpleasantness that surrounds it. He was a little vague about just how deep his own entanglement was, but he was certainly more than an innocent bystander. Quiché owned a house and a BMW in Honduras, which he couldn't have bought on the savings from his salary as a National Guard corporal.

Making Quiché second in command was a risky venture in terms of American politics—the contras' critics in Congress were already trying to paint them as a vast drug-smuggling conspiracy—but within the movement Bermúdez couldn't have made a better choice. The complaints of the campesino commanders were further muted when Bermúdez and the ex-Guard faction ceded four general staff positions (personnel, logistics, civil affairs, and the largely ceremonial post of inspector general) to them. Meanwhile, the ex-Guardsmen retained the three key posts: intelligence, counterintelligence, and operations.

On March 2, just after the balloting for the new general staff was completed, the Sandinistas sent their version of a congratulatory message: several of their An-26 planes streaked through the sky over San Andrés de Bocay, unleashing a score of five-hundred-pound bombs that left awesome scars in the jungle but landed too far away to do any real harm. Nine days later, 1,500 FSLN troops surged into the Bocay area. Though the contras were badly outnumbered, they used their superior knowledge of the terrain to good advantage. The Sandinistas were also hobbled by mine fields they themselves planted during their May 1987 occupation of San Andrés de Bocay; incredibly, they hadn't kept charts of their own mines, and 80 FSLN soldiers were killed or wounded in explosions. By March 17, the offensive was at a standstill, and when six Honduran F-5 jet fighters bombed FSLN positions at Bermudez's request, the Sandinistas withdrew.

The Sandinista incursion, just ten days before the Sapoá peace talks were to begin, should have paid propaganda dividends to the contras. But the Reagan administration, in the kind of hysterical overkill that so often marred its Central American policy, botched the opportunity: 3,200 U.S. soldiers were airlifted to Honduras as what the Pentagon called a "deterrent." The

227

implication—that the Sandinista incursion somehow threatened Honduras—was absurd. It was a thirty-day trek through the jungle from San Andrés de Bocay to the nearest Honduran village. The insane disproportion of the administration's response caused many congressmen to speculate that the incursion was an invention of the State Department. The Sandinistas got off the hook.

Between the aid cutoff, the Sandinista incursion, and the disquietude in his own ranks, Bermúdez had hardly given a thought to the Sapoá peace talks. Like most other contra officials, he hadn't taken any of the peace negotiations seriously. They were just a propaganda game. And during the first few weeks of March, Bermúdez didn't think much of the way contra politicians were playing their hand.

The Sandinistas had committed two provocations, Bermúdez believed, that should have prompted the contras to cancel peace talks: when they fired Obando, and when they attacked San Andrés de Bocay. But the political directors wouldn't do it; their lust for the spotlight at peace talks, Bermúdez thought, was overwhelming their good sense, if they had any. The contras would be in a much better position to talk peace if U.S. aid was flowing. And the way to get the aid flowing was to make the Sandinistas look like the communist aggressors they were, instead of giving them a forum to posture as flaming pacifists.

The fact was that Bermúdez didn't trust most of the people on the five-member political directorate. He viewed most of the directors as dilettantes or opportunists, imposed by the gringos in their eternal (and futile) quest for a contra political organization that would please liberal Democrats in Congress.

The current political structure was the fourth, and in Bermúdez's opinion, the worst. From 1981 to 1985, the political arm of the contras based in Honduras was the FDN, the only one Bermúdez believed had any claim to legitimacy. The FDN political directorates (first the three-member group headed by Chicano Cardenal, then the six-member delegation that included Bermúdez and Adolfo Calero) were created at the insistence of the Americans and the Argentines, it was true, but at least the members were chosen by Nicaraguans.

That was much more than could be said for the next political organization, the United Nicaraguan Opposition, known by its Spanish acronym UNO. It was created in 1985, when the CIA was banned from contact with the contras and the State Department stepped into the act. Elliott Abrams, the assistant secretary of state for inter-American affairs and the Reagan administration's point man on Nicaraguan policy, became Washington's proconsul to the contras.

Abrams and his aides were determined to package the contras in a way that would win votes in Congress—regardless of the wishes of the Nicaraguans and despite the effect it had on the war effort. Their first project was UNO, which placed the FDN's troops under the authority of a three-man political junta that included Calero and two politicians who had worked with Edén Pastora, Alfonso Robelo, and Arturo Cruz, Sr.

The only qualifications Robelo and Cruz had for the jobs were that they spoke good English and could chant all the buzzwords (social democracy, mixed economy, nonalignment) that made congressional liberals feel warm and happy. Cruz, though handy at Washington cocktail parties, was almost unknown inside Nicaragua, where he had lived only occasionally during the past forty years. A one-time Sandinista supporter who served briefly on the postrevolutionary junta, among Nicaraguans Cruz was known contemptuously as El Casi—"the almost." He attended the National Guard military academy but never got his commission; studied to be an economist, but never won his doctorate; planned to run for the Nicaraguan presidency in 1984, but never officially declared his candidacy. Most of his adult life had been spent in the United States.

On the surface, Robelo's political qualifications were more impressive. A well-known opponent of the Somoza regime, he had organized his own small political party before serving on the first postrevolutionary junta. But as the political chief of Pastora's ARDE, Robelo's record was one of uninterrupted failure. He wasn't able to gain ARDE the support of a single Latin American government, his supposed clout with congressional liberals had not saved U.S. aid to the contras, and he didn't win the loyalty of a single ARDE soldier— when he joined UNO, no troops came with him.

UNO's two-year run was a complete catastrophe. Robelo spent most of his time sniping at Calero and demanding an accounting of the money that he was convinced flowed secretly into the contra coffers from the NSC's Oliver North. In fact, by 1985, North was no longer sending cash to the contras, just supplies. The only exceptions were $50,000 a month to Robelo for political activities, and a $6,000-a-month salary to Cruz.

Robelo, for the most part, did not meddle in military affairs. But Cruz did. For two years he tried to have Bermúdez replaced by Wicho Rivas, one of Pastora's less-distinguished former commanders. Cruz presented no bill of particulars against Bermúdez; he just wanted the army under the command of one of his personal loyalists. In public, Cruz talked loftily of working for political reforms in the contras; in private, he pursued a petty personal agenda that included forcing the purchase of all of UNO's commercial airline tickets through his wife's travel agency.

Meanwhile, UNO's civilian bureaucracy grew by Promethean leaps and bounds. The contras' office on Connecticut Avenue in Washington, which subsisted on $3,000 a month when the FDN ran it, was devouring a $25,000 monthly budget and bellowing for more.[3] The Miami office, disguised by an innocuous sign that read "Pan American Information Service," sprawled over two entire floors of an office building across from the airport on Northwest 36th Street.

In February 1987, Adolfo Calero engineered the destruction of UNO with a single move: He resigned. As Calero had privately predicted, within weeks Cruz and Robelo were fighting each other over the spoils. For a solid month, Cruz issued daily threats to quit if he didn't get his way. Abrams publicly begged him to stay. "Nobody's irreplaceable, but he comes as close as you can get," Abrams told the *Washington Post*.[4] Cruz repaid him by resigning from UNO in a letter to the editor of the *Miami Herald* on March 9, 1987.

The next political umbrella devised for the contras by the State Department was called the Nicaraguan Resistance. It was to have seven directors, elected by exiles from four Nicaraguan political parties—the Liberals, Conservatives, Social Democrats, and Social Conservatives—as well as the minority populations of the Atlantic coast, and the Southern Bloc of Opposition, or BOS, a group of politicians who stayed with Pastora when UNO was formed. A seventh director would be chosen at-large.[5]

The Nicaraguan Resistance was yet another sham organization designed to appeal to the U.S. Congress by accommodating so-called liberal contra politicians who had no authentic popular following. The Social Democrats and Social Christians were both tiny splinter parties that could have held a joint national convention in a shower stall. BOS was a mirage, a personal vehicle for Alfredo César, a cunning young Stanford-educated economist who ran the Central Bank for the Sandinistas in the early days after the revolution. César's king-sized ambition was so apparent that almost no one trusted him, except Senator Nancy Kassebaum of Kansas. She was so smitten that she managed to have $5 million of the $100 million aid package approved in 1986 reserved for César's army—which then could have afforded to buy a tank for each one of its twenty soldiers.

The mistrust that Bermúdez felt for the American-imposed politicians drove him closer to the director he knew the gringos disliked the most: Arístides Sánchez. Sánchez had been a member of the original three-member FDN directorate until the CIA demanded that the contras unload him. It was not his politics that the Agency objected to, but his personality. Sánchez was a malicious gossip who constantly stirred up one faction against another.

While the CIA succeeded in banishing him temporarily, Sánchez ultimately outsmarted the Agency. He spent more time in the camps than any other contra civilian, and he convinced the commanders—including Bermúdez—that they needed him to defend their interests against conniving politicians in Tegucigalpa and Miami. In fact, he was a poor advocate—meetings bored him and he rarely spoke if he attended at all—and a worse political adviser. Nonetheless, Sánchez slipped back onto the FDN directorate, and in 1987 he was elected as the Liberal Party representative to the Resistance directorate.

As the Sapoá peace talks approached, Sánchez counseled Bermúdez to stay away, as usual playing to his suspicions about the other politicians. The peace talks were just a way for them to get their names in the paper. The Managua communists weren't going to offer any deals. Sánchez would keep the others from giving away the farm; and, in the one-in-a-million chance that a bad treaty was signed, Bermúdez could always renounce it on the grounds that he hadn't been a party to it. What was there to lose?

Bermúdez was already leaning in that direction, and the Sandinista offensive against San Andrés de Bocay made the decision easier. How would it look to his men, he wondered, if he sat down with Sandinista commanders who, just a few days before, tried to wipe them out? He decided not to go to Sapoá.

The directorate tried to change his mind, although not as hard as it might have. Three of the directors—Sánchez, Calero, and César—were too busy fighting over who would head the negotiating team. Three times in two weeks the contra press office issued communiqués changing the identity of the delegation's chief. Finally, on March 16, just five days before the talks were to begin, the contras announced that Sánchez, Calero, and César would alternate as leaders. When they should have been devising a negotiating strategy and working up a cease-fire plan, the politicians were fighting about who got to sit in the best chair.

Sapoá was not much more than a wide place in the Pan-American Highway on Lake Nicaragua's western shore where trucks stopped for customs inspections, chosen because it met the contras' demand for a site inside Nicaragua—barely—but still isolated them from the civilian population. The contras found hotels in Liberia, Costa Rica, an hour south, and journeyed to the talks each morning by bus.

The first session convened a little past 9 A.M. on Monday, March 21. Humberto Ortega asked Cardinal Obando (attending the talks as an official witness, along with Joao Baena Soares, secretary-general of the Organization of American States) for a prayer that the negotiations would be fruitful. As Obando prayed, several contras eyed the militantly atheist Ortega. When the prayer was over, Ortega met their gaze. "I don't believe in it," he acknowledged. "But my mother believes, and she prays both for you and for us."

As the talks began, the atmosphere was cordial. Sandinista delegates (they included Joaquín Cuadra, the army's chief of staff; Lenín Cerna, the second in command at the Interior Ministry; and Ricardo Wheelock, the head of military intelligence) carefully avoided the word "mercenary," their ordinary term for the contras. In fact, they didn't even use the word "contra." Instead, they talked about "the resistance." For their part, the contras skirted the term *piricuaco*. And in discussing Sandinista ideology, they dropped "communist" for "Marxist-Leninist," which seemed somehow more polite.

But if the room was free of deliberate insult, the language sometimes still grew rough. Early the first day, a Sandinista delegate made a reference to contra camps in Honduras.

"What are you talking about?" Sánchez interrupted. "We don't have any camps in Honduras."

On the Sandinista side of the table, some negotiators openly snickered. Even several contras had to smother their laughter. But Ortega's lips were thin and white.

"Goddamn it, this is a serious discussion," he growled. "We're not going to get anywhere if you're just going to talk a lot of bullshit." Sánchez hardly spoke again until the final day of talks.

For Toño, it was a surreal experience to sit across from the Sandinista high command. *If these people knew what I did here,* he thought, staring at the Sandinista officers, *they would never let me leave here alive.* Just a couple of miles from Sapoá, in December 1978, Toño's National Guard unit was ambushed. He led his squad charging up a hill, hoping to overrun one leg of the ambush, and as the Guardsmen topped the slope they came face to face with a man in a black beret cradling a machine gun. He jerked the trigger, but the weapon jammed, and Toño and the Guardsmen fired their rifles, blowing most of his face off. When Toño read the papers he found in the corpse's pockets, his hands shook. They had just killed Gaspar García Laviana, a radical Spanish priest who was one of the most famous Sandinista commanders.

It was not just memories that made Toño uncomfortable. For nearly four months now, he had been faithfully attending peace talk sessions, analyzing Sandinista proposals, trying to dope out FSLN intentions, devising cease-fire schemes. But he felt like a ghost in a play, standing at the edge of the stage and making comments that the other characters couldn't hear. No one seemed to care what the commanders thought. The politicians rarely let them speak, and when Bermúdez wanted a report, he called his buddy Arístides Sánchez, even though Sánchez didn't attend any of the negotiations until Sapoá.

Since the disgrace and ostracism he suffered after the La Trinidad operation in 1985, Toño had completely rehabilitated himself. His unit fought hard and well in repelling the Sandinista incursions into Honduras in March and December of 1986. And in July 1987, Toño nearly captured San José de Bocay during a ferocious daylong attack. The accusations of cowardice that dogged him after La Trinidad were all but forgotten. In the general staff elections in San Andrés de Bocay, he was voted chief of operations—third in command of the contra army.

The election should have been a triumphant moment for Toño, but instead he was frustrated. Once again he had failed to get Bermúdez to attend a briefing on the peace talks. Toño wanted to talk about a set of plans he had drawn up after the last negotiations in Guatemala City, where the contras had accepted Cardinal Obando's proposal that they withdraw into enclaves while the Sandinistas democratized Nicaragua. The contras went along with Obando blindly, gambling that the Sandinistas would turn down the proposal, and it worked. Toño believed the idea of enclaves would come up again, though, and the contras should have a workable plan. He spent several days working up maps and charts. But Bermúdez had no time to listen. "He's not taking us seriously," Toño complained to Fernando. "No matter how hard we work, he only cares about the commanders who are personally loyal to him."

In Sapoá, it was the same old story. The civilian negotiators were ignoring the commanders. In fact, the civilians were so involved in their own intrigues that they hadn't even bothered to prepare a written cease-fire plan. The FSLN gave a detailed presentation of its own plan, which called for an in-place, thirty-day cease-fire while the contras disarmed. As contra troops turned in their guns, the Sandinistas would free a proportional number of political prisoners. Once the contra army was disbanded, its leaders could join a dialogue between the Sandinistas and their political opponents on constitutional reforms and new elections. The contra negotiators listened politely and, when it was their turn, winged it, offering a vague, impromptu plan that resembled Cardinal Obando's Guatemala City proposal.

After six hours of talks the first day, it was clear that the two sides had fundamentally different ideas about the negotiations. The Sandinistas wanted an agreement that would end the war for good, with any changes in the Nicaraguan political landscape left for future discussions. The contras, however, were there to negotiate an intermediate accord: a provisional break in hostilities while the Sandinistas democratized Nicaragua. On the surface, at least, there was a wide gap between the two positions.

But as they rode the bus back to Costa Rica, the contra negotiators felt their expectations stirring. They sensed desperation in the Sandinistas. The contras stayed up late that night, getting the details of their own plan on paper. It seemed the Sapoá talks might be more than a propaganda exercise after all.

On Tuesday, the contras' suspicions became certainties. At all the other talks, the Sandinistas had rejected any discussion of politics and insisted on sticking to military matters. Now, however, they changed tack. They might be willing, Humberto Ortega said, to break the FSLN's monopoly on television broadcasting and permit a private station. And they would allow the contras to join the constitutional dialogue in Managua as soon as the first rebel unit disarmed.

Even more telling, the contras felt, was the way Ortega reacted to some harsh words from the commanders. When the general made an offhand comment about his contempt for the National Guard, Toño spoke up for the first time. "I was in the National Guard," he said, his voice level but intense. "And I'll tell you something: I wouldn't be fighting with you today if you hadn't confused justice with revenge, if you hadn't put everybody who wore a National Guard uniform in jail. As long as my friends are in jail, I will never—*never*—put down my gun."

Instead of bristling, Ortega's tone was deferential. "I've never heard it described quite that way," he replied. "You have a point. . . . We made a lot of mistakes at the beginning. We were stubborn. But the revolution is still young, and it's changing. We are more flexible now."

"We've heard that a thousand times before," Toño scoffed. Still Ortega remained calm. And during breaks in the talks, it was apparent that the Sandinistas were trying to placate the contra commanders. A Sandinista officer named Manuel Calderón (in one of the war's common ironies, he was Toño's cousin) approached Commander Fernando. "You must still have some family inside Nicaragua," Calderón said. "Wouldn't you like to see them?" Fernando, suspecting a trick, changed the subject. But the next day during a break, the contra commanders discovered that the Sandinistas had flown a helicopter full of their relatives from Managua for a visit.

Ortega's conciliatory tone convinced the contras that an agreement was possible. But not until Wednesday morning, as the final day began, did the talks zero in on specific differences in the two plans. There was general agreement that the contras would move into enclaves and that the Sandinistas would immediately lift some restrictions on civil liberties. And there was sharp disagreement over how the contras would be supplied inside the enclaves, and the manner in which the Sandinistas would release political prisoners.

The Sandinistas adamantly insisted that the contras receive only "humanitarian" supplies in the enclaves—food, clothing, and medicine—channeled through a refugee-aid organization. The contra commanders, however, were steadfast that military aid be permitted under their own supervision. The commanders also refused to go along with any agreement that linked the number of political prisoners released to the number of contra soldiers laying down their arms. "It sounds like you're trading hostages for our guns," Fernando told Ortega. "It's trafficking in human beings."

As the talks broke for lunch, hope for an agreement was fading. And a division was developing in the contra delegation between the commanders and the politicians. "Why do you keep demanding that the troops be allowed to get military aid inside the enclaves?" César asked the commanders at lunch. "What difference does it make? The Americans aren't going to give us any military aid anyway."

To the commanders, however, there was a big difference. The contras had some military supplies stockpiled in Honduras that could be delivered to the enclaves. Toño and Fernando knew that no matter how big the enclaves were, without military resupply, field commanders would never agree to enter them for fear of being surrounded and massacred.

No matter how often the commanders repeated their argument, however, the contra civilians didn't understand. They believed an agreement would give the contra troops a chance to rest, regroup, and organize new networks of civilian supporters inside the enclaves, much as they did in the three zones where the Sandinistas declared a unilateral cease-fire in October 1987. The politicians were certain that the U.S. Congress would restore humanitarian aid instantly if there was a cease-fire agreement; then, later, when the Sandinistas violated the agreement—as they were certain to do—the Americans would restore military aid as well.

After lunch the talks resumed, fruitlessly, for another three hours. As early evening approached, the negotiators gave up. They sent a small working group to another room to prepare a joint communiqué listing areas of agreement, and scheduling further talks in April.

The rest of the negotiators smoked, chatted, or wandered outside. César stood in one corner of the room, talking animatedly with his childhood friend Joaquín Cuadra. Calero was in another corner with Humberto Ortega. "You know, we could still reach an agreement," Ortega said. After several minutes, Calero beckoned Sánchez over, then César and Cuadra as well. The conversation went on for an hour. Just as the working group returned with its joint communiqué, Calero announced: "We've got an agreement." The working group went right back to the table to put it in writing.

None of the commanders took part in either the informal conversation with Ortega or the working group. They had no idea what was in the agreement until the working group emerged again, more than three hours later, and a Sandinista negotiator began reading it aloud. As they listened, the commanders realized in horror that every single one of their objections had been overridden. The agreement still contained a phased release of political prisoners tied to disarmament; it barred military aid in the enclaves; and, worst of all, it talked about definitive contra disarmament within sixty days.

"Toño," Fernando whispered, "we can't accept this." Toño felt sick, betrayed. "You're right," he muttered back. He interrupted the reading. "This is not going to be acceptable to the men in the mountains," Toño warned. "And if they don't accept it, then it's just a bunch of bullshit."

"Toño's right," Lenín Cerna murmured to Ortega, loudly enough that everyone in the room heard. "Well, then," Ortega asked the commanders, "what do you propose?"

The four commanders huddled. "It's already past 11 P.M., and we don't have time to renegotiate the whole agreement," Toño whispered. "The press is waiting, and if there's no agreement now, everyone will say that the commanders fucked it up. What if we just tell them to remove the language about disarmament in sixty days and say that this will be the subject of continuing negotiations? We can live with the rest of it." The agreement said the size and location of the cease-fire enclaves would be worked out in technical talks the next week; they could try to win back military supplies for the enclaves in those negotiations. The other commanders agreed, and Toño told Ortega what they wanted. The change was made with no further discussion.

A few minutes later, Daniel Ortega arrived from Managua for the signing ceremony. The negotiators filed out and climbed onto a makeshift stage in the customs shed where journalists waited. For the Sandinistas, only Humberto Ortega and the two foreigners, Paul Reichler and Hans-Jürgen Wischnewski, signed. But Calero insisted that every member of his delegation sign it. Sánchez, who supported the agreement inside the negotiating room, was overwhelmed with doubt and remorse the moment he put his name on it; he climbed down from the stage to sit in the audience. Expressionlessly, the commanders sighed then moved to the rear. After the Nicaraguan national anthem was sung, they walked out to the bus. While everyone inside celebrated, they cried.

The final document that emerged from Sapoá was, arguably, far better than the contras had any right to expect, given that their U.S. aid had been cut off and they were negotiating from a position of weakness. A sixty-day truce was to begin immediately. Within fifteen days the contras were to withdraw into enclaves; the size and location of the zones would be established during another meeting in Sapoá on March 28. Inside the zones they could receive humanitarian—but not military—aid, delivered by "neutral organizations." The Sandinistas agreed that "neutral organizations" included any air delivery company not associated with the Pentagon or the CIA.

Contra troops in the enclaves did not have to disarm. Terms of their eventual disarmament, if there was to be one, would be negotiated in Managua during the sixty-day truce. As soon as all the troops were inside the enclaves, the contras would get eight delegates to the talks on constitutional reforms between the FSLN and its political opponents in Managua. That would give the opposition and the contras a total of sixteen delegates to only eight for the Sandinistas.

Meanwhile, the Sandinistas had to withdraw all restrictions on freedom of the press and freedom of speech, including their ban on private television stations. They had to permit their political opponents to return to Nicaragua without imposing restrictions or loyalty oaths. The Sandinistas would release 100 political prisoners on March 27, half of the remainder when the contras were inside the enclaves, and the rest as soon as a permanent cease-fire agreement was signed.

In short, the Sandinistas agreed to make a substantial number of political reforms immediately, before a single contra put down his gun. The contras, meanwhile, got a sixty-day free look while tucked safely away from the Sandinista army. If they didn't like what they saw—if the Sandinistas were lying—they could go back to war. The most significant part of the accord, overlooked by nearly everyone, was the provision giving anti-Sandinista forces two-thirds of the seats in the constitutional talks in Managua, a majority that would permit them to set the ground rules for the next election, including international supervision. Free elections: exactly what the contras had been demanding for six years.

Many Nicaraguans instinctively grasped that the Sapoá agreement was not only an important contra victory but, even more significantly, a decisive Sandinista defeat. It punctured forever the myth of FSLN inevitability, the slogans like "Men pass and die, but the Front goes on forever." The Sandinistas had not only been forced to sit down with men that they had, since the first moments of the revolution, branded murderers, thieves, and rapists; they had made *concessions* to them. Even Nicaraguans who wanted no part of the contras were electrified to see the FSLN treat them as equals. Sapoá proved that, for all their Soviet and Cuban backing, the Sandinistas could be beaten.

Only two groups of people did not believe the agreement was an impressive contra achievement. One was the U.S. State Department, which reacted like a plantation overseer to a slave revolt. The political section of the U.S. embassy in Honduras, the day after the pact was signed, dashed off a cable to Washington indignantly accusing the contras of surrendering without permission. Concluded the cable: "The contras have a lot to answer for."

The other group that did not approve of the Sapoá accord included a substantial number of the contras themselves—even some of those who signed it.

Bermúdez was lying in a hammock in a thatched hut along the Río Bocay, listening, as he did every night, to shortwave radio broadcasts from around Central America. When an announcer said an agreement had been signed in Sapoá, the words struck his ears like a thunderclap. With no communications link between San Andrés de Bocay and the peace negotiators, Bermúdez had no idea an accord was imminent. The next morning he took a helicopter to Tegucigalpa, expecting that some of the politicians would come there to explain what was going on. But none did. Bermúdez flew on to Miami where the contra political assembly was meeting.

As he walked through the lobby of the Viscount Hotel, where the meeting was being held, Bermúdez saw Nicaraguan exiles thronging the lobby and hallways. Every time one of the cease-fire negotiators appeared, angry shouts of "Assassin!" and "Betrayer!" rang out. At least one fistfight had already broken out.

Inside, Bermúdez grew angrier by the minute as he listened to the cease-fire negotiators. The agreement was terrible. It prohibited military supplies for his men, yet didn't say a word about the guns and bullets that flowed into Nicaraguan ports every day from the Soviet and Cubans. What kind of parity was that? And all the negotiators blamed someone else. The commanders said the civilians shoved the agreement down their throats. The civilians said the commanders should have refused to sign it if they felt that strongly.

The most vitriolic denunciations came from the man who told Bermúdez not to attend the negotiations, who promised he wouldn't let anything go wrong, Arístides Sánchez. Attempting to explain why he signed the agreement, Sánchez lashed out at everyone. It was Toño and Fernando's fault, for not warning him how badly it was flawed. It was Calero's fault, for dominating the discussions. "I felt like a student in a schoolroom," Sánchez complained. "I could only talk when they gave me permission."

In acid terms, Bermúdez expressed his disgust. The negotiators had acted like rank amateurs, each pursuing his own agenda. Now there was no choice but to make the best of a bad situation. The members of the assembly were threatening to reject the agreement. Bermúdez urged against that. It was a lousy agreement, he said, but the cost of not complying would be far greater. The assembly, reluctantly, ratified it. But Bermúdez, with his anger at the agreement, his caustic words to the negotiators, and his refusal to accept a good part of the blame for not attending the talks, had already started a chain reaction that would soon rocket out of control.

The first link in the chain was Sánchez. Seething at the criticism he endured for signing the accord, Sánchez embarked on a campaign to destroy it. He told Bermúdez he wanted to head the commission that was going back to Sapoá on March 28 and 29 to negotiate the details of the cease-fire enclaves. If the boundaries of the enclaves and the supply routes were never established, then the Sapoá agreement would never take effect.

Bermúdez would later deny that he was part the scheme, but at the very least he acquiesced in it. He only reluctantly kept Fernando and Toño on the negotiating team, and the new commanders that he added—Mike Lima, Aureliano, and Johnson—were militant opponents of the Sapoá agreement. They believed it was a sellout by the politicians, who gave up everything the commanders had won on the battlefield. And they felt Fernando and Toño had let them down by not blocking the agreement. Sánchez encouraged the ill feelings. "Toño and Fernando aren't really commanders anymore," he told the others. "They've gotten used to staying in expensive hotels and drinking fine wine. They're politicians now." Sánchez even suggested that Toño and Fernando signed the agreement in return for being allowed to see their family members in Sapoá.

Sánchez and the new commanders made no secret of their intent to wreck the technical talks. They arrived late to every session, called for frequent breaks, and argued endlessly over trivial points. Toño and Fernando, however, worked to repair some of the weaknesses in the original accord. The first thing to do was to settle on the dimensions of the enclaves. Toño brought out the maps he drew up after the Guatemala City talks.

He had three proposals. The first one was a deliberately outrageous opening demand: The contras would get about 60 percent of Nicaragua. The second, Toño believed, would be an excellent arrangement for the contras: seven enclaves covering about 8,500 square miles, some on the fringes of the Pacific coast urban areas. The third was the minimum acceptable deal: seven enclaves more remotely located but still covering about 7,700 square miles—far too large for the Sandinistas to effectively surround.

The Sandinistas, as expected, rejected the first one. But on March 29, the final day of talks, they accepted Toño's second plan. After the Sandinistas signed the agreement, however, Sánchez refused. "We need to think about it," he said. "I think we'll have to schedule another meeting to iron out some details."

Joaquín Cuadra was stupefied. "Are you joking?" he asked. "This was *your* plan." Sánchez just shook his head. At the other end of the table, Toño kept his face straight, but a wave of sick rage rolled through his stomach. *All right,* he silently addressed Sánchez, *fuck you.*

Back in Honduras a few days later, Toño was pondering his next move when Commander Rigoberto walked into his hut. "Toño, I heard what they did at the technical talks," he said. "We've got to get rid of these guys." And the conspiracy was hatched. Fernando and Tigrillo quickly joined it.

The dissidents, as they came to be known, had just one demand: Bermúdez must go. (Sánchez, as far as they were concerned, was just one of Bermúdez's goons who would disappear along with him.) They planned a three-pronged strategy to depose Bermúdez. They would get the majority of the field commanders to sign a letter demanding his ouster; at the same time, they would warn the CIA and the Honduran military that Bermúdez no longer had the support of his own army. The gringos and the Hondurans, they were confident, would pull the plug on Bermúdez rather than risk a public mutiny.

Throughout the last two weeks of April, the dissidents met with other commanders and made speeches to the units of sympathetic officers. Sometimes they found receptive audiences; sometimes they mistook polite disinterest for agreement. In late April, after a meeting of commanders in Danlí, they got fifty-one signatures on a letter calling for Bermúdez to resign.

Emboldened, Rigoberto and Fernando made an appointment on April 28 with Terry, the CIA's Tegucigalpa station chief. He listened to their complaints, then offered a suggestion.

"Launching a rebellion against the leadership while it's negotiating with the Sandinistas is a terrible idea," Terry observed. "You're playing into Ortega's hands. Why don't you declare a truce with Bermúdez for sixty days, until the Sapoá cease-fire period is over? I'll give you the money for a vacation in Miami or wherever you want to go. At the end of the sixty days, when the negotiations with the Sandinistas are over, you can challenge Bermúdez. I give you my word the CIA won't take sides—if the men support you, then Bermúdez will go."

To Rigoberto, it sounded like a trick to separate the commanders from their troops. He suspected the sixty days in Miami would stretch into sixty years.

"You have the right idea," he told Terry, "but backwards. You send *Bermúdez* to Miami for sixty days, and let *us* run the peace talks."

Terry gazed at Rigoberto. "In that case," the CIA man said, "I must tell you that the interests of the United States, which has armed you and supported you, are represented by Bermúdez." The meeting was over. Honduran military officers were no more receptive.

Bermúdez tried, belatedly, to talk to the dissidents, to soothe injured feelings. But there had been too many harsh words, too many grudges nursed too long. They refused to see him. So Bermúdez sent his most loyal officers—Mike Lima, Aureliano, Mack, Quiché—out to lobby the men in the camps.

Among the contra field commanders, about 20 percent detested Bermúdez and the former National Guardsmen and another 20 percent were ardently pro-Guard. The rest could be persuaded or pressured, and Bermúdez's lieutenants zealously pursued both avenues. The dissidents were secret Sandinistas, they argued, who were sabotaging the contra army. Why else launch a mutiny right in the middle of peace talks? There was even proof of their cozy relations with the FSLN; the pro-Bermúdez forces passed out thousands of copies of a photo of Toño and Fernando posing at Sapoá with Toño's cousin Manuel Caldcrón, the Sandinista commander. Some men who thought the photo unconvincing had their family-assistance payments cut off. Soon Bermúdez had a letter of support with seventy-three signatures on it, including many of those who signed the dissident letter.

The charge that the dissidents were communists was ridiculous, but so were many of their accusations against Bermúdez. They said he represented the National Guard, a fascist institution. (But Toño himself was a former Guardsman.) They said he turned a blind eye to human rights violations. (But Tigrillo had one of the worst human rights records of any commander.) They said he was a tyrant who ruled with an iron fist. (A real tyrant would have had them shot.) On both sides the slanders escalated out of control.

Both the CIA and the Hondurans were hoping this feud, like so many others, would blow over. But when stories about the dissidents started appearing in newspapers in Miami and Washington, they decided to act. On May 4, Honduran soldiers burst into a Tegucigalpa hotel room and arrested Toño, Rigoberto, and four other dissidents. Along with Tigrillo, arrested in Danlí, they were put aboard an airliner bound for Miami. A few days later, Fernando—the last of the dissident ringleaders—was also arrested and bundled off to Miami.

Shortly after that, Commander Poffi—Toño's executive officer—called the dissidents in Miami. He wanted authorization to lead an attack on Bermúdez's headquarters. Rigoberto, Fernando, and Toño debated it for several hours then called him back.

"We can't support that," Toño said. "Don't do it."

There was a long silence on the line. "All right," Poffi finally answered. "Then I guess there is nothing left for me to do except come to Miami." The dissident movement was finished.

Toño's girlfriend, Judith, also flew to Miami. Toño picked her up in a borrowed car then continued to an office where he could get his American driver's license renewed. The line was long; he gave Judith a $20 bill and sent her to a ncarby Kmart store to pass the time.

Judith had joined the contras in 1982, when she was fifteen years old. Now, at the age of twenty-one, she had killed more men than she had dated. Nearly all the young recruits who joined at the same time she did were dead, and so were most of her relatives: Four dozen members of her family had perished fighting the Sandinistas. In the jungle, sometimes, Toño had wondered if Judith would live long enough to have a life.

She came back from the Kmart half an hour later, clutching a shopping bag, but she wouldn't let Toño see what was inside. It was only later, when they were alone at a friend's apartment, that she opened it to show Toño her new doll.

Peace talks continued all spring. But now the Sandinistas were playing the same game as the contras, arguing about trivia, stalling, making outrageous demands. It didn't matter; the contras were so irreparably fractured that their delegation wouldn't have agreed to a stipulation that the sky was blue. Both sides abandoned everything that had been agreed to at Sapoá.

Because the negotiations were such a sham, the contra delegation was not even dismayed to learn that Alfredo César had been negotiating secretly with the Sandinistas for four months. At the final session of talks, on June 9, the American attorney Paul Reichler revealed to reporters that he had met with César half a dozen times since February, in Washington, Miami, and Managua. "He told me it was his ambition to come back [to Nicaragua] and run for president in 1990 and start his own party," Reichler said. César, Reichler claimed, promised that if the Sandinistas offered guarantees to make that possible, he could get Bermúdez to sign a peace treaty.

Reichler expected his revelation to cause an upheaval among the contras. But it didn't. For one thing, they already knew César had been up to something; during negotiations in late April, he was caught sneaking over the back wall of their hotel at 2 A.M. More fundamentally, it didn't matter what César was doing. The contras knew they weren't going to sign anything at all.

Purges rocked the contra ranks, including the political staff, for the rest of the year. Bermúdez believed that Calero had tried to use the dissidents as a lever to take over the entire movement. Calero denied it. "The only thing I thought was that these dissident commanders were among our best and brightest, and we couldn't just discard them," Calero told me. "They had to be listened to." Perhaps he was telling the truth. But there was no question that Calero, like the dissidents, was angry with the way Bermúdez acted after Sapoá.

In August, the contras elected a new directorate. Bermúdez, against the advice of nearly everyone—including the Americans—decided to run and won easily. But it was a useless victory. Sapoá and its aftermath left the relationships between the directors hopelessly poisoned. They rarely met; after a time, they rarely spoke. The directorate was dead. So were the prospects of new U.S. military aid. Congress resumed dispensing food and medicine—no one wanted to be accused of letting the contras starve to death as the 1988 American presidential election approached—but there was no money for weapons or ammo. As the contra troops inside Nicaragua ran low on bullets, they headed for the border, just as they had in 1984.

The contra retreat, so quick on the heels of their apparent political victory in Sapoá, crushed the spirit of many anti-Sandinista Nicaraguans. Throughout 1988 the numbers of Nicaraguan refugees entering the United States steadily rose. They slipped across the Rio Grande near Brownsville, Texas, then called relatives to wire money for bus tickets to Miami. On a single weekend in January 1989, two thousand refugees surged into Miami; the city had to open its baseball stadium to house them. Congressmen, city officials, and the State Department began trading accusations about who was to blame and pondering what to do about the hundreds of thousands of refugees who might follow.

Almost unnoticed in the hubbub was the fact that while the contra political apparatus had disintegrated, the contra *army* was intact. It sat in the Honduran base camps, waiting. The only people who seemed aware of it were the Sandinistas.

16 | "You Won, But Nobody Knows It"

It was a languid Saturday afternoon in Sweetwater, a careworn clump of apartment buildings and shopping plazas nestled precariously between Miami and the Everglades. A sleepy village founded by Russian circus midgets, Sweetwater during the 1980s became the exile capital of Nicaragua. Thousands of refugees settled there, dominating the town so completely that more than once the Sweetwater City Council voted to send all illegal guns confiscated by its police department to the contras.

On this March afternoon, three weeks after Daniel Ortega and the Sandinistas lost elections in Nicaragua, Sweetwater was just getting over its collective hangover. For three delirious nights in a row, people danced in the streets, jamming traffic for miles. Lounging across an armchair in the small, tidy apartment he shared with two other ex-contras, Toño laughed just thinking about it. "The best part about it, to me, was listening to all the American politicians and reporters talking about what a surprise it was," he said. "Why should it have been surprising? Why did they think we were fighting the war?"

The shrill ring of the telephone interrupted him. One of his men was calling collect from a pay phone in Danlí, Honduras. Nearly two years had passed since Toño and the other dissidents were arrested and deported, and still these calls came, three or four times a week. To many of his men, Toño was still the commander.

This call, like most of the recent ones, was from a contra soldier befuddled by political developments. Violeta Chamorro, the new president, wouldn't be inaugurated for another month. But the gringos and the UN people were coming around the camps, telling the contras to disarm immediately. Was that a good idea, the soldier wondered? How could anyone be sure that the Sandinistas would really let Doña Violeta take office? If the contras refused to put down their guns, would the Americans try to take them? Maybe they should slip back into Nicaragua, where the gringos couldn't find them, and wait to see what happened.

242

"Look, the important thing is to remain calm and don't do anything crazy," Toño advised. "There will be a lot of cheap talk, but the Americans aren't going to get their hands dirty trying to take your guns. It's just that everyone is confused right now. They didn't expect things to turn out like this."

He paused, shaking his head sympathetically. "The thing is," Toño counseled, "you won the war. But nobody knows it."

For the contras, 1988 and 1989 were a long twilight. Troops inside Nicaragua, conserving their limited ammunition, tried to avoid combat. The Sandinistas, unwilling to risk provoking the resumption of U.S. military aid, did not attempt frontal assaults. The contras called the resulting delicate, almost ritualistic, series of probes and retreats *una guerra silenciosa*—a silent war. Sandinista patrols methodically penetrated close enough to contra positions to ignite firefights; the contras quickly disengaged and withdrew a little bit closer to the Honduran border.

Few men died, but inch by inch, the contras lost everything they gained during 1987. By the end of 1988, no more than two thousand contra troops remained inside Nicaragua. Worse yet, after the Sandinistas murdered some of their campesino supporters, the contras began evacuating entire villages as they pulled out. If the war ever revived, their support network would no longer exist.

As the contras flowed out of Nicaragua, speculation in U.S. embassies throughout Central America focused on the "Beirut scenario": the fear that the contra army would disintegrate and southern Honduras would become a tropical version of the ruined Lebanese capital, ruled by bands of armed outlaws. The scenario never unfolded. Though the population of the camps around Yamales reached thirty-five thousand, they stayed orderly. Commanders kept up military discipline with endless drills, giving new recruits sticks to carry instead of guns.

The gringos kept a surprised eye on developments. After military aid was cut off, the already-waning influence of the CIA declined even further. The Agency's Central American Task Force was reduced to a mere shell; Alan Fiers, the last of the fire-breathing, can-do CIA men, went on to another assignment after a tearful farewell to contra leaders in Miami. By mid-1988, the small group of aides in Elliott Abrams's sixth-floor offices at the State Department was in almost total control of U.S. contra policy.

With the 1988 election approaching, neither Congress nor the Reagan administration had any stomach for fighting about a military aid bill. The Abrams group saw its job as preserving the contras for the next president. The Republican candidate, Vice President George Bush, had always been a strong contra supporter and would presumably want to reactivate them. The Democrat, Massachusetts governor Michael Dukakis, was wildly anticontra; if he won, the Abrams group reasoned, let him suffer the headache of disarming fifteen thousand guerrillas and forcing them to return, defenseless, to a communist country.

The contras understood the equation. On the night of November 8, as early election returns pointed to Bush's victory, the sharp stutter of AK-47s echoed

243

around Yamales. The contras were firing their guns in jubilation. With Ronald Reagan, Jr. (as many commanders called Bush) in the White House, they would be going back to war.

As the new administration took shape, however, plenty of warning signals sounded that Nicaragua was going onto the back burner. The first was when Bush named his campaign manager, James Baker, secretary of state. During the campaign, Baker had steered Bush away from saying anything at all about Central America or the contras. First and foremost a politician, Baker had no use for complicated issues that carried little weight with voters but consumed an inordinate amount of time, resources, and political capital—a perfect description of Nicaragua.

The second was the failure to appoint a new assistant secretary for Latin American affairs promptly. Although Bush had hundreds of appointments ready to go when he took over on January 22, 1989, there was still no nominee for the job of overseeing U.S. policy in Central America, a clear sign that the region would not be near the center of the Bush administration's world view, as it always had been for Reagan.

The administration's failure to name a point man had already spooked the presidents of the four Central American democracies. They expected an unofficial message from the incoming Bush team about the direction of U.S. policy before a scheduled January 15 summit meeting with Daniel Ortega. When none came, they rescheduled the summit for February 13. As the new date approached with no one in place at State, several of the presidents quietly asked if the Americans wanted another postponement. No, go ahead, the gringos said, expecting it to be just one more unproductive grumbling session. But Ortega, who so often had launched surprise military offensives at unlikely moments, was preparing a political sneak attack.

Bush's election stunned the Sandinistas. Perhaps because their view of U.S. politics was gleaned largely from visiting congressional liberals, they were certain that Dukakis would win and cut the contras off cold turkey. When Bush won, the Sandinistas—like the contras—assumed he would continue Reagan's policies. The Sandinistas, desperate to avoid another military confrontation, frantically searched for a way to eliminate the contras before Bush had a chance to squeeze more aid from Congress.

In February 1989, when nearly every leader in Latin America gathered in Caracas for the inauguration of Venezuelan president Carlos Andrés Pérez, Ortega sent up a trial balloon to the Central American presidents. "We could move up elections in Nicaragua to allow all those who so wish to participate," Ortega offered. "However, I am asking your support to remove the contras from Honduras, to disband the contras in Honduras." Big deal, the other presidents scoffed, Somoza held elections too. So Ortega sweetened the pot: To make sure the elections were honest, he would invite international observers from the UN and the OAS. Now the presidents were interested, and Ortega believed he could get a formal agreement at the Central American summit.[1]

The meeting took place in El Salvador, at the Tesoro Beach resort on the Pacific, twenty-five miles southeast of San Salvador. The State Department sent only a single, low-level observer; the field was left to liberal congressmen like Connecticut's Senator Christopher Dodd, who relentlessly spread the message that Congress would never pass another military aid bill for the contras. In less than two days, Ortega had his agreement.

He promised to amend the Nicaraguan constitution so that elections scheduled for November 1990 could be held nine months earlier. International observers would be invited to monitor the voting. Restrictions that made it nearly impossible for opposition parties to organize or campaign would be eased. And, as he had done regularly since signing the Arias peace plan in August 1987, Ortega promised to release all political prisoners.

In exchange, Ortega got what he wanted: a commission appointed by the five presidents would produce, within ninety days, a plan to disarm the contras and return them to Nicaragua or ship them outside Central America.

The announcement stupefied the contra directors, who had come to Tesoro Beach in a futile attempt to lobby. The presidents had, in the past, called for a halt to U.S. military aid. But they had never before suggested forced disarmament. And in return for what? Promises from Ortega? How could anyone demobilize an army based on a promise from a communist?

The contra delegation huddled inside a hotel room to put together a public response. It would be the directorate's last meeting; the four most powerful directors—Adolfo Calero, Arístides Sánchez, Alfredo César, and Enrique Bermúdez—could no longer stand one another. Literally nothing was too childish or insignificant for them to blow up into a full-scale vendetta. "I'm sick of that fucking Calero," Sánchez confided to Bermúdez one day. "Whenever we come out of a meeting, the reporters always go to him first because he's so tall. If we go to the camps in a helicopter, he always gets to sit in front because his legs are so long."

The contras didn't believe for a minute that the Sandinistas would permit free elections; the FSLN would lose in a landslide. But perhaps the contras could play along with Ortega's phony promise, at least temporarily. The Central American presidents weren't going to come up with a disarmament plan for ninety days; meanwhile, Nicaragua's opposition parties would demand guarantees from Ortega and complain loudly when they didn't get them. If the parties refused to participate in a stacked election, as they had in 1984, the agreement of the presidents would self-destruct.

The directors issued a statement calling the Tesoro Beach agreement "a triumph both for the Resistance and for the internal opposition." If there were free elections in Nicaragua, the statement added, the contras would be happy to put down their arms and go home. Calero, though, couldn't help voicing his skepticism to reporters. "Any agreement that is based on a promise by Ortega," he observed, "is like leashing a dog with a string of sausages."

The Tesoro Beach agreement prodded the Bush administration into shaping its Latin American policy. On March 1, a new assistant secretary of state for Latin American affairs was nominated: Bernard Aronson, a former Jimmy Carter speechwriter and onetime organizer for the United Mine Workers who nonetheless supported the contras. Aronson not only broke ranks with the Democratic party on the issue, he even wrote one of Ronald Reagan's more successful televised speeches pleading for more aid.

The contras, nonetheless, mistrusted him. Aronson was a tenacious supporter of Arturo Cruz, Sr., and other ex-Sandinista politicians, and he lobbied constantly to purge all former National Guardsmen from the contra ranks. In a 1985 essay in *New Republic*, Aronson flatly declared that the Guardsmen should be replaced by former Sandinistas:[2]

Bermúdez and his top commanders were chilled by the news of Aronson's nomination. Three weeks later, the chill turned icy. In a televised appearance at the White House, Bush announced an agreement with the Democratic congressional leaders. Congress would appropriate $4.5 million a month for food, clothing, shelter, and medical supplies for the contras until the Nicaraguan presidential election in February 1990. In return, Bush would freeze aid to any contra unit that staged an attack.

The Bush administration was putting its chips on the election promised by Daniel Ortega. The contras were reduced to a hedge—a threat that could be unveiled later if the Sandinistas reneged or stole the election.

The contra political directors learned of the agreement from one of Aronson's staffers, who briefed them in a Miami hotel room as Bush was announcing it on television. What they weren't told was that the State Department had decided to get rid of most of them, including Bermúdez.

Connoisseurs of fine ironies could appreciate it: the State Department, after years of taking sides in every contra argument, found itself sucked into a political black hole of its own making. In January 1989, in the dying hours of the Reagan administration, I visited the suite of offices where Elliott Abrams and his men were holed up to see if any last-second conspiracies were afoot. One of Abrams's henchmen was bellowing incoherently into a phone. After he finally slammed it down, he explained that he was settling a dispute between Calero, César, Bermúdez, and Sánchez.

"You know what I'm doing today?" he asked. "I'm trying to find tickets to an inaugural ball for Sánchez, César, and Bermúdez. You know why? Because that fucking Calero got tickets from Jack Kemp [a conservative Republican congressman], and then he ran down to Miami and started prancing around, waving them under everyone's nose: 'I got tickets because I'm the one that really counts.' Now I have to find three more sets, or it will be a major political incident . . . over a goddamn fucking ticket to an inaugural ball." Truly, it was the principle of "Everybody has his own gringo" refined to its purest essence.

Throughout 1988, as the political superstructure the State Department had imposed atop the contra army turned cannibal and devoured itself, the Abrams group grew progressively angrier and more frustrated. The bureaucracy that State had created to win political support from Congress was doing the very opposite. Its constant public feuds delighted contra opponents in both Washington and Managua. The contra political arm, stitched together in a Washington laboratory, had turned into an uncontrollable public relations Frankenstein.

The contra leadership needed radical surgery, the Abrams aides believed. The lesson they drew from the collapse of the directorate was not that the State

Department had interfered too much in contra politics, but too little. They often lamented that if only State had been in control from the beginning, instead of those Langley lunkheads, the contras would be in Managua by now. Nothing could convince them otherwise, not even the total failure of State's experiment at managing the Indian army on the Atlantic coast in 1987.

When Aronson arrived at State, he retained most of the Abrams aides. He liked their approach and was delighted to learn that they shared his suspicions about the ex-Guardsmen. Neither Aronson nor his aides had much contact with the military side of the contras. They knew nothing of the role the Guardsmen played in organizing logistics or planning operations. (Nor did they understand that a campesino commander might be popular and a spectacular recruiter, yet militarily erratic and a disaster on human rights.) As far as they were concerned, the Guardsmen were just another bit of leftover evidence of the CIA's ham-handed approach to the contras—goons put in place because they could salute and click their heels when one of the Agency's knuckledraggers barked an order.

If the contras had a future, Aronson and his aides believed, it lay neither with the politicians nor the military command structure dominated by ex-Guardsmen. Regardless of whether the contras were going back to war or demobilizing, the State Department wanted them led by young campesino commanders. Aronson's office scurried to unload everyone else.

The contra politicians were the easiest to drive away. Most of them realized they had no role left; because Bush would not be asking for military aid, there was no congressional lobbying, and because field commanders were no longer permitted to launch attacks, there was no use in seeking military aid from other governments.

Pushing aside Bermúdez (and, by extension, the other ex-Guardsmen) was more difficult. But Aronson's office began a steady campaign of destabilization. Several associates of Arturo Cruz, Sr., were hired as "consultants" on human rights or politics. Bermúdez no longer has the support of the Americans, they told commanders during meetings in Honduran base camps. In fact, the gringos think he's an obstacle, a Somocista relic. Don't be afraid to challenge him.

At the same time, Aronson's office—without consulting Bermúdez or anyone else in the military chain of command—began bringing campesino commanders to Washington for friendly chats that were anything but subtle. When Commander Emiliano accepted an invitation to visit the State Department, an Aronson aide made polite conversation for a few minutes and then asked bluntly: "When are you guys going to get rid of Bermúdez?"

Bermúdez watched these maneuvers in amazement. Just a year after dissident commanders nearly touched off one armed mutiny, the State Department was courting another. Aronson and his aides, Bermúdez thought, had no idea how tenuous the structure of a guerrilla army really was, how fragile the chain of command. When Bermúdez challenged him, Aronson said as much. "I no longer recognize you as the interlocutor for the Resistance," Aronson replied. "We will deal with many different voices." He obviously didn't see that an army that spoke with many different voices might also move in many different directions.

247

To Bermúdez, Aronson's talk about "a new generation of commanders" was a flimsy mask for his real agenda: putting the contra army in hands that were more easily manipulated. A young campesino like Franklyn, who had only been to Managua once or twice in his life—how could he put on a new suit and tie, fly to Washington, be escorted to an elegant office atop the State Department, and then say no? Bermúdez had been dealing with the gringos for eight years; he didn't win every argument, by any means, but he knew how to dig his heels in. If Bermúdez were gone, it would much easier for State to get its way, especially in the worst-case scenario: if the Sandinistas stole the presidential elections with fraud, but not blatantly enough to anger the U.S. Congress. Then State would have the difficult task of forcing the contras to accept the election and disarm.

Bermúdez had fought off countless attempts to oust him. This time, however, he had one hand tied behind his back. Joining the directorate in 1988 had forced him to spend more time in Miami and Washington and less in the camps with the troops. He counted on a handful of his most loyal commanders to act as his eyes and ears and to represent him to the men.

In early 1989, however, the system was breaking down. One of his trusted commanders—Aureliano, the former doctor who set up an internal front in Managua early in the war—was murdered under mysterious circumstances.[3] And two others, Mike Lima and Mack, were under assault by the State Department's human-rights hit team.

From the moment it was born, Bermúdez distrusted the Nicaraguan Association for Human Rights (known by its Spanish abbreviation, ANPDH). A last-minute invention of the State Department just before the congressional vote on the $100 million aid package in 1986, it was created without any consultation with the contras themselves. Hoping to sway a few wavering congressmen, State stipulated that $3 million of the money would go to set up an independent human-rights monitoring organization.

Bermúdez was immediately skeptical. What military organization provided outside investigators free access to its bases and commanders? Certainly not the Sandinistas. The director of ANPDH was Marta Patricia Baltodano, and that made Bermúdez uneasy as well. During the early 1980s, Baltodano's independent human-rights group in Nicaragua was so critical of the revolutionary goverment that the Sandinistas shut it down. But Bermúdez remembered her group from the late 1970s, when it constantly pilloried the National Guard. A lot of the criticism, Bermúdez thought, had been unfair and unbalanced and weakened the Guard's ability to fight the Sandinista insurgency.

Bermúdez and Baltodano clashed almost immediately when ANPDH staffers moved into the base camps. Baltodano—twenty-eight years old when she took the job in 1986—was a slim, soft-spoken attorney whose mild appearance often led her adversaries to underestimate her intelligence and tenacity. Accustomed to monitoring governments, for which there are well-defined standards of behavior when it comes to civil liberties and due process of law, Baltodano believed the same yardstick could be applied to a guerrilla movement. Any time evidence of misbehavior surfaced, charges should be brought before a tribunal of commanders, convictions obtained, and stern punishments imposed, all without fear or favor, exceptions or extenuations. I once asked her if a contra patrol, deep behind Sandinista lines, had the right to execute a spy discovered in its midst. "Of course not," she replied, eyeing me as though foam dripped from my mouth. "He should be arrested and then brought back to Honduras for trial."

Bermúdez, on the other hand, believed that allowances had to be made, not only for extraordinary circumstances in which a guerrilla commander might find himself, but for the delicate political ties that bound the contras together. Perfect justice was of course the goal, but it might be tempered by any number of things. Would a verdict touch off a family feud that might lead to more violence? Would it upset the tenuous truce between campesinos and National Guardsmen? If charges were filed against a commander, would his troops accept a guilty verdict? Or would they mutiny?

Bermúdez and Baltodano continued their prickly coexistence on a more or less even footing until the final months of 1988. But as the State Department's influence increased, so did Baltodano's. And late in the year, two human-rights scandals erupted that led to a direct confrontation.

The first arose when reports filtered out of the camps that a teenaged contra soldier who called himself Managua 2 had been tortured to death and buried in an unmarked grave in the Yamales campsite of the Quilalí Regional Command. When contra military police began inquiring, they learned that Managua 2 hadn't been seen since he was called in for questioning by the counterintelligence office headed by Mike Lima.

Baltodano's investigators tried hard to build a case against Lima. It wasn't easy. The counterintelligence office was in Tegucigalpa, six hours from Yamales, and Lima only occasionally visited the camp. Moreover, witnesses who saw Managua 2 taken away said he was in the custody of a contra named Israelita. Israelita worked not for Lima but his rival, Commander Mack, head of the intelligence office.

Then a new set of charges surfaced. In December 1988, the contras released 104 prisoners to the International Red Cross. When ANPDH staffers interviewed them, a number of the prisoners held as suspected Sandinista infiltrators claimed to have been tortured during their interrogation. Young female soldiers fell under suspicion of espionage with dubious frequency; they were put in a separate jail where they were raped regularly.

Most of the accusations of torture and rape were lodged against six contra interrogators—including Israelita, the intelligence officer who arrested Managua 2. But three of the men claimed to have been tortured by Mike Lima.

The accusations against Lima contained various discrepancies, and, unlike the charges against the interrogators, could not be corroborated by other witnesses. Two prisoners could not be questioned further because they had already returned to Nicaragua. Ordinarily, such a weak case wouldn't have been pursued.

But Lima's name had already come to the ANPDH's attention during the investigation of Managua 2's death. And although the ANPDH staffers had found little to link Lima to the killing, they detested him. They knew he regarded the ANPDH's work as irrelevant, even destructive. He didn't believe

249

moral standards could be applied to war. His only ethical obligation, Lima believed, was to his men—to keep as many of them alive as long as possible. Anything that furthered that end was permissible; anything that detracted from it was unacceptable. Lima was the antithesis of Baltodano and her belief that law is the underpinning of civilization, even in war. The ANPDH forwarded the evidence it had accumulated to the military prosecutor's office and asked that charges be filed against Lima for mistreatment of prisoners.

Meanwhile, the investigation of Managua 2's death moved ahead. Witnesses came forward to confirm that he died while being tortured by Israelita. And evidence arose that Israelita's boss Mack had helped cover up the killing.

Mack's real name was José Benito Bravo. A former sergeant in the National Guard, he joined the contras at the very beginning. He was often quoted in newspaper stories—he was always available to reporters—and a casual reader in the United States might think that Commander Mack was not only the bravest contra officer but possibly the most erudite as well.

The truth was that Mack was hardly a commander at all. When he participated in the December 1987 attack on Las Minas, it was his first trip inside Nicaragua in more than three years. And his rare ventures into combat were almost always disastrous. In October 1983 Mack bolted from a Sandinista sneak attack on his Honduran base camp, abandoning his briefcase. Inside, the Sandinistas found snapshots of all the principal contra commanders posing alongside their (secret) Argentine advisers and a (even more secret) CIA officer; a phone book with a complete list of contra contacts in Honduras; and a treasure trove of documents and receipts.

From 1983 to 1987, Mack was in charge of contra training. But he had actually spent most of his time setting up his own little rackets in the border camps. Whores, card games, liquor—you name it, Mack ran it. Dissatisfied customers could take their complaints to his goon squad. By 1988, business was so good that Mack could hire managers to stay in the camps while he spent most of his time in Tegucigalpa gambling at the Hotel Honduras Maya or romping with his three girlfriends.

Mack finagled control of the intelligence section because he wanted the $2,500-a-month budget the CIA provided. (U.S. law still permitted the Agency to support contra intelligence-gathering.) He also planned to wrest the counter-intelligence office from Mike Lima so he could siphon away its budget, too. That was the real story behind the death of Managua 2; Mack ordered his thug Israelita to find some Sandinista spies and drag confessions out of them. Catching Sandinista infiltrators was the job of Mike Lima's counterintelligence office, not Mack's intelligence section. But Mack wanted to show he could do a better job than Lima.

Bermúdez didn't know every seamy detail of Mack's activities, but he knew enough that he should have taken some action. Mack represented Bermudez's greatest single flaw as a commander—the excessive value he put on loyalty. A commander who was loyal to Bermúdez could expect Bermúdez to be loyal to him, even when it was obvious that something was wrong. Too many times throughout the war he turned a blind eye to officers who were killers, like Chino

Lau, or thieves, like Juan Gómez, the head of the contra air force who somehow always had spare parts to sell even when contra aircraft were grounded for lack of them.[4]

Now Bermúdez would have to pay the price. The ANPDH and the State Department were pressing for the conviction of a commander. Word leaked out on Capitol Hill, and in early March several pro-contra congressmen summoned Bermúdez to a meeting. This could be the end, they warned him, if you don't move fast. Bermúdez did. Within ten days, a contra tribunal returned six convictions in Managua 2's murder: Israelita and three other men who tortured him; the Quilalí commander, for dereliction of duty; and Mack, for covering up the death. The Honduran government had recently outlawed contra jails, so the only possible penalty was expulsion from the movement.

At the same time, the State Department and the ANPDH were pushing the case against Mike Lima forward. The military prosecutor's office twice declined to file charges for lack of evidence. Both times Baltodano and the State Department launched a barrage of bitter protests. When a tribunal was convened and acquitted Lima, Baltodano and her State Department allies complained of procedural errors. Lima was left in legal limbo.

By July 1989, Lima had been under constant investigation for nine months. The gringos had cut off his family-assistance payments months earlier, so his wife, Aracely, was supporting their two toddlers on nothing but her minimum-wage sewing job in Miami. Lima wasn't sure how to satisfy these people, who talked all the time about the law but didn't mind bending it in order to get him. He went to see an old friend, one of the few CIA officers remaining at Yamales.

"When is this going to end?" Lima asked.

"It's never going to end," the CIA man answered softly. "Don't you see, Mike? It's not you they're after, it's Bermúdez."

Lima nodded. He had sensed it for a long time, of course, but he hadn't wanted to admit it. This war had taken seven years of his life, taken his arm, taken so many of his friends. He had always hoped to end it by walking into Managua with a rifle in his hand.

Lima dug up the travel document the gringos had provided him to fly back and forth to Miami for medical care. He told everyone he was going to see his American doctor to have his prosthesis adjusted. Two weeks after he arrived, he landed a job as a security guard.

As 1989 wore on, the contras' Tesoro Beach gamble looked like it might be a winner. The contras endorsed the agreement of the five Central American presidents—internationally supervised Nicaraguan elections in exchange for contra disarmament—in the expectation that the opposition parties inside Nicaragua would denounce election plans as a sham and cause the deal to collapse. That was exactly what happened. As Ortega ignored the opposition's complaints, the other four presidents lost enthusiasm; their mid-May deadline for devising a contra disarmament plan passed with no announcement. If the presidents failed to set concrete plans and timetables for demobilization at their

251

next summit, in Tela, Honduras, on August 6 and 7, the whole disarmament scheme might die.

Ortega was determined not to let that happen. The Bush administration was putting a new economic squeeze on him. In May, Ortega toured Western Europe, hoping to bring back $250 million in aid; thanks to strong U.S. lobbying, he came home with only $20 million.[5] The Americans were also pushing the Soviet Union hard, making it clear that if Mikhail Gorbachev wanted U.S. support for his economic "new thinking" at home, he would have to rein in the Sandinistas. And, for the first time, the Soviets were responding. They cut off direct weapons shipments to Nicaragua and told Fidel Castro to do the same.[6]

Once again, Ortega resorted to desperate measures. On August 2, four days before the presidential summit, he met in Managua with representatives of twenty opposition parties. The talks continued, uninterrupted, for twenty-five hours. Ortega pledged to suspend the military draft for five months, stop arrests of political activists, grant equal television time to opposition parties, end the ban on opinion polls, and amend the constitution yet again to cut the transition time between elections and the inauguration of the new president from ten months to two. The opposition parties, in return, signed a statement calling for disarmament of the contras.

That was enough to get the Central American presidents back on board. They agreed to ask the UN and the OAS to begin disarming the contras on September 7 and finish by December 7. Like all the other presidential accords, the agreement was made without consulting the contras themselves. Despite two years' worth of evidence to the contrary, the presidents simply assumed that the contras would do as they were told.

The Sandinistas made no attempt to conceal their glee. "The contras' death sentence has been signed," declared Daniel Ortega. His brother Humberto added: "It won't be sudden, like an earthquake. They'll just dry up."

The Tela agreement did send a ripple of panic through the contra commanders. Some wanted to reinfiltrate Nicaragua immediately and survive through banditry. Others, however, counseled staying cool. Who, after all, was going to make them disarm? A couple dozen UN *maricones* in blue berets? The Honduran army, which opposed disarmament, wouldn't lift a finger to help. The best course of action was to just squat in the camps, as they had for eighteen months now, and wait. They had defied a Soviet-backed army for seven years; they could certainly handle a few politicians and social workers.

It worked. The UN didn't even venture into the camps until mid-October, when Francesc Vendrell, the head of the disarmament commission, addressed a large group of contras in Yamales. "Don't let yourselves become the subject of a policy that perhaps has already become an anachronism," he urged them. "Don't stay here to be abandoned by a country that once helped you." The contras just stood there, impassive, unyielding; they would not be moved.

Ortega's decision to permit elections caused some grumbling among Sandinista militants who considered voting a bourgeois distraction from the revolution. Even with the concessions he made to the opposition parties, however, there was little reason to think an election was a serious threat to the FSLN. The Somozas, after all, staged regular elections for forty years without a close call. The key was the opposition's corruption. Every opposition politician wanted to be the star, the *caudillo*. So instead of working together, they splintered into dozens of microparties, each with its own candidate. On the rare occasions that unity threatened to break out, a few leaders could easily be bribed with the promise of a token role in the government.

The FSLN anticipated as many as twenty opposition candidates on the ballot, competing for resources and carving up the anti-Sandinista vote. Whichever candidate finished with the highest number of votes, regardless of whether he had a majority, would be president, meaning that Ortega could probably win with as little as 30 percent.

Shortly after the Tela agreement, however, the Japanese ambassador to Nicaragua invited the heads of all the opposition parties to a private meeting at his embassy. Expecting a cocktail party, they were instead treated to a stern lecture. I'm warning you, the ambassador admonished the politicians. The international community, including my government, is going to resume aid to Nicaragua after this election, regardless of who wins. So don't imagine that, if you screw around and miss your chance to unseat the Sandinistas, the Western world will bail you out by strangling them economically.

Coming from such an unexpected source, the ultimatum had muzzle-velocity impact. By late August, fourteen parties had agreed on ground rules for fashioning a common platform and slate of candidates. The group—which called itself the National Opposition Union, or UNO, Spanish for "one" —was certainly among the most bizarre political coalitions in Latin American history. It ran the ideological gamut from the Communist Party of Nicaragua to the openly authoritarian Liberal Constitutionalist Party. About the only belief the parties held in common was that anything would be better than the Sandinistas.

There were three contenders for the UNO presidential nomination: Virgilio Godoy of the Independent Liberal Party, who collaborated with the Sandinistas as labor minister for four years; Violeta Chamorro, the publisher of *La Prensa,* who served on the first revolutionary junta; and Enrique Bolaños, the fiercely conservative businessman who warned Violeta within weeks of the revolution that the junta was letting the Sandinistas accrue too much power. Godoy was an experienced politician, but still had many enemies from his days in the government. Bolaños was the country's most articulate and ferocious critic of the FSLN, but his unyielding conservatism appalled the coalition's leftist parties. Doña Violeta, as Chamorro was respectfully known, had little grasp of either politics or ideology, but polls showed her as the most popular of all opposition figures.

The UNO parties convened on September 1 to pick their candidate. For hours they argued, haggled, bargained. But they couldn't break a three-way deadlock. As the meeting moved into its second day, Godoy prepared to throw his support to Bolaños. Before he could, Costa Rican president Oscar Arias called to warn that if UNO wanted financial support from parties in Venezuela and Costa Rica, not to mention the gringos, it had better nominate Doña Violeta. Meanwhile, State Department representatives were on the phone with a similar message to some of the parties backing Bolaños. By the evening of September 2, Doña Violeta was the nominee.

The calls were engineered by Alfredo César, the former contra politician. He had returned to Nicaragua four months earlier to promote Doña Violeta's candidacy. Just as he had with the contras, César used his connections with Arias, the State Department, and liberal U.S. congressmen to compensate for his lack of political clout among Nicaraguans. And once Doña Violeta had the nomination, César quickly sealed her off from the UNO coalition.

Despite his reputation as a yuppie technocrat, César erected his palace guard around the candidate using the oldest Nicaraguan political currency: blood-lines. Doña Violeta's closest adviser was her daughter, Cristiana. Her campaign director was businessman Antonio Lacayo, Cristiana's husband and César's brother-in-law. The campaign office manager was Silvia César, César's wife and Lacayo's sister. Together they spun a cocoon so tight around Doña Violeta that even her running mate Godoy rarely saw her.

By conventional political yardsticks, the Sandinistas had a lopsided advan-tage. Despite the promises from Arias, little outside help reached UNO. With much hoopla, the U.S. Congress appropriated $9 million for the campaign. But only about $3.3 million was intended for UNO. The rest was for international observers, poll-watchers, administrative costs, and $1.8 million in taxes levied by the Sandinista government. While the government got its share of the money immediately, it snared the UNO contribution in so much red tape that, three weeks before the election, Doña Violeta's campaign had received only $278,000.[7]

Meanwhile, the Sandinistas spent wildly—$7 million by their own account, several times that if the state resources poured into the campaign were counted. There were Daniel Ortega T-shirts, posters, cigarette lighters, briefcases, handkerchiefs, scarves, baseball caps, even condoms. Mariachi bands and pop singers from across Latin America were flown in for campaign appearances where Ortega was marketed as El Gallo, the rooster. Gone were the olive fatigues and thick glasses; Ortega's new uniform was Italian leather jackets, designer blue jeans, and contact lenses.

Although the Sandinistas made strategic use of dirty tricks and bullyboy threats (more than 150 UNO candidates dropped out of the election), they seldom resorted to violence as they had during the 1984 presidential election. The reason, undoubtedly, was the international observers who cascaded into the country as the voting approached. They began arriving in October; by election day, there were 435 staffers from the Organization of American States, 239 from the UN, 39 from a group put together by Jimmy Carter, and at least a dozen smaller delegations from foreign political parties and move-ments. Together they were able to monitor about 70 percent of the 4,394 polling places.

As the sun rose on February 25, long lines had already formed at hundreds of polling stations. More than 80 percent of the 1.7 million eligible voters cast ballots before the polls closed at 6 P.M. Three hours later both parties had enough totals from their own poll-watchers to sense the outcome. The nine

FSLN *comandantes* entered a closed-door meeting and didn't emerge until 11 P.M. About half an hour later, Ortega got the official word from the international observers: Violeta Chamorro had won the election with 55 percent of the vote to Ortega's 41 percent.

The UNO victory was as broad as it was deep. In Chontales and Boaco departments, UNO won every single mayoral race; Doña Violeta even carried a Sandinista military base in Jinotega and a housing complex in Managua reserved for high-ranking army officials. If absentee voting had been permitted, the gigantic Nicaraguan exile communities in Costa Rica, Honduras, and the United States would have lifted Doña Violeta's victory margin from 14 percentage points to 25.

A haggard Ortega emerged around sunrise to face television cameras. His meandering, halting speech never mentioned Violeta Chamorro by name. But in the end, he answered the question everyone wanted to ask. "The president and government of Nicaragua," Ortega rasped, "are going to respect and abide by the people's mandate as shown in the voting in these elections." A few minutes later, perhaps inadvertently, he mentioned what the defeat of the Sandinistas would mean for Nicaragua.

"Now a new road is being opened," Ortega said. "War will end. The contras will disappear."

However much the Sandinistas were tempted to annul the election, it was obviously impossible. They would never have gotten another penny from Western Europe or Japan, their allies in Eastern Europe were toppling right and left, and the Soviet Union would not risk its amicable new relationship with the United States on a Nicaraguan adventure. The FSLN's last remaining friend, Fidel Castro, was beset with his own problems stemming from the tumbling communist dominoes. Moreover, just three months before, George Bush had invaded Panama to rid himself of Manuel Noriega. The Sandinistas could not be certain he wouldn't do the same in Nicaragua.

Instead, the Sandinistas set out to make sure that they retained all the power, if not the government itself. In a speech two days after the election, Ortega was forthright about their strategy. "We will continue to rule from below," he announced. As he spoke, crates of AK-47s were being trucked into the countryside to be parceled out like deadly CARE packages. The Sandinista army gave away an estimated twenty thousand weapons in the month after the election, handing them out with such abandon that many wound up in the hands of contras.

While the army emptied its arsenals, FSLN civilian officials looted every nook and cranny of the government in an avaricious binge later known as "the big piñata." Opulent homes confiscated by the government after the revolution were sold to individual Sandinistas for prices as low as $1,000. So were dozens of radio stations and movie theaters. The Sandinistas also sold themselves half an hour of time on the government television station, every night for the next five years. The regular price would have been $9,000 a night; they charged themselves $25. Meanwhile, they granted huge raises to government workers

255

and encouraged squatters to move onto thousands of acres of government land, much of it confiscated from exiled businessmen who would be returning when Doña Violeta took office.

Other ripoffs were less publicized but far more insidious. Using a network of four hundred dummy corporations scattered across the world, coupled with the government's import-export monopoly, the Sandinistas sold themselves most of Nicaragua's next cotton crop, deliberately timing the transaction for the low ebb of the futures market. Not only did the transaction mean a potential profit of tens of millions of dollars for FSLN members, it removed the new government's only source of quick foreign exchange.

Nothing the Sandinistas did, however, prepared Nicaraguans for the shock they received on April 25 during Doña Violeta's inaugural address. She talked about reconciliation, putting down the guns to rebuild Nicaragua. She proclaimed a general amnesty for political crimes. She suspended the draft. And then she dropped her bombshell. "While the demobilization of the resistance forces that has been agreed to is completed, as well as the demobilization of youth in the military services and recovery of weapons in the hands of civilians," Doña Violeta announced, "I have instructed Army Gen. Humberto Ortega to remain at his post." She had to pause then; the ecstatic shouts of the Sandinistas in the audience and the angry screams of their enemies drowned out her words.

Negotiations between the Sandinistas and Doña Violeta's coterie had begun even before the election, in mid-January. "They're talking about the rules of the game," a Nicaraguan with intimate knowledge of the discussions told me at the time. "You know—what happens if I win, what happens if you win. Antonio [Lacayo] and Alfredo [César] don't want a situation where Violeta starts to abolish the army and the Sandinistas have to stage a coup. They know you can't corner a cat and not leave a door open, unless you are willing to kill that cat. And maybe it scratches your eyes out in the process."[8]

Lacayo and César did considerably more than leave a door open; they gave away the store. All they won were a few cosmetic concessions: Ortega would lose his title as defense minister (but keep his rank as general), and he had to officially resign from the FSLN. When the plan was presented to Doña Violeta's cabinet ministers and senior aides two days before her inauguration, they revolted. For seven hours they railed at Antonio Lacayo for suggesting the deal. Doña Violeta sat quietly, saying little, until one of her cabinet appointees asked point-blank what she thought.

"The same as you think, Antonio," she answered in a timid, little-girl voice.

The group voted against Ortega's appointment by forty-three to two and left the meeting thinking it was dead. But Lacayo and César leaked word to the Sandinistas that Doña Violeta was wavering. The Ortega brothers came to her home. We won't be able to control the army if you go ahead with this, Humberto Ortega warned her.

It was a crucial moment. Doña Violeta's answer would determine if she would rule Nicaragua or if the country would be just one more banana republic where a figurehead civilian government sits in the palace while the army wields the real power. And the timing of this confrontation did not favor the Sandinistas. They had the guns. But would they really dare to defy Doña Violeta at a moment when dignitaries from eighty-three countries and nine international organizations were in Managua for her inauguration? A Sandinista regime that seized power through a coup after an election cheered by the whole world would be an international pariah.

Doña Violeta backed down. In the wink of an eye, she gave away a victory that had cost Nicaragua a decade of war and twenty thousand lives.

The announcement that Ortega would stay at the head of the army cast a pall over the transition. Two of the new cabinet ministers quit. In Miami, thousands of exiles postponed plans to return home. And many Sandinista officials, as they turned over their office keys to their replacements, wore mocking smiles.

Héctor Briceño, the new chief of the government television station, was moving into his offices when the outgoing director, Iván García, knocked on the door. "Excuse me," he said, "but I think I forgot something." He went to the desk, opened the bottom drawer, and pulled out a Makarov pistol. Then he walked back out, politely waving goodbye. Or, perhaps, see you later.[9]

No one greeted the news that Ortega was staying more angrily than the contras. Reporters who visited a campsite in Estelí Department the next day found Commander Rubén addressing his men. "There can't be reconciliation with Humberto Ortega," Rubén shouted as his troops murmured their approval. "The same people who have assassinated and imprisoned people continue with a part of the power. And it's the most important part, because they have the weapons."

Rubén, Franklyn, and a handful of other commanders were in charge of the contras now. Two weeks before the election, they issued a communiqué relieving Bermúdez of command. Arístides Sánchez, the last remaining civilian official in the movement, had informed the commanders the gringos wanted it done before the election. It seemed plausible to the commanders; the State Department had, after all, been undermining Bermúdez for more than a year. They were sick of talking about it. They sent out the communiqué.

Sánchez, apparently, was lying. News of the communiqué came as a complete surprise to Bernard Aronson's aides in Washington. And Aronson himself seemed dismayed. "You always have to be careful," he told the assistant who brought him the cable containing the news. "Sometimes you might get what you want." The prospect of an upheaval in the contras with the election just two weeks away was appalling to the State Department. What if Bermúdez decided to fight?

In Tegucigalpa, Bermúdez pondered the communiqué. He knew that if he resisted the dismissal, many commanders would support him. Rubén, Franklyn, and the others were not widely known outside their own units. Family feuds and old jealousies would keep some commanders from embracing this new leadership, and others would be skeptical that their men would get a fair break on dividing up supplies. His political skills, Bermúdez knew, were more important than the State Department thought. But a struggle would divert

257

attention from the election in Nicaragua; it might even provide the Sandinistas an excuse to cancel it.

Bermúdez called the wire services. "I am the leader of the armed Nicaraguan resistance, and I continue being the leader," he decreed. His pride salved, he spent the next two days quietly burning documents and closing down the safe house that for nine years had been the contras' Tegucigalpa nerve center. He called together the half-dozen remaining staff members. "If you want to come to Miami with me," Bermúdez told them, "I think I can get you travel documents and work permits. But after that you'll be on your own. I'm not a commander there, I'm just another exile looking for a job." A few days later, he led them on a final, lonely mission to the airport.

Both the State Department and Doña Violeta would soon wish Bermúdez were still around. Within days of the election, a team of gringos and Chamorro aides was urging the contra commanders to disarm. Seemingly there was little to argue about. The contras fought for free elections and an end to Sandinista rule; they had gotten both. But the younger commanders who had replaced Bermúdez were far more radical. Many said they would disarm only when the Sandinista army did the same. Others wanted a new army, integrated from both forces.

The attitude of Antonio Lacayo and Doña Violeta's other negotiators did not help. They acted, the commanders noted, as if they'd won the election all by themselves and didn't owe so much as a thank-you to anyone—as though the Sandinistas would have permitted their pipsqueak campaign if there hadn't been a gun to their head. One of the government negotiators bluntly told the contra commanders he hoped they never returned to Nicaragua.

"We don't want you back," the government man said. "You'll be an economic and a security problem. It would be better if the gringos take you. Once you've got jobs, we figure you'll send home $50 million a year."

"Gee," a contra commander said later, relating the conversation to a State Department official, "we're reduced to a cash crop."

Lacayo had evidently promised the Sandinistas the contras would be disarmed before Doña Violeta took office in April. He kept insisting that the contras turn in their weapons immediately, as though he faced a deadline. Lacayo's anxiety, and his arrogance, played into the contras' hands. Their American aid was set to expire on March 31. Assuming, as the Sandinistas often had, that the contras were mercenaries who would quit the minute the money ran out, Lacayo made a deal he thought would solve most of his problems. The government would pay pensions to contra widows, orphans, and disabled soldiers. In return, the contras in Honduras would turn over their arms to the UN by April 20, five days before the inauguration. Those inside Nicaragua would enter secure enclaves in the countryside while arrangements for their disarmament were completed.

There was, however, a gaping loophole. The agreement did not prohibit contras in Honduras from reinfiltrating Nicaragua. Within days, thousands of them rolled across the border. By the time UN teams arrived at Yamales, just the lame and crippled remained. The only weapons they surrendered were rusty and broken, except for one heavy Soviet antiaircraft cannon that gleamed so brightly it looked brand-new. It was. The contras, embarrassed by the few guns they had to turn in, pulled the cannon out of a warehouse where it had been sitting unassembled in a crate for more than two years and put it together the night before the UN teams arrived.

Outfoxed, Doña Violeta's government opened new negotiations. On April 19, after a marathon ten-hour session, a new agreement called for the contras inside Nicaragua to begin disarmament on April 25 and finish by June 10. But the news that Humberto Ortega was staying with the army derailed that plan before it got started. A third agreement, on May 5, called for both the contras and the Sandinistas to begin reducing their forces.

But ten days into the agreement, the contras again suspended disarmament. They offered various excuses, but it was increasingly obvious that no one or two or even ten of the commanders could bargain for the entire army. Doña Violeta's government would have to negotiate with a broad spectrum of commanders to get a deal that would stick. At the end of May, the government invited about two dozen of them to Managua to hammer out a definitive agreement.

For the first time, the government offered to give the contras territory where they could resettle. But the talks bogged down over the quantity of land, its location, and the degree of political control the contras would have over it. That night, two of the most vocal dissenters—Franklyn and Mack, who had rejoined the contras in the final days in Honduras—were invited to a small party at Doña Violeta's home.

It was a lively affair. The president told mildly ribald jokes to the commanders, sang Mexican songs with them, and kept the rum flowing freely. Around midnight, she excused herself briefly to make a phone call. A few minutes later, Humberto Ortega arrived. You know, he said to Mack as he poured himself a drink, there's no reason we can't work this out. You don't want to live out in the mountains eating worms forever, do you? If we could end this war, a smart guy like you could make some money.

Mack, his eyes shining brightly, summoned Franklyn over. The conversation lasted nearly until dawn.

The next day, Mack and Franklyn circulated among the commanders, arguing that the government's offer wasn't so bad. Within twenty-four hours the agreement was signed. The government would turn over 7,722 square miles in Nueva Segovia, Madriz, Estelí, Matagalpa, Zelaya, Chontales, and Río San Juan departments. About $47 million from the $300 million promised Doña Violeta's government by the United States would go to "development zones" in the contra territory. And the contras could form police forces in their zones, so they wouldn't be at the mercy of the Sandinista police.

On Wednesday, June 27, the commanders gathered in San Pedro de Lóvago. Fittingly, it was a hardscrabble mountain town in a distant section of Chontales Department, a place where campesinos had long since abandoned any hope that a government in Managua would help them and asked nothing more than to be left alone. These were the people the Sandinistas claimed their revolution had been for; and these were the people who had resisted the FSLN most fiercely.

Doña Violeta flew in by helicopter to accept their weapons in front of the town church. The first one to hand over his gun was Franklyn. Then he turned to face the crowd of people gathered around the church. "It's an honor to say," he told them, "mission accomplished."

Franklyn's words were not widely reported. As the Nicaragua story faded out to a happy ending—so it seemed to the rest of the world, anyway—the contras were regarded as an embarrassing historical artifact. No one had any interest in acknowledging them: not Doña Violeta or her palace guard, who boasted that they single-handedly won the election with their political acumen and sheer moral force; not the Latin American social democrats in countries like Venezuela and Costa Rica, who helped install the Sandinistas and spent the next decade averting their gaze from the results; not the journalists who never took the contra cause seriously and were still puzzled by the election returns; and certainly not the American politicians who used the contras as a club to batter the Reagan administration without bothering to understand them. It was fashionable, in the wake of the election, to give all the credit to the Central American peace plan devised by Oscar Arias. The obvious question—how could there have been a peace plan without, first, a war?—was never asked.

But the contra mission *was* accomplished. The contras got nearly everything they were fighting for. The "popular church," which viewed Jesus as a Marxist revolutionary, all but disappeared. The government coffee-purchasing agents who set prices on whims, then paid worthless cordobas for beans they would sell for dollars, vanished. The draft, which shipped baby-faced teenagers into the mountains and gray corpses back home, ended. The demands of petty tyrants that farmers leave their fields to attend political meetings ceased. The political prisoners, who languished years in jail for publicly contradicting government policy or for wearing National Guard uniforms, were released. The identification of the government with a single political party stopped. The total dependence on the Soviet Union shattered. The exportation of subversion to neighboring countries was reined in.

The single contra goal that remained unattained—the drastic reduction of the largest, best-equipped army in Central America and its removal from party control—was the fault of Doña Violeta and her government, not the contras. She had the opportunity to take decisive steps to bring the army under the direction of the Nicaraguan government instead of the Sandinista party, and she was too cowardly, or perhaps too confused, to take it.

In fact, the government's knuckling under to the Sandinista army was arguably just one more defeat for the same political class that had failed the contras so abjectly throughout the war. Doña Violeta's government was riddled with the same politicians that the State Department jammed down the contras' collective throat: Alfredo César, Arturo Cruz, Sr., Alfonso Robelo, and their friends. They were no more effective at corralling the Sandinistas than they had been winning support for the contras from Latin American governments or U.S. Democrats.

The politicians did immense damage to the contra cause—and, because their failures prolonged the war, to Nicaragua. They were brought into the movement to provide an articulate voice for the campesinos dying in lonely jungles and muddy mountainsides. Instead, they began to imagine that *they* were the movement, that their chats with congressmen and reporters were the stuff of heroism. They not only failed at their task, but their nasty public spats and underhanded jabs at one another were largely responsible for the public perception of the contras as dilettantes and mercenaries who had to be paid to fight.

The contra troops were as successful as the politicians were ineffective. They began resisting the Sandinistas within months of the revolution, without encouragement or aid from anyone. Between 1979 and 1988, they had U.S. military backing only four years, and yet by 1987, they had made serious inroads against an army with massive and consistent support from the Soviet Union. By contrast, it took the Sandinistas seventeen years to mount a genuine military challenge to Somoza.

The Sandinistas, of course, always denied that the contras represented a genuine threat. But their actions said otherwise. As early as 1982, they began relocating campesinos to keep them from joining the contras; by the war's end they had displaced at least three hundred thousand. They agreed first to cease-fire talks and then to outright political negotiations with a force that they insisted was strategically defeated. They amended their constitution, abandoned their controls over news media and political organizing, and in the end virtually ceded authority over their own national elections in a desperate attempt to win a victory in the international political arena that they could not achieve on the battlefield.

American military aid was an important factor in the war but not, in the final analysis, the most important one. The contras built themselves into the largest guerrilla army in Latin America, much bigger than the region's most vaunted communist groups. (They were nearly three times the size of El Salvador's guerrilla movement, double that of the insurgencies in Colombia or Peru.) And then they simply refused to go away, even when their fickle allies in the United States abandoned them.

And, as 1990 drew to a close, there were signs that the contras still hadn't gone away.

A total of 21,863 contras disarmed, according to the final UN report. They handed over 17,883 weapons, including 112 antiaircraft missiles, 134 mortars, 1,265 grenade launchers, 4 machine guns, and 14,920 rifles and pistols. In Miami, Bermúdez snorted when he heard the figures. At least half a dozen missiles, hundreds of machine guns and grenade launchers, and thousands of rifles were missing.[10]

The Sandinistas, having won the confrontation over control of the army, continued to challenge the government at every turn. Between May and August, Sandinista unions shut the government down three times with strikes accompanied by takeovers of government buildings. Doña Violeta, powerless to evict the strikers—the Sandinista police and army certainly weren't going to move against FSLN unions—had no choice but to capitulate with wage increases of 100 percent and more. Finally the government abandoned any attempt to

261

shrink the enormous state payroll, chaining itself to a wildly featherbedded bureaucracy that was, almost to a person, loyal to an opposition party.

The decision left government economic strategy in ruins. By the end of 1990, Nicaragua's annual inflation rate was more than 9,000 percent. International lending agencies refused to provide aid without structural reforms; the exiled business and professional class, appalled by the inflation and the disruptive strikes, stayed in Costa Rica and the United States. Friendly foreign governments, distracted first by the opening of Eastern Europe and then by gathering war clouds in the Persian Gulf, turned their attention elsewhere.

Doña Violeta's government made no attempt at all to honor the promises it made to the contras. Land titles were never delivered; neither were tools and material needed to build roads, furnish electricity, and pipe in drinking water. By July 1990, fewer than three thousand contras remained in the development zones, with more leaving daily. Among the first to depart were Mack and Franklyn. The government gave them several new trucks and a plush office in Managua.

Soon the contras were reappearing in Boaco, Chontales, Nueva Segovia, Matagalpa, and all the other places they knew so well from the war. They brought guns with them. At first there were small clashes, mostly at underutilized Sandinista cooperatives where the contras tried to move in. In November, bands of contras began putting up roadblocks along the Rama Road in Zelaya Department. They spread steadily west through Chontales into Boaco and even attempted to set up roadblocks in the city of Masaya, just outside Managua.

Mayors of eighteen towns throughout Chontales and Boaco announced their support, and soon an informal organization was born: Let's Save Democracy. What began as an inarticulate shout of frustration turned into a political movement with specific goals—the fulfillment of the government's promises to the contras and the dismissal of Antonio Lacayo and Humberto Ortega. Even after Doña Violeta sent the army to open the Rama Road, the leaders of Let's Save Democracy continued to meet and formulate strategy for the next confrontation. That there would be another armed encounter, the group's leaders had no doubt. Doña Violeta's government talked incessantly of national reconciliation, but only with the Sandinistas.

By the time the Sandinista army cleared the Rama Road, using two hundred troops backed by helicopter gunships and armored cars, twenty-four people had been killed and another fifty wounded during skirmishes around the roadblocks. A month later, after another of Doña Violeta's attempts to make peace with the Sandinistas by vetoing a National Assembly bill to cut the military budget, new fighting broke out. This time, in the battle-scarred northern town of Jalapa, eleven died and twenty were wounded. Where men gathered in the mountain towns, the talk about the government was dark. These people were going to drag the country back into another civil war.

Epilogue:
February 16, 1991

The lobby of Managua's Inter-Continental Hotel was a swirl of music and colors. Two different parties were going on in the hotel's banquet rooms, and the lobby was jammed with people. Even so, Carlos García, the Chamorro government's minister of sports, easily recognized his old friend walking toward the hotel bar. "Enrique!" he shouted. "*Hermano!*" Enrique Bermúdez turned in surprise, then rushed across the hallway to embrace García.

"Why haven't you called me?" García demanded. He hadn't even known Bermúdez was in Managua.

"I know you're trying to get a better job in the government," Bermúdez replied. "I don't want to get you in trouble. A lot of people don't like me." He eyed the crowd, then turned back to García. "We'll see each other later," Bermúdez promised. "I'm looking for someone." Abruptly he plunged back into the throng of party-goers, leaving García standing by himself in puzzlement.

It was the second time Bermúdez had visited Managua since the end of the war. His first trip, in September 1990, was supposed to last just a few days while he tried to get the Chamorro government to return the title to his house, seized by the Sandinistas shortly after the revolution. But the days stretched into three months. Everywhere Bermúdez went he was waylaid by former contras disillusioned at their treatment by the Chamorro government and bitter at the representation they were getting from the commanders who succeeded him. Come back, the men urged him. Be our voice to Doña Violeta. In mid-December, eight hundred former contras signed a letter to the Chamorro government designating Bermúdez "as the only representative of members of the Nicaraguan Resistance."

When he returned to Miami for Christmas, nearly all of his friends urged Bermúdez not to go back to Managua. "It's not safe, Enrique," his old CIA adviser Jim Adkins said over a seafood lunch in early January. "The Sandinistas are killers." Bermúdez knew that; several dozen ex-contras had been murdered since the war ended. But whenever he talked about the letter his men sent to the government, his eyes were bright. It was a chance to show that the State Department was wrong. The men still wanted *him*. On January 29, he flew back to Managua. His wife Elsa argued all the way to the airport. As his flight took off, she cried.

Bermúdez stayed in his sister's empty house, so barren there wasn't even a refrigerator. Some days he worked on reclaiming the title to his home. But several times he drove a borrowed Jeep to the mountains up north to see his old troops and find out exactly what they wanted from Doña Violeta. The trips did not go unnoticed. "Three men have been following me for four days," Bermúdez wrote on a small yellow note pad he kept in his briefcase. "They travel on a motorcycle and a Lada car, license plate 5036, color white." Later he jotted down the colors and license plates of three more Ladas, the small Soviet-made cars used by Sandinista police.

Bermúdez spent February 16 quietly at the townhouse; when a neighbor stopped by to say hello, Bermúdez said he planned to stay home that night. But something, or someone, drew him to the Inter-Continental Hotel, adjacent to the Sandinista military headquarters located in Somoza's old Bunker.

After he left Carlos García in the Inter-Continental lobby, Bermúdez disappeared. But García saw him again later, poking his head into the hotel's La Cita bar. "Come on, have a beer with us," García cajoled him. Bermúdez sat down with García's small group of drinking buddies and joined in their mild political argument. But he seemed preoccupied, expectant. Around 9:30, García went to take care of a problem with the bar bill; when he came back, Bermúdez was gone.

He didn't go far. A hotel employee found him a few minutes before 10 P.M., lying beneath the open door of his Jeep in the Inter-Continental parking lot. As Bermúdez had opened the vehicle's door, a gunman standing behind him fired two shots through the back of his head.

Elsa Bermúdez flew to Managua to bring her husband's body back to Miami. But she had to delay her return an extra day to accommodate the thousands of mourners who wanted to parade past the casket. And when she accompanied it to the airport, more than a thousand ex-contras overran a police line to escort the casket to the plane.

In Miami, the U.S. government didn't send a representative to the funeral. Oliver North, looking haggard and worn from weeks of questioning by a federal grand jury, sat in an alcove of the church. Scattered more anonymously through the pews were a handful of CIA men, saying their goodbyes, as they do everything else, secretly.

Enrique Bermúdez was just one of more than fifty ex-contras murdered in Nicaragua during the first six months of 1991. But his assassination—carried out so brazenly, in a crowded hotel parking lot right next to Sandinista military headquarters—carried an unmistakable message. Ex-contras began retrieving weapons from hidden caches; by mid-April, bands of so-called "recontras" were moving openly through the countryside in Estelí and Jinotega departments. On April 30, the recontras launched their first attack, ambushing a Sandinista military construction battalion near Ayapal, a village on the Honduran border in Jinotega Department. By mid-December, the recontras had staged about twenty attacks.

There were six groups of recontras in the north, with a seventh organizing southeast of Managua in Chontales and Zelaya departments. The commanders —they included Tigrillo and his brother Dimas—formed a loosely knit umbrella organization called the Enrique Bermúdez Democratic Force of National Salvation. Altogether, they commanded about one thousand armed troops. But openly supported by the campesinos, the recontras could clearly quintuple their numbers overnight if necessary.

The most aggressive of the recontra commanders was a campesino named José Angel Morán, whose nom de guerre was El Indomable, the indomitable one. He spoke in the hollow cadences of someone who had nothing left to lose. He didn't. In December 1990, a Sandinista army patrol machine-gunned his house. He wasn't home, but his pregnant wife was killed. Like the other recontras, El Indomable did not expect negotiations with the government to go anywhere.

"Here in Nicaragua," he observed, "the only dialogue we ever have is with bullets."

Notes

1. Maldito País

1. José Román, *Maldito País* (Managua: Editorial Union, 1983).
2. Alejandro Bolaños-Geyer, *William Walker, The Gray-Eyed Man of Destiny, Book Two: The Californias* (Lake St. Charles, Mo.: privately published, 1989), p. 349.
3. Neill Macaulay, *The Sandino Affair* (Durham, N.C.: Duke University Press, 1985), pp. 82, 239.
4. Macaulay, *Sandino,* p. 65.
5. Macaulay, *Sandino,* pp. 93–97, 213.
6. Donald C. Hodges, *Intellectual Foundations of the Nicaraguan Revolution* (Austin, Texas: University of Texas Press, 1986), p. 60.
7. Macaulay, *Sandino,* p. 247.
8. Bernard Diedrich, *Somoza and the Legacy of U.S. Involvement in Central America* (Maplewood, N.J.: Waterfront Press, 1989), p. 48.
9. Diedrich, *Somoza,* p. 23.
10. Robert A. Pastor, *Condemned to Repetition: The United States and Nicaragua* (Princeton, N.J.: Princeton University Press, 1987), p. 30.
11. Alain Rouquie, *The Military and the State in Latin America* (Berkeley, Calif.: University of California Press, 1987), p. 168; Walter LaFeber, *Inevitable Revolutions* (New York: W. W. Norton & Company, 1984), p. 73.
12. Pastor, *Condemned,* p. 43.
13. Diedrich, *Somoza,* p. 61.
14. Carlos Fonseca, *Un nicaragüense en Moscu* (Managua: Secretaria Nacional de Propaganda y Educación Política del FSLN, 1980).
15. In fact, no convincing evidence linking Somoza to the murder ever surfaced. In later years several members of the Chamorro family—including his widow, Violeta, now president of Nicaragua—began to suspect that the Sandinistas (who considered the editor a bourgeois handmaiden of imperialism) had committed the murder, knowing Somoza would be blamed. See Jaime Chamorro, *La Prensa: The Republic of Paper* (New York: Freedom House, 1988), pp. 65–75.
16. Humberto Belli, *Breaking Faith* (Westchester, Ill.: Crossway Books, 1985), p. 33; David Nolan, *The Ideology of the Sandinistas and the Nicaraguan Revolution* (Coral Gables, Fla.: Institute of Interamerican Studies, University of Miami, 1984), p. 68.
17. All quotations are from *The 72-Hour Document* (Washington D.C.: U.S. Department of State, 1986). Although the State Department is hardly a disinterested observer, the Sandinistas never challenged the authenticity of the document or its translation.

18. *The 72-Hour Document*, p. 6.
19. *The 72-Hour Document*.
20. Belli, *Breaking Faith*, pp. 95–98.

2. The Volcano Rumbles

1. Guy Gugliotta, "Argentines Reveal Details of Somoza Assassination," *Miami Herald*, July 17, 1989, pp. 1A, 7A.
2. Anastasio Somoza as told to Jack Cox, *Nicaragua Betrayed* (Boston: Western Islands, 1980), p. 386.

3. An Interview with a Tape Recorder

1. Roy Gutman, *Banana Diplomacy* (New York: Simon and Schuster, 1988), p. 28. Allen left the Reagan administration a year later when $1,000 in cash—a gift from a Japanese reporter—was discovered in his safe at the National Security Council. But he apparently continued to jinx the anti-Sandinista forces for years. His safe was given to NSC staffer Oliver North, who stuffed it full of politically embarrassing documents on the contras that were found when North was fired in 1986. *Report of the Congressional Committees Investigating the Iran-Contra Affair* (Washington, D.C.: Government Printing Office, 1988), app. B, vol. 20, p. 660.
2. Bob Woodward, *Veil* (New York: Simon and Schuster, 1987), p. 113.
3. Robert F. Turner, *Nicaragua v. United States: A Look at the Facts* (McLean, Va.: Pergamon-Brassey's, 1987), p. 59.
4. Nat Hamrick says he doesn't recall the interview with the tape recorder. Walters denies having anything to do with the contras at all. But two Nicaraguans who participated in the strange encounter with the tape recorder and the chat with Walters confirmed the details to me; so did a former American diplomat.

4. War

1. Don Oberdorfer and Patrick E. Tyler, "U.S.-Backed Nicaraguan Rebel Army Swells to 7,000 Men," *Washington Post*, May 8, 1983, pp. A1, A10–11. Robert C. Toth and Doyle McManus, "Contras and CIA: A Plan Gone Awry," *Los Angeles Times*, March 3, 1985, p.1.
2. The published "confession" of an Argentine officer who was kidnapped and interrogated by the Sandinistas in 1982 said Villegas's real name was José Hoyas. Edgar Chamorro, *Packaging the Contras* (New York: Institute for Media Analysis, 1987), p. 61.

5. Commander Zero

1. Doyle McManus and Robert C. Toth, "The Contras: How U.S. Got Entangled," *Los Angeles Times*, March 4, 1985, p. 1.
2. Beatriz Parga, "Interviewing Edén Pastora," *Caribbean Review* 11 (Summer 1982): 30.
3. Edén Pastora, oral history, International Security Studies Program, Fletcher School of Law and Diplomacy, transcript, p. 26.
4. Parga, *Caribbean Review*, p. 31.
5. Parga, *Caribbean Review*, p. 31.
6. Clarridge has frequently been identified in the U.S. news media and testified publicly during the Iran-contra hearings.
7. After the United States invaded Grenada in 1983, Clarridge added a bumper sticker to the jeep: Nicaragua's Next.
8. These figures come from Pastora's own ledgers.
9. Edén Pastora, "The Watchful Eye," in Robert S. Leiken and Barry Rubin, eds., *The Central American Crisis Reader* (New York: Summit Books, 1987), pp. 252–256.
10. In 1984, Alvarez was ousted in a barracks coup and flew to exile in Miami. Publicly, Pastora praised the coup as a righteous blow against an incipient fascist. Privately, he flew to Miami himself and offered his army to help restore Alvarez to command. Alvarez politely declined.

11. Edén Pastora, "Proclamation (April 1983)," in Leiken and Rubin, *Crisis Reader*, pp. 263–64.

6. The Monkey-Eaters

1. In one of the most baseless bits of character assassination to appear in the American press during the war, *Newsweek* reported that "380" was a "derisive nickname" applied to Bermúdez by his troops because it was his preferred model of Mercedes-Benz. Gordon Mott, "No More Mr. Nice Guy," *Newsweek* 112 (August 1, 1988): 31. In fact, when visiting his wife in Miami, Bermúdez drove an old Honda Civic; in Honduras, he used an FDN-owned Toyota.
2. For a detailed account of the Enders talks, see Gutman, *Banana Diplomacy*, pp. 66–73.
3. In the early days of the war as many as 10 percent of the FDN's combat troops were women. But they became pregnant so frequently that, by the end, women made up less than 2 percent of the combatants. In 1983, when *Soldier of Fortune* magazine asked one FDN official what the contras needed most, she promptly replied: "Diapers."

7. Growing Pains

1. The Sandinistas insisted that the first Nicaraguan military draft was created in September 1983, and they denied there was any prior conscription. But in June and July of that year, I talked to hundreds of Nicaraguan refugees at the UN camps in Jacaleapa and Teupasenti, Honduras, who swore that there was.
2. Gruner's name was first disclosed in Jane Mayer and Doyle McManus, *Landslide* (Boston: Houghton Mifflin Company, 1988), p. 288.
3. Edgar Chamorro with Jefferson Morley, "Confessions of a 'Contra,'" *New Republic* 193 (August 5, 1985): pp. 18–23.
4. The problem was not necessarily limited to the general staff. One contra politician was notorious for visiting the brothel across from the Hotel Prado in Tegucigalpa to make drunken speeches proclaiming himself the next president of Nicaragua.
5. Christopher Dickey, "Well-Armed Units Show Strongholds," *Washington Post,* April 3, 1983, pp. A1, A14; Dickey, "Nothing Ragtag About Nicaraguan Rebels," *Washington Post,* April 3, 1983, p. A14.
6. Christopher Dickey, *With the Contras* (New York: Simon and Schuster, 1985).
7. Winters has frequently been identified in print as a CIA officer at least as far back as 1968.
8. Doty was first identified as a CIA officer in Woodward, *Veil*, p. 230.
9. Interestingly, most of them accepted Echaverry's claim that if they could hold the territory for seventy-two hours, other Central American countries would intervene on their behalf. But there seems to have been no factual basis for this claim; no contra official from that time remembers any such agreement.
10. Alvarez was not the only casualty of the coup. Don Winters, the CIA station chief, was so close to Alvarez that he had no idea anything was brewing in the barracks. (Alvarez was the godfather of Winters's adopted Honduran child.) There were some fiery cables from Langley over that, and Winters was removed from his post ahead of schedule.

8. Down South

1. Pastora even bragged to his men that he had put a gun to his head during an argument with General Alvarez during the unity negotiations in Honduras and screamed, "You can't conquer me . . . because the man who is determined to die is invincible!" Everyone else who was at the meeting in Honduras denies it. "If he had ever done that with me," sniffed Chicano Cardenal, "I would have said, 'Go ahead, Edén, shoot.'"
2. Brenton R. Schlender, "Nicaraguan Exile Units Feud with Each Other as well as Sandinistas," *Wall Street Journal,* July 27, 1983, pp. 1, 18.
3. Cohen and Hart were less than amused. That night they bawled out the chief of Managua's CIA station for several hours. Woodward, *Veil*, pp. 272–275.

4. I don't suggest that I had any special immunity from Pastora's charm. See Glenn Garvin, "Commander Zero: Still Chasing the Smell of Gunpowder," *Washington Times*, November 17, 1983, pp. 1B, 2B, and "The Return Of Commander Zero," *Washington Times*, February 28, 1985, pp. 1B, 2B.

5. So, for that matter, did the northern front. In 1986, when the State Department contracted with aviation companies to deliver $27 million in nonlethal aid to the contras, four of the firms selected were owned and operated by narco-traffickers. Senate Subcommittee on Terrorism, Narcotics and International Communications, *Drugs, Law Enforcement and Foreign Policy* (Washington, D.C.: Government Printing Office, 1989), pp. 41–49.

6. Senate Subcommittee, *Drugs,* p. 50.

7. Senate Subcommittee, *Drugs,* p. 136.

8. *Report*, pp. 630–2.

9. The García Family

1. Joseph Persico, *Casey: From the OSS to the CIA* (New York: Viking, 1990), p. 290.

2. John Brecher, "A Secret War for Nicaragua," *Newsweek* 100 (November 8, 1982): 42.

3. Adkins was first publicly identified as a CIA officer in *CovertAction Information Bulletin* in 1980.

4. Adkins eventually won this argument in rather dramatic fashion. In November 1983, Bosch was sent back to the United States after trying to swindle the embassy out of about $150,000 in exchange-rate manipulations. In January 1984, he was forced out of the CIA. And soon after that, he—perhaps unintentionally—passed Agency secrets to his friend Edward Lee Howard, a former CIA officer who defected to the Soviets. See David Wise, *The Spy Who Got Away* (New York: Random House, 1988). Bosch and Howard were publicly identified as former CIA officers by federal authorities during the investigation.

5. Enders was first publicly identified as a CIA officer in Steven Emerson, *Secret Warriors* (New York: Putnam, 1988), p. 9.

6. To say that "Casey and Clarridge decided" is not to imply that the CIA was a rogue elephant, acting on its own without the knowledge or approval of the Reagan administration. Most of the war's major escalations were approved by various national security organs, most prominent among them the National Security Planning Group, which included President Reagan himself as well as the secretaries of state and defense. Nonetheless, Nicaragua policy in general, and the conduct of the contra war particularly, were clearly spearheaded by the CIA from 1981 to 1984.

7. Casey, too, seemed to suffer a mysterious memory lapse about Vietnam. When he was running for Congress in 1966, Casey opposed mining Haiphong as "a reckless action that would risk escalation into a big land war in Asia." Persico, *Casey,* pp. 124, 371.

8. Robert A. Rankin, "CIA Actions in Nicaragua Revive Fears of the Past," *Miami Herald,* April 16, 1984, p. 19A.

9. Not the least of the reasons for refusing to accept the court's jurisdiction was that Nicaragua itself had never accepted it—that is, the Sandinistas were attempting to sue in a court where they themselves could not be sued. For a full discussion of the legal issues surrounding the World Court's jurisdiction, see John Norton Moore, *The Secret War in Central America* (Frederick, Md.: University Publications of America, 1987), pp. 83–90; and "Reflections of the State Department on the U.S. and the World Court," *World Affairs* 148 (Summer 1985): 53–60.

10. *Report*, app. B, vol. 17, pps. 205–214.

11. It has a particularly close resemblance to *Armed Psyop,* a 1968 lesson book used at the Army Special Warfare School at Fort Bragg, North Carolina, and *Handbook on Aggressor Insurgent War,* a 1967 field manual.

12. Chamorro claims he decided, on his own, to cut out the pages that contained the references to criminals and martyrs. But his story makes no sense; Chamorro's secretary translated Kirkpatrick's work into Spanish, and Chamorro approved it section by section. If he

objected to the language, he could have changed it. No other contra official supports Chamorro's version of the story.

13. Robert Parry, "CIA Manual Tells Nicaraguan Rebels to Hire Criminals," Associated Press wire, October 14, 1984.

14. The 1966 *U.S. Army Handbook of Counterinsurgency Guidelines,* for instance, forthrightly advocated assassinations and kidnappings. It struck a single cautionary note: "You may not employ mass counter-terror, as opposed to selective counter-terror, against the civilian population, i.e., genocide is not an alternative." Aryeh Neier, "Exporting Persecution," *Nation* 241 (September 7, 1985): 183. At the same time Kirkpatrick was putting together his manual, a group of officers at the CIA's Central American Task Force in Langley was preparing a comic book demonstrating sabotage techniques for distribution to civilians inside Nicaragua. It was titled *Manual Del Combatiente Por La Libertad*—in English, *Freedom Fighter's Manual.* The task force officers were also drawing on old military manuals for material, including one from the World War I era that showed how to destroy railroad tracks and derail trains. The officer who headed the project, however, vetoed all the really spectacular stuff. "This program is so unpopular with Congress," he warned the men working with him, "that if we use anything like that, they'll use it to hang us." Instead, the *Freedom Fighter's Manual* wound up looking more like a list of exam-week fraternity pranks: Throw tools in sewers. Leave open the corral gates at state farms. Call in phony hotel reservations. Break light bulbs. (The single exception was a set of instructions for making Molotov cocktails.) When the comic book was finished, the officer confided to friends that he was embarrassed at how silly it was, but confident that it wouldn't end anyone's career, either.

15. All quotations come from the unexpurgated version of the manual translated by the Congressional Research Service. Tayacán, *Psychological Operations in Guerrilla Warfare* (Washington, D.C.: Library of Congress, 1984).

16. Humberto Ortega, *Sobre la Insurrección* (Havana: Editorial de Ciencias Sociales, 1986), p. 34.

17. Cannistraro has frequently been identified in print as a CIA officer, going back at least to 1979; Fernández was publicly identified many times during the Iran-contra scandal.

10. The Last Hurrah of Commander Zero

1. After I learned of the executions in 1986 and began asking questions about them, Pastora never spoke to me again. He directed his top aides to do the same.

2. Arturo Cruz, Jr., *Memoirs of a Counterrevolutionary* (New York: Doubleday, 1989), pp. 136–7.

3. Pastora has variously accused the Sandinistas, the CIA, Oliver North, North's courier Rob Owen, and then-Vice President George Bush of authorizing the attack. Occasionally he even says he doesn't know. See Andrew Cockburn, "Who Tried to Kill Edén Pastora?" *Washington Post,* July 5, 1977, pp. D1, D4; Glenn Garvin, "Pastora Accuses Owen in Bombing," *Washington Times,* May 20, 1987, p. 6A, and "Three Years Later, Nicaraguan Bombing Is Still an Enigma," *Washington Times,* May 29, 1987, p. 13A; and Beth Hawkins, "Pastora: North Was Behind Bombing," *Tico Times* (San José, Costa Rica), May 15, 1987, p. 4.

4. Tim Golden, "Pastora's Goals Remain an Elusive Dream," *Miami Herald,* September 17, 1986, pp. 1A, 4A.

5. Pastora stole his first Rolex from one of Somoza's nephews, a hostage during the National Palace takeover. The Cubans gave him a second one as a present. The rest he collected simply by asking for them. In 1982, when Pastora was negotiating with Chicano Cardenal over unity with the FDN, Cardenal noticed that Pastora was staring fixedly at his right wrist. "Chicano, that's a Rolex," he blurted. "Give me that." Cardenal, succinct as ever, invited Pastora to "go fuck yourself."

6. Edward Cody, "Pastora's Lonely Battle," *Washington Post,* January 18, 1985, pp. A1, A31.

7. The FDN, like ARDE, had been cut off from U.S. government funds. But Calero was

getting money through Oliver North's fund raising.

8. "Testimony of Tomás Castillo," *Joint Hearings on the Iran-Contra Investigation* (Washington, D.C.: Government Printing Office, 1988), vol. 100-4, p. 43. Pastora said later that Fernández told him there was a CIA agent aboard the boat. Alfonso Chardy, Sam Dillon, and Tim Golden, "Agent Led Rebels for CIA," *Miami Herald*, February 28, 1987, pp. 1A, 7A.

9. *Report*, app. B, vol. 3, p. 249.

10. *Report*, app. B, vol. 3, pp. 501–2.

11. Fernández was certainly aware of this episode; he answered the phone in Langley. *Report*, app. B, vol. 3, p. 307. His undignified retreat notwithstanding, El Negro's reputation was so formidable in those days that when the Sandinistas discovered a dead contra who resembled him, they hitched the corpse to a pickup truck and dragged it all around the border for the next two days, boasting that they had killed Chamorro.

12. *Report*, app. B, vol. 3, pp. 404–5.

11. The Dry Years

1. Michael Maclear, *The Ten Thousand Day War: Vietnam, 1945–1975* (New York: St. Martin's Press, 1981), pp. 172–88.

2. Macaulay, *Sandino*, p. 153.

3. John Lantigua, "Sandinistas to Mobilize Against Rebels," *Washington Post*, August 22, 1985, pp. A25, A34; Tim Golden, "2 Nicaragua Citics React Differently to Rebel Threat," *Miami Herald*, August 8, 1985, p. 22A.

4. All Sandinista military statistics are taken from *The Sandinista Military Build-up* (Washington, D.C.: Departments of State and Defense, 1985). Although the U.S. government certainly had a motive for exaggerating numbers, the Sandinistas never challenged American estimates. So many arms arrived in Nicaragua that Humberto Ortega deliriously suggested that even nuclear missiles were a possibility. See Stephen Kinzer, "Nicaraguan Warns Honduras On Raids," *New York Times*, April 10, 1983, p. 1. The Soviets maintained a polite silence to the proposition.

12. Not-Too-Private Enterprise

1. *Report*, pp. 45, 63, 85, 101. The CIA, for its part, sent Duane Clarridge to South Africa to seek money but nervously called off the discussion before it bore fruit. *Report*, p. 38. The single State Department foray into the fund-raising field was a $10 million request to tiny-but-filthy-rich Brunei, an oil-producing island off the coast of Borneo. Assistant Secretary of State Elliott Abrams made a successful pitch but then gave the Bruneians an incorrect Swiss bank account number. The contras never saw a penny of the Brunei money, but the passbook holder of Credit Suisse account number 368-430-22-1 became a very happy man. *Report*, pp. 352–3.

2. *Report*, p. 343.

3. Christopher Robbins, *The Ravens* (New York: Crown, 1987), p. 124.

4. For a detailed description of The Enterprise's assets and financial practices, see *Report*, pp. 331–53.

5. North, again displaying a fondness for cloak-and-dagger if not an aptitude, sent Rodriguez a letter, marked AFTER READING THIS LETTER PLEASE DESTROY IT, providing him with code words to use in "this compartmented operation" and warning him not to breathe a word of North's involvement. North dispatched this secret message through the ultra-secure channels of. . . . Federal Express. And he sent it to Rodriguez's home in Miami, where his wife simply stuffed it in an envelope and dropped it in the mail to El Salvador.

6. *Report*, app. B, vol. 7, p. 1163.

7. The Reagan administration used the incursion as an excuse to give the Hondurans $20 million in military aid that by law was only available in an "emergency." Honduran president José Azcona dutifully swore that the incursion was an emergency. It *was* an emergency for the contras, but not for Honduras; Azcona did not even interrupt his

traditional Holy Week at the beach. At the U.S. embassy in Tegucigalpa, the incursion became known as The Easter Egg War.

8. "Testimony of Robert C. Dutton," *Joint Hearings,* vol. 100-3, pp. 533–47; "Testimony of Richard V. Secord," *Joint Hearings,* vol. 100-1, p. 190.

9. *Report,* p. 73.

10. For the markup on arms prices, see *Report,* p. 347. For the accounting on the Iranian arms sales and The Enterprise's surplus cash, see *Report,* pp. 337, 343. For Secord's refusal to abandon El Salvador, see "Testimony of Robert C. Dutton," *Joint Hearings,* p. 548. For the accounting of the profits generated by The Enterprise, see *Report,* pp. 344, 348–9.

13. Spies and Lovers

1. The General Directorate for State Security was just one—albeit the largest—of the organizations controlled by Borge's Interior Ministry. The ministry had another 5,000 employees, including a highly trained 1,200-man counterinsurgency battalion. See *Nicaragua's Interior Ministry: Instrument of Political Consolidation* (Washington, D.C.: Department of State, 1987), pp. 2, 4, 10.

2. The mobs were given their name by Daniel Ortega, who with mock innocence insisted that the Sandinistas had nothing to do with them. Shirley Christian, *Nicaragua: Revolution In The Family* (New York: Random House, 1985), p. 228.

3. The book is a collection of interviews with contras; although the authors claim they were done throughout Central America, nearly all were conducted in Sandinista prisons. *The Contras: Interviews with Anti-Sandinistas* (San Francisco: Synthesis Publications, 1985), pp. 134–53.

4. La Garza fell in love with one of the contra doctors whose wife had left him when he joined the FDN. Eventually La Garza and the doctor got married. "And now they have two little baby contras," another doctor told me in November 1990.

5. Later Astorga claimed the Sandinistas only intended to kidnap the general, Reynaldo Pérez, and he was killed in the struggle. But his body was found with wads of cotton taped over the eyes and a handkerchief taped over the mouth. His throat had been cut and the body had "many piercing puncture wounds," as though from an ice pick. By some accounts, the general had been castrated and his penis placed inside his mouth. "Cronología de la cita mortal," *La Prensa* (Managua, Nicaragua), March 10, 1978, p. 1; Norman L. Wolfson, "The Lost Cause of a PR Man," *National Review* (July 20, 1979): 907. And Astorga herself, in a letter to *La Prensa* a week after the murder, said the "execution" of Pérez was planned for "several months" by Daniel Ortega, Victor Tirado, and Henry Ruiz, all members of the FSLN directorate. "Aparece Nora Jenkins," *La Prensa* (Managua, Nicaragua), March 16, 1978, p. 1. After the revolution, the FSLN rewarded Astorga by making her ambassador to the United Nations.

6. Elizabeth Reimann, *Yo Fui Un Contra* (Managua: Editorial Vanguardia, 1987).

7. Readers surprised by this revelation may console themselves with the fact that Stansfield Turner, CIA director under Jimmy Carter, didn't know it either. One of the most awkward moments of Turner's stewardship at the Agency came during a luncheon of Latin American station chiefs. Everyone was brooding about the CIA's failure to predict the Mariel exodus that brought 120,000 Cuban refugees to the United States in just a few weeks. "Why can't you just recruit someone who lives in one of those houses overlooking Mariel Harbor?" Turner demanded of the Havana station chief. "Then they could get word to us if they see the boats massing again." There was a painful silence in the room, broken only by the Havana chief's stuttered explanation that "we don't really, uh, work that, uh, way. . . ."

8. I have not included the journalist's name because I haven't seen the transcript of the tape personally, and I have no other evidence to confirm that the reporter was helping the Sandinistas. But there is no doubt that the FSLN had some agents working for foreign news media. María Lourdes Pallais was one. And Miguel Bolaños, a State Security officer

who defected in 1983, said that he was case officer for two journalists who reported to the Sandinistas. He has only identified one: Juan Maltes, a Nicaraguan who is a reporter for the Associated Press. Bolaños said he used Maltes to plant misinformation in AP stories "only a couple of times." Mainly, according to Bolaños, the Sandinistas used Maltes to gather information on the activities of Nicaraguan opposition leaders. Miguel Bolaños, oral history, International Security Studies Program, Fletcher School of Law and Diplomacy, Tufts University, transcript pp. 17–19.

9. There was a second spy reporting on the activities of the El Salvador supply operation. Felix Rodriquez, the former CIA contract officer who acted as a liaison between the supply operation and the Salvadoran air force, hired a friend of his named Luis Posada Carriles to take care of the logistical details: renting houses for the air crews, hiring maids and cooks, paying the bills and, so forth. Posada Carriles, a Cuban-American veteran of the Bay of Pigs, had been involved in every conceivable type of Latin American spookery. The Venezuelan government accused him of the midair bombing of a Cuban airliner in 1976, and imprisoned him nine years without trial. In 1985, he escaped and found his way to El Salvador, where Rodriguez gave him a job. But a year later, Rodriguez fired him after he discovered that Posada Carriles was meeting regularly with an officer of the DGI, Fidel Castro's intelligence agency, which cooperated extensively with the Sandinistas.

10. What the contras really needed were the services of the California Highway Partrol, which reduced detection of Sandinista infiltrators to a science. In a September 1988 bulletin to its officers, the CHP warned that Sandinista agents permeated San Francisco. "FSLN members favor large American luxury cars stolen from Budget car rental," the bulletin said, and were usually "dressed in military garb." One was even spotted in "a Soviet military field jacket," the CHP added in ominous tones. See "And They'll Smell Of Russian Vodka," *Harper's Magazine* 277 (December 1988): 26-27.

11. Many commanders told me they thought the problem was that Nicaraguans are congenital liars. "The lie detector may work well on Americans, because Americans don't lie," Mike Lima said. "But Nicaraguans lie all the time, every day. For us, lying is normal."

The American mania for polygraphs reached all the way back to Washington, where contra political adviser Arturo Cruz, Jr., was dating Fawn Hall, Oliver North's lissome blonde secretary. The CIA asked Cruz to take a lie detector test, and he agreed. One of his jobs with the Sandinistas, after all, had been acting as liaison with Cuban intelligence officers in Washington. He passed, but the romance with Hall broke up anyway. "I loved Fawn, I really did," he explained to me. "But I couldn't see spending the rest of my life with someone who didn't know who Eisenhower was."

12. Belli, *Breaking Faith*, p. 90.

13. "Dos mil se alzaron en Managua," *La República* (San José, Costa Rica), November 20, 1986, p. 36.

14. 1987

1. Because it fought deep inside Nicaragua in areas where the Sandinistas had not forced all the campesinos into relocation camps, the Jorge Salazar recruited more heavily than any other contra unit. Over the years it divided, again and again, until there were five Jorge Salazar Regional Commands.

2. Mrazek knew that all the contra camps were inside the twenty-mile buffer zone and was well aware of the anomaly of a provision that blocked CIA flights into contra camps but permitted them into Nicaragua itself. "Believe me, we would have liked to stop the flights into Nicaragua, too," one of his staffers told me, "but we didn't have the votes."

3. Playing tour guide for visiting American congressmen was the duty most despised by CIA officers in Honduras. Many of the visitors were anti-contra congressmen making sure they weren't vulnerable to the charge that they didn't know anything about the program they were voting against. That meant CIA escorts often had to endure long anti-contra harangues as they shepherded the congressmen around. The congressmen frequently treated CIA

officers and other embassy staffers as personal valets; the embassy security force had a particular distaste for a liberal New England senator who on every trip forced them to stand guard during his overnight visits to the brothel across from the Hotel Prado.

Occasionally, however, something happened that made the duty worthwhile. CIA officers treasured the time George Miller, a Democratic congressman from California, visited a contra hospital and was surprised to find an American nurse working there during her vacation. "So," Miller inquired, "you're patching these contras up so they can go back into Nicaragua and murder civilians?" The nurse, a hefty woman, reared back. "Someone has to stand up to communism," she roared, "and it certainly isn't going to be you spineless sons of bitches in Congress!" She chased Miller back to the refuge of the CIA's helicopter, shouting at him every step of the way.

4. Late in 1991, the investigation of Iran-contra independent counsel Lawrence Walsh began to topple other CIA dominoes. Former Central American Task Force chief Alan Fiers pled quilty to a charge of withholding information from Congress, and former director of operations Clair George was indicted on ten similar charges. Duane Clarridge, the wildest of the CIA cowboys, was indicted on seven charges.

5. For a description of Wright's back-channel dealings with the Sandinistas and other Central American governments, see Gutman, *Banana Diplomacy*, pp. 346–9.

6. The Sandinistas had closed down nearly all the independent radio news programs in the country, too. They also tried to shut down the stations themselves, indirectly, by refusing to supply them foreign exchange to buy replacement parts and were clearly puzzled that the strategy hadn't worked. They didn't know the U.S. embassy was importing replacement parts through its diplomatic pouch and giving them to the independent radio stations.

15. Self-Destruction

1. Several hours of one session were consumed by an argument over the Spanish word for "stenographer." Gutman, *Banana Diplomacy*, p. 219.

2. Although their Soviet-bloc allies provided the Sandinistas with hundreds of shoulder-fired anti-aircraft missiles, as well as dozens of larger fixed-position weapons, the FSLN's defensive record against contra aircraft was undistinguished. In six years, the Sandinistas shot down seven planes. They included an ARDE twin-engine Beechcraft downed on a supply mission in 1983, the FDN C-47s piloted by Roberto Amador in 1983 and José Luis Gutiérrez in 1984, an FDN helicopter that was assisting in an air attack on a Sandinista base in Nueva Segovia in 1984, the Hasenfus plane in 1986, and the DC-6 in 1988.

The other incident involved a CIA plane that, two years before Hasenfus was shot down, came within a hair's breadth of touching off a Hasenfus-like scandal. The plane was a C-47, mounted with special powerful engines that enabled it to fly from Ilopango Air Force Base in El Salvador, over the Pacific Ocean, east across Costa Rica, and then north into Nicaragua, where it dropped supplies to ARDE.

In March 1984, the plane flew the same route several days in a row. A Sandinista patrol, armed with SAM-7s, charted the flights and decided the plane could be shot down—but the best vantage point for firing a missile, the Sandinistas soldiers concluded, was on the Costa Rican side of the border. They made their way across, and on March 24, 1984, shot the plane down.

When the C-47 didn't make its drop on time, ARDE sent patrols to search for it. Within two hours, they located the wreckage—and captured one member of the Sandinista patrol that shot the plane down. ARDE officials frantically ordered their men to clean up the wreckage before Costa Rican security forces arrived. Not only did it contain thousands of pounds of weapons and ammunition, but the crew members had been carrying various identification cards and documents that would link them to Ilopango Air Force Base and the CIA. ARDE troops managed to carry away the supplies and the bodies of the crewmen (two Salvadorans, two Nicaraguans, and a Panamanian) and destroy all the incriminating documents. The wreckage itself, however, was too big to hide, and a major scandal erupted when Costa Rican authorities found it. But there was no evidence left to pin the plane on anyone—and the Sandinistas, who could have provided details, would have had to admit that their patrol crossed into Costa Rican territory. They kept silent.

3. *Report*, app. B, vol. 14, pp. 753–5. The bureaucracy eventually employed more than three hundred personnel on a monthly budget of $750,000.

4. Lloyd Grove, "Arturo Cruz at the Nicaraguan Crossroads," *Washington Post,* February 19, 1987, pp. B1, B4.

5. The contra organizations for the Atlantic coast Indian and Creole populations were so hopelessly divided that nearly eighteen months passed before they named their representative to the Nicaraguan Resistance directorate, leaving it with only six members.

16. "You Won, But Nobody Knows It"

1. Ortega described the Caracas talks during a press conference on February 22, 1990. See "President Ortega Holds News Conference," Foreign Broadcast Information Service *Daily Report* (FBIS-LAT-90-037), February 23, 1990, p. 22. In a document prepared for a secret meeting of Sandinista militants in August 1989, Bayardo Arce—one of the nine FSLN *comandantes*—was just as explicit. The Sandinistas decided "to offer democratization in exchange for demobilization. That is what we went to El Salvador to do—to negotiate. We offered to move up the date of the elections with all the guarantees for our adversaries." See "FSLN 'Confidential Document' for Cadre School," Foreign Broadcast Information Service *Daily Report* (FBIS-LAT-89-214), November 7, 1989, pp. 30–34.

2. Bernard Aronson, "Another Choice in Nicaragua," *New Republic* 192 (May 27, 1985): 22.

3. Aureliano was killed on January 7, 1989, by two men who followed him from a Tegucigalpa bar, forced his Toyota Landcruiser off a deserted stretch of highway just outside the city, and riddled him with sixteen shots from an Israeli-made Uzi machine gun.

4. In 1990, Gómez began selling off entire aircraft, including the *Lady Ellen* — a helicopter purchased with $60,000 donated to the contras by Texas heiress Ellen Garwood after she heard one of Oliver North's pep talks.

5. "FSLN 'Confidential Document' for Cadre School," *Daily Report*, p. 31.

6. The change in Soviet behavior was due to extensive jawboning by both James Baker and Aronson of their USSR counterparts. See Michael Kramer, "Anger, Bluff—and Cooperation," *Time* 135 (June 4, 1990), pp. 38–45.

7. Robert Pear, "U.S. Aid Just Dribbles in to Nicaragua Opposition, but the Sandinistas Profit," *New York Times,* February 4, 1990, p. 3.

8. After the election, Lacayo announced he would begin transition talks with the Sandinistas. He has always denied that there were earlier, secret discussions. But my source reported to me regularly on discussions that began around January 15.

9. Pedro Sevcec, "Crece división en coalición nica," *El Nuevo Herald,* April 28, 1990, pp. 1A, 6A.

10. The UN figures were reported in "Los contras eran más de 20,000," *El Nuevo Herald,* July 3, 1990, p. 1A.

Index